THE CHALLENGE OF
Democracy

Government in America

Brief Edition

Second Edition

Kenneth Janda
Northwestern University

Jeffrey M. Berry
Tufts University

Jerry Goldman
Northwestern University

Abridged by

Earl Huff
California Polytechnic State University,
San Luis Obispo

Houghton Mifflin Company **Boston** **Toronto**
Dallas   Geneva, Illinois   Palo Alto   Princeton, New Jersey

Sponsoring Editor: Margaret Seawell
Development Editor: Susan Granoff
Project Editor: Jean Levitt
Electronic Production Specialist: Victoria Levin
Production/Design Coordinator: Sarah Ambrose
Art Editor: Karen Lindsay
Cover Design: Ron Kosciak, Dragonfly Design
Senior Manufacturing Coordinator: Priscilla Bailey
Marketing Manager: Karen Natale

Illustration Credits

Illustrations by Illustrious, Inc.
Cover Photo: Chris Collins-The Stock Market

Chapter 1: **Page 1 (opener):** © Rhoda Galyn/Photo Researchers, Inc.; **8:** Wide World Photos; **19:** Baldev/Sygma; **21:** Bob Daemmrich/The Image Works; **27:** Paul Conklin.

Chapter 2: **Page 36 (opener):** © Beringer/Dratch/The Image Works; **37:** J.P. Laffont/Sygma; **41:** Courtesy of the John Carter Brown Library at Brown University; **56:** Tracy W. McGregor Library, Manuscripts Division, Special Collections Department, University of Virginia Library; **63:** National Archives.

Chapter 3: **Page 71 (opener):** © Kenneth Martin/Amstock; **82:** National Archives; **83:** Peter Blakely/SABA; **87:** © 1990 Robert Fox/Impact Visuals; **95:** Wide World Photos.

Chapter 4: **Page 98 (Opener):** © Michael Lyon/TexaStock; **104:** St. Louis Globe; **107:** Wide World Photos; **127:** Historical Still of the King beating provided courtesy of Social Reform, Inc.; **129:** James D. Wilson/The Gamma Liaison Network.

(Illustration credits continue after page I-17.)

Printed in the U.S.A.

Library of Congress Catalog Card Number: 93-78686

ISBN: 0-395-66879-4

23456789-AM-98 97 96 95 94

CONTENTS

4

PUBLIC OPINION, POLITICAL SOCIALIZATION, AND THE MASS MEDIA   98

6

POLITICAL PARTIES, CAMPAIGNS, AND ELECTIONS   166

7

INTEREST GROUPS   209

8

CONGRESS   233

9

THE PRESIDENCY   263

10

THE BUREAUCRACY   290

11

THE COURTS   316

PREFACE

The second edition of *The Challenge of Democracy*, Brief Edition, is an abridged and updated version of the very popular Election Printing of the Third Edition of *The Challenge of Democracy*. In creating this Brief Edition our goal was to streamline the larger text without diminishing any of the qualities that have made it so successful. Additionally, we sought to make the text as current as possible by incorporating examples from events of spring 1993 and by including coverage of the Clinton Administration.

We considered all deletions carefully. Some Third Edition chapters were shortened and combined in the Brief Edition; others—chapters that discussed economic, domestic, and foreign policy—were omitted entirely. Generally, we examined individual sections and paragraphs closely to remove small bits of material—pruning language, multiple examples, and details, for instance.

The resulting text is almost half as long as the full-length edition and is ideally suited for short courses or courses in which additional readings are assigned. At the same time, *The Challenge of Democracy*, Brief Edition, retains the important information students need to understand the American political process. It also retains the thematic framework that structured the full-length edition.

Thematic Framework

Our theoretical framework provides a way for students to put the information they learn in their introductory American government course into a broader perspective. More important, it enables students to recognize and think critically about the difficult choices we face as citizens and voters.

Two enduring themes in American politics run throughout the book; both are introduced in Chapter 1, "Dilemmas of Democracy." First, we suggest that American politics often reflects conflicts between the values of freedom and order, and between the values of freedom and equality. These conflicts have been powerful forces throughout American history and continue to explain current political issues and controversies.

The second theme asks students to consider two different models of democracy. In one, government makes decisions by means of majoritarian principles—that is, by taking the actions desired by a majority of citizens. A contrasting model of democratic government, pluralism, is built around the interaction of decision makers in government with competing interest groups concerned about issues that affect them.

As appropriate in each chapter, we use he themes to illustrate the dynamics of the American political system and to discuss relevant issues. For instance, Chapter 2 examines how the Constitution was designed to promote order and virtually ignored issues of political and social equality. However, as we show in Chapter 12, "Civil Liberties and Civil Rights," equality was later promoted by several amendments to the Constitution. In Chapter 4, "Public Opinion, Political Socialization, and the Mass Media," we explore the media's role in reporting public opinion, which advances the cause of majoritarianism. Pluralism is a focus of our discussion of issue networks in Chapter 10, "The Bureaucracy."

Throughout the book we stress that students must make their own choices among the competing values and models of government. We want our readers to learn firsthand that a democracy requires difficult choices. That is why we titled our book *The Challenge of Democracy.*

Features of the Revised Edition

It's remarkable how much change can take place in the span of a few years. In this second edition of *The Challenge of Democracy*, Brief Edition, we examine the implications of 1992's three-way race for the presidency and discuss the ramifications of a new president, a new Congress, and a changing Supreme Court.

We have retained the basic structure of the previous edition but have added a wealth of new information; extensively updated charts, tables, and photos; and incorporated numerous recent examples throughout—including coverage of the Clinton administration, the Somalia relief operation, and other timely events and issues. For example, in Chapter 6, "Political Parties, Campaigns, and Elections," we have expanded the coverage of modern campaign strategy and technology to take account of recent innovations.

As in the previous edition, each chapter begins with a vignette that draws students into the substance of the material that chapter examines and suggests one of the themes of the book. For example, we begin Chapter 12, "Civil Liberties and Civil Rights," by discussing the debate over the exhibition of Robert Mapplethorpe's photographs at Cincinnati's Contemporary Arts Center. Were the efforts of city officials to ban these photographs, which they considered obscene, an appropriate attempt to maintain order or an infringement on freedom of expression?

Because we believe that students can better evaluate how our political system works when they compare it with politics in other countries, we have increased the number of "Compared with What?" inserts. This feature provides a comparative perspective on such topics as: How much importance do citizens in other parts of the world place on freedom and equality? How do other multicultural societies deal with the question of affirmative action? Are Americans more or less likely to perceive the media as politically powerful than are citizens of other Western democracies?

We also make frequent use of other boxed features throughout the text. They allow us to explore some topics in more detail or discuss matters that don't fit easily into the regular flow of text. Examples include a historical account of Martin Luther King, Jr.'s "I Have a Dream" speech and an explanation of the constitutional mechanism for replacing a president who is unable to carry out the duties of the office.

Each chapter concludes with a brief summary, a list of key terms, and a short list of annotated recommended readings. At the end of the book, we have included an appendix with the complete text of the Declaration of Independence and the Constitution.

The Teaching Package

The Challenge of Democracy, Brief Edition, is part of a tightly integrated set of instructional materials. We have worked closely with some very talented people to produce what we think is a superior set of ancillary materials to help both students and instructors.

The *Instructor's Resource Manual with Test Items* provides teachers with material that relates directly to the thematic framework and organization of the book. The Resources section includes learning objectives, chapter synopses, detailed lecture outlines, and suggested classroom and individual activities. The Test Items section provides identification, multiple-choice, and essay questions. The *Study Guide* contains an overview of each chapter, exercises on reading tables and graphs, topics for student research, and multiple-choice questions for practice. The transparency package, containing forty full-color overhead transparencies, is available to adopters of the book. Adopters may also receive videotapes from Houghton Mifflin's Videotape Program in American Government, written and produced by Ralph Baker and Joseph Losco of Ball State University. The most recent additions to the program are *Making It Work: The Clean Air Act* and *Campaign and Election, 1992*. A corresponding *Video Guide* contains summaries and scripts of each tape, definitions of key terms, multiple-choice questions, and ideas for class activities.

Software ancillaries available to adopters include *LectureBank*, an inventory of complete lectures, and Test Generator, a test generation program containing all the items in the printed *test item bank*. Other software ancillaries are designed to improve students' understanding: *MicroGuide*, a computerized study guide, and *IDEAlog*, an interactive exercise introducing students to the value-conflicts theme in the book. For instructors who want to introduce students to data analysis, a disk and workbook called *Crosstabs* allows students to do research using survey data on the 1988 presidential election and data on voting in Congress, updated after the 1990 election. The *Crosstabs* materials were prepared in collaboration with Philip Schrodt of the University of Kansas. The *Supreme Court Tutorial*, a Hypercard tour of the Supreme Court and its history, includes information on key decisions, biographical material, and photos of twentieth-century justices.

We invite your questions, suggestions, and criticisms. You may contact us at our respective institutions, or, if you have access to an electronic mail service, such as BITNET or INTERNET, you may contact us through the following e-mail address: *cod@nwu.edu.*

Acknowledgments

In the Third Edition of *The Challenge of Democracy* we acknowledged the contributions of many individuals whose advice and assistance have been of great value. We remain in their debt. We have also been fortunate to obtain the help of many outstanding political scientists who reviewed drafts of chapters for the second Brief Edition. Their comments have been tremendously helpful. Our thanks go to

Robert Albritton
Northern Illinois University

Gordon Alexandre
Glendale Community College

Thomas J. Bellows
University of Texas at San Antonio

Jim Case
Sul Ross State University

Alan Clem
University of South Dakota

Frank J. Coppa
Union County College—Cranford

Grady S. Culpepper
Atlanta Metropolitan College

John Culver
California Polytechnical State University

Jim Duke
Richland College

Larry Elowitz
Georgia College

Jerri Gussis
Richland College

Roger Hamburg
Indiana University at South Bend

Samuel Hoff
Delaware State College

Jon Hurwitz
University of Pittsburgh—Main Campus

Fred Kramer
University of Massachusetts—Amherst

Robert Lane
Saginaw Valley State University

Kathryn A. Lee
Seattle Pacific University

David S. Mann
College of Charleston

Maureen Romans
Rhode Island College

Karen Woodward
Burlington County College

Bruce A. Wallin
Northeastern University

In addition, we want to thank the many capable people at Houghton Mifflin who helped make this Brief Edition a reality. We are especially indebted to our development editor, Susan Granoff, whose suggestions were enormously beneficial. The very professional efforts of Margaret Seawell, Michele Casey, and Jean Levitt have also been instrumental.

K.J., J.B., J.G., E.H.

DILEMMAS OF DEMOCRACY

1

Which is better: to live under a government that allows individuals complete freedom to do whatever they please or to live under one that enforces strict law and order? Which is better: to allow businesses and private clubs to choose their customers and members or to pass laws that require them to admit and serve everyone, regardless of race or sex?

For many people, none of these alternatives is satisfactory. All of them pose difficult dilemmas of choice. These dilemmas are tied to opposing philosophies that place different values on freedom, order, and equality.

This book explains American government and politics in light of these dilemmas. It does more than explain the workings of our government; it encourages you to think about what government should—and should not—do. And it judges the American government against democratic ideals, encouraging you to think about how government should make its decisions. As the title implies, *The Challenge of Democracy* argues that good government often involves tough choices.

College students frequently say that American government and politics are hard to understand. In fact, many people voice the same complaint. Seventy percent of a national sample interviewed after the 1988 presidential election agreed with the statement "Politics and government seem so complicated that a person like me can't understand what's going on."[1] With this book, we hope to improve your understanding of "what's going on" by analyzing and evaluating the norms, or values, that people use to judge political events. Our purpose is not to preach what people ought to favor in making policy decisions; it is to teach what values are at stake.

Teaching without preaching is not easy; no one can exclude personal values completely from political analysis. But our approach minimizes this problem by concentrating on the dilemmas that confront governments when they are forced to choose between policies that threaten equally cherished values. An example: Americans value both the U.S. flag and the Bill of Rights to the U.S. Constitution. In a split decision, the U.S. Supreme Court ruled in 1989 that burning the flag as a form of protest is a valid expression of "freedom of speech" and is thus protected under the First Amendment in the Bill of Rights. Dissenting justices argued that the people and their representatives should be entitled to safeguard the nation's symbol. Should the government act to uphold the Constitution or to protect the flag?

Every government policy reflects a choice between conflicting values. We want you to understand this idea, to understand that all government policies reinforce certain values (norms) at the expense of others. We want you to interpret policy issues (for example, should flag burning go unpunished?) with an understanding of the fundamental values in question (freedom of expression versus order and protection of national symbols) and the broader political overtones (liberal or conservative politics).

By looking beyond specifics to underlying normative principles, you should be able to make more sense out of politics. Our framework for analysis does not encompass all the complexities of American government, but it should help your knowledge grow by improving your digestion of political information. We begin by considering the basic purposes of government. In short, why do we need it?

The Purposes of Government

Most people do not like being told what to do. Fewer still like being coerced into acting a certain way. Yet every day, millions of American motorists dutifully drive on the right-hand side of the street and obediently stop at red lights. Every year, millions of U.S. citizens struggle to complete their income tax forms before midnight, April 15. In both these examples, the coercive power of government is at work. If people do not like being coerced, why do they submit to it? In other words, why do we have government?

Government can be defined as the legitimate use of force—including imprisonment and execution—within territorial boundaries to control human behavior. All governments require citizens to surrender some freedom in the process of being governed. But why do people surrender their freedom to this control? They do so to obtain the benefits of government. Throughout history, government seems to have served two major purposes: maintaining order (preserving life and protecting property) and providing public goods. More recently, some governments have pursued a third purpose: promoting equality.

Maintaining Order

Maintaining order is the oldest objective of government. **Order** in this context is rich with meaning. Let us start with the notion of "law and order." Maintaining order in this sense means establishing the rule of law to preserve life and to protect property. To the seventeenth-century philosopher Thomas Hobbes (1588–1679), preserving life was the most important function of government. In his classic philosophical treatise, *Leviathan* (1651), Hobbes described life without government as life in a "state of nature." Without rules, people would live like predators, stealing and killing for personal benefit. In Hobbes's classic phrase, life in a state of nature would be "solitary, poor, nasty, brutish, and short." He believed that a single ruler, or sovereign, had to possess unquestioned authority to guarantee the safety of the weak against the attacks of the strong. He believed that complete obedience to the sovereign's strict laws was a small price to pay for the security of living in a civil society.

Most of us can only imagine what a state of nature would be like. We might think of the "Wild West" in the days before a good guy with a white hat rode into town and established law and order. But in some parts of the world today, people actually live in a state of lawlessness. In this decade the anarchy and resulting famine in Somalia and the conflict that accompanied the break-up of Yugoslavia suggested what a state of nature might be like. Throughout history, authoritarian rulers used people's fears of civil disorder to justify their governments as the "established order."

In his focus on life in the cruel state of nature, Hobbes saw government primarily as a means for survival. Other theorists, taking survival for granted, believed that government protected order by preserving private property (goods and land owned by individuals). Foremost among them was John Locke (1632–1704), an English philosopher. In *Two Treatises on Government* (1690), he wrote that the protection of life, liberty, and property was the basic objective of government. His thinking strongly influenced the Declaration of Independence, which identified "life, liberty, and the pursuit of happiness" as "unalienable rights" of citizens under government.

Not everyone believes that the protection of private property is a valid objective of government. The German philosopher Karl Marx (1818–1883) rejected the private ownership of property that is used in the production of goods or services. Marx's ideas form the basis of **communism**, a complex theory that gives ownership of all land and productive facilities to the people—in effect, to the government. Today, Russia and other states that were once included within the Soviet Union are moving haltingly toward free-market economies that permit the private ownership of land. However, in line with communist theory, the 1977 constitution of the former Soviet Union enunciated the following principles of government ownership:

> State property, i.e., the common property of the Soviet people, is the principal form of socialist property. The land, its minerals, waters, and forests are the exclusive property of the state. The state owns the basic means of production in industry, construction, and agriculture; means of transport and communication; the banks; the property of state-run trade organizations and public utilities, and other state-run undertakings; most urban housing; and other property necessary for state purposes.[2]

Outside communist societies, the extent to which government must protect property or can take it away is a political issue that forms the basis of much ideological debate.

Providing Public Goods

After governments have established basic order, they can pursue other ends. Using their coercive powers, they can tax citizens to raise funds to spend on **public goods**—benefits and services that are available to everyone such as education, sanitation, and parks. Public goods benefit all citizens but are not likely to be produced by the voluntary acts of individuals. The government of ancient Rome, for example, built aqueducts to carry fresh water from the mountains to the city. Road building is another public good that has been provided by governments since ancient times.

Some government enterprises that have been common in other countries—running railroads, operating coal mines, generating electric power—are politically controversial or even unacceptable in the United States. Many people believe public goods and services should be provided by private businesses operating for profit.

Promoting Equality

The promotion of equality has not always been a major objective of government. It gained prominence only in this century in the aftermath of industrialization and urbanization. Confronted by the contrast of poverty amid plenty, some political leaders in European nations pioneered extensive government programs to improve life for the lower classes. Under the emerging concept of the **welfare state**, government's role expanded to provide individuals with medical care, education, and a guaranteed income "from the cradle to the grave." Sweden, Britain, and other nations adopted welfare programs aimed at reducing social inequalities. This relatively new purpose of government has been by far the most controversial. Taxation for public goods (building roads and schools, for example) is often opposed because of its cost alone. Taxation for government programs to promote economic and social equality is opposed more strongly on principle.

The key issue here is the government's role in redistributing income—taking from the wealthy to give to the poor. Charity (voluntary giving to the poor) has a strong basis in Western religious traditions; using the power of the state to support the poor does not. Using the state to redistribute income was originally a radical idea set forth by Marx as the ultimate principle of developed communism: "from each according to his ability, to each according to his needs."[3] This extreme has never operated in any government, not even in communist states. But over time, taking from the rich to help the needy has become a legitimate function of most governments. In the United States, food stamps and Aid to Families with Dependent Children (AFDC) are typical examples of government programs that tend to redistribute income—and generate controversy.

Government can also promote social equality through policies that do not redistribute income. For example, it can regulate social behavior to enforce equality—as it did when the Supreme Court ruled in 1987 that Rotary Clubs must admit women members. Policies that regulate social behavior, like those that redistribute income, inevitably clash with the value of personal freedom.

A Conceptual Framework for Analyzing Government

Citizens have very different views on how vigorously they want government to maintain order, provide public goods, and promote equality. Of the three objectives, providing for public goods is usually less controversial than maintaining order or promoting equality. After all, government spending for highways, schools, and parks carries benefits for nearly every citizen. Moreover, these services merely cost money. The cost of maintaining order and promoting equality is greater than money; it usually means a trade-off of basic values.

To understand government and the political process, you must be able to recognize these trade-offs and identify the basic values they entail. You need to take a broad view, a much broader view than that offered by examining specific political events. You need to employ political concepts.

A *concept* is a generalized idea about a class of items or thoughts. It groups various events, objects, or qualities under a common classification or label. The conceptual framework that guides this book consists of five concepts that figure prominently in political analysis. We regard these five concepts as especially important to a broad understanding of American politics, and we use them repeatedly throughout the book. This framework will help you evaluate political happenings long after you have read this text.

The five concepts that we emphasize deal with the fundamental issues of *what* government tries to do and *how* government decides to do it. The concepts that relate to what government tries to do are *order, freedom,* and *equality.* All governments by definition value order; maintaining order is part of the meaning of government. Most governments at least claim to preserve individual freedom while they maintain order, although they vary widely in the extent to which they succeed. Very few governments even profess to guarantee equality, and governments differ greatly in policies that pit equality against freedom. Our conceptual framework should help you evaluate the extent to which the United States pursues all three values through its government.

How government chooses the proper mix of order, freedom, and equality in its policymaking has to do with the *process* of choice rather than with the outcome of it. We evaluate the American governmental process using two models of democratic government: the *majoritarian* and the *pluralist.* Most governments profess to be democracies. Whether they are depends on how the term is defined. Even countries that Americans agree are democracies—for example, the United States and Britain—differ substantially in the type of democracy they practice. We use our conceptual models of democratic government both to classify the type of democracy practiced in the United States and evaluate the government's success in fulfilling that model.

These five concepts can be organized into two groups: concepts that identify the *values* pursued by government and concepts that describe *models* of democratic government. Freedom, order, and equality fall in the first category; majoritarian democracy and pluralist democracy take their place in the second. First we will examine freedom, order, and equality as conflicting values pursued by government. Later in this chapter we will discuss majoritarian democracy and pluralist democracy as alternative institutional models for implementing democratic government.

The Concepts of Freedom, Order, and Equality

These three terms—*freedom, order,* and *equality*—have different connotations in American politics. Both freedom and equality are positive terms that politicians have learned to use to their own advantage. Consequently, freedom and equality mean different things to different people at different times—depending on the political context in which they are used. Order, in contrast, has negative connotations for many people, for it symbolizes government intrusion in private lives. Except during periods of social strife, few politicians in Western democracies call openly for more order. Because all governments infringe on freedom, we examine that concept first.

Freedom.   Freedom can be used in two major senses: *freedom to* and *freedom from*. Franklin Delano Roosevelt used the word in both senses in a speech he made shortly after the United States entered World War II. He described four freedoms—freedom of religion, freedom of speech, freedom from fear, and freedom from want.

Freedom to is the absence of constraints on behavior. In this sense, freedom is synonymous with *liberty*. **Freedom from** suggests immunity from fear and want. In the modern political context, *freedom from* often symbolizes the fight against exploitation and oppression. The cry "Freedom Now!" of the civil rights movement in the 1960s conveyed this meaning. If you recognize that freedom in this sense means immunity from discrimination, you can see that it comes close to the concept of equality.[4] We avoid using the word *freedom* to mean "freedom from"; for this meaning, we simply use the word *equality*.

Order.   When order is viewed in the narrow sense of preserving life and protecting property, most citizens would concede the importance of maintaining order and thereby grant the need for government. However, when order is viewed in the broader sense of preserving the social order, people are more likely to argue that maintaining order is not a legitimate function of government. *Social order* refers to established patterns of authority in society and to traditional modes of behavior. However, it is important to remember that social order can change. Today, perfectly respectable men and women wear bathing suits that would have caused a scandal at the turn of the century.

A government can protect the established order under its **police power**—its authority to safeguard citizens' safety, health, welfare, and morals. The extent to which government should use this authority is a topic of ongoing debate in the United States and is constantly being redefined by the courts. There are those who fear the evolution of a *police state*—government that uses its power to regulate nearly all aspects of behavior.

Most governments are inherently conservative; they tend to resist social change. But some governments have as a primary objective the restructuring of the social order. Social change is most dramatic when a government is overthrown through force and replaced by a revolutionary government. Governments can work at changing social patterns more gradually through the legal process. Our use of the term *order* in this book includes all three aspects of the term: preserving life, protecting property, and maintaining traditional patterns of social relationships.

Rosa Parks: She Sat for Equality
Rosa Parks had just finished a day's work as a seamstress and was sitting in the front of a bus in Montgomery, Alabama, going home. A white man claimed her seat, which in December 1955 he could do according to the law. When she refused to move and was arrested, angry blacks led by Dr. Martin Luther King, Jr. began a boycott of the Montgomery bus company.

Equality.   Like *freedom* and *order*, *equality* is used in different senses to support different causes.

Political equality in elections is easy to define: Each citizen has one and only one vote. This basic concept is central to democratic theory (a subject we explore at length later in this chapter). But when some people advocate political equality, they mean more than "one person, one vote." These people contend that an urban ghetto dweller and the chair of the board of General Motors are not politically equal even though each has one vote. Through occupation or wealth, some citizens are more able than others to influence political decisions. For example, wealthy citizens can exert influence by advertising in the mass media or by contacting friends in high places. Lacking great wealth and political connections, most citizens do not have this kind of influence. Thus, some analysts argue that equality in wealth, education, and status—that is, **social equality**—is necessary for true political equality. There are two routes to achieving social equality: providing equal opportunities and ensuring equal outcomes.

Equality of opportunity means that each person has the same chance to succeed in life. This idea is deeply ingrained in American culture. The Constitution prohibits titles of nobility, property ownership is not a requirement for holding public office, and public schools and libraries are free to all. To many people, the concept of social equality is satisfied just by offering opportunities for people to advance themselves. It is not essential that people end up being equal after using those opportunities.

For others, true social equality means nothing less than **equality of outcome**.[5] They believe that society must see to it that people *are* equal. It is not enough for governments to provide people with equal opportunities; they must also design policies to redistribute wealth and status so that economic equality and social equality are actually achieved.

Some link equality of outcome with the concept of governmental **rights**—the idea that every citizen is entitled to certain benefits of government, that government should guarantee its citizens adequate (if not equal) housing, employment, medical care, and income as a matter of right. If citizens are entitled to government benefits as a matter of right, then government efforts to promote equality of outcome become legitimized.

Clearly, the concept of equality of outcome is very different from that of equality of opportunity and requires a much greater degree of government activity. It is also the concept of equality that clashes most directly with the concept of freedom. By taking from one to give to another—which is necessary for the redistribution of income and status—the government clearly creates winners and losers. The winners may believe that justice has been served by the redistribution. The losers often feel strongly that their freedom to enjoy their income and status has suffered.

Two Dilemmas of Government

The two major dilemmas facing American government in the 1990s stem from the oldest and the newest objectives of government. The oldest is maintaining order; the newest, promoting equality. Both order and equality are important social values, but government cannot pursue either without sacrificing a third important value: individual freedom. The clash between freedom and order forms the *original* dilemma of government; the clash between freedom and equality, the *modern* dilemma of government. Although the dilemmas are very different, each involves trading off some amount of freedom for another value.

The original dilemma: Freedom versus order.   The conflict between freedom and order originates in the very meaning of government as the legitimate use of force to control human behavior. How much freedom must a citizen surrender to government? This dilemma has occupied philosophers for hundreds of years.

The original purpose of government was to protect life and property, to make citizens safe from violence. How well is the American government doing today in providing law and order to its citizens? Many people living in large cities would say not too well. Surveys indicate that Americans do not trust their urban governments to protect them from crime when they go out alone at night.[6]

When the old communist governments still ruled in Eastern Europe, the climate of fear in urban America stood in stark contrast with the pervasive sense of personal safety in such cities as Moscow, Warsaw, and Prague. Then it was common to see old and young strolling along late at night on the streets and in the parks. The old communist regimes gave their police great powers to control guns, monitor citizens' movements, and arrest and imprison suspicious people—which enabled them to do a better job of maintaining order. Communist governments deliberately chose order over freedom.

The value conflict between freedom and order represents the original dilemma of government. In the abstract, people value both freedom and order; but in real life, any policy that works toward one of these values by definition takes away from the other. In a democracy, policy choices hinge on how much citizens value freedom and how much they value order.

The modern dilemma: Freedom versus equality.   Popular opinion has it that freedom and equality go hand in hand. In reality, these two values usually clash when governments enact policies to promote social equality. Because social equality is a relatively recent government objective, deciding between policies that promote equality at the expense of freedom and vice versa is the modern dilemma of politics. Consider these examples:

- During the 1970s, the courts ordered the busing of schoolchildren to achieve equal proportions of blacks and whites in public schools. This action was motivated by concern for educational equality, but it also impaired freedom of choice.

- During the 1980s, some states passed legislation that went beyond giving men and women equal pay for equal work to the more radical notion of *pay equity*—equal pay for *comparable* work. Women had to be paid at a rate equal to men's—even if they had different jobs—providing the women's jobs were of "comparable worth" (meaning the skills and responsibilities were comparable).

- In the 1990s, Congress prohibited discrimination in employment, public services, and public accommodations on the basis of a person's physical or mental disability. Under the 1990 Americans with Disabilities Act, businesses with twenty-five or more employees could not pass over an otherwise qualified person with a handicap in employment or promotion, and new buses and trains had to be made accessible to them.

These examples illustrate the problem of using government power to promote equality. The clash between freedom and order is obvious, but that between freedom and equality is more subtle. Often it goes unnoticed by the American people, who think of freedom and equality as complementary, rather than conflicting, values. When forced to choose between the two, however, Americans tend to choose freedom over equality more often than do people in other countries. The emphasis on equality over freedom was especially strong in the Soviet Union, which traditionally guaranteed its citizens medical care, inexpensive housing, and other social services.

The clashes among freedom, order, and equality explain a great deal of the political conflict in the United States. These conflicts also underlie the ideologies that people use to structure their understanding of politics.

Ideology and the Scope of Government

People hold different opinions about the merits of government policies. Sometimes their views are based on self-interest and sometimes on individual values and beliefs. Some people hold an assortment of values and beliefs that produce contradictory opinions on government policies. Others organize their opinions into a **political ideology**—a consistent set of values and beliefs about the proper purpose and scope of government.

Political writers often describe the ideologies of politicians and voters as "liberal" or "conservative." In popular usage, liberals favor an active, broad role for government in society; conservatives, a passive, narrow role. People often divide sharply on ideological grounds over the desirability of government programs. By carefully analyzing their political ideologies, we can explain their support of and opposition to seemingly diverse government policies. To gain perspective regarding the range of ideologies, imagine a continuum. At one end is the belief that government should do everything; at the other, the belief that government should not exist. These extreme ideologies—from most government to least government—and those that fall between them are shown in Figure 1.1.

Totalitarianism

Totalitarianism is a belief that government should have unlimited power. A totalitarian government controls all sectors of society: business, labor, education, religion, sports, the arts. A true totalitarian favors a network of laws, rules, and regulations that guides every aspect of individual behavior. The object is to produce a perfect society serving some master plan for "the common good." A list of societies that have

MOST   LEAST
GOVERNMENT   GOVERNMENT

POLITICAL THEORIES		
Totalitarianism	Libertarianism	Anarchism

ECONOMIC THEORIES		
Socialism	Capitalism	Laissez Faire

POPULAR POLITICAL LABELS IN AMERICA	
Liberal	Conservative

FIGURE 1.1   Ideology and the Scope of Government
We can classify political ideologies according to the scope of action that people
are willing to give government in dealing with social and economic problems.
In this figure, the three lines map out various philosophical positions along an
underlying continuum ranging from "most" to "least" government. Notice
that conventional politics in the United States spans only a narrow portion of
the theoretical possibilities for government action.

In popular usage, liberals favor a greater scope of government; conserva-
tives, a narrower scope. But over time, this traditional distinction has eroded
and now oversimplifies the differences between liberals and conservatives. See
Figure 1.2 on page 16 for a more discriminating classification of liberals and
conservatives.

come perilously close to "perfection" would include Germany under
Adolf Hitler and the Soviet Union under Joseph Stalin.

Socialism

Whereas *totalitarianism* refers to government in general, *socialism* per-
tains to government's role in the economy. Like communism, socialism
is an economic system based on Marxist theory. Under **socialism** (and
communism), the scope of government extends to ownership or control
of the basic industries that produce goods and services (communications, heavy industry, transportation, and so on). Although socialism
favors a strong role for government in regulating private industry and
directing the economy, it allows more room than communism does for
private ownership of productive capacity.

Communism in theory was supposed to result in a "withering
away" of the state, but communist governments in practice tended toward totalitarianism, controlling both political and social life through
a dominant party organization. Some socialist governments, however,

practice **democratic socialism**. They guarantee civil liberties (such as freedom of speech and freedom of religion) and allow their citizens to determine the extent of government activity through free elections and competitive political parties. The governments of Britain, Sweden, Germany, and France, among other democracies, have at times since World War II been avowedly socialist.

Capitalism

Capitalism also relates to the government's role in the economy. In contrast to both socialism and communism, **capitalism** supports *free enterprise*—private businesses operating without government regulations. Some theorists, most notably economist Milton Friedman, argue that free enterprise is necessary for free politics.[7] Whether this argument is valid depends in part on a person's understanding of democracy (a subject we discuss later in this chapter).

The United States is decidedly a capitalist country, more so than most other Western nations. Despite the U.S. government's enormous budget, it owns or operates relatively few public enterprises. For example, railroads, airlines, and television stations are privately owned in the United States; these businesses are frequently owned by the government in other countries. But the U.S. government does extend its authority into the economic sphere, regulating private businesses and directing the overall economy. American liberals and conservatives both embrace capitalism, but they differ on the nature and amount of government intervention in the economy they consider necessary and appropriate.

Libertarianism

Libertarianism opposes all government action except that which is necessary to protect life and property. Libertarians grudgingly recognize the necessity of government but believe that it should be as limited as possible. For example, libertarians grant the need for traffic laws to ensure safe and efficient automobile travel. But they oppose laws, for instance, that set a minimum drinking age as a restriction on individual actions. Libertarians believe that social programs that provide food, clothing, and shelter are outside the proper scope of government. They also oppose any government intervention in the economy. This kind of economic policy is called **laissez faire**—a French phrase that means "let [people] do [as they please]."

Anarchism

Anarchism stands opposite totalitarianism on the political continuum. Anarchists oppose all government in any form. As a political philosophy, anarchism values freedom above all else. Because all government involves some restriction on personal freedom (for example, forcing people to drive on one side of the road), a pure anarchist would even object to traffic laws. Like totalitarianism, anarchism is not a popular philosophy, but it does have adherents on the political fringes.

Liberals and Conservatives—The Narrow Middle

As shown in Figure 1.1, practical politics in the United States ranges over only the central portion of the continuum. The extreme positions—totalitarianism and anarchism—are rarely argued in public debate. And in this era of distrust of "big government," few American politicians would openly advocate socialism—although one did in 1990 and won election to Congress. Nevertheless, more than fifty people ran for Congress in 1992 as candidates of the Libertarian party. Although none won, American libertarians are sufficiently vocal to be heard in the debate over the role of government.

Most of that debate, however, is limited to a narrow range of political thought. On one side are people commonly called *liberals*; on the other, *conservatives*. In popular usage, liberals favor more government; conservatives, less. This distinction is very clear when the issue is government spending to provide public goods. Liberals favor generous government support for education, wildlife protection, public transportation, and a whole range of social programs.* Conservatives want smaller government budgets and fewer government programs. They support free enterprise, arguing against government job programs, regulation of business, and legislation of working conditions and wage rates.

But in other areas, liberal and conservative ideologies are less consistent. In theory, **liberals** favor government activism, yet they oppose government regulation of, for example, abortions. In theory, **conservatives** oppose government activism, yet they support government control over the publication of sexually explicit material. What is going on? Are American political attitudes hopelessly contradictory, or is something missing in our analysis of these ideologies today? Actually, something is missing. To understand the liberal and conservative stances on political issues, we have to look not only at the scope of government action but also at the purpose. That is, to understand a political ideology, we must understand how it incorporates the values of freedom, order, and equality.

---

* Don't confuse *libertarians* with *liberals*. The words are similar, but their meanings are very different. *Libertarianism* draws on *liberty* as its root and means "absence of governmental constraint." In American political usage, *liberalism* evolved from the root word *liberal*. Over time, liberal has come to mean something closer to "generous" and "tolerant" in the sense that liberals are willing to support government spending on social programs as well as to respect different lifestyles.

American Political Ideologies and the Purpose of Government

Much of American politics revolves around the two dilemmas just described: freedom versus order and freedom versus equality. These two dilemmas do not account for all political conflict, but they offer insight into the workings of politics and organize the seemingly chaotic world of political events, actors, and issues.

Liberals Versus Conservatives: The New Differences

Liberals and conservatives are different, but their differences no longer hinge on the narrow question of the government's role in providing public goods. Liberals still favor more government and conservatives still want less, but this is no longer the critical difference between them. Today that difference stems from their attitudes toward the purpose of government. Conservatives support the original purpose of government, maintaining social order. They are willing to use the coercive power of the state to force citizens to be orderly. Conservatives do not stop with defining, preventing, and punishing crime, however. They want to preserve traditional patterns of social relations—the domestic role of women and the importance of religion in school and family life, for example.

Liberals are less likely than conservatives to use government power to maintain order. In general, liberals are more tolerant of alternative lifestyles—for example, homosexual behavior. Liberals do not shy away from using government coercion, but they use it for a different purpose—to promote equality. They support laws that ensure homosexuals receive equal treatment in employment, housing, and education; that require the busing of schoolchildren to achieve racial equality; that force private businesses to hire and promote women and members of minority groups; that require public carriers to provide equal access to people with handicaps.

Conservatives do not oppose equality, but they do not value it to the extent of using the government's power to enforce equality. For liberals, the use of that power to guarantee equality is both valid and necessary.

A Two-dimensional Classification of Ideologies

To classify liberal and conservative ideologies more accurately, we have to incorporate freedom, order, and equality in the classification. We do this using the model in Figure 1.2. It depicts these conflicting values along two separate dimensions, each anchored in maximum freedom at the lower left. One dimension extends horizontally from maximum freedom on the left to maximum order on the right. The other extends vertically from maximum freedom at the bottom to maximum equality

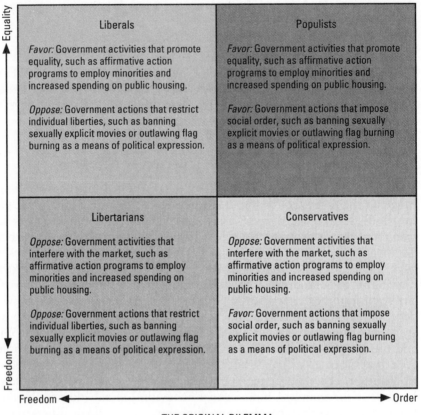

FIGURE 1.2   Ideologies: A Two-dimensional Framework
The four ideological types above are defined by the values they favor in resolving the two major dilemmas of government: How much freedom should be sacrificed in pursuit of order? And how much freedom should be sacrificed in pursuit of equality? Test yourself by thinking about the values that are most important to you. Which box in the figure best represents your combination of values?

at the top. Each box represents a different ideological type: libertarians, liberals, conservatives, and populists.*

Libertarians value freedom more than order or equality. (We use this term for people who have libertarian tendencies but who may not accept the whole philosophy.) In practical terms, libertarians want mini-

---

* The ideological groupings we describe here conform to the classification in William S. Maddox and Stuart A. Lilie, *Beyond Liberal and Conservative: Reassessing the Political Spectrum* (Washington, D.C.: Cato Institute, 1984), p. 5. However, our formulation—in terms of the values of freedom, order, and equality—is quite different.

mal government intervention in both the economic and the social spheres. For example, they oppose food stamp programs and laws against abortion.

Liberals value freedom more than order but not more than equality. Liberals oppose laws against abortion but support food stamp programs. **Conservatives** value freedom more than equality but are willing to restrict freedom to preserve social order. Conservatives oppose food stamp programs but favor laws against abortion.

Finally, there is the ideological type positioned at the upper right in Figure 1.2. This group values *both* equality and order more than freedom. Its members support both food stamp programs and laws against abortion. We will call this new group **populists**. The term populist derives from a rural reform movement that was active in the United States in the late 1800s. Populists thought of government as an instrument to promote the advancement of common people against moneyed or vested interests. They used their voting power both to regulate business and enforce their moral judgments on minorities whose political and social values differed from the majority's.[8] Today the term aptly describes those who favor government action both to reduce inequalities and ensure social order.

By analyzing political ideologies on two dimensions, rather than one, we can explain why people seem to be liberal on one issue (favoring a broader scope of government action) and conservative on another (favoring less government action). The answer hinges on the action's *purpose*: Which value does it promote—order or equality? According to our typology, only libertarians and populists are consistent in their attitudes toward the scope of government activity, whatever its purpose. Libertarians value freedom so highly that they oppose most government efforts to enforce either order or equality. Populists are inclined to trade off freedom for both order and equality. Liberals and conservatives, in contrast, favor or oppose government activity depending on its purpose. As you will learn in Chapter 4, large groups of Americans fall into each of the four ideological categories. Because Americans choose four different resolutions to the original and modern dilemmas of government, the simple labels *liberal* and *conservative* no longer describe contemporary political ideologies as well as they did in the 1930s, 1940s, and 1950s.

To this point, our discussion of political ideologies has centered on conflicting views about the values government should pursue. We now turn our attention to alternative institutional models for implementing democratic government.

The American Governmental Process: Majoritarian or Pluralist

On January 17, 1989, a drifter named Patrick Purdy opened fire with his AK-47 on students in a crowded elementary school playground in Stockton, California. Five children were killed, and twenty-nine students and one teacher were injured.[9]

The Stockton massacre prompted some members of Congress to push for a ban on semiautomatic weapons such as the AK-47. The National Rifle Association (NRA) vehemently disagreed, claiming that such a ban was an infringement on the constitutional right of the people to "bear arms." The 2.6-million-member group has been very successful in defeating gun control measures proposed in Congress. Indeed, in 1986 the organization was successful in getting Congress to pass a law weakening a very modest gun control bill that was passed in 1968 in the wake of the assassinations of Robert Kennedy and Martin Luther King, Jr.

The NRA's ability to thwart gun control efforts is particularly interesting in light of the American people's opinion on the subject. Seventy percent of the public favors stricter gun control laws, and 72 percent favors a ban on assault rifles.[10] The Senate managed to include (by a 1-vote margin) a ban on nine types of assault rifles in its 1990 anticrime bill, but the House refused to go along. The provision on semiautomatics was stripped from the final version of the legislation by a House-Senate conference committee.[11]

Over the years, Congress has regularly backed the interests of this particular minority opposed to gun control over the preferences of the majority, which favors gun control. Is it democratic for policymakers to favor an intensely vocal minority at the expense of a less-committed majority?

To assist you in answering this question, we examine *how* government should decide what to do. In particular, we set forth criteria for judging whether a government's decision-making process is democratic.

The Theory of Democratic Government

The origins of democratic theory lie in ancient Greek political thought. Greek philosophers classified governments according to the number of citizens involved in the process. Imagine a continuum running from rule by one person, through rule by a few, to rule by many. At one extreme is an **autocracy**, in which one individual has the power to make all important decisions. Some argue that Hitler ruled Germany autocratically.

Oligarchy puts government power in the hands of "the few." At one time, it was common for the nobility or the major landowners of a country to rule as an aristocracy. Today, military leaders are often the rulers in countries governed by an oligarchy.

At the other extreme of the continuum is **democracy**, which means "authority in, or rule by, the people."[12] Most scholars believe that the United States, Britain, France, and other countries in Western Europe are genuine democracies.

Freedom, the Universal Language
These 1989 demonstrators in Beijing hoped to embarrass the authoritarian Chinese government during a state visit by former Soviet leader Mikhail Gorbachev. Their message was, if freedom could come to the Soviet Union, why not to China?

The Meaning and Symbolism of Democracy

Americans have a simple answer to the question "Who should govern?" They respond, "The people." Unfortunately, this answer is too simple. It fails to define who "the people" are. Are young children included? Recent immigrants? Illegal aliens? This answer also fails to tell us how the people should do the governing. Should they be assembled in a stadium? Vote by mail? Choose others to govern for them? Let us take a closer look at what *government* by the *people* really means.

The word *democracy* originated in Greek writings around the fifth century B.C. *Demos* referred to the common people, the masses; *kratos* meant "power." The ancient Greeks were afraid of democracy—rule by the people. That fear is evident in the term *demagogue*. We use the term today to refer to a politician who appeals to and often deceives the masses by manipulating their emotions and prejudices.

Many centuries after the Greeks first defined democracy, the idea still carried the connotation of mob rule. When George Washington was president, opponents of a new political party disparagingly called it a "democratic" party. Today, however, democracy has become the apple pie and motherhood of political discourse. Like *justice* and *decency*, *democracy* is used reverently by politicians of all persuasions. Even totalitarian regimes use it. North Korea calls itself the Democratic People's Republic of Korea, even though by American standards it is one of the most undemocratic places on earth. Like other complex concepts, democracy means different things to different people.

There are two major schools of thought about what constitutes democracy. The first believes democracy is a form of government. It emphasizes the *procedures* that enable the people to govern—meeting to discuss issues, voting in elections, running for public office. The second sees democracy in the *substance* of government policies—in guaranteeing freedom of religion and providing for human needs. The *procedural* approach focuses on *how* decisions are made; the *substantive* approach is concerned with *what* government does.[13]

The Procedural View of Democracy

Procedural democratic theory sets forth principles that describe how government should make decisions. These principles address three distinct questions:

1. *Who* should participate in decision making?
2. *How much* should each participant's vote count?
3. *How many* votes are needed to reach a decision?

According to procedural democratic theory, all adults within the boundaries of the political community should participate in government decision making. We refer to this principle as **universal participation**. How much should each participant's vote count? According to procedural theory, all votes should be counted *equally*. This is the principle of **political equality**. Notice that universal participation and political equality are two distinct principles. It is not enough for everyone to participate in a decision; all votes must carry equal weight.

Finally, how many votes are needed to reach a decision? Procedural theory prescribes that a group should decide to do what the *majority* of its participants wants to do. This principle is called **majority rule**. (If participants divide over more than two alternatives and none receives a simple majority, the principle usually defaults to *plurality rule*, in which the group should do what most participants want.)

A Complication: Direct Versus Indirect Democracy

These three principles—universal participation, political equality, and majority rule—are widely recognized as necessary for democratic decision making. In small, simple societies, these principles can be met in a **direct democracy**, in which all members of the group meet to make decisions while observing political equality and majority rule. Some-

Speak Right Up
At this neighborhood meeting a citizen speaks out regarding airport noise
abatement issues. Such citizen participation in the democratic process occurs
throughout the United States. It may be done directly, as in the town meetings
of some small New England villages, or indirectly, as citizens make their
views known to elected officials at all levels of government.

thing close to direct democracy is practiced in some New England villages, where citizens gather in town meetings to make community
decisions.

In large, complex societies, however, the people cannot assemble in
one place to participate directly in government. An alternative is indirect democracy, or what is commonly called **representative democracy.**
Here citizens participate in government by electing public officials to
make government decisions for them.

Within the context of representative democracy, we adhere to the
principles of universal participation, political equality, and majority rule
to guarantee that elections are democratic. But what happens after the
election? The elected representatives might not make the same decisions the people would have made if they had gathered for the same
purpose. To cope with this possibility in representative government,
procedural theory specifies a fourth decision-making principle: **respon-**

siveness. According to this principle, elected representatives should follow the general contours of public opinion as complex pieces of legislation are formulated.

With responsiveness added to deal with the case of indirect democracy, there are now four principles of procedural democracy:

- Universal participation
- Political equality
- Majority rule
- Government responsiveness to public opinion

The Substantive View of Democracy

According to procedural theory, the principle of responsiveness is absolute. The government should do what the majority wants, regardless of what that is. At first, this seems a reasonable way to protect the rights of citizens in a representative democracy. But think for a minute. Christians account for more than 90 percent of the U.S. population. Suppose that the Christian majority backs a constitutional amendment to require Bible reading in public schools, that the amendment is passed by Congress, and that it is ratified by the states. From a strictly procedural view, the action would be democratic. But what about freedom of religion? What about the rights of minorities? To limit the government's responsiveness to public opinion, we must look outside procedural democratic theory to substantive democratic theory.

Substantive democratic theory focuses on the substance of government policies, not on the procedures followed in making those policies. It argues that in a democratic government, certain principles must be embodied in government policies. Substantive theorists would reject a law that requires Bible reading in schools because it would violate a substantive principle, the freedom of religion.

In defining the principles that underlie democratic government—and the policies of such government—most substantive theorists agree on a basic criterion: Government policies should guarantee civil liberties (guaranteed freedoms of action, such as freedom of religion and freedom of expression) and civil rights (social treatment to which citizens are entitled, such as protection against discrimination in employment and housing). According to this standard, the claim that the United States is a democracy rests on its record in ensuring its citizens these liberties and rights. (We look at how good this record is in Chapter 12.)

Agreement among substantive theorists breaks down when discussion moves from civil rights to *social* rights (adequate health care, quality education, decent housing) and *economic* rights (private property, steady employment). They disagree most sharply on whether a government must promote social equality to qualify as a democracy. For example, must a state guarantee unemployment benefits and adequate public housing to be called democratic? Some insist that policies that promote social equality are essential to democratic government.[14] Others reject expanding the requirements of substantative democracy beyond those policies that safeguard civil liberties and civil rights. The core of this nation's substantive principles of democracy is, of course, embedded in the Bill of Rights and other amendments to the Constitution.

The political ideology of a theorist tends to explain his or her position on what democracy really requires in substantive policies. Conservative theorists have a narrow view of the scope of democratic government and a narrow view of the social and economic rights guaranteed by that government. Liberal theorists believe that a democratic government should guarantee its citizens a much broader spectrum of social and economic rights.

Procedural Democracy Versus Substantive Democracy

There is a problem with the substantive view of democracy. It does not provide clear, precise criteria for determining whether a government is democratic. Thus, theorists are free to promote their pet values—separation of church and state, guaranteed employment, equal rights for women, whatever—under the guise of substantive democracy.

There is also a problem with the procedural viewpoint. Although it presents specific criteria for democratic government, those criteria can produce undesirable social policies that prey on minorities. This situation clashes with **minority rights**—the idea that citizens are entitled to certain rights that cannot be denied by majority decisions. One way to protect minority rights is to limit the principle of majority rule by, for instance, requiring a two-thirds majority or some other extraordinary majority when decisions must be made on certain subjects or to put the issue in the Constitution and thereby beyond the reach of majority rule.

Clearly, procedural and substantive democracy are not always compatible. In choosing one over the other, we are also choosing to focus on either procedures or policies. As authors of this text, we favor a compromise between the two. On the whole, we favor the procedural conception of democracy because it more closely approaches the classical definition of *democracy*—"government by the people." And procedural democracy is founded on clear, well-established rules for decision making. But the theory has a serious drawback: It allows a democratic government to enact policies that can violate the substantive principles of democracy. Thus, pure procedural democracy should be diluted so that minority rights guaranteeing civil liberties and civil rights are part of the structure of government.

In the real world of politics, drawing the appropriate line between which issues should be subject to procedural democracy and which should fall under the coverage of substantive democracy is not always easy. People frequently disagree over this division. But if they realize that democratic government and desirable policies are not necessarily synonymous, then they should be able to live with a political system that sets standards for the decision-making process, if not for the decisions themselves.

Institutional Models of Democracy

Some democratic theorists favor institutions that tie government decisions closely to the desires of the majority of citizens. If most citizens want laws against the sale of pornography, then the government should outlaw pornography. If citizens want more money spent on defense and less on social welfare (or vice versa), then the government should act accordingly. For these theorists, the essence of democratic government is majority rule and responsiveness.

Other theorists place less importance on these principles. They do not believe in relying heavily on mass opinion. Instead, they favor institutions that allow groups of citizens to defend their interests in government decisions.

Both schools of thought hold a procedural view of democracy but differ in how they interpret *government by the people*. We can summarize these theoretical positions using two alternative models of democracy. As a model, each is a hypothetical plan, a blueprint, for achieving democratic government through institutional mechanisms. The *majoritarian model* values participation by the people in general; the *pluralist model* values participation by the people in groups.

The Majoritarian Model of Democracy

The **majoritarian model of democracy** relies on the classical, textbook theory of democracy. It interprets *government by the people* as government by the *majority* of the people. To force the government to respond to public opinion, the majoritarian model depends on several mechanisms that allow the people to participate directly in the political system.

The popular election of government officials is the primary mechanism for democratic government in the majoritarian model. Citizens are expected to control their representatives' behavior by choosing wisely in the first place and by re-electing or defeating public officials according to their performance.

Majoritarian theorists also see elections as a means for deciding government policies. An election on a policy issue is called a **referendum**. When a policy question is put on the ballot by the action of citizens circulating petitions and gathering a required minimum number of signatures, it is called an **initiative**. Twenty-one of the states allow their legislatures to put referenda before the voters as well as give citizens the right to place initiatives on the ballot. Five other states make provision for one or the other mechanism.[15]

In the United States, there are no provisions for referenda at the national level. However, Americans are strongly in favor of a system of national referenda.[16] The most fervent advocates of majoritarian democracy would like to see modern technology used to maximize the government's responsiveness to the majority. Indeed, in his 1992 bid for the presidency, Ross Perot advocated electronic "town meetings" to regularly gauge public opinion on major issues.

The majoritarian model contends that citizens can control their government if they have adequate mechanisms for popular participation. It also assumes that citizens are knowledgeable about government and politics, that they want to participate in the political process, and that they make rational decisions in voting for their elected representatives.

If these factors are truly necessary to the functioning of majoritarian democracy, then the majoritarian model in the United States is in trouble. Only 22 percent of a national sample of voters said that they "followed what's going on" in government "most of the time." In contrast, 40 percent said that they followed politics "only now and then" or "hardly at all."[17] Furthermore (as discussed in Chapter 5), voter turnout in presidential elections has fallen to around one-half of the eligible electorate. And those who do vote often choose candidates more from habit (along party lines) than from a close examination of the candidates' positions on the issues.

An Alternative Model: Pluralist Democracy

For years, political scientists struggled valiantly to reconcile the majoritarian model of democracy with polls that showed a widespread ignorance of politics among the American people. If most voters do not know enough to make rational political judgments, why pretend that they should govern at all? In short, why argue for democracy?

In the 1950s, an alternative interpretation of democracy evolved, one tailored to the limited knowledge and participation of the *real* electorate. It was based on the concept of *pluralism*—that modern society consists of innumerable groups of people who share economic, religious, ethnic, or cultural interests. Often people with similar interests organize formal groups. When an organized group seeks to influence government policy, it is called an **interest group**. Many interest groups regularly spend a great deal of time and money trying to influence government policy (see Chapter 7). Among them are the AFL-CIO, the American Hospital Association, the National Association of Manufacturers, the National Organization for Women (NOW), and, of course, the NRA.

The **pluralist model of democracy** interprets *government by the people* to mean government by people operating through competing interest groups. According to this model, democracy exists when many (plural) organizations operate separately from the government, press their interests on the government, and even challenge the government.[18] Compared with majoritarian thinking, pluralist theory shifts the focus of democratic government from the mass electorate to organized groups. It changes the criterion for democratic government from responsiveness to mass public opinion to responsiveness to organized groups of citizens.

A decentralized, complex government structure offers the access and openness necessary for pluralist democracy. The ideal is a system that divides government authority among numerous institutions with overlapping authority. Under such a system, competing interest groups have alternative points of access to present and argue their claims.

The U.S. Constitution approaches the pluralist ideal in the way it divides authority among the branches of government. When the National Association for the Advancement of Colored People (NAACP) could not get Congress to outlaw segregated schools in the South, it turned to the federal court system, which did what Congress would not. According to the pluralist democracy ideal, if all opposing interests are allowed to organize, and if the system can be kept open so that all substantial claims have an opportunity to be heard, then the diverse needs of a pluralist society will be served when an issue is decided.

The Majoritarian Model Versus the Pluralist Model

In majoritarian democracy, the mass public, not interest groups, controls government actions. The citizenry must be knowledgeable about government and willing to participate in the electoral process. Majoritarian democracy relies on electoral mechanisms that harness the power of the majority to make decisions. Conclusive elections and a centralized structure of government are two mechanisms that aid majority rule.

Pluralism does not demand much knowledge from citizens in general. It requires specialized knowledge only from groups of citizens, in particular their leaders. Unlike majoritarian democracy, pluralist democracy seeks to limit majority action so that interest groups can be heard. It relies on strong interest groups and a decentralized government structure—mechanisms that interfere with majority rule and thereby protect minority interests. We could even say that pluralism allows minorities to rule.

An Undemocratic Model: Elite Theory

If pluralist democracy allows minorities to rule, how does it differ from **elite theory**—the view that a small group of people (a minority) makes most important government decisions? According to elite theory, important government decisions are made by an identifiable and stable

The Power Elite?   *This picture symbolizes the underlying notion of elite theory that government is driven by wealth. In truth, wealthy people usually have more influence in government than do people of ordinary means. Critics of elite theory point out that it is difficult to demonstrate that an identifiable ruling elite usually sticks together and gets its way in government policy.*

minority that shares certain characteristics, usually vast wealth and business connections.*

Elite theory contends that these few individuals wield power in America because they control its key financial, communications, industrial, and governmental institutions. Their power derives from the vast wealth of America's largest corporations and the perceived importance of the continuing success of those corporations to the growth of the economy. An inner circle composed of the top corporate leaders provides not only effective advocates for individual companies and for the interests of capitalism in general but also supplies people for top government jobs—from which they can further promote their interests.[19]

According to elite theory, the United States is not a democracy but an oligarchy. Although the voters appear to control government through elections, elite theorists argue that the powerful few in society manage to define the issues and to constrain the possible outcomes of government decisions to suit their own interests. Clearly, elite theory describes a government that operates in an undemocratic fashion.

---

* The classic book on elite theory in American politics is C. Wright Mills, *The Power Elite* (New York: Oxford University Press, 1956). Actually, elite theory argues that elite rule is inevitable in every government, indeed in every large organization. See Thomas R. Dye, *Who's Running America? The Bush Era*, 5th ed. (Englewood Cliffs, N.J.: Prentice-Hall, 1990), especially pp. 2–6, for a summary of elite theory.

Elite theory appeals to many people, especially those who believe that wealth dominates politics. The theory breaks down, however, when an attempt is made to use it to explain a broad range of political decisions. Careful studies of decision making in American cities, which should be even more susceptible to elite rule than the nation as a whole, have shown that different groups win on different issues.[20] This also seems to be true in some cases at the national level. For instance, the giant oil, chemical, and steel industries do not always triumph over environmental groups on the issue of air pollution. And what was once the nation's largest corporation, AT&T, was forced to break up its telephone monopoly in suits brought by much smaller communications companies.

The available evidence of government decisions on many different topics does not generally support elite theory—at least in the sense that an identifiable ruling elite usually gets its way on government policy.[21] Not surprisingly, elite theorists reject this logic. They argue that studies of decision making on individual issues does not adequately test the influence of the power elite. Rather, they contend that much of the elite's power comes from its ability to keep things off the political agenda. That is, it is powerful because it manages to maintain its privileged position by keeping people from questioning fundamental assumptions about American capitalism.[22]

Consequently, elite theory is not dead; it is still forcefully argued by radical critics of American politics.[23] Although we don't feel that the scholarly evidence supports elite theory, we do recognize that contemporary American pluralism favors some segments of society over others. The poor are chronically unorganized and are not well represented by interest groups. On the other hand, business is very well represented in the political system. As many interest group scholars who reject the elitist theory have documented, business is better represented than any other sector of the public.[24] Thus one can endorse pluralist democracy as a more accurate description of American politics than elitism without believing all groups are equally well represented in the political system.

Elite Theory Versus Pluralist Theory

The key difference between elite and pluralist theory lies in the durability of the ruling minority. Unlike elite theory, pluralist theory does not define government conflict in terms of a minority versus *the* majority; instead, it sees many minorities vying with one another in different policy areas. Although some groups with "better connections" in government may win more often in individual arenas, no identifiable elite wins consistently across a broad range of issues. The pluralist model, then, rejects the primary implication of elite theory: that a single group dominates government decisions.

Instead, pluralist democracy makes a virtue of the struggle among minority interests. It argues for government that accommodates this struggle and channels the result into government action. According to pluralist democracy, the public is best served if the government structure provides access for different groups to press their claims in competition with one another. Notice that pluralist democracy does not insist that all groups have equal influence on government decisions. In the political struggle, wealthy, well-organized groups have an inherent advantage over poorer, inadequately organized groups. In fact, unorganized segments of the population may not even get their concerns placed on the agenda for government consideration. This is a critical weakness of pluralism. However, pluralists contend that as long as all groups are able to participate vigorously in the decision-making process, it is democratic.

Democracies Around the World

We have proposed two models of democratic government. The majoritarian model conforms to classical democratic theory for a representative government. According to this model, democracy should be a form of government that features responsiveness to majority opinion. According to the pluralist model, a government is democratic if it allows minority interests to organize and freely press their claims on government.

No government actually achieves the high degree of responsiveness demanded by the majoritarian model. It is also true that no government offers complete and equal access to the claims of all competing groups, as required by an optimally democratic pluralist model. Nevertheless, some nations approach these ideals closely enough to be considered practicing democracies.

Testing for Democratic Government

How can one determine which countries qualify as practicing democracies? A government's degree of responsiveness or access cannot be measured directly, so indirect tests of democracy must be used. One test is to look for traits normally associated with democratic government—whether defined from a procedural or from a substantive viewpoint. One scholar, for example, established five criteria for a democracy:[25]

1. *Most adults can participate in the electoral process.* (Embodies the principle of universal participation)

2. *Citizens' votes are secret and not coerced.* (Embodies the principle of political equality)

3. *Leaders are chosen in free elections, contested by at least two viable political parties.* (Embodies the principle of majority rule)

4. *The government bases its legitimacy on representing the desires of its citizens.* (Embodies the principle of responsiveness)

5. *Citizens, leaders, and party officials enjoy basic freedoms of speech, press, assembly, religion, and organization.* (Substantive policies that create conditions for the practice of the other criteria)

Because the United States fits all these criteria to a fairly high degree, it qualifies as a democracy. How about the other nations of the world? Applying standards similar to these to all nations with a population of more than 3 million, one writer identified just eighteen nations in addition to the United States as democracies.[26] Those nations have government traditions of widespread participation, political equality, and free elections to choose representatives who pay close attention to public opinion.

By any reckoning, democratic government is relatively rare across the world. Yet with many of the former East bloc countries taking significant steps toward becoming real democracies, the trend in world politics is toward democratization rather than away from it.

Four of the five preceding criteria apply to government procedures rather than to government policy. But all these criteria apply equally to the majoritarian and pluralist models of democracy. Although the United States clearly qualifies as a democracy according to these criteria, they cannot be used to judge whether it is closer to a majoritarian or to a pluralist democracy.

American Democracy: More Pluralist Than Majoritarian

It is not idle speculation to ask what kind of democracy is practiced in the United States. The answer to this question can help us understand why our government can be called *democratic* despite a low level of citizen participation in politics and despite government actions that run contrary to public opinion. The answer may also help us understand why many Americans are not satisfied with the democratic form of government here. As shown in Compared with What? 1.1, only 59 percent of a national sample reported that they were satisfied with the way democracy works in the United States.

Throughout the rest of this book, we probe more deeply to determine how well the United States fits the two alternative models of democracy, majoritarian and pluralist. If the answer is not already apparent, it soon will be. We argue that the political system in the United States rates relatively low according to the majoritarian model of democracy but that it fulfills the pluralist model very well. It should not be surprising, then, that 80 percent of the wealthiest group of respondents in a national survey were satisfied with the way democracy works in the United States compared with only 43 percent of the poorest group.[27] Indeed, an advocate of majoritarian democracy once wrote,

Compared with What? 1.1

The Importance of Freedom and Equality as Political Values

Compared with citizens' views of freedom and equality in eleven other nations, Americans value freedom more than others do. Respondents in each country were asked which of the following statements came closer to their own opinion:

- "I find that both freedom and equality are important. But if I were to make up my mind for one or the other, I would consider personal freedom more important, that is, everyone can live in freedom and develop without hindrance."
- "Certainly both freedom and equality are important. But if I were to make up my mind for one of the two, I would consider equality more important, that is, that nobody is underprivileged and that social class differences are not so strong."

Americans chose freedom by a ratio of nearly 3 to 1, followed closely by the British. No other nations showed such a strong preference for freedom, and citizens in three countries favored equality instead. When we look at this finding, the importance of freedom as a political concept in the United States is very clear.

(continued)

"The flaw in the pluralist heaven is that the heavenly chorus sings with a strong upper-class accent."[28]

This evaluation of the pluralist nature of American democracy may not mean much to you now. But you will learn that the pluralist model makes the United States look far more democratic than does the majoritarian model. Eventually, it will be up to you to decide the answers to these three questions: Is the pluralist model really an adequate expression of democracy, or is it a perversion of classical ideals designed to portray America as democratic when it really is not? Does the majoritarian model result in a "better" type of democracy? If so, is it possible to devise new mechanisms of government to produce a desirable mix of majority rule and minority rights? These questions should play in the back of your mind as you read more about the workings of American government in meeting the challenge of democracy.

Summary

The challenge of democracy is making difficult choices—choices that inevitably bring important values into conflict. The *Challenge of Democracy* outlines a normative framework for analyzing the policy choices that arise in the pursuit of the purposes of government.

Compared with What? 1.1 (continued)

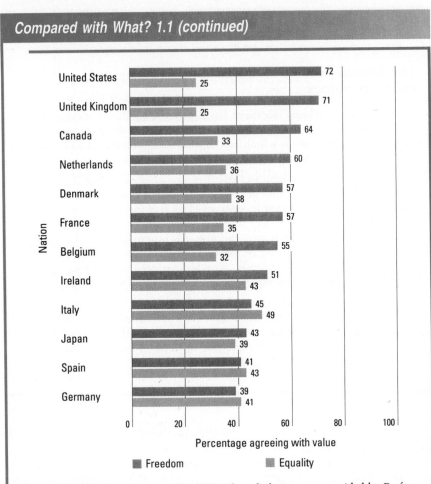

Source: *World Values Survey, 1981–1982.* The tabulation was provided by Professor Ronald F. Inglehart.

The three major purposes of government are maintaining order, providing public goods, and promoting equality. In pursuing these objectives, every government infringes on individual freedom. But the degree of that infringement depends on the government's (and by extension, its citizens') commitment to order and equality. What we have, then, are two dilemmas. The first—the original dilemma —centers on the conflict between freedom and order. The second—the modern dilemma—focuses on the conflict between freedom and equality.

Some people have political ideologies that help them resolve the conflicts that arise in political decision making. These ideologies outline the scope and purpose of government. At opposite extremes of the continuum are totalitarianism, which supports government intervention in every aspect of society, and anarchism, which rejects government entirely. An important step back from totalitarianism is socialism. Democratic socialism favors government ownership of basic industries but preserves civil liberties. Capitalism, another economic system, promotes free enterprise. A significant step short of anarchism is libertarianism, which allows government to protect life and property but little else.

In the United States, the terms *liberal* and *conservative* are used to describe a narrow range toward the center of the political continuum. That is, liberals support a broader role for government than do conservatives. But it is easier to understand the differences between liberals and conservatives and their views on the scope of government if the values of freedom, order, and equality are incorporated into this description of political ideologies. Libertarians choose freedom over both order and equality. Populists are willing to sacrifice freedom for both order and equality. Liberals value freedom and equality more than order. Conservatives value freedom and order more than equality.

In evaluating the process of government in the United States, most scholars would include this country among the very few democracies of the world. But what kind of democracy is it? The answer depends on the definition of *democracy*. Some believe democracy is procedural in nature; they define *democracy* as a form of government in which the people govern through certain institutional mechanisms. Others hold to substantive theory, claiming a government is democratic if its policies promote civil liberties and rights.

In this book, we use the procedural conception of democracy, distinguishing between direct and indirect (representative) democracy.

Procedural democratic theory has produced rival institutional models of democratic government. The classical majoritarian model assumes that people are knowledgeable about government, that they want to participate in the political process, and that they carefully and rationally choose among candidates. The pluralist model of democracy argues that democracy in a complex society requires only that government allow private interests to organize and press their competing claims openly in the political arena.

- Which is better: to live under a government that allows individuals complete freedom to do whatever they please or to live under one that enforces strict law and order?

- Which is better: to allow businesses and private clubs to choose their customers and members or to pass laws that require them to admit and serve everyone, regardless of race or sex?

- Which is better: a government that is highly responsive to public opinion on all matters or one that responds deliberately to organized groups that argue their cases effectively?

If by the end of this book, you understand the issues involved in answering these questions, you will have learned a great deal about American government.

Key Terms

government	freedom to
order	freedom from
communism	police power
public goods	political equality
welfare state	social equality

equality of opportunity
equality of outcome
rights
political ideology
totalitarianism
socialism
democratic socialism
capitalism
libertarianism
laissez faire
anarchism
libertarians
liberals
conservatives
populists
autocracy
oligarchy

democracy
procedural democratic theory
universal participation
political equality
majority rule
direct democracy
representative democracy
responsiveness
substantive democratic theory
minority rights
majoritarian model of democracy
referendum
initiative
interest group
pluralist model of democracy
elite theory

Selected Readings

Barber, Benjamin R. *Strong Democracy: Participatory Politics for a New Age.* Berkeley and Los Angeles: University of California Press, 1984. Barber favors a "strong democracy," a government that features a high degree of participation by individuals, much as a direct democracy does. He suggests specific institutional reforms to stimulate civic discussion and popular participation in government.

Cronin, Thomas E. *Direct Democracy.* Cambridge, Mass.: Harvard University Press, 1989. Cronin thoroughly examines the experience of the states with referenda and initiatives, and concludes that they have been used in a sensible, moderate manner.

Dahl, Robert A. *Democracy and Its Critics.* New Haven, Conn.: Yale University Press, 1989. The nation's leading expert on pluralist theory examines the basic foundations of democracy and defends democracy against a variety of criticisms that have focused on its shortcomings.

Ebenstein, William, and Edwin Fogelman. *Today's Isms: Communism, Fascism, Capitalism, Socialism.* 9th ed. Englewood Cliffs, N.J.: Prentice-Hall, 1985. This standard source describes the history of each of the four major "isms" and relates each to developments in contemporary politics. This is a concise, informative, and readable book.

Green, Philip. *Retrieving Democracy: In Search of Civic Equality.* Totowa, N.J.: Rowman and Allanheld, 1985. Green contends that representative government is "pseudodemocracy" because government is not under the direct control of the people. He argues for "egalitarian democracy," a society of truly equal citizens, and urges fundamental economic reforms to produce a redistribution of wealth, which would facilitate direct democracy.

Institute for Cultural Conservatism. *Cultural Conservatism: Toward a New National Agenda.* Washington, D.C.: Free Congress Research and Education Foundation, 1987. This book assumes that traditional values are necessary for individual fulfillment and that society and government must play an active role in upholding traditional culture.

King, Desmond S. *The New Right: Politics, Markets and Citizenship.* Chicago: Dorsey Press, 1987. King uses the concepts of freedom, order, and equality to analyze ideological tendencies in Margaret Thatcher's government in Britain and in Ronald Reagan's government here. He uses liberalism in the European sense to mean "limiting" state intervention in the economy. (In fact, contrary to American practice, this is the way most of the world uses the term.)

Maddox, William S., and Stuart A. Lilie. *Beyond Liberal and Conservative: Reassessing the Political Spectrum.* Washington, D.C.: Cato Institute, 1984. Not satisfied with the conventional labels *liberal* and *conservative,* Maddox and Lilie have devised a typology of ideologies based on two dimensions: expansion of personal freedom and government intervention in economic affairs. It is similar to our framework but less theoretical.

Medcalf, Linda J., and Kenneth M. Dolbeare. *Neopolitics: American Political Ideas in the 1980s.* Philadelphia: Temple University Press, 1985. This slim volume reviews the history of ideological labels in American politics. It explains the changing meanings of various labels and updates their usage in contemporary politics. It also describes more recent ideologies, among them the "New Right."

Skogan, Wesley G. *Disorder and Decline: Crime and the Spiral of Decay in American Neighborhoods.* New York: Free Press, 1990. This study of neighborhood crime and disorder in six cities explores the nature of disorder and the limits to the state's police powers in dealing with urban decline.

Spitz, Elaine. *Majority Rule.* Chatham, N.J.: Chatham House, 1984. Spitz reviews the various meanings of majority and rule and the place of majority rule in democratic theory. She then goes beyond the narrow definition of majority rule as a method of deciding among policies. She argues that majoritarianism should be viewed as a "social practice" among people who want to hold their society together when making decisions.

Verba, Sidney et al. *Elites and the Idea of Equality: A Comparison of Japan, Sweden, and the United States.* Cambridge, Mass.: Harvard University Press, 1987. The authors surveyed leaders in each country representing established organizations, challenging groups, and mediating institutions to determine their views on equality and to learn how economics and politics affect the distribution of income in the modern welfare state.

Westen, Peter. *Speaking of Equality: An Analysis of the Rhetorical Force of "Equality" in Moral and Legal Discourse.* Princeton, N.J.: Princeton University Press, 1990. This philosophical treatise is not easy to read, but it has an especially useful chapter on "equal opportunity," which Westen says does not mean the "same" opportunity.

THE CONSTITUTION

2

The midnight burglars made a mistake. It led to their capture in the early hours of June 17, 1972, and triggered a constitutional struggle that eventually involved the president of the United States, Congress, and the Supreme Court. The burglars' mistake seems small: They left a piece of tape over the lock they had tripped to enter the Watergate office and apartment complex in Washington, D.C. But a security guard discovered their tampering and called the police, who surprised the burglars in the offices of the Democratic National Committee at 2:30 A.M. and arrested five men.

The events that followed are described in Feature 2.1. Here it need only be noted that the Watergate affair posed one of the most serious challenges to the constitutional order of modern American government. The incident ultimately developed into a struggle over the rule of law between the presidency, on the one hand, and Congress and the courts, on the other. President Richard Nixon attempted to use the powers of his office to hide his tampering with the electoral process. In the end, the cover-up was thwarted by the Constitution and by leaders who believed in it. The constitutional principle of separation of powers among the executive, legislative, and judicial branches prevented the president

Senators Investigate a President
The Select Committee on Presidential Campaign Activities, shown here, was created by the Senate in 1973 to investigate events surrounding Watergate. Its chairman was Democrat Sam Ervin (seated at the center); its ranking minority member was Republican Howard Baker (to Ervin's right). Baker was prominent during another congressional investigation into possible abuses of executive power, but not as a senator. He was President Ronald Reagan's chief of staff during the Iran-Contra hearings in 1987.

from controlling the Watergate investigation. The principle of checks and balances allowed Congress to threaten Nixon with impeachment and removal from office. The belief that Nixon had violated the Constitution finally prompted members of his own party to support impeachment.

Nixon resigned the presidency after little more than a year and a half into his second term. In some countries, such an irregular change in government leadership provides an opportunity for a palace coup, an armed revolution, or a military dictatorship. But here, significantly, there was no political violence after Nixon's resignation; in fact, none was expected. Constitutional order in the United States had been put to a test, and it had passed with high honors.

This chapter poses some questions about the Constitution. How did it evolve? What form did it take? How is it altered? What values does it reflect? And which model of democracy—majoritarian or pluralist—does it fit best?

Watergate

The frightening details of the Watergate story did not unfold until after President Nixon's re-election in November 1972. Two months later, in January 1973, seven men went to trial for the break-in itself. They included the five burglars and two men closely connected with the president: E. Howard Hunt (a former CIA agent and White House consultant) and G. Gordon Liddy (counsel to the Committee to Re-elect the President [CREEP]). The burglars entered guilty pleas. Hunt and Liddy were convicted by a jury. In a letter to the sentencing judge, one of the burglars charged that they had been pressured to plead guilty, that perjury had been committed at the trial, and that others were involved in the break-in. The Senate launched its own investigation of the matter. It set up the Select Committee on Presidential Campaign Activities, chaired by Democratic Senator Sam Ervin from North Carolina.

The testimony before the Ervin committee was shocking. The deputy director of Nixon's re-election committee, Jeb Magruder, confessed to perjury and implicated John Mitchell, Nixon's campaign manager and former attorney general, in planning the burglary. Special Counsel to the President John Dean said that the president had been a party to a cover-up of the crime for eight months. And there were more disclosures of other political burglaries and of forged State Department cables.

A stunned nation watching the televised proceedings learned that the president had secretly tape-recorded all his conversations in the White House. The Ervin committee asked for the tapes. Nixon refused to produce them, citing the separation of powers between the legislative and executive branches and claiming "executive privilege" to withhold information from Congress.

In the midst of all this, Nixon's vice president, Spiro T. Agnew, resigned while under investigation for income tax evasion. The Twenty-fifth Amendment to the Constitution (1967) gave the president the power to choose a new vice president with the consent of Congress. Nixon nominated Gerald Ford, then the Republican leader in the House of Representatives. On December 6, 1973, Ford became the first appointed vice president in the nation's history.

Meanwhile, Nixon was fighting subpoenas demanding the White House tapes. Ordered by a federal court to deliver specific tapes, Nixon proposed a compromise. He would release written summaries of the taped conversations. Archibald Cox, the special prosecutor of the attorney general's office, refused the compromise. Nixon retaliated with the "Saturday Night massacre," in which Attorney General Elliot L. Richardson and his deputy resigned, Cox was fired, and the special prosecutor's office was abolished.

The ensuing furor forced Nixon to appoint another special prosecutor, Leon Jaworski, who eventually brought indictments against Nixon's closest aides. Nixon himself was named as an unindicted co-conspira-

continued

tor. Both the special prosecutor and the defendants wanted the White House tapes, but Nixon continued to resist. Finally, on July 24, 1974, the Supreme Court ruled that the president had to hand over the tapes. At almost the same time, the House Judiciary Committee voted to recommend to the full House that Nixon be impeached for, or charged with, three offenses: impeding and obstructing the investigation of the Watergate break-in, abuse of power and repeated violation of the constitutional rights of citizens, and defiance of House subpoenas.

The Judiciary Committee vote was decisive but far from unanimous. On August 5, however, the committee and the country finally learned the contents of the tapes released under the Supreme Court order. They revealed that Nixon had been aware of a cover-up on June 23, 1972, just six days after the break-in. He had also issued an order to the FBI, saying, "Don't go any further in this case, period!"[*] Now even the eleven Republican members of the House Judiciary Committee, who had opposed the first vote to impeach, were ready to vote against Nixon.

Faced with the collapse of his support and likely impeachment by the full House, Nixon resigned the presidency on August 9, 1974. Vice President Gerald Ford became the first unelected president of the United States. A month later, acting within his constitutional powers, Ford pardoned private citizen Richard Nixon for all federal crimes that he had committed or may have committed. Others were not so fortunate. Three members of the Nixon cabinet (two attorneys general and a secretary of commerce) were convicted and sentenced for their crimes in the Watergate affair. Nixon's White House chief of staff, H. R. Haldeman, and his domestic affairs adviser, John Ehrlichman, were convicted of conspiracy, obstruction of justice, and perjury. Other officials were tried, and most were convicted, on related charges.[**]

[*] The Encyclopedia of American Facts and Dates (New York: Crowell, 1979), p. 946.
[**] Richard B. Morris, ed., *Encyclopedia of American History* (New York: Harper and Row, 1976), p. 544.

The Revolutionary Roots of the Constitution

The Constitution itself is just 4,300 words. But those 4,300 words define the basic structure of our national government. It is a comprehensive document that divides the government into three branches and describes the powers of those branches, their relationships, and the interaction between government and governed. The Constitution makes itself the supreme law of the land and binds every government official to support it.

Most Americans revere the Constitution as political "scripture." To charge that a political action is unconstitutional is like claiming that it is unholy. And so the Constitution has taken on a symbolism that has strengthened its authority as the basis of American government. A strong belief in the Constitution has led many politicians to abandon party for principle when constitutional issues are in question.

The U.S. Constitution, written in 1787 for an agricultural society huddled along the coast of an unknown new land, now guides the political life of a massive urban society in the nuclear age. To fully understand the reasons for the stability of the Constitution—and of the political system it created—we must first look at its historical roots, roots that lie in colonial America.

Freedom in Colonial America

Although British subjects, the American colonists in the eighteenth century enjoyed a degree of freedom denied most people in the world. They were able to inherit property, attend church (but perhaps not any church), and enter a trade or profession with few of the restrictions imposed by Europe's feudal past.

By 1763, Britain and the colonies had reached a compromise between imperial control and colonial self-government. America's foreign affairs and overseas trade were controlled by the king and Parliament (the British legislature); the rest was left to home rule. But the cost of administering the colonies was substantial. Because Americans benefited the most, contended their English countrymen, Americans should bear that cost.

The Road to Revolution

The British believed that taxing the colonies was the obvious way to meet administrative costs; the colonists did not agree. Like most people, they did not want to be taxed. And they especially did not want to be taxed by a distant government in which they had no representation. During the decade preceding the outbreak of hostilities in 1775, this issue was to convert increasing numbers of colonists from loyal British subjects seeking the rights of Englishmen to revolutionaries seeking the end of British rule over the American colonies.

On the night of December 16, 1773, colonists reacted to a British duty on tea by giving the Boston Tea Party. A mob boarded three ships and emptied 342 chests of that valuable substance into Boston Harbor. In an attempt to reassert British control over the recalcitrant colonists, Parliament passed the Coercive (or Intolerable) Acts (1774). One of the acts imposed a blockade on Boston until the tea was paid for; another gave royal governors the power to quarter British soldiers in private homes. Now the taxation issue was secondary; more important was the conflict between British demands for order and American demands for liberty. In response, the Virginia and Massachusetts assemblies summoned a **continental congress**, an assembly that would speak and act for the people of all the colonies.

A Uniquely American Protest
Americans protested the Tea Act (1773) by holding the Boston Tea Party (see background, left) and by employing a unique form of punishment—tarring and feathering. An early treatise on the subject offered the following instructions: "First, strip a person naked, then heat the tar until it is thin, and pour upon the naked flesh, or rub it over with a tar brush. After which, sprinkle decently upon the tar, whilst it is yet warm, as many feathers as will stick to it."

The First Continental Congress met in Philadelphia in September 1774. The objective of the assembly was to restore harmony between Great Britain and the American colonies. A leader, called the "president," was elected. (The terms *president* and *congress* in American government trace their origins to the First Continental Congress.) In October 1774, the delegates adopted a statement of rights and principles, many of which later found their way into the Declaration of Independence and the Constitution. For example, the congress claimed a right "to life, liberty, and property" and a right "peaceably to assemble, consider of their grievances, and petition the king." Then the congress adjourned, planning to reconvene in May 1775.

Revolutionary Action

By early 1775, however, a movement that the colonists themselves were calling a revolution had already begun. The colonists in Massachusetts were fighting the British at Concord and Lexington. Delegates to the Second Continental Congress, meeting in May, faced a dilemma: Should they prepare for war? Or should they try to reconcile with Britain? As conditions deteriorated, the Second Continental Congress remained in session to serve as the government of the colony-states.

On June 7, 1776, the Virginia delegation called on the Continental Congress to resolve "that these United Colonies are, and of right ought to be, Free and Independent States, that they are absolved from all allegiance to the British Crown, and that all political connection between them and the State of Great Britain is, and ought to be, totally dissolved." A committee of five men was appointed to prepare a proclamation expressing the colonies' reasons for declaring independence.

The Declaration of Independence

Thomas Jefferson, a young farmer and lawyer from Virginia, prepared a draft of the proclamation. The document Jefferson drafted—the **Declaration of Independence**—expressed simply, clearly, and rationally the arguments in support of separation from Great Britain.

The principles underlying the declaration were rooted in the writings of the English philosopher John Locke and were expressed many times by speakers in congress and in the colonial assemblies. Locke argued that people have God-given, or natural, rights that are inalienable—that is, they cannot be taken away by any government. In addition, Locke believed that all legitimate political authority exists to preserve these natural rights and that such authority is based on the consent of those who are governed. The idea of consent is derived from **social contract theory**, which states that the people agree to set up rulers for certain purposes and that they have the right to resist or remove rulers who persist in acting against those purposes.[1]

Jefferson used similar arguments in the Declaration of Independence. His "impassioned simplicity of statement" reverberates to this day with democratic faith:

> We hold these truths to be self-evident: That all men are created equal; that they are endowed by their creator with certain unalienable rights; that among these are life, liberty, and the pursuit of happiness.

The First Continental Congress had declared in 1774 that the colonists were entitled to "life, liberty, and property." Jefferson reformulated the objectives of government as "life, liberty, and the pursuit of happiness." And he continued:

> That, to secure these rights, governments are instituted among men, deriving their just powers from the consent of the governed; that whenever any form of government becomes destructive of these ends, it is the right of the people to alter or to abolish it, and to institute new government, laying its foundation on such Principles, and organizing its power in such form, as to them shall seem most likely to effect their safety and happiness.

He went on to list the many deliberate acts of the king that were working against the legitimate ends of government. Finally, he declared that the colonies were "FREE AND INDEPENDENT STATES," with no political connection to Great Britain.

The major premise of the Declaration of Independence is that the people have a right to revolt when they determine that their govern-

Compared with What? 2.1

Exporting the American Revolution

For more than forty years, Czechoslovakia lay in the grip of the Soviet Union. But over the course of a few weeks at the end of 1989, a revolution rooted in the demand for freedom brought Czechoslovakia to independence. Here is how it began:

> PRAGUE, Nov. 27—Soon after the strike began today, Zdenek Janicek, a brewery worker, rose on a platform in grimy overalls and began to speak.
>
> "We hold these truths to be self-evident," he said, "that all men are created equal, that they are endowed by their creator with certain unalienable rights, that among these rights are life, liberty, and the pursuit of happiness."
>
> For the nearly 1,500 workers who gather to listen to him, today was a day of declaring independence from the stifling Communist leadership that has ruled Czechoslovakia for 40 years. Like millions of workers throughout the nation, workers here walked off their jobs at noon today in a two-hour general strike demanding greater democracy and an end to the Communist Party's monopoly on power.
>
> "Americans understood these rights more than 200 years ago," Mr. Janicek said after reciting part of the Declaration of Independence to his co-workers. "We are only now learning to believe that we are entitled to the same rights."

Today Czechs and Slovaks have peacefully splintered into separate republics.

Source: "Millions of Czechoslovaks Increase Pressure on Party with 2-Hour General Strike," *New York Times*, November 28, 1989, p. 1. Copyright © 1989 by The New York Times Company. Reprinted by permission.

ment is denying them their legitimate rights. The long list of the king's actions was evidence of that denial. And so the people had the right to rebel, to form a new government. (See Compared with What? 2.1.)

On July 2, 1776, the Second Continental Congress finally voted for independence. The vote was by state, and the motion carried 11 to 0. (Rhode Island was not present, and the New York delegation, lacking instructions, did not cast its "yea" vote until July 15.) Two days later, the Declaration of Independence was approved with very few changes.

The War of Independence lasted far longer than anyone had expected. It began in a moment of confusion, when a shot rang out while British soldiers approached the town of Lexington on the way to Concord, Massachusetts, on April 19, 1775. It ended with Lord Cornwallis's surrender of his 6,000-man army at Yorktown, Virginia, on October 19, 1781. It was a costly war: There were more dead and wounded in relation to the population than in any other conflict except the Civil War.[2]

From Revolution to Confederation

By declaring independence from England, the colonies were leaving themselves without any real central government. So the revolutionaries proclaimed the creation of a republic. Strictly speaking, a **republic** is a government without a monarch, but the term had come to mean a government rooted in the consent of the governed in which power was exercised by representatives responsible to the governed. A republic did not have to be a democracy, and this was fine with the founders; at that time democracy was associated with mob rule and instability (see Chapter 1). The revolutionaries were less concerned with who would control their new government than with limiting the powers of that government. They had revolted in the name of liberty, and now they wanted a government with sharply defined powers. To make sure they got one, they meant to define its structure and powers in writing.

The Articles of Confederation

Barely a week after the Declaration of Independence was signed, the Second Continental Congress received a committee report on "Articles of Confederation and Perpetual Union." A **confederation** is a loose association of independent states that agree to cooperate on specified matters. In a confederation, the states retain their **sovereignty**, which means that each has supreme power within its borders. The central government is weak; it can only coordinate, not control, the actions of its sovereign states.

The **Articles of Confederation**, which were finally adopted on November 15, 1777, jealously guarded state sovereignty; their provisions clearly reflected the delegates' fears of a strong central government. Under the Articles, each state, regardless of its size, had one vote in the congress. Votes on financing the war against Britain and other important issues required the consent of at least nine of the thirteen states. The common danger—the war—forced the young republic to function under the Articles, but this first try at a government was inadequate to the task. The delegates had succeeded in crafting a national government that was largely powerless.

The Articles failed for at least four reasons. First, they did not give the national government the power to tax. As a result, the congress had to plead for funds with which to conduct the continuing war with Great Britain and to carry on the affairs of the new nation. Second, except for the appointment of a presiding officer of the congress (the president), the Articles made no provision for an independent leadership position to direct the government. This omission was planned—the colonists feared the re-establishment of a monarchy—but it left the nation without a leader. Third, the Articles did not allow the national government to regulate interstate and foreign commerce. (When John Adams proposed that the confederation enter into a commercial treaty with Britain after the war, he was asked, "Would you like one treaty or thirteen, Mr. Adams?")[3] Fourth, the Articles themselves could not be amended without the unanimous agreement of the congress and the assent of all the state legislatures; thus, each state had the power to veto any changes in the confederation.

The goal of the delegates who drew up the Articles of Confederation was to retain power in the states. This was consistent with republicanism, which viewed the remote power of a national government as a danger to liberty. In this sense alone, the Articles were a grand success. They completely hobbled the infant government.

Disorder Under the Confederation

Once the Revolution ended and independence was a reality, it became clear that the national government had neither the economic nor the military power to function. Americans, freed from wartime austerity, rushed to purchase goods from abroad. Debt mounted and, for many, bankruptcy followed.

The problem was particularly severe in Massachusetts, where high interest rates and high state taxes were forcing farmers into bankruptcy. In 1786 and 1787, farmers under the leadership of Daniel Shays, a Revolutionary War veteran, carried out a series of insurrections to prevent the foreclosure of their farms by creditors. With the congress unable to secure funds from the states to help out, the governor of Massachusetts eventually called out the militia and restored order.[4] **Shays' Rebellion** demonstrated the impotence of the confederation and the urgent need to suppress insurrection and maintain domestic order.

From Confederation to Constitution

Order, the original purpose of government, was breaking down under the Articles of Confederation. The "league of friendship" envisioned in the Articles was not enough to hold the nation together in peacetime.

In 1786, Virginia invited the states to attend a convention at Annapolis to explore revisions to the Articles of Confederation. The meeting was both a failure and a success. Although only five states sent delegates to Annapolis, the delegates seized the opportunity to call for another meeting in Philadelphia the next year. The congress later agreed to the convention but limited its mission to "the sole and express purpose of revising the Articles of Confederation."

Shays' Rebellion lent a sense of urgency to the task before the Philadelphia convention. The congress's inability to confront the rebellion was evidence that a stronger national government was necessary to preserve order and property—to protect the states from internal as well as external dangers. "While the Declaration was directed against an excess of authority," remarked Supreme Court Justice Robert H. Jackson some

150 years later, "the Constitution [that followed the Articles of Confederation] was directed against anarchy."[5]

The Constitutional Convention officially opened on May 25, 1787. Its delegates were authorized only to "revise" the Articles of Confederation. Within the first week of debate, Edmund Randolph of Virginia had presented a long list of changes, suggested by fellow Virginian James Madison, that would replace the weak confederation of states with a powerful national government. The delegates unanimously agreed to debate Randolph's proposal, which was called the *Virginia Plan*. Almost immediately, then, they rejected the idea of amending the Articles of Confederation and began working instead to create an entirely new constitution.

The Virginia Plan

The **Virginia Plan** served as the basis of the convention's deliberations for the rest of the summer. It made several important proposals:

- That the powers of the government be divided among three separate branches: a **legislative branch**, for making laws; an **executive branch**, for enforcing laws; and a **judicial branch**, for interpreting laws.

- That the legislature consist of two houses. The first would be chosen by the people; the second by the members of the first house from among persons nominated by the state legislatures.

- That representation in the legislature be in proportion to taxes paid to the national government or in proportion to the free population of each state.

- That an executive of unspecified size be selected by the legislature and serve for a single term.

- That the national judiciary include one or more supreme courts and other lower courts, with judges appointed for life by the legislature.

- That the executive and a number of national judges serve as a council of revision to approve or veto (disapprove) legislative acts. Their veto could be overridden, however, by a vote of both houses of the legislature.

- That the range of powers of all three branches be far greater than that assigned the national government by the Articles of Confederation and include the power of the legislature to override state laws.

By proposing a powerful national legislature that could override state laws, the Virginia Plan clearly advocated a new form of government. It was a mixed structure, with more authority over the states and new authority over the people.

Madison was a monumental force in the ensuing debate on the proposals. However, the constitution that emerged from the convention bore only partial resemblance to the document Madison wanted to create. Of the seventy-one specific proposals that Madison endorsed, he ended up on the losing side on forty of them.[6] And the parts of the Virginia Plan that were ultimately adopted in the Constitution were not adopted without challenge. Conflict revolved primarily around the basis of representation in the legislature, the method of choosing legislators, and the structure of the executive branch.

The New Jersey Plan

When it appeared that much of the Virginia Plan would be carried by the large states, the smaller states united in opposition. William Paterson of New Jersey introduced an alternative set of nine resolutions written to preserve the spirit of the Articles of Confederation by amending, rather than replacing, them. His **New Jersey Plan** included the following proposals:

- That a single-chamber legislature have the power to raise revenue and regulate commerce.

- That the states have equal representation in the legislature and choose the members of that body.

- That a multiperson executive be elected by the legislature, with powers similar to those listed in the Virginia Plan but without the right to veto legislation.

- That a supreme judiciary be created with a very limited jurisdiction. (There was no provision for a system of national courts.)

- That the acts of the legislature be binding on the states; that is, be regarded as the "supreme law of the respective states," with force used to compel obedience.

The New Jersey Plan was defeated in the first major convention vote by 7 to 3. However, the small states had enough support to force a compromise on the issue of representation in the legislature.

The Great Compromise

The Virginia Plan's provision for a two-chamber legislature was never seriously challenged, but the idea of representation according to population stirred up heated debate. The smaller states demanded equal representation for all states.

A committee was created to resolve the deadlock. It consisted of one delegate from each state, chosen by secret ballot. The committee worked through the Independence Day recess, then reported the **Great Compromise** (sometimes called the *Connecticut Compromise*): The House of Representatives would initially consist of fifty-six members, apportioned *according to the population of each state*. Revenue-raising acts would originate in the House. Most important, *the states would be* *represented equally in the Senate,* with two senators each. Senators would be selected by their state legislatures, not directly by the people.

The delegates accepted the Great Compromise. The smaller states got their equal representation; the larger states, their proportional representation. The small states might dominate the Senate and the large states might control the House, but because all legislation had to be approved by both chambers, neither group would be able to dominate the other.

Compromise on the Presidency

Contention replaced compromise when the delegates turned to the executive branch. They did agree on a one-person executive—a president—but they disagreed on how the executive would be selected and what the term of office would be. The delegates distrusted the people's judgment, fearing that public passions might be aroused. Consequently, the delegates rejected the idea of popular election. At the same time, representatives of the smaller states feared that election by the legislature would allow the larger states to control the executive.

Once again the states compromised, creating the cumbersome election system that we know today as the **electoral college.** The college consists of a group of electors who are chosen for the sole purpose of selecting the president and vice president. Each state legislature would choose a number of electors equal to the number of representatives it had in Congress. Each elector would then vote for two people. The person with the most votes would become president, provided that that person had a majority of the votes; the person with the next greatest number of votes would become vice president. (This procedure was changed in 1804 by the Twelfth Amendment, which mandates separate votes for each office.) If no candidate won a majority, then the House of Representatives would choose a president, with *each state having one vote.*

The electoral college compromise removed the fear of a popular vote for president. At the same time, it satisfied the smaller states. If the electoral college failed to produce a president—which the delegates expected would happen—then an election by the House would give every state the same voice in the selection process.

Finally, the delegates agreed that the president's term of office should be four years and that the president should be eligible for re-election.

The delegates also realized that removing a president from office would be a very serious political matter. For that reason, they involved the other two branches of government in the process. The House alone was empowered to charge a president with "treason, bribery, or other high crimes and misdemeanors," by a majority vote. The Senate was given the sole power to try such impeachments. It could convict, and thus remove, a president only by a two-thirds vote. And the chief justice of the United States was required to preside over the Senate trial.

The Final Product

Once the delegates resolved their major disagreements, they dispatched the remaining issues relatively quickly. A committee was appointed to draft a constitution. The Preamble, which was the last section to be drafted, begins with a phrase that would have been impossible to write when the convention opened. This single sentence contains four elements that form the foundation of the American political tradition.[7]

- *It creates a people:* "We the people of the United States" was a dramatic departure from a loose confederation of states.

- *It explains the reason for the Constitution:* "in order to form a more perfect union" was an indirect way of saying that the first effort, under the Articles of Confederation, had been inadequate.

- *It articulates goals:* "establish justice, insure domestic tranquility, provide for the common defence, promote the general welfare, and secure the blessings of liberty to ourselves and our posterity" meant that government would exist to promote order and freedom.

- *It fashions a government:* "do ordain and establish this Constitution for the United States of America."

The Basic Principles

In creating the Constitution, the founders relied on four political principles that together established a revolutionary new political order. These principles were republicanism, federalism, separation of powers, and checks and balances.

Republicanism. **Republicanism** is a form of government in which power resides in the people and is exercised by their elected representatives. The framers were determined to avoid aristocracy (rule by a hereditary class), monarchy (rule by one), and direct democracy (rule by the people). A republic was both new and daring: No people had ever been governed by a republic on so vast a scale. Indeed, the framers themselves were far from sure that their government could be sustained. After the convention, Benjamin Franklin was asked what sort of government the new nation would have. "A republic," he replied, "if you can keep it."

Federalism. **Federalism** is the division of power between a central government and regional units. It stands between two competing government schemes. On the one side is **unitary government**, in which all power is vested in a central government. On the other side stands confederation, a loose union with powerful states. The Constitution embodies a division of power but confers substantial powers on a national government at the expense of the states.

According to the Constitution, the powers vested in the national and state governments are derived from the people, who remain the ultimate sovereign. National and state governments can exercise their powers over persons and property within their own spheres of authority. But at the same time, the people can preserve their liberty by participating in the electoral process or amending their governing charters and thereby restrain both the national government and the state governments.

The Constitution lists the powers of the national government and the powers denied to the states. All other powers remain with the states. However, the Constitution does not clearly describe the spheres of authority within which these powers can be exercised. As we discuss in Chapter 3, limits on the exercise of power by the national government and the states have evolved as a result of political and military conflict; moreover, these limits have continually changed.

Separation of powers.   **Separation of powers** is the assignment of the lawmaking, law-enforcing, and law-interpreting functions to independent legislative, executive, and judicial branches of government. Nationally, the lawmaking power resides in Congress, the law-enforcing power resides in the presidency, and the law-interpreting power resides in the courts. Service in one branch prohibits simultaneous service in the others. Separation of powers safeguards liberty by ensuring that all government power does not fall into the hands of a single person or group of people. But the framers' concern with protecting the liberty of the people did not extend to the election process. The Constitution constrains majority rule by limiting the direct influence of the people on that process (see Figure 2.1).

In theory, separation of powers means that one branch cannot exercise the powers of the other branches. In practice, however, the separation is far from complete. One scholar has suggested that what the country has instead is "separate institutions *sharing* powers."[8]

Checks and balances.   The constitutional system of **checks and balances** is a means of giving each branch of government some scrutiny of and control over the other branches. The framers reasoned that these checks and balances would prevent one branch from ignoring or overpowering the others.

Separation of powers and checks and balances are two distinct principles, but both are necessary to ensure that one branch does not dominate the government. Separation of powers divides government re-

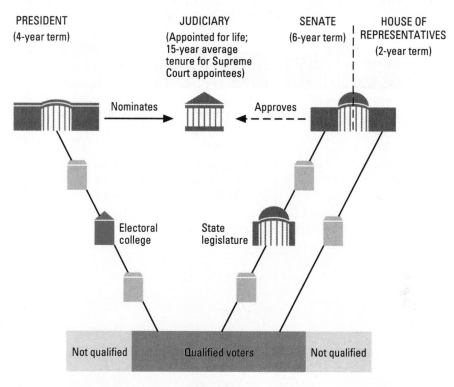

Ballot
box

FIGURE 2.1   The Constitution and the Electoral Process
The framers were afraid of majority rule, and that fear is reflected in the electoral process described in the Constitution. The people, speaking through the voters, had direct input only in the choice of their representatives in the House. The president and senators were elected indirectly through the electoral college and state legislatures. (The direct election of senators did not become law until 1913, when the Seventeenth Amendment was ratified.) Judicial appointments are, and always have been, far removed from representative links to the people. Judges are nominated by the president and approved by the Senate.

sponsibilities among the legislative, executive, and judicial branches; checks and balances prevent the exclusive exercise of those powers by any one of the three branches. For example, only Congress can enact laws. But the president (through the power of the veto) can cancel them, and the courts (by finding a law in violation of the Constitution) can nullify them. And the process goes on. In a "check on a check," Congress can override a president's veto by an extraordinary (two-thirds) ma-

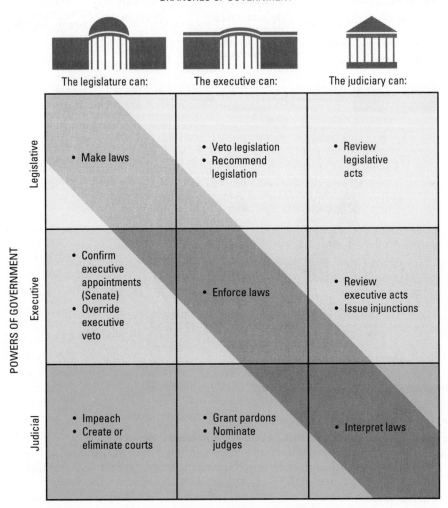

FIGURE 2.2   Separation of Powers and Checks and Balances
Separation of powers *is the assignment of lawmaking, law-enforcing, and law-interpreting functions to the legislative, executive, and judicial branches. This is illustrated by the diagonal grid in the figure.* Checks and Balances *give each branch some power over the other branches. For example, the executive branch possesses some legislative power, and the legislative branch possesses some executive power. These checks and balances are illustrated within the columns and outside the diagonal grid.*

jority in each chamber; and it is empowered to propose amendments to the Constitution, counteracting the courts' power to find a national law invalid. Figure 2.2 depicts the relationship between separation of powers and checks and balances.

The Articles of the Constitution

In addition to the Preamble, the Constitution includes seven articles. The first three establish the internal operation and powers of the separate branches of government. The remaining four define the relationships among the states, explain the process of amendment, declare the supremacy of national law, and explain the procedure for ratifying the Constitution.

Article I: The legislative article.   In structuring the new government, the framers began with the legislative branch because they thought law-making was the most important function of a republican government. Article I is the most detailed and therefore the longest of all the articles. It defines the **bicameral** (two-chamber) character of Congress and describes the internal operating procedures of the House of Representatives and the Senate. Section 8 of Article I expresses the principle of **enumerated powers**, which means that Congress can exercise only the powers that the Constitution assigns to it. Eighteen powers are enumerated; the first seventeen are specific powers (for example, the power to regulate interstate commerce).

The last clause in Section 8, known as the **necessary and proper clause** (or the **elastic clause**), gives Congress the means to execute the enumerated powers (see the Appendices). This clause is the basis of Congress's **implied powers**—those powers that Congress must have in order to execute its enumerated powers. The power to levy and collect taxes (Clause 1) and the power to coin money and regulate its value (Clause 5), when joined with the necessary and proper clause (Clause 18), *imply* that Congress has the power to charter a bank. Otherwise, the national government would have no means of managing the funds it collects through its power to tax. Implied powers clearly expand the enumerated powers conferred on Congress by the Constitution.

Article II: The executive article.   Article II sets the president's term of office, the procedure for electing a president through the electoral college, the qualifications for becoming president, and the president's duties and powers. The last include acting as commander in chief of the military, making treaties (which must be ratified by a two-thirds vote of the Senate), and appointing government officers, diplomats, and judges (again, with the advice and consent of the Senate).

The president also has legislative powers—part of the constitutional system of checks and balances. For example, the Constitution requires that the president periodically inform the Congress of the "state of the Union" and of the policies and programs that the executive branch intends to advocate in the forthcoming year. Today this is done annually in the president's State of the Union address. Under special circumstances, the president can also convene or adjourn Congress. Additionally, the duty to "take care that the laws be faithfully executed" in Section 3 has provided presidents with a reservoir of power.

Article III: The judicial article.   The third article was purposely vague. The Constitution established the Supreme Court as the highest court in the land. But beyond that, the framers were unable to agree on the need for, the size of, or the composition of a national judiciary or on the procedures it should follow. They left these issues to Congress, which resolved them by creating a system of national courts separate from that of the states.

Short of impeachment, federal judges serve for life. They are appointed to indefinite terms on "good behavior," and their salaries cannot be lowered while they hold office. These stipulations reinforce the separation of powers; they see to it that judges are independent of the other branches, that they do not have to fear retribution in their exercise of judicial power.

The judicial branch can be checked by Congress through its power to create (and eliminate) lower federal courts. Congress can also restrict the power of the lower courts to decide cases. And, as we have noted, the president appoints—with the advice and consent of the Senate—the justices of the Supreme Court and the judges of the lower federal courts.

Article III does not explicitly give the courts the power of **judicial review**, the authority to invalidate congressional or presidential actions. That power has been inferred from the logic, structure, and theory of the Constitution.

The remaining articles.   The remaining four articles of the Constitution cover a lot of ground. Article IV requires that the citizens, judicial acts, and criminal warrants of each state be honored in all other states. This is a provision that promotes equality; it keeps the states from treating outsiders differently from their own citizens. The origin of this clause can be traced to the Articles of Confederation. Article IV also allows the addition of new states and stipulates that the national government will protect the states against invasion and domestic violence.

Article V specifies the methods for amending (changing) the Constitution. (We have more to say about this shortly.)

An important component of Article VI is the **supremacy clause**, which asserts that in the case of conflict, the Constitution, national laws, and treaties take precedence over state and local laws. This stipulation is vital to the operation of federalism. In keeping with the supremacy clause, Article VI also requires that all national and state officials, elected or appointed, take an oath to support the Constitution. The article also mandates that religion cannot be a qualification for holding government office.

Finally, Article VII describes the ratification process, stipulating that approval by conventions in nine states was necessary for the "establishment" of the Constitution.

The Framers' Motives

What forces motivated the framers? Surely economic issues were important, but they were not the major issues. The single most important factor leading to the Constitutional Convention was the inability of the national or state governments to maintain order under the loose structure of the Articles of Confederation. Certainly order involved the protection of property, but the framers had a broader view of property than their portfolios of government securities. They wanted to protect their homes, their families, and their means of livelihood from impending anarchy.

Although they disagreed bitterly on structure, mechanics, and detail, the framers agreed on the most vital issues. For example, three of the most crucial parts of the Constitution—the power to tax, the necessary and proper clause, and the supremacy clause—were approved unanimously without debate. The motivation to create order was so strong that the framers were willing to draft clauses that protected the most undemocratic of all institutions—slavery.

The Slavery Issue

The institution of slavery was well ingrained in American life at the time of the Constitutional Convention, and slavery helped shape the Constitution, although the term is not mentioned anywhere in it. It is doubtful, in fact, that there would have been a Constitution if the delegates had had to resolve the slavery issue.

The question of representation in the House of Representatives brought the issue close to the surface of the debate leading to the Great Compromise. Representation according to population was an element of the accord. But who counted in the "population"? Eventually, the delegates agreed unanimously that in the apportionment of representatives in the House and in the assessment of direct taxes, the population of each state was to be determined by adding "the whole number of free persons" and "three-fifths of all other persons" (Article I, Section 2). The phrase "all other persons" is, of course, a substitute for slaves.

The three-fifths clause gave states with large slave populations (the South) greater representation in Congress than states with small slave populations (the North). This overrepresentation translated into greater influence in presidential selection because electoral votes were determined by the size of each state's congressional delegation. The clause also undertaxed states with large slave populations.

All Were Not Created Equal
This 1845 photograph of Isaac Jefferson, who had been one of Thomas Jefferson's slaves at Monticello, reminds us that the framers of the Constitution did not extend freedom and equality to all. Slavery was a widely accepted social norm in the eighteenth century.

Another issue centered on the slave trade. Several southern delegates were uncompromising in their defense of the slave trade, while some delegates favored prohibition. The delegates compromised, agreeing that the slave trade could not be ended before twenty years had elapsed (Article I, Section 9).

Finally, the delegates agreed, without serious challenge, that fugitive slaves be returned to their masters (Article IV, Section 2).

In addressing these points, the framers in essence condoned slavery. Clearly, slavery existed in stark opposition to the idea that "all men are created equal," and although many slaveholders, including Jefferson and Madison, agonized over the issue, few made serious efforts to free their own slaves. Most Americans seemed indifferent to slavery. Nevertheless, the eradication of slavery proceeded gradually in the states. By 1787, Connecticut, Massachusetts, New Jersey, New York, Pennsylvania, Rhode Island, and Vermont had abolished slavery or had provided for gradual emancipation. This slow but perceptible shift on the slavery issue in many states masked a volcanic force capable of destroying the Constitutional Convention and the Union.

Selling the Constitution

On September 17, 1787, nearly four months after the Constitutional Convention had opened, the delegates convened for the last time to sign the final version of their handiwork. Because several delegates were unwilling to sign the document, the last paragraph was craftily worded to give the impression of unanimity: "Done in Convention by the unanimous consent of the *States* present." However, before the Constitution could take effect, it had to be ratified by a minimum of nine state conventions.

The proponents of the new charter, who wanted a strong national government, called themselves *Federalists*. The opponents of the Constitution were quickly dubbed *Antifederalists*. They claimed, however, that they were true federalists because they wanted to protect the states from the tyranny of a strong national government. The viewpoints of the two groups formed the bases of the first American political parties.

The *Federalist Papers*

Beginning in October 1787, an exceptional series of eighty-five newspaper articles defending the Constitution appeared under the title *The Federalist: A Commentary on the Constitution of the United States*. The essays were reprinted extensively during the ratification battle. They bore the pen name "Publius" and were written primarily by James Madison and Alexander Hamilton, with some assistance from John Jay. Rationally and quietly, Publius argued in favor of ratification. *The Federalist* (also called the *Federalist Papers*) remains the best single commentary we have on the meaning of the Constitution and the political theory it embodies.

The Antifederalists, not to be outdone, offered their own intellectual basis for rejecting the Constitution. In several essays, the most influential authored under the pseudonyms "Brutus" and "Federal Farmer," they attacked the centralization of power in a strong national government, claiming it would obliterate the states, violate the social contract of the Declaration of Independence, and destroy liberty in the process.

These essays defended the status quo, maintaining that the Articles of Confederation established true federal principles.[9]

Of all the *Federalist Papers*, the most magnificent and most frequently cited is "Federalist No. 10," which was written by James Madison. In it, he argued that the proposed constitution was designed "to break and control the violence of faction": "By a faction, I understand a number of citizens, whether amounting to a majority or minority of the whole, who are united and actuated by some common impulse of passion, or of interest, adverse to the rights of other citizens, or to the permanent and aggregate interests of the community."

Of course, Madison was discussing what we described in Chapter 1 as *pluralism*. What Madison called *factions* today are interest groups or even political parties. According to Madison, "The most common and durable source of factions has been the various and unequal distribution of property." Madison was concerned, not with reducing inequalities of wealth (which he took for granted), but with controlling the seemingly inevitable conflict stemming from them. The Constitution, he argued, was "well constructed" for this purpose.

Through the mechanism of *representation*, wrote Madison, the Constitution would prevent the tyranny of the majority (mob rule). Government would not be controlled directly by the people but would be governed indirectly by their elected representatives. And those representatives would have the intelligence and the understanding to serve the larger interests of the nation. Moreover, the federal system would require that majorities form first within each state and then organize for effective action at the national level. This and the vastness of the country would make it unlikely that a majority would form "to invade the rights of other citizens."

The purpose of "Federalist No. 10" was to demonstrate that the proposed government was not likely to be ruled by any faction. Contrary to conventional wisdom, Madison argued, the key to controlling the evils of faction is to have a large republic—the larger, the better. The more diverse the society, the less likely it is that an unjust majority can form. Madison certainly had no intention of creating a majoritarian democracy; his view of popular government was much more consistent with the model of pluralist democracy discussed in Chapter 1.

Madison pressed his argument from a different angle in "Federalist No. 51." Asserting that "ambition must be made to counteract ambition," he argued that the separation of powers and checks and balances would control tyranny from any source. If power is distributed equally across the three branches, then each branch has the capacity to counteract the other. In Madison's words, "Usurpations are guarded against by a division of the government into distinct and separate departments." Because legislative power tends to predominate in republican governments, legislative authority is divided between the Senate and the House of Representatives, with different methods of selection and terms of office. Additional protection comes through federalism, which divides power "between two distinct governments"— national and state—and subdivides "the portion allotted to each . . . among distinct and separate departments."

The Antifederalists wanted additional separation of powers and additional checks and balances, which, they maintained, would entirely eliminate the threat of tyranny. The Federalists believed that these additions would make decisive national action virtually impossible. But to ensure ratification, they agreed to a compromise.

A Concession: The Bill of Rights

Despite the eloquence of the *Federalist Papers*, many prominent citizens, including Thomas Jefferson, were unhappy that the Constitution did not list basic civil liberties—the individual freedoms guaranteed to citizens. The omission of a bill of rights was the chief obstacle to the adoption of the Constitution by the states. The colonists had just rebelled against the British government to preserve their basic freedoms— why did the proposed Constitution fail to spell out those freedoms?

The answer was rooted in logic, not politics. Because the national government was limited to those powers that were granted to it and because no power was granted to abridge the people's liberties, then a list of guaranteed freedoms was not necessary. Hamilton, in "Federalist No. 84," went even further, arguing that the addition of a bill of rights would be dangerous. Because it was not possible to list all prohibited powers, wrote Hamilton, any attempt to provide a partial list would make the remaining areas vulnerable to government abuse.

But logic was no match for fear. Many states agreed to ratify the Constitution only after Washington suggested that a list of guarantees be added through the amendment process. Well over a hundred amendments were proposed by the states. These were eventually narrowed down to twelve, which were approved by Congress and sent to the states. Ten of them became part of the Constitution in 1791 after securing the approval of the required three-fourths of the states. Collectively, these ten amendments are known as the **Bill of Rights**. They restrain the national government from tampering with fundamental rights and civil liberties and emphasize the limited character of national power (see Table 2.1).

Ratification

The Constitution officially took effect with its ratification by the ninth state, New Hampshire, on June 21, 1788. However, the success of the new government was not assured until August 1788, when the Consti-

TABLE 2.1   The Bill of Rights

The first ten amendments to the Constitution are known as the Bill of Rights. *The following is a list of those amendments grouped conceptually. For the actual order and wording of the Bill of Rights, see the Appendix.*

Guarantees	Amendment
Guarantees for Participation in the Political Process	
No government abridgement of speech or press; no government abridgement of peaceable assembly; no government abridgement of petitioning government for redress.	1
Guarantees Respecting Personal Beliefs	
No government establishment of religion; no government prohibition of free religious exercise.	1
Guarantees of Personal Privacy	
Owners' consent necessary to quarter troops in private homes in peacetime; quartering during war must be lawful.	3
Government cannot engage in unreasonable searches and seizures; warrants to search and seize require probable cause.	4
No compulsion to testify against oneself in criminal cases.	5
Guarantees Against Government Overreaching	
Serious crimes require a grand jury indictment; no repeated prosecution for the same offense; no loss of life, liberty, or property without due process; no government taking of property for public use without just compensation.	5
Criminal defendants will have a speedy public trial by impartial local jury; defendants informed of accusation; defendants confront witnesses against them; defendants use judicial process to obtain favorable witnesses; defendants have legal assistance for their defense.	6
Civil lawsuits can be tried by juries if controversy exceeds $20; in jury trials, fact-finding is a jury function.	7
No excessive bail; no excessive fines; no cruel and unusual punishment	8
Other Guarantees	
No government trespass on unspecified fundamental rights.	9
The states or the people reserve the powers not delegated to the national government or denied to the states.	10
The people have the right to bear arms.	2

tution was ratified by the key states of Virginia and New York after lengthy debate.

The reflection and deliberation that attended the creation and ratification of the Constitution signaled to the world that a new government could be launched peacefully. The French observer Alexis de Tocqueville (1805–1859) later wrote:

> That which is new in the history of societies is to see a great people, warned by its lawgivers that the wheels of government are stopping, turn its attention on itself without haste or fear, sound the depth of the ill, and then wait for two years to find the remedy at leisure, and then finally, when the remedy has been indicated, submit to it voluntarily without its costing humanity a single tear or drop of blood.[10]

Constitutional Change

The founders realized that the Constitution would have to be changed from time to time. To this end, they specified a formal amendment process in Article V—a process that was used almost immediately to add the Bill of Rights. With the passage of time, the Constitution also has been altered through judicial interpretation and changes in political practice.

The Formal Amendment Process

There are two stages in the amendment process, **proposal** and **ratification**; both are necessary for an amendment to become part of the Constitution. The Constitution provides two alternative methods for completing each stage (see Figure 2.3). Amendments can be proposed (1) by a two-thirds vote of the House of Representatives and of the Senate or (2) by a national convention summoned by Congress at the request of two-thirds of the state legislatures. All constitutional amendments to date have been proposed by the first method; the second has never been used.

A proposed amendment can be ratified (1) by a vote of the legislatures of three-fourths of the states or (2) by a vote of constitutional conventions held in three-fourths of the states. Congress chooses the method of ratification. It has used the state convention method only once, for the Twenty-first Amendment, which repealed the Eighteenth (Prohibition).

Calling a national convention to propose an amendment has never been tried. Certainly the method raises several thorny questions, the most significant of which concerns what limits, if any, there are on the business of the convention. Would a national convention called to consider a particular amendment be within its bounds to rewrite the Constitution? No one really knows.

A movement to convene a constitutional convention to write an amendment that would require a balanced budget was well under way

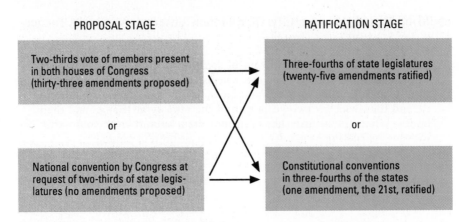

FIGURE 2.3   *Amending the Constitution*
There are two stages in amending the Constitution: proposal and ratification. Congress has no control over the proposal stage, but it prescribes the ratification method. Once it has ratified an amendment, a state cannot retract its action. A state's rejection of an amendment does not bar future reconsideration, however.

when, in 1988, it faltered and appeared to reverse its course, at least in part because many state legislators feared that a convention would become a Pandora's box loosing a whirlwind of political change and fundamentally altering the national government. However, continued interest in the budget issue led to a vigorous effort within Congress to propose a balanced budget amendment to the states in 1992. That effort also failed when the proposal was unable to muster the necessary two-thirds vote in the House of Representatives.

Most of the Constitution's twenty-seven amendments were adopted to help keep it abreast of changes in political thinking. The first ten amendments (the Bill of Rights) were the price of ratification, but they have been important to our current system of government. The last seventeen amendments fall into three main categories: those that make *public policy*, those that correct deficiencies in *government structure*, and those that promote *equality* (see Table 2.2).

Since 1787, about ten thousand constitutional amendments have been introduced; only a fraction have passed through the proposal stage. Once an amendment has been voted by the Congress, chances of ratification are high. The Twenty-seventh Amendment, which prevents members from voting themselves immediate pay increases, was ratified in 1992. It was submitted to the states in 1789. Only six amendments submitted to the states have failed to be ratified. Two such failures occurred in the 1980s: the Equal Rights Amendment and full congressional representation for Washington, D.C.

Roll Out the Barrels
The Eighteenth Amendment, which was ratified by the states in 1919, banned the manufacture, sale, or transportation of alcoholic beverages. The amendment was spurred by moral and social reform groups, like the Women's Christian Temperance Union, founded by Evanston, Illinois, resident Frances Willard in 1874. The amendment proved to be an utter failure. People continued to drink, but their alcohol came from illegal sources.

Interpretation by the Courts

In 1803, in its decision in *Marbury* v. *Madison,* the Supreme Court declared that the courts have the power to nullify government acts when they conflict with the Constitution. (We elaborate on the power of *judicial review* in Chapter 11.) The exercise of judicial review forces the courts to interpret the Constitution. In a way, this makes a lot of sense. The judiciary is the law-interpreting branch of the government; the Constitution is the supreme law of the land, fair game then for judicial interpretation. But in interpreting the Constitution, the courts cannot help but give new meaning to its provisions. This is why judicial interpretation is a principal form of constitutional change.

Political Practice

The Constitution remains silent on many issues. For example, it says nothing about political parties or the president's Cabinet, yet both par-

Table 2.2   Constitutional Amendments 11 Through 27 ━━━

No.	Proposed	Ratified	Intent	Subject
11	1794	1795	G	Prohibits an individual from suing a state in a federal court without the state's consent
12	1803	1804	G	Requires the electoral college to vote separately for president and vice present
13	1865	1865	E	Prohibits slavery
14	1866	1868	E	Gives citizenship to all persons born or naturalized in the United States (former slaves); prevents states from depriving any "person of life, liberty, or property, without due process of law"
15	1869	1870	E	Guarantees that citizens' right to vote cannot be denied "on account of race, color, or previous condition of servitude"
16	1909	1913	E	Gives Congress power to collect an income tax
17	1912	1913	E	Provides for popular election of senators, who were formerly elected by state legislatures
18	1917	1919	P	Prohibits making and selling intoxicating liquors
19	1919	1920	E	Gives women the right to vote
20	1932	1933	G	Changes the presidential inauguration from March 4 to January 20 and sets January 3 for the opening date of Congress
21	1933	1933	P	Repeals the Eighteenth Amendment
22	1947	1951	G	Limits a president to two terms
23	1960	1961	E	Gives citizens of Washington, D.C., the right to vote for president
24	1962	1964	E	Prohibits charging citizens a poll tax to vote

(continued)

ties and cabinets have exercised considerable influence in American politics. Some constitutional provisions have fallen out of use. The electors in the electoral college, for example, were supposed to exercise their

Table 2.2   *Cont.*

No.	Proposed	Ratified	Intent	Subject
25	1965	1967	G	Provides for presidential succession, disability, and vice-presidential vacancy
26	1971	1971	E	Lowers the voting age to eighteen
27	1789	1992	G	Bars immediate pay increases to members of Congress

P   Amendment legislating public policy
G   Amendment correcting perceived deficiencies in government structure
E   Amendment advancing equality

own judgment in voting for president and vice president. Today the electors simply rubber-stamp the outcome of election contests in their states.

Political practice has altered the distribution of power without changes in the Constitution. The framers intended Congress to be the strongest branch of government. But the president has come to overshadow Congress. Presidents such as Abraham Lincoln and Franklin Roosevelt used their powers imaginatively to respond to national crises. And their actions served as springboards for future presidents to further enlarge the powers of the office.

An Evaluation of the Constitution

The U.S. Constitution is one of the world's most praised political documents. It is the oldest written national constitution and one of the most widely copied, sometimes word for word. It is also one of the shortest. The brevity of the Constitution may be one of its greatest strengths. The framers simply laid out a structural framework for government; they did not describe relationships and powers in detail. For example, the Constitution gives Congress the power to regulate "commerce . . . among the several states" (Article I, Section 8) but does not define interstate commerce. This kind of general wording allows interpretations that reflect contemporary political, social, and technological developments.

The generality of the U.S. Constitution stands in stark contrast to the specificity of most state constitutions. The constitution of California, for example, provides that "fruit and nut-bearing trees under the age of four years from the time of planting in orchard form and grapevines under the age of three years from the time of planting in vineyard form . . . shall be exempt from taxation" (Article XIII, Section 12). Because of this specificity, most state constitutions are much longer than the U.S. Constitution.

Freedom, Order, and Equality in the Constitution

The revolutionaries constructed a new form of government—a *federal* government—that was strong enough to maintain order but not so strong that it could dominate the states or infringe on individual freedoms. In short, the Constitution provided a judicious balance between order and freedom. It paid virtually no attention to equality.

Consider social equality. The Constitution never mentioned slavery —a controversial issue even then. As we discussed earlier, the Constitution implicitly condoned slavery in the wording of several articles. Not until the ratification of the Thirteenth Amendment in 1865 was slavery prohibited.

The Constitution was designed long before social equality was ever thought of as an objective of government. In fact, in "Federalist No. 10," Madison held that protection of the "diversities in the faculties of men from which the rights of property originate" is "the first object of government." More than a century later, the Constitution was changed to incorporate a key device for the promotion of social equality—the income tax. The Sixteenth Amendment (1913) gave Congress the power to collect an income tax; it was proposed and ratified to replace a law that had been declared unconstitutional in an 1895 court case. The idea of **progressive taxation** (in which the tax rate increases with income) had long been closely linked to the income tax, and the Sixteenth Amendment gave that idea a constitutional basis.[11] Progressive taxation later helped promote social equality through the redistribution of income. That is, higher-income people are taxed at higher rates to help fund social programs that benefit low-income people. Social equality itself has never been, and is not now, a prime *constitutional* value. The Constitution has been much more effective in securing order and freedom.

The Constitution also did not take a stand on political equality. It left voting qualifications to the states, specifying only that people who could vote for "the most numerous branch of the State Legislature" could also vote for representatives to Congress (Article I, Section 2). In most states at that time, only taxpaying or property-owning white males could vote. With few exceptions, blacks and women were universally excluded from voting. These inequalities have been rectified by several amendments.

The Constitution did not guarantee blacks citizenship until the Fourteenth Amendment was ratified (1868) and did not give them the right to vote until the Fifteenth Amendment (1870). Women were not guaranteed the right to vote until the Nineteenth Amendment (1920). Finally, the *poll tax* (a tax that people had to pay in order to vote and that tended to disenfranchise blacks) was not eliminated until the Twenty-fourth Amendment (1964). Two other amendments expanded the Constitution's grant of political equality. The Twenty-third Amendment (1961) allowed citizens of Washington, D.C., who are not considered residents of any state, to vote for president. The Twenty-sixth Amendment (1971) extended voting rights to all citizens who are at least eighteen years old.

The Constitution and Models of Democracy

Think back to our discussion of the models of democracy in Chapter 1. Which model does the Constitution fit: the pluralist or the majoritarian? Actually, it is hard to imagine a government framework better suited to the pluralist model of democracy than the Constitution of the United States. It is also hard to imagine a document more at odds with the majoritarian model. Consider Madison's claim in "Federalist No. 10" that government inevitably involves conflicting factions. This concept fits perfectly with the idea of competing groups in pluralist theory (see Chapter 1). Think about his description in "Federalist No. 51" of the Constitution's ability to guard against the concentration of power in the majority through its separation of powers and checks and balances. This concept—avoiding a single center of government power that might fall under majority control—also fits perfectly with pluralist democracy.

The delegates to the Constitutional Convention intended to create a republic, a government based on majority consent; they did not intend to create a democracy, which rests on majority rule. They succeeded admirably in creating that republic. Along the way, they also produced a government that grew into a democracy, but a particular type of democracy. The framers neither wanted nor got a democracy that fit the majoritarian model. They perhaps wanted and certainly did get a government that conforms to the pluralist model.

Summary

The U.S. Constitution is more than a historic document, an antique curiosity. Although more than two hundred years old, it still governs the politics of a mighty modern nation. It still has the power to force from office a president who won re-election by a landslide and the power to see the country through government crises.

The Constitution was the end product of a revolutionary movement aimed at preserving existing liberties. That movement began with the Declaration of Independence, a proclamation that everyone is entitled to certain rights (among them, life, liberty, and the pursuit of happiness) and that government exists for the good of its citizens. When government denies those rights, the people have the right to rebel.

War with Britain was only part of the process of independence. Some form of government was needed to replace the British monarchy. The Americans chose a republic and defined the structure of that republic in the Articles of Confederation. The Articles, however, were a failure. Although they guaranteed the states their coveted independence, the Articles left the central government too weak to deal with disorder and insurrection.

The Constitution was the second attempt at limited government. It replaced a loose union of powerful states with a strong national government incorporating four political principles: republicanism, federalism, separation of powers, and checks and balances. Republicanism is a form of government in which power resides in the people and is exercised by their elected representatives. Federalism is a division of power between the national government and the states. The federalism of the Constitution conferred substantial powers on the national government at the expense of the states. Separation of powers is a further division of the power of the national government into legislative (lawmaking), executive (law-enforcing), and judiciary (law-interpreting) branches. Finally, the Constitution established a system of checks and balances, giving each branch some scrutiny of and control over the others.

Once the document had been written, work began on ratification. A major stumbling block was the failure of the Constitution to list the individual liberties that Americans had fought to protect. With the promise of a bill of rights, the Constitution was ratified. These ten amendments guaranteed

participation in the political process, respect for personal beliefs, and personal privacy. They also embodied guarantees against government overreaching in criminal prosecutions. Over the years, the Constitution has evolved through the formal amendment process, through the exercise of judicial review, and through political practice.

The Constitution was designed to strike a balance between order and freedom. It was not designed to promote equality; in fact, it had to be amended to redress inequality. The framers did not set out to create a democracy. There was little faith in government by the people two centuries ago. Nevertheless, the framers produced a democratic form of government. That government, with its separation of powers and checks and balances, is remarkably well suited to the pluralist model of democracy. Simple majority rule, which lies at the heart of the majoritarian model, was precisely what the framers wanted to avoid.

The framers also wanted a government that would balance the powers of the national government and those of the states. The exact balance was a touchy issue and had been skirted by the delegates at the Constitutional Convention. Some seventy years later, a civil war was fought over that balance of power. That war and countless political battles before and after it have demonstrated that the national government dominates the state governments in our political system. In the next chapter, we look at how a loose confederation of states has evolved into a "more perfect Union."

Key Terms

Continental Congress
Declaration of Independence

social contract theory
republic

confederation
sovereignty
Articles of Confederation
Shays' Rebellion
Virginia Plan
legislative branch
executive branch
judicial branch
New Jersey Plan
Great Compromise
electoral college
republicanism
federalism
unitary government

separation of powers
checks and balances
bicameral
enumerated powers
necessary and proper clause
elastic clause
implied powers
judicial review
supremacy clause
Bill of Rights
proposal
ratification
progressive taxation

Selected Readings

Beard, Charles A. *Economic Interpretation of the Constitution of the United States.* New York: Macmillan, 1913. Beard argues that the framers' economic self-interest was the motivating force behind the Constitution.

Becker, Carl. *The Declaration of Independence: A Study in the History of Political Ideas.* New York: Knopf, 1942. This classic work examines the theory and politics of the Declaration of Independence.

Bowen, Catherine Drinker. *Miracle at Philadelphia.* Boston: Atlantic–Little, Brown, 1966. This is an absorbing, well-written account of the events surrounding the Constitutional Convention.

Kammen, Michael. *A Machine That Would Go of Itself: The Constitution in American Culture.* New York: Knopf, 1986. In this remarkable examination of the Constitution's cultural impact, the author argues that Americans' reverence for the Constitution is inconsistent with their ignorance of its content and meaning.

Kurland, Philip B., and Ralph Lerner, eds. *The Founders' Constitution.* 5 vols. Chicago: University of Chicago Press, 1987. This thorough collection of primary documents is designed to explain the Constitution and is organized around the structure of the Constitution from Preamble through Amendment XII.

McDonald, Forrest. *Novus Ordo Seclorum: The Intellectual Origins of the Constitution.* Lawrence: University Press of Kansas, 1985. This is an authoritative examination of the intellectual ferment surrounding the birth of the U.S. Constitution.

Rakove, Jack N. *The Beginnings of National Politics: An Interpretive History of the Continental Congress.* New York: Knopf, 1979. This book traces the history of the Continental Congress and the difficulties of governing under the Articles of Confederation.

Storing, Herbert J. *What the Anti-Federalists Were For.* Chicago: University of Chicago Press, 1981. Storing analyzes the arguments against the Constitution.

Wills, Garry. *Explaining America: The Federalist.* Garden City, N.Y.: Doubleday, 1981. This arresting work analyzes the intellectual background of the framers.

Wood, Gordon S. *The Creation of the American Republic, 1776–1787.* Chapel Hill: University of North Carolina Press, 1969. This is a penetrating study of political thought in the early period of the new republic.

FEDERALISM

3

Steve Oligmueller, age nineteen, Highmore High School class of 1986, had returned home to South Dakota for the summer. At night, he would get together with old friends and swap stories about freshman year at college. They would meet at The Stable, a local bar, to sit, talk, listen to music, and have a couple of beers. In the spring of 1987, South Dakota was one of four states that still allowed people under twenty-one to drink beer. Soon, however, the cost of letting nineteen-year-olds drink beer would go up drastically—not just for Steve and his friends but also for all the taxpayers of South Dakota. The state stood to lose nearly $10 million in federal highway funds unless it raised its minimum drinking age to twenty-one.

Just three years earlier, twenty-nine states and the District of Columbia had allowed people younger than twenty-one to purchase and consume some forms of alcoholic beverages. In 1984, however, an action taken in Washington, D.C., marked the beginning of the end of legalized drinking for those under twenty-one. What happened? Did Congress establish a national minimum drinking age? No, at least not directly. Congress simply added a provision to a highway bill. Under that provision, states would lose 5 percent of their federal highway funds in 1986 and 10 percent in 1987 if they allowed the purchase or consumption of alcohol by those under twenty-one. States themselves would have to change their own laws or risk losing federal funds. This was a round-about method of achieving a national objective. If the national government wanted to set twenty-one as a national drinking age, why not act directly and pass legislation to do so?

The simplest answer has to do with the federal system of government. The Constitution divided power between the national government and the state governments. With only one sobering exception (Prohibition and the Eighteenth Amendment), regulating liquor sales and setting minimum drinking ages had always been the responsibilities of state governments. But over the years, the national government has found ways to extend its influence into areas well beyond those originally defined in the Constitution.

Supporters of the legislation believed that the national government's responsibility to maintain order justified intervention. The lives and safety of people were at stake. Opponents of the plan argued that it constituted age discrimination and infringed on states' rights. They claimed the act was an unwarranted extension of national power, that it limited the freedom of the states and of their citizens.

President Reagan, who had campaigned on a pledge to reduce the size and scope of the national government, strongly opposed replacing state standards with national ones. When confronted with this issue, which pitted order against freedom and national standards against state standards, he first opposed the bill; later, he changed his position. At the signing ceremony, he said:

> This problem is bigger than the individual states. It's a grave national problem and it touches all our lives. With the problem so clear cut and the proven solution at hand we have no misgiving about this judicious use of federal power. I'm convinced that it will help persuade state legislators to act in the national interest.[1]

Several states took the matter to court, hoping to have the provision declared unconstitutional under the Tenth and the Twenty-first Amendments. In June 1987, the Supreme Court reached its decision in *South Dakota* v. *Dole*.[2] The justices conceded that direct congressional control of the drinking age in the states would be unconstitutional. Nevertheless, there was no constitutional barrier to the indirect achievement of such objectives. The 7–2 majority argued that far from being an infringement on states' rights, the law was a "relatively mild encouragement to the states to enact higher minimum drinking ages than they otherwise would choose."

These events show how much the role of the national government has changed since the Constitution was adopted. In the early part of the last century, presidents routinely vetoed bills authorizing roads, canals, and other interstate improvements because they believed these kinds of projects exceeded the constitutional authority of the national government. In 1991, the national government contributed more than $15 billion to cost-sharing projects with the states for road research, planning, and construction.[3]

An important element of federalism was at work here: the respective sovereignty of national and state governments. (Sovereignty is the quality of being supreme in power or authority.) Congress acknowledged the sovereignty of the states by not legislating a national drinking age. And the states were willing to barter their sovereignty in exchange for needed revenues. As long as this remains true, there are few areas where national power cannot reach.

Sovereignty also affects political leadership. A governor may not be the political equal of a president, but a governor and a president represent different sovereignties. Consequently, presidents rarely command governors; they negotiate, even plead.

In this chapter, we examine American federalism in theory and in practice. Is the division of power between nation and states a matter of constitutional principle or practical politics? How does the balance of power between nation and states relate to the conflicts between freedom and order and between freedom and equality? Does federalism reflect the pluralist or the majoritarian model of democracy?

Theories of Federalism

The delegates who met in Philadelphia in 1787 tackled the problem of making one nation out of thirteen independent states by inventing a new political form—federal government—that combined features of a confederacy with features of unitary government (see Chapter 2). Under this principle of **federalism**, two or more governments would exercise power and authority over the same people and the same territory. For example, the governments of the United States and Pennsylvania would share certain powers (the power to tax, for instance), while other powers would belong exclusively to one or the other. As James Madison wrote in "Federalist No. 10," "The federal Constitution forms a happy combination . . . the great and aggregate interests being referred to the national, and the local and particular to state governments." So the power to coin money belongs to the national government; the power to grant divorces remains a state prerogative. By contrast, authority over the state militia may sometimes belong to the national government and sometimes to the state government. The history of American federalism reveals that it has not always been easy to draw a line between what is "great and aggregate" and what is "local and particular."*

---

* The everyday phrase Americans use to refer to their central government—federal government—muddies the waters even more. Technically speaking, the United States has a federal system of government that includes both the national and the state governments. To avoid confusion from here on, we use the term *national government*, rather than *federal government*, when we are talking about the central government.

Nevertheless, federalism offered a solution to the problem of diversity in America. It also provided a new political model. A leading scholar of federalism estimated that today 40 percent of the world's population lives under a formal federal constitution, while another 30 percent lives in polities that apply federal principles or practices without formal constitutional acknowledgment.[4]

The history of American federalism is full of attempts to capture its true meaning in an adjective or metaphor. By one recent reckoning, scholars have generated nearly five hundred ways to describe federalism.[5] Let us concentrate on two such representations: dual federalism and cooperative federalism.

Dual Federalism

The expression **dual federalism** sums up a theory about the proper relationship between the national government and the states. This theory has four essential parts. First, the national government rules by enumerated powers only. Second, the national government has a limited set of constitutional purposes. Third, each government unit—nation and state—is sovereign within its sphere. And fourth, the relationship between nation and states is best characterized by tension rather than cooperation.[6]

Dual federalism portrays the states as powerful components of the federal system—in some ways, the equals of the national government. Under dual federalism, the functions and responsibilities of the national government and the state governments are theoretically different and practically separate from each other. Dual federalism sees the Constitution as a compact among sovereign states. Of primary importance in dual federalism are **states' rights**, a concept that reserves to the states all rights not specifically conferred on the national government by the Constitution. Claims of states' rights often come from opponents of a national government policy. Their argument is that the people have not delegated the power to make such policy, and thus the power remains with the states or the people. Proponents of states' rights believe that the powers of the national government should be interpreted very narrowly. They insist that, despite the **elastic clause**, which gives Congress the **implied powers** needed to execute its enumerated powers (see Chapter 2), the activities of Congress should be confined to the enumerated powers only. They support their view by quoting the Tenth Amendment: "The powers not delegated to the United States by the Constitution, nor prohibited by it to the States, are reserved to the states respectively, or to the people."

Political scientists use a metaphor to describe dual federalism. They call it *layer-cake federalism*. The powers and functions of national and state governments are as separate as the layers of a cake (see Figure 3.1). Each government is supreme in its own "layer," or sphere of action; the

Dual Federalism:
The Layer-Cake Metaphor

Citizens cutting into the political system will find clear differences between state and national powers, functions, and responsibilities.

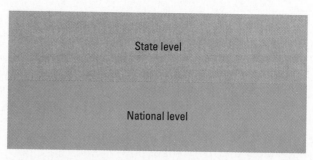

Cooperative Federalism:
The Marble-Cake Metaphor

Citizens cutting into the political system at any point will find national and state powers, functions, and responsibilities mixed and mingled.

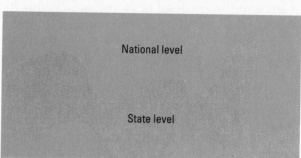

FIGURE 3.1   Metaphors for Federalism
The two views of federalism can be represented graphically.
Dual Federalism: The Layer-Cake Metaphor
Citizens cutting into the political system will find clear differences between state and national powers, functions, and responsibilities.
Cooperative Federalism: The Marble-Cake Metaphor
Citizens cutting into the political system at any point will find national and state powers, functions, and responsibilities mixed and mingled.

two layers are distinct; and the dimensions of each layer are fixed by the Constitution.

Dual federalism—the theory that underlies the layer-cake metaphor—has been challenged on historical and other grounds. Some critics argue that if the national government is really a creation of the states, it is a creation of only thirteen states—those that ratified the Constitution. The other thirty-seven states were admitted after the national government came into being and were created by that government out of land it had acquired. Another challenge concerns the ratification process. Remember, the original thirteen states ratified the Constitution in special conventions, not in state legislatures. Ratification, then, was an act of the *people*, not of the *states*. Moreover, the Preamble to the Constitution begins, "We the people of the United States," not "We the States." The question of just where the people fit into the federal system is not handled very well by dual federalism.

Cooperative Federalism

Cooperative federalism, a phrase coined in the 1930s, embraces a different theory of the relationship between the national and the state governments. It acknowledges the increasing overlap in state and national functions and rejects the idea of separate spheres, or layers, for the states and the national government. Cooperative federalism includes three elements. First, national and state agencies typically undertake governmental functions jointly rather than exclusively. Second, nation and states routinely share power. And third, power is not concentrated at any government level or in any agency; this fragmentation of responsibilities gives people and groups access to many centers of influence.

Cooperative federalism blurs the distinction between national and state powers. The bakery metaphor used to describe this kind of federalism is a *marble cake*. The national and the state governments do not act in separate spheres; they are intermingled. Their functions are mixed in the American federal system. Critical to cooperative federalism is an expansive view of the Constitution's supremacy clause (Article VI), which specifically subordinates state law to national law and charges every judge with disregarding state laws that are inconsistent with the Constitution, national laws, and treaties.

Some scholars argue that the layer-cake metaphor has never accurately described the American political structure.[7] National and state governments have many common objectives and have often cooperated to achieve them. In the nineteenth century, for example, cooperation, not separation, made it possible to develop transportation systems and to establish land-grant colleges.

A critical difference between the theories of dual and cooperative federalism is the way they interpret two sections of the Constitution that set out the terms of the relationship between the national and the state governments. Article I, Section 8 lists the enumerated powers of the Congress and then concludes with the **elastic clause**, which gives Congress the power to "make all laws which shall be necessary and proper for carrying into execution the foregoing powers." The Tenth Amendment, as we have seen, reserves to the states or the people "powers" not given to the national government or denied to the states by the Constitution. Dual federalism postulates an inflexible elastic clause and a capacious Tenth Amendment. Cooperative federalism postulates suppleness in the elastic clause and confines the Tenth Amendment to a self-evident, obvious truth.

In efforts to limit the scope of the national government, conservatives have given much credence to the layer-cake metaphor. In contrast, liberals, believing that one of the functions of the national government is to bring about equality, have argued that the marble-cake metaphor is more accurate. Nevertheless, the Constitution is only the starting point in the debate. The real meaning of American federalism must be found in its implementation.

The Dynamics of Federalism: Legal Sanctions and Financial Incentives

Although the Constitution defines a kind of federalism, the actual balance of power between nation and states has always been more a matter of politics than of formal theory. A discussion of federalism, then, must do more than simply list the powers that the Constitution assigns to the levels of government. The balance of power has shifted substantially since President Madison agonized over the proper role the national government should play in funding roads. Today, that government has assumed functions never dreamed of in the nineteenth century.

Why has power shifted so dramatically from the states to the national government? The answer lies in historical circumstances, not in debates over constitutional theory. For example, the greatest test of states' rights came when several Southern states attempted to secede from the union. The threat of secession challenged the supremacy of the national government, a supremacy that Northern armies established militarily in the nation's greatest bloodbath, the Civil War.

Some changes in the balance of power were the product of constitutional amendments. For example, the due process and equal protection clauses of the Fourteenth Amendment* (1868) limited states' rights, as did the income tax mandated by the Sixteenth Amendment (1913) and the Seventeenth Amendment's provision for the direct election of senators (1913). Most of the national government's power, however, has come to it through legislation, judicial interpretation, and political coercion. It has relied primarily on two distinct approaches to expand its power: incentives to win state cooperation and sanctions (that is, mechanisms of social or economic control) designed to "pinch" in an effort to secure cooperation. Here we look at these tools of political change.

Legislation and the Elastic Clause

The elastic clause of the Constitution gives Congress the power to make all laws that are "necessary and proper" to carry out its responsibilities. By using this power in combination with its enumerated powers, Congress has been able to increase the scope of the national government tremendously over the last two centuries. Change has often come in times of crisis and national emergency—the Civil War, the Great Depression, the world wars. The role of the national government has grown as it has responded to needs and demands that state and local governments were unwilling or unable to meet.

Legislation is one of the prods the national government has used to achieve goals at the state level, to force the states to comply. The Voting

---

* The Fourteenth Amendment was itself a product of the Civil War.

Rights Act of 1965 is a good example. Section 2 of Article I of the Constitution gives the states the power to set voter qualifications. But the Fifteenth Amendment (1870) provides that no person shall be denied the right to vote "on account of race, color, or previous condition of servitude." Before the Voting Rights Act, states could not specifically deny blacks the right to vote, but they could require that voters pass literacy tests or pay poll taxes, requirements that virtually disenfranchised blacks in many states. The Voting Rights Act was designed to correct this political inequality (see Chapter 12).

The act gives officials of the national government the power to decide whether individuals should be allowed to vote in all elections—including primaries and national, state, and local elections. The constitutional authority for the act rests on the second section of the Fifteenth Amendment, which gives Congress the power to enforce the amendment through "appropriate legislation."

Judicial Interpretation

The Voting Rights Act was not a unanimous hit. Its critics, adopting the language of dual federalism, insisted that the Constitution gave the states the power to determine voter qualifications. Its supporters claimed that the Fifteenth Amendment guarantee of voting rights took precedence over states' rights and gave the national government new responsibilities. In this instance, the states tried to defend their freedom to set voter qualifications against the national government's effort to promote political equality.

The conflict was ultimately resolved by the Supreme Court, the arbiter of the federal system. The Court settles disputes over the powers of the national and the state governments by deciding whether actions of the national or state governments are constitutional (see Chapter 11). Since 1937, the Supreme Court has almost always supported the national government in contests involving the balance of power between nation and states.

The growth of national power has been accomplished through a variety of routes. One is the Supreme Court's interpretation of the Constitution's **commerce clause**. Clause 3 of Article I, Section 8 states that "Congress shall have the power . . . to regulate commerce . . . among the several States. . . ." Although the Court's interpretation of the clause varied in the past, today the only limit on the exercise of the commerce power is Congress itself.

During Chief Justice Earl Warren's tenure (1953–1969), the Supreme Court used the Fourteenth Amendment to extend various provisions of the Bill of Rights to the states, thereby shifting power from the states to the national government. Through the Court, the national government set minimum standards for due process in criminal cases that the states would have to meet. These standards provide equality before the law for individuals who are suspected of crimes, but critics argue that they hamper state officials in trying to maintain order.

A series of decisions concerning *reapportionment*—resetting the boundaries of electoral districts—also eroded the power of the states in the early 1960s.[8] Until that time, states had set the boundaries of voting districts, but some had failed to adjust those boundaries to reflect changes in population. As a result, in certain areas small numbers of rural voters were able to elect as many representatives as were large numbers of urban voters. In deciding cases involving reapportionment, the Court set down a new standard of one person, one vote and forced the states to apply this principle in redrawing their districts and apportioning their legislatures.

In the due process and reapportionment cases, the Supreme Court protected individual rights and in the process championed political equality. But remember, the Supreme Court is part of the national government. When it defends the rights of an individual against a state, it also substitutes a national standard for the state standard governing that relationship.

Grants-in-Aid

In the last three decades, the national government's use of financial incentives has rivaled its use of legislation and judicial interpretation as a means of shaping relationships between the national and the state governments. The principal method the national government uses to make money available to the states is through grants-in-aid.

A **grant-in-aid** is money paid by one level of government to another to be spent for a specific purpose. Most grants-in-aid come with standards or requirements prescribed by Congress. Many are awarded on a matching basis; that is, recipient governments must make some contribution of their own, which is then matched by the national government. Grants-in-aid take two general forms: categorical grants and block grants.

Categorical grants are targeted for specific purposes, such as library literacy or weatherization assistance for low-income persons. Restrictions on the use of such grants often leave the recipient government relatively little discretion. Recipients today include state governments, local governments, and public and private nonprofit organizations. There are two kinds of categorical grant: formula grants and project grants. **Formula grants**, as their name implies, are distributed according to a particular formula, which specifies who is eligible for the grant and how much each eligible applicant will receive. The formulas may weigh such factors as state per capita income, number of school-age children, urban population, and number of families below the poverty line. In 1989, 155 of the 478 categorical grants offered by the national government were formula grants, a 13 percent increase in two years. The remaining 323 grants were **project grants**—grants awarded on the basis of competitive applications.[9] New grants have focused on acquired immune deficiency syndrome (AIDS), homelessness, and substance abuse.

In contrast to categorical grants, **block grants** are awarded for broad, general purposes, such as urban mass transit, criminal justice, or community services. They allow recipients considerable freedom in deciding how to allocate money to individual programs. Whereas a categorical grant may be given to promote a specific activity—say, ethnic heritage studies—a block grant can be offered for elementary, secondary, and vocational education. The state or local government receiving the block grant then chooses the specific educational programs to fund with it.

Grants-in-aid are a method of redistributing income. Money is collected by the national government from citizens of all fifty states and is then allocated to other citizens, supposedly for worthwhile social purposes. And, indeed, many grants have worked to remove gross inequalities among states and their citizens. But the formulas used to redistribute this income are not impartial; they are themselves highly political and often subject to debate in Congress.

Whatever its form, grant money comes with strings attached. Many of the strings are there to ensure that the money is used for the purpose for which it was given; others are designed to evaluate how well the grant is working. Still others are instituted to achieve some broad national goal, which is not always closely related to the specific purpose of the grant. For example, as noted earlier, the Highway Act of 1984 reduced the amount of money available to states that allowed those younger than twenty-one to purchase and consume alcoholic beverages. The lure of financial aid has proved to be a powerful incentive for states to relinquish the freedom to set their own standards and to accept those set by the national government.

The Developing Concept of Federalism

A student of federalism once remarked that "each generation faced with new problems has had to work out its own version of federalism." Succeeding generations have used judicial and congressional power in varying degrees to shift the balance of power back and forth between the national and the state governments.

McCulloch v. Maryland

Early in the nineteenth century, the nationalist interpretation of federalism triumphed over states' rights. In 1819, under Chief Justice John Marshall, the Supreme Court expanded the role of the national government in its decision in *McCulloch* v. *Maryland*.[10] The Court was asked to rule whether Congress had the power to establish a national bank and, if so, whether states had the power to tax that bank. In a unanimous opinion written by Marshall, the Court conceded that Congress had only the powers that the Constitution conferred, and it nowhere mentioned banks. However, Article I granted to Congress the authority to enact all laws necessary and proper to the execution of Congress's enumerated powers. Marshall gave a broad interpretation to this elastic clause: "Let the end be legitimate, let it be within the scope of the constitution, and all means which are appropriate, which are plainly adapted to that end, which are not prohibited, but consistent with the letter and spirit of the constitution, are constitutional."

The Court clearly agreed that Congress had the power to charter a bank. But did the states—in this case, Maryland—have the power to tax the bank? Arguing that "the power to tax is the power to destroy," Marshall insisted that states could not tax the national government because the powers of the national government came, not from the states, but from the people. Marshall here was embracing cooperative federalism.

States' Rights and Dual Federalism

Many people assume that the Civil War was fought over slavery. It was not. The real issue was the character of the federal union, of federalism itself. At the time of the Civil War, regional variations between Northern and Southern states were considerable. With the Southern economy based on labor-intensive agriculture, Southerners supported both low tariffs on imported goods and slavery. Northerners, to protect their own economy, wanted high tariffs. When they sought national legislation that threatened Southern interests, Southerners demanded states' rights. They even introduced the theory of **nullification**—the idea that a state could declare a particular action of the national government null and void. The Civil War rendered the idea of nullification null and void, but it did not settle the balance between national and state power.

In the decades after the Civil War, the Supreme Court placed limits on national power, particularly when the national government attempted to regulate industry. The Court rejected the idea that the power to regulate interstate commerce could be used to justify policies not directly related to the smooth functioning of such commerce—policies such as setting a national minimum wage or abolishing child labor. In the late nineteenth and early twentieth centuries, the justices were influenced by laissez-faire economic theory, a hands-off approach to business. Time and again the Court ruled that congressional legislation that limited the activities of corporations was unconstitutional because it invaded the domain of the states.

The New Deal and Its Consequences

It took the Great Depression to place dual federalism in repose. The problems of the Depression proved too extensive for either state govern-

Made in the U.S.A.
A young factory worker in the early part of this century. The Supreme Court decided in 1918 that Congress had no power to limit child labor. According to the Court, that power belonged to the states, which resisted imposing limits for fear such legislation would drive businesses to other (less restrictive) states.

ments or private businesses to handle. So the national government assumed a heavy share of responsibility for providing relief and directing efforts toward economic recovery. Under the New Deal, President Franklin D. Roosevelt's response to the Depression, Congress enacted various emergency relief programs to restore economic activity and help the unemployed. Many of these measures required the cooperation of the national and the state governments. Through regulations attached to funds, the national government extended its power and control over the states.[11]

At first, the Supreme Court's view of the Depression was different from that of the other branches of the national government. In the Court's opinion, the whole structure of federalism was threatened when collections of local troubles were treated as one national problem. Justice Owen Roberts, in the decision in *United States* v. *Butler* (1936), wrote:

It does not help that local conditions throughout the nation have created a situation of national concern; for this is but to say that when-

"It's the Economy, Stupid!"
To what degree does government have a responsibility to provide for the economic well-being of the citizenry? To what degree is this a responsibility of the national government? The Preamble of the U.S. Constitution states that a major objective of that government is to "promote the general Welfare." But precisely what does this mean? Perhaps that question was answered in 1992 by the voters who seemed to agree with the wording of a sign in Bill Clinton's Little Rock campaign headquarters: "It's the economy, stupid!"

ever there is a widespread similarity of local conditions, Congress may ignore constitutional limitations on its own powers and usurp those reserved to the states.[12]

In this decision and others, the Court struck down several pieces of regulatory legislation, including the National Industrial Recovery Act, which would have regulated wages, working hours, and business competition.

In 1937, however, with no change in personnel, the Court began to alter its course. It upheld the Social Security Act and the National Labor Relations Act—both New Deal measures. Perhaps the Court had studied the 1936 election returns and was responding to the country's endorsement of the use of national policies to address national problems. In any event, the Court gave up its effort to set a rigid boundary between national and state power. From then on, the division of power in the federal system became less relevant, and the relationship between governments became increasingly important.

Some call the New Deal era "revolutionary." There is no doubt that the period was critical in reshaping federalism in the United States. But perhaps the most significant change was in the way Americans thought about both their problems and the role of the national government in solving them. Difficulties that at one time had been seen as personal or local problems were now national problems requiring national solutions. The *general welfare*, broadly defined, became a legitimate concern of the national government.

In other respects, however, the New Deal was not very revolutionary. Congress, for example, did not claim that any new powers were needed to deal with the nation's economic problems; it simply used the constitutional powers it had to suit the circumstances. And with one brief exception, from the late 1930s onward the Supreme Court upheld Congress's power on virtually every issue.

Desegregation and the War on Poverty

During the 1950s and 1960s, the national government assumed the task of promoting social equality by combating racism and poverty. Both problems had seemed impossible to solve at the state level.

Matters of race relations had generally been left to the states, which more or less ignored them despite the constitutional amendments passed after the Civil War. Moreover, when the Supreme Court adopted the separate-but-equal doctrine in 1896,* states were free to do as much, or as little, as they pleased about racial inequality.[13]

In 1954, however, in *Brown* v. *Board of Education*, the Supreme Court decided that racially separate but objectively equal public schools were inherently *unequal*.[14] This put the national government in the position of ordering the desegregation of public schools. As the civil rights movement focused increasing attention on the problems of discrimination, Congress passed two important pieces of legislation: the Civil Rights Act of 1964 and the Voting Rights Act of 1965. Through these acts, the national government used its legislative sanction to outlaw racial discrimination in employment, in public accommodations, and in voter qualifications. The acts themselves sharply limited states' rights where the effect of those rights had been to deny equality.

In the 1960s, President Lyndon Johnson's War on Poverty generated an enormous amount of social legislation and a massive increase in the scope of the national government. In an attempt to provide equality of opportunity and improve the quality of life throughout the United

---

* In *Plessy* v. *Ferguson* (1896), the Supreme Court upheld state-imposed racial segregation, ruling that separate facilities for blacks and whites could be maintained as long as they were "equal" (see Chapter 12).

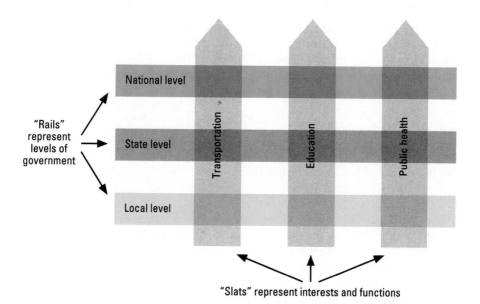

National level

State level

Local level

"Rails" represent levels of government

Transportation

Education

Public health

"Slats" represent interests and functions

FIGURE 3.2   Picket-Fence Federalism
The picket-fence model shows how functions cross government lines and also connect the officials who work at different levels of government.

States, the national government used money inducements to introduce a number of new programs, ranging from increased aid to higher education and aid to elementary and secondary schools to food stamps and employment-training projects.

Johnson's recipe for marble-cake federalism included some new ingredients. Before 1960, nearly all intergovernmental assistance (that is, aid from one level of government to another) had gone from the national government to state governments. But the War on Poverty often gave aid directly to local governments or even to community groups.

As the role of the national government grew larger and was more generally accepted, the focus of the debate over federalism changed. National, state, and local governments were no longer separate, distinct layers; they interacted. But how? The search for answers to this question placed **intergovernmental relations** at center stage. The study of intergovernmental relations looks at that interdependence and the connections among personnel and policies at different levels of government. It also examines the ways that national, state, and local governments influence one another.

The political dynamics of intergovernmental relations since the 1960s suggested a new metaphor for federalism: **picket-fence federalism** (see Figure 3.2). Here, the fence rails are the levels of government—national, state, and local—and the fence slats are the interests of lobbies and groups, both inside and outside of government, and the functions of government. The communities of interest (or functions) represented by each slat make contact at each of the three levels of government. They are able to share information, develop common standards, and exert pressure on each level of government. Government officials themselves may move along the interest slats to influence officials on other rails. On a typical trip to Washington, for instance, the head of a state department of education may have a morning meeting with members of the state's congressional delegation to make them aware of the state's educational needs and priorities, then go to lunch with lobbyists from the National Education Association (NEA), and after that testify in front of a congressional committee on education and meet with officials from the U.S. Department of Education. This tired official may return to the office the next day to find an education chief from a neighboring state on the phone, hoping to find out how the visit went.

Since the 1960s, the national government has provided money for all sorts of local programs—rat control, crime control, rural fire protection, solid waste disposal, home insulation. Far from being unresponsive, Congress has become hyperresponsive. And its willingness to spend national funds has increased the importance of existing interest groups and has led to the creation of new ones. The result is not just pluralist democracy but *hyperpluralism*—every conceivable interest has its group.

The growth of government programs, the hyperresponsiveness of Congress, and the pressure of interest groups have created a federal system that critics describe as "overloaded and out of control." When the Advisory Commission on Intergovernmental Relations (ACIR), a group created by Congress to monitor the federal system, reviewed the operation of that system in 1980, it concluded that the system just did not work. Over the previous two decades, the ACIR said, the system of intergovernmental relations had become "more pervasive, more intrusive, more unmanageable, more ineffective, more costly and more unaccountable."[15]

A New, Newer, Newest Federalism

Every president since Richard Nixon has expressed disenchantment with the unmanageability of the federal system and has pledged to cut the size of the bureaucracy and return power to the states. Yet reform has been difficult to implement. At the national level, a growing body of rules and regulations often places new responsibilities on state and local governments without providing adequate resources to carry out the national mandate.

Nixon's New Federalism: Revenue Sharing

When Nixon came into office in 1969, he pledged to change a national government he characterized as "overly centralized, overbureaucratized

A Victory for "Socialism?"
Only a few decades ago health care was generally seen as a personal responsibility. Proposals for national government involvement were often condemned as "socialized medicine." As health care has become more and more sophisticated—and more expensive—attitudes have changed. Here a demonstration organized by a coalition of New York area labor unions call for a national health care system.

. . . unresponsive as well as inefficient." He dubbed his solution to the problem "New Federalism" and claimed it would channel "power, funds and authority . . . to those governments closest to the people." He expected New Federalism to help restore control of the nation's destiny "by returning a greater share of control to state and local authorities."[16] New Federalism was nothing more than dual federalism in modern dress.

The centerpiece of Nixon's New Federalism was *revenue sharing,* in which the national government would turn tax revenues over to the states and localities to spend as they pleased. The plan had two parts: general revenue sharing and special revenue sharing. **General revenue sharing** provided new money to be used as state and local governments saw fit, with very few strings attached. When general revenue sharing began in 1972, the program was very popular with the governments it helped, but over the years members of Congress became less enamored of it. They did not have the same control over revenue sharing funds that they had over the more traditional categorical grants. And they preferred the good will derived from narrowly focused grants to their districts. As a result, Congress did not allow the funding for general revenue sharing to grow as categorical grant funds had. In 1986, general revenue sharing was phased out completely.

The second part of Nixon's New Federalism, **special revenue sharing**, was a plan to consolidate existing categorical grant programs. Money available under several categorical programs in a particular area (for example, health services) would be combined into one large block grant. But Congress was reluctant to lose the political credit and control it had under the existing grant system. In addition, the dynamics of intergovernmental relations worked against the consolidation of programs: Interest groups lobbied hard to keep their pet projects from being consolidated. All this combined to slow the progress of special revenue sharing during the Nixon years.

Nixon's New Federalism, then, was not very successful in stemming the flow of power from the states to the national government. The national government gave more aid to the states, and that aid carried more and more strings.

A perception that the federal system was bloated and out of control began to take hold. In 1976, Jimmy Carter campaigned for president as an outsider who promised to reduce the size and cost of the national government. And he did have some success. After 1978, national government aid to states and localities actually did begin to drop.

New Federalism Under Reagan and Bush

Ronald Reagan took office in 1981 promising a "new New Federalism" that would "restore a proper constitutional relationship between the federal, state and local governments." He charged that "the federal system had been bent out of shape." The national government had become the senior partner in intergovernmental relations, treating "elected state and local officials as if they were nothing more than administrative agents for federal authority."

Reagan's commitment to reduce taxes as well as government spending meant he could not offer the incentive of new funding to make his New Federalism palatable. He did resurrect an element of Nixon's New Federalism, however, in the use of block grants. In the first year of the Reagan administration, Congress agreed to combine fifty-seven categorical grants into nine block grants. State officials were enthusiastic about the prospect of having greater control over grant funds; they were less enthusiastic when they realized that the amounts they received would be cut by approximately 25 percent. The share of state and local bills footed by the national government began to fall.

In 1982, Reagan proposed a more thorough overhaul of the federal system. This time he offered a program swap in which some forty-four programs previously funded or administered by the national government would be put under state control. At the same time, the national government would take over responsibility for Medicaid, a program of health care for the poor. Initially, Washington would provide the states with the money needed to run the new programs. Eventually, however, the states would be expected to pick up the costs themselves or eliminate the programs.

Reagan's proposed exchange of programs aroused intense opposition. He could not build a winning coalition in support of the plan, and as a result, his most ambitious effort to remake American federalism failed. In fact, many new grant programs were added to respond to new problems and national priorities—for example, halting the spread of AIDS and fighting drug abuse. But if the Reagan administration did not achieve a wholesale reorganization of the federal system, it did prompt a re-evaluation of the role of the national government in that system. George Bush, during his presidency, reaffirmed Reagan's New Federalism and reasserted Reagan's policy of assuring that proposed policies and legislation give maximum discretion to state and local governments.[17]

Some Consequences of New Federalism

New Federalism has changed dramatically since 1960. Until 1978, there was nearly steady growth in aid to states and local communities. But then a period of decline began, which bottomed out in 1982. Aid has increased only slightly since then (see Figure 3.3). Furthermore, the components of aid for states and cities have changed substantially compared to earlier periods. Payments for the poor now take an increasing share of the national government's contribution to the states. And that trend is likely to continue.

Today spending pressures on state and local governments are enormous. Yet the sober reality of national budget deficits erases hope of increased aid. For the first time in decades, many state and local governments are raising taxes or adopting new ones to pay for public services that were once the shared responsibility of cooperative federalism.

Other Governments in the Federal System

We have concentrated here on the roles the national and the state governments play in shaping the federal system. Although the Constitution explicitly recognizes just national and state governments, the American federal system has spawned a multitude of local governments as well. In a recent count, the number exceeded eighty-three thousand![18]

The Kinds of Local Government

Americans are citizens of both nation and state, but they also come under the jurisdiction of various local government units. These units

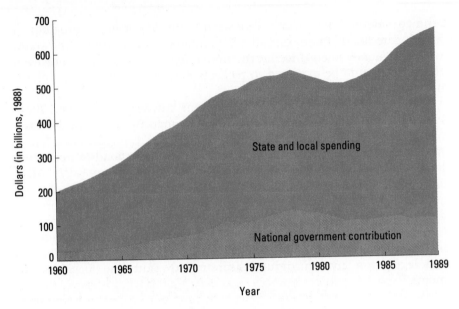

FIGURE 3.3   *National Government's Contribution Fades*
In the 1970s, the national government contributed 25 percent of state and lo-
cal government spending. By the end of the 1980s, the national government's
contribution had declined to about 17 percent. As the national government's
spending declined, state and local government spending accelerated, espe-
cially for Medicaid, welfare, prisons, and education. (Source: "80's Leave States
and Cities in Need," New York Times, *December 30, 1990, Sec. 1, p. 1. Copyright © 1990*
by The New York Times Company. Reprinted by permission.)

include **municipal governments**, the governments of cities and towns.
Municipalities, in turn, are located in (or may contain or share boundaries with) counties, which are administered by **county governments**. In
addition, most Americans also live in a **school district**, which is responsible for administering local elementary and secondary educational programs. They may also be served by one or more **special districts**,
government units created to perform particular functions when those
functions are best performed across jurisdictional boundaries. Examples
of special districts include the Port Authority of New York, the Chicago
Sanitation District, and the Southeast Pennsylvania Transit Authority.
    These local governments are created by state governments either
through their constitutions or through legislation. This means local
governments' organization, powers, responsibilities, and effectiveness
vary considerably from state to state. About forty states provide their
cities with various forms of **home rule**—the right to enact and enforce
legislation in certain administrative areas. In contrast, county governments, which are the main units of local government in rural areas,

tend to have relatively little legislative power or none at all. Instead, county governments generally serve as administrative units, performing the specific duties assigned to them under state law.

The functions of national, state, city, and county governments and of school and special districts often overlap. In practice, it is now virtually impossible to distinguish among them by using Madison's criteria of great and aggregate interests and local and particular interests. How can the ordinary citizen be expected to make sense of this maze of governments? And does the ordinary citizen really benefit from all these governments?

So Many Governments: Advantages and Disadvantages

In theory at least, one benefit of localizing government is that it brings government closer to the people; it gives them an opportunity to participate in the political process, to have a direct impact on policy. From this perspective, overlapping governments appear compatible with a majoritarian view of democracy.

The reality is somewhat different, however. Studies have shown that people are much more likely to vote in national elections than in local elections. Voter turnout in local contests tends to be very low, even though the impact of individual votes is much greater. Furthermore, the fragmentation of powers, functions, and responsibilities among national, state, and local governments makes government as a whole seem very complicated and hence less comprehensible and accessible to ordinary people. In addition, citizens who are busy with the daily matter of making a living have only limited time to devote to public affairs. All these factors tend to keep individual citizens out of politics and to make government more responsive to organized groups, which have the resources—time, money, and know-how—to influence policymaking (see Chapter 7). Instead of bringing government closer to the people and reinforcing majoritarian democracy, the system's enormous complexity tends to encourage pluralism.

One possible benefit of having many governments is that they enable the country to experiment with new policies on a small scale. New programs or solutions to problems can be tested in one city or state or in a few cities or states. Successful programs can then be adopted by other cities or states or by the nation as a whole. For this reason, states are sometimes called the "laboratories of democracy." For example, when President Reagan asked for a constitutional amendment requiring a balanced national budget—that is, one in which expenditures cannot be greater than income—he had a precedent. Many states have such a constitutional provision.

The large number of governments also enables government to respond to the diverse conditions that prevail in different parts of the country. States and cities differ enormously in population, size, economic resources, climate, and other characteristics. Smaller political units are better able to respond to particular local conditions and can generally do so quickly. Nevertheless, smaller units may not be able to muster the economic resources to meet such challenges. Consequently, the national government has used its funds to equalize disparities in wealth and development among states (see Feature 3.1).

Contemporary Federalism and the Dilemmas of Democracy

When President Reagan came to the White House, conservatives were delighted. They believed his preference for layer-cake federalism would mean the dismantling of the liberal welfare state and the end of the national government's efforts to promote social and political equality at the expense of freedom. They argued that different states had different problems and resources and asserted that returning control to state governments would encourage diversity. States would be free to experiment with alternatives for meeting their problems. States would compete with one another. And people would be free to choose the state government they preferred by simply "voting with their feet"—moving to another state.

In addition, conservative proponents of New Federalism argued that the national government was too remote, too tied to special interests, and too unresponsive to the public at large. The national government overregulated and tried to promote too much uniformity. Moreover, they added, the size and complexity of the federal system led to waste and inefficiency. States, in contrast, were closer to the people and better able to respond to specific local needs. If state governments were revitalized, individuals might believe that they could have a greater impact on decision making. The quality of political participation would improve. Furthermore, conservatives believed that shifting power to the states would help them achieve other parts of the conservative political agenda. States, they thought, would work harder to keep taxes down, they would not be willing to spend a lot of money on social welfare programs, and they would be less likely to pass stiff laws regulating businesses. Reagan's New Federalism would bring back the days of laissez faire, when states found it difficult to regulate businesses for fear that industries might move to less-restrictive states.

What conservatives hoped for liberals feared. They remembered that the states' rights model allowed political and social inequalities, that it supported racism. Blacks and city dwellers were often left virtually unrepresented by white state legislators, who disproportionately served rural interests. Liberals believed the states were unwilling or unable to protect the rights or provide for the needs of their citizens, whether

Feature 3.1

Who Should Make the Rules? Federalism and Public Opinion

Where do American citizens stand on the question of the distribution of power between the national and the state governments? What areas do they believe require uniform national standards? A *New York Times/CBS News* poll taken in May 1987 put questions like these to 1,254 people and found some deep divisions on the issues. Only a few respondents (5 percent) believed that the states have too much power; most (47 percent) thought the balance between states and nation is about right; a sizable minority (39 percent) claimed that the national government has too much power.

When it came down to deciding whether national or state standards are better, respondents were divided (respondents with no opinion are not cited).

In the matter of pollution control, 49 percent favored a national policy, while 46 percent wanted individual state policies. In the setting of murder penalties, 62 percent looked to the national government; 34 percent, to the states. On the issue of registration and voting, 64 percent of respondents wanted one national policy; 31 percent were in favor of state policies. In the case of selecting textbooks in public schools, 35 percent wanted a single, nationwide policy; 61 percent opted for state choices. As for minimum wage, 51 percent of respondents wanted a national standard; 45 percent, individual state standards. As for the establishment of safety standards in factories, 65 percent opted for national standards; 31 percent, for state ones. And in the matter of setting highway speed limits, 42 percent said yes to a national specification; 56 percent wanted to leave it to the states.

Ironically, this evidence says that Americans want the national government to assume greater responsibility for such matters as penalties for murder, registration and voting, and safety standards, all of which have traditionally fallen within the states' domain. Yet most Americans hold to the view that the national government already has either enough or too much power.

Source: William K. Stevens, "Pagentry and the Ideals of 200 Years," *New York Times*, May 26, 1987, pp. A1, A20. Copyright © 1987 by The New York Times Company. Reprinted by permission.

those citizens were consumers seeking protection from business interests, defendants requiring guarantees of due process of law, or poor people seeking a minimum standard of living.

To what extent were conservative hopes and liberal fears realized as federalism developed in the 1980s? And how did the development of federalism during this period relate to the dilemmas of democracy?

Federalism and the Values of Freedom, Order, and Equality

Neither the conservatives' hopes nor the liberals' fears were fully real-ized under the New, Newer, or Newest Federalism, nor did the array of recent conservative presidents always embrace the states' rights posi-tion. Federalism of the Bush-Reagan variety was used mainly as a tool for cutting the national budget by offering less money to the states. Contrary to the expectations of conservatives and liberals alike, how-ever, states themselves proved willing to approve tax increases to pay for social services and education. In an era when Washington was less willing to enforce antitrust legislation, civil rights laws, or affirmative action plans, state governments were more likely to do so. At a time when a conservative national government put little emphasis on the value of equality, state governments did more to embrace it.

Conservatives had thought that the value of freedom would be en-hanced if more matters were left to the states. Traditionally, state gov-ernments had been relatively small, lacking the wherewithal to limit large corporate interests, for example. But since the 1970s, state govern-ments have become "big governments" themselves. They are better able to tackle problems, and they are not afraid to use their power to pro-mote equality.

To the surprise of liberals, who had originally looked to the national government to protect individuals by setting reasonable minimum stan-dards for product safety, welfare payments, and employee benefits, states are now willing to set higher standards than the national govern-ment has. As states take a more active role in setting these standards, they highlight another challenge for our democracy—the need to main-tain order by protecting the lives of citizens.

Thus, the relationship among the federal system, political ideology, and the values of freedom, order, and equality is no longer as simple as it appeared when the 1970s began. Then, liberals could look to the na-tional government and marble-cake federalism to help secure equality. Conservatives could wish for a return to small government, states' rights, and layer-cake federalism. In the 1980s, conservatives gave lip service to the ideals of New Federalism but were often reluctant to give up the national power that helped them achieve their vision of order. After all, if they returned power to the states, they might well do more to promote equality than freedom. As one prominent conservative put it, "The Great Society may be over in Washington, but it has just begun in the states."[19]

Federalism and Pluralism

As discussed in Chapter 1, the system of government in America today supports the pluralist model of democracy. Federalism is an important part of that system. How has it contributed to American pluralism? Does each of the competing views of federalism support pluralism?

The First Lady Goes to School
In our federal system, education remains primarily a state responsibility. However, the national government has increased its involvement dramatically since the 1960s when, as a part of President Lyndon Johnson's War on Poverty, the national government provided massive assistance in an effort to promote greater equality of opportunity. In this picture First Lady Hillary Rodham Clinton meets children at a New York public school to symbolize the continuing interest of the national government in education.

Our federal system of government was designed to allay citizens' fears that they might be ruled by majorities of citizens who were residents of distant regions and with whom they did not necessarily agree or share interests. By recognizing the legitimacy of the states as political divisions, the federal system also recognized the importance of diversity. The existence and cultivation of diverse interests are hallmarks of pluralism.

Each of the two competing theories of federalism supports pluralism but in somewhat different ways. Dual federalism, which has evolved into New Federalism, wants to decentralize government, to shift power to the states. It recognizes the importance of local, rather than national, standards and applauds the diversity of those standards. This variety allows people, if not a voice in policymaking, at least the choice of policy under which to live. These factors tend to support pluralist democracy.

In contrast, cooperative federalism is perfectly willing to override local standards for a national standard in the interest of promoting equality. Yet this view of federalism, particularly in its picket-fence version, also supports pluralist democracy. It is highly responsive to all manner of group pressures, including pressure at one level from groups unsuccessful at other levels. By blurring the lines of national and state responsibility, this kind of federalism encourages petitioners to try their luck at whichever level of government offers the best chance of success.

Summary

The government framework outlined in the Constitution was the product of political compromise, an acknowledgment of the states' fear of a powerful central government. The division of powers sketched in the Constitution was supposed to turn over "great and aggregate" matters to the national government, leaving "local and particular" concerns to the states. Exactly what was great and aggregate and what was local and particular were not fully explained.

Federalism comes in many varieties. Two stand out because they capture valuable differences between the original and modern vision of a federal government. Dual, or layer-cake, federalism wants to retain power in the states and keep the levels of government separate. Cooperative, or marble-cake, federalism emphasizes the power of the national government and sees the national and the state governments working together to solve national problems. Each view, in its own way, supports the pluralist model of democracy.

Over the years, the national government has used both its enumerated and implied powers to become involved in virtually every area of human activity. The tools of political change include direct legislation, judicial decisions, and financial rewards in the form of grants.

As its influence grew, so did the government itself. At the same time, intergovernmental relations became more complex. New Federalists, generally conservative, suggested cutting back the size of the national government, reducing federal spending, and turning programs over to the states as a solution to the problem of unwieldy government. Liberals worried that New Federalists, in their haste to decentralize and cut back, would turn over important responsibilities to states that were unwilling or unable to assume them. Government, rather than being too responsive, would become unresponsive. But neither conservative hopes nor liberal fears were fully realized in the 1980s. The states proved both willing and able to tackle some major problems. More than this, they were willing to fund many programs that promoted equality.

The debate over federalism will continue in the 1990s and beyond. Cooperative federalism will surely be replaced by another theory of intergovernmental relations, and the ghost of dual federalism may still return. One truth emerges from this overview of federalism: The balance of power between the national and the state governments will be settled by political means, not by theory.

Key Terms

federalism	block grants
dual federalism	nullification
states' rights	intergovernmental relations
elastic clause	picket-fence federalism
implied powers	general revenue sharing
cooperative federalism	special revenue sharing
commerce clause	municipal governments
grant-in-aid	county governments
categorical grants	school district
formula grants	special districts
project grants	home rule

Selected Readings

Berger, Raoul. *Federalism: The Founder's Design.* Norman: University of Oklahoma Press, 1987. Berger, a constitutional historian, argues that the states preceded the nation and that the states and the national government were to have mutually exclusive spheres of sovereignty.

Dye, Thomas R. *American Federalism: Competition Among Governments.* Lexington, Mass.: Lexington Books, 1990. Dye presents a theory of competitive federalism that encourages rivalry among states and local governments to offer citizens the best array of public services at the lowest cost.

Gittell, Marilyn, ed. *State Politics and the New Federalism.* New York: Longmans, 1986. This collection of works on intergovernmental relations emphasizes the role of the states.

Hall, Kermit L., ed. *Federalism: A Nation of States.* New York: Garland, 1987. This is a collection of the most important historical and political science scholarship on federalism.

Nathan, Richard P., and Fred C. Doolittle. *Reagan and the States.* Princeton, N.J.: Princeton University Press, 1987. This overview and set of case studies examine fiscal federalism as a part of Reagan's New Federalism.

O'Toole, Laurence J., ed. *American Intergovernmental Relations.* Washington, D.C.: Congressional Quarterly Press, 1985. This collection of readings includes classics on the subject as well as analyses of intergovernmental relations in the Reagan administration.

Reagan, Michael, and John Sanzone. *The New Federalism.* New York: Oxford University Press, 1981. This classic analysis of fiscal federalism emphasizes grants.

Walker, David B. *Toward a Functioning Federalism.* Cambridge, Mass.: Winthrop, 1981. Walker analyzes the overloaded system of intergovernmental relations and offers alternatives to it.

PUBLIC OPINION, POLITICAL SOCIALIZATION, AND THE MASS MEDIA

4

Fridays are different in Saudi Arabia. After prayers, criminals are paraded in the streets and then punished publicly. Murderers are beheaded, adulterers are flogged, and thieves have their hands chopped off. The Saudi government wants its citizens to get the message: Crime will not be tolerated. Moreover, what constitutes a crime in Saudi Arabia may not be a crime in the United States. Members of the U.S. armed forces sent there in 1990 during the Persian Gulf crisis learned this as their mail from home was opened to keep out alcohol and sexually oriented magazines, both of which are illegal. It is also illegal for a woman to drive a car there. Saudi Arabia, which claims the lowest crime rate in the world, is a country that greatly values order.

In contrast, the United States has one of the highest crime rates in the world. Its homicide rate, for example, is three to ten times that of most other Western countries. Although no one is proud of this record, our government would never consider beheading, flogging, or dismembering as a means of lowering the crime rate. First, the Eighth Amendment to the Constitution forbids "cruel and unusual punishment." Second, the public would not tolerate this kind of punishment.

However, the public definitely is not squeamish about the death penalty (capital punishment), at least for certain crimes. The Gallup organization has polled the nation on this issue for fifty years. Except in 1966, most respondents have consistently supported the death penalty for murder.[1] In fact, public support for capital punishment has increased dramatically since the late 1960s. In 1988, 79 percent of all respondents were in favor of the death penalty for murder, while only 16 percent opposed it. Substantial segments of the public also were in favor of the death penalty for an attempt to assassinate the president (63 percent), rape (51 percent), and hijack of an airplane (49 percent).

Government has been defined as the legitimate use of force to control human behavior. Throughout most of American history, the execution of people who threaten the social order has been a legal practice of government. In colonial times, capital punishment was imposed not only for murder but also for antisocial behavior—for denying the "true" God, cursing one's parents, committing adultery, practicing witchcraft, or being a rebellious child.[2] In the late 1700s, some writers, editors, and clergy argued for abolishing the death sentence. The campaign intensified in the 1840s, and again in 1890, when New York State adopted a new technique, electrocution, as the instrument of death. By 1917, twelve states had passed laws against capital punishment. But the outbreak of World War I fed the public's suspicion of foreigners and fear of radicals, leading to renewed support for the death penalty. Reacting to this shift in public opinion, four states restored it.

The security needs of World War II and postwar fears of Soviet communism fueled continued support for capital punishment. After the Red Scare subsided in the late 1950s, public opposition to the death penalty increased. But public opinion was neither strong enough nor stable enough to force state legislatures to outlaw the death penalty. In keeping with the pluralist model of democracy, abolition efforts shifted from the legislative arena to the courts.

One of the major arguments the abolitionists used was that the death penalty is cruel and unusual punishment and therefore unconstitutional. Certainly the public in the 1780s did not think capital punishment was either. But two hundred years later, opponents contended that execution by the state had become cruel and unusual by contemporary standards. Their argument had some effect on public opinion; in 1966 a plurality of respondents opposed the death penalty for the first (and only) time since the Gallup surveys began.

The states responded to this shift in public opinion by reducing the number of executions each year until, in 1968, they were stopped completely in anticipation of a Supreme Court decision. By then, public opinion had again reversed itself in favor of capital punishment. Nevertheless, in 1972 the Court ruled in a 5–4 vote that the death penalty as imposed by existing state laws was unconstitutional.[3] The Court's decision was not well received in many states, and thirty-five state legislatures passed new laws to get around the ruling. Meanwhile, the nation's homicide rate increased. Public approval of the death penalty jumped almost 10 points and began climbing higher.

In 1976, the Supreme Court changed its position and upheld three new state laws that provided for consideration of the defendant and the offense before imposition of the death sentence.[4] The Court also rejected the argument that punishment by death itself violated the Constitution while noting that public opinion favored the death penalty. Now endorsed by the courts as well as the public, the death penalty was again available to the states. Through the end of the 1970s, however, few states applied the penalty: Only three criminals were executed. Eventually, however, the states began to heed the clamor, executing about twenty criminals a year by the mid-1980s.

The history of public thinking on the death penalty reveals several characteristics of public opinion:

1. *The public's attitudes toward a given government policy can vary over time, often dramatically.* Opinions about capital punishment tend to fluctuate with threats to the social order. The public is more likely to favor capital punishment in times of war and fear of foreign subversion and when crime rates are high.

2. *Public opinion places boundaries on allowable types of public policy.* Chopping off a hand is not acceptable to the public (and surely to courts interpreting the Constitution) as a punishment for theft in the United States, but electrocuting a murderer in private (not in public) is all right.

3. *Citizens are willing to register opinions on matters outside their expertise.* People clearly believe execution by lethal injection is more humane than electrocution, asphyxiation in the gas chamber, or hanging. How can the public know enough about execution to make these judgments?

4. *Governments tend to react to public opinion.* State laws for and against capital punishment have reflected swings in the public mood. Moreover, the Supreme Court's decision in 1972 against capital punishment came when public opinion on the death penalty was sharply divided; the Court's approval of capital punishment in 1976 coincided with a rise in public approval of the death penalty.

5. *The government sometimes does not do what the people want.* Although public opinion overwhelmingly favors the death penalty for murder, few states actually punish murderers with execution.

The last two conclusions bear on our discussion of the majoritarian and pluralist models of democracy in Chapter 2. Here we probe more deeply into the nature, shape, depth, and formation of public opinion in a democratic government. What is the place of public opinion in a democracy? How do people acquire their opinions? What are the major lines of division in public opinion? How do individuals' ideology and knowledge affect their opinions? What is the relationship between public opinion and ideological type?

Public Opinion and the Models of Democracy

The majoritarian and pluralist models of democracy differ greatly in their assumptions about the role of public opinion in democratic government. According to the classic majoritarian model, the government should do what a majority of the public wants. In contrast, pluralists argue that the public as a whole seldom demonstrates clear, consistent opinions on the day-to-day issues of government. At the same time, pluralists recognize that subgroups within the public do frequently and vigorously express opinions on specific issues. The pluralist model requires that government institutions allow the free expression of opinions by these "minority publics." Democracy is at work when the opinions of many different publics clash openly and fairly over government policy.

Thanks to opinion polling, we can better understand the conflict between these two institutional models of democracy. *Polling* involves interviewing a sample of citizens to estimate public opinion as a whole. **Public opinion** is simply the collected attitudes of citizens on a given issue or question. Opinion polling is such a common part of contemporary life that we often forget it is a modern invention, dating only from the 1930s (see Figure 4.1). In fact, survey methodology did not develop into a powerful research tool until the advent of computers in the 1950s.

Before polling became an accepted part of the American scene, politicians, journalists, and everyone else could argue about what "the people" wanted, but no one really knew. Today, sampling methods and opinion polling have altered the debate over the majoritarian and pluralist models of democracy. Now that we know how often government policy runs against majority opinion, it becomes harder to defend the U.S. government as democratic under the majoritarian model.

Each of the two models of democracy makes certain assumptions about public opinion. The majoritarian model assumes that a majority of people hold clear, consistent opinions on government policy. The pluralist model insists that public opinion is often divided, and opinion polls certainly give credence to that claim. What are the bases of these divisions? What principles, if any, do people use to organize their beliefs and attitudes about politics? Exactly how do individuals form their political opinions? We look for answers to these questions in this chapter. In later chapters, we assess the effect of public opinion on government policies. The results should help you make up your own mind about the viability of the majoritarian and pluralist models in a functioning democracy.

Public opinion in America *is* capable of massive change over time, however. Moreover, change can occur on issues that were once highly controversial. A good example of a dramatic change in American public opinion is race relations, specifically integrated schools. A national sur-

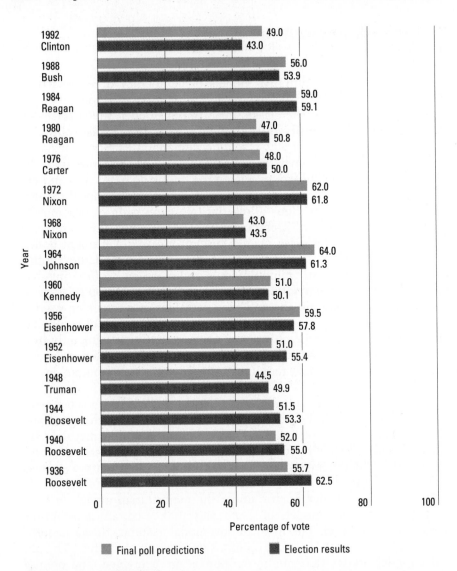

FIGURE 4.1   Gallup Poll Accuracy

One of the nation's oldest polls was started by George Gallup in the 1930s. The accuracy of the Gallup Poll in predicting presidential elections over nearly fifty years is charted here. Although not always on the mark, its predictions have been fairly close to election results. The poll was most notably wrong in 1948, when it predicted that Thomas Dewey, the Republican candidate, would defeat the Democratic incumbent, Harry Truman, underestimating Truman's vote by 5.4 percentage points. In 1992, the last Gallup poll before the election estimated that Bill Clinton would obtain 49 percent of the vote; George Bush, 37 percent; and Ross Perot, 14 percent. The actual vote was Clinton, 43; Bush, 37; and Perot, 19. Gallup substantially overestimated Clinton's vote while underestimating Perot's showing. (Source: Gallup Report, December 1988, p. 44. Used by permission of The Gallup Poll. Updated by the author.)

vey in 1942 asked whether "white and Negro students should go to the same schools or separate schools."[5] Only 30 percent of white respondents said that students should attend schools together. When virtually the same question (substituting black for Negro) was asked in 1984, 90 percent of the white respondents endorsed integrated schools.[6]

However, white Americans have not become "color-blind." Despite their endorsement of integrated schools, only 23 percent of the whites surveyed in 1984 were in favor of busing to achieve racial balance. And whites were more willing to bus their children to a school with a few blacks than to one that was mostly black.[7] So white opinion changed dramatically with regard to the principle of desegregated schools, but whites seemed divided on how that principle should be implemented. Trying to explain this contradiction and the way in which political opinions in general are formed, political scientists cite the process of political socialization, the influence of cultural factors, and the interplay of ideology and knowledge. In the next several sections, we examine how these elements combine to create and affect public opinion.

Political Socialization

Public opinion is grounded in political values. People acquire their values through **political socialization**, a complex process through which individuals become aware of politics, learn political facts, and form political values. Think for a moment about your political socialization. What is your earliest memory of a president? When did you first learn about political parties? If you identify with a party, how did you decide to do so? If you do not, why not? Who was the first liberal you ever met? The first conservative?

Obviously, the paths to political awareness, knowledge, and values differ among individuals, but most people are exposed to the same influences, or *agents of socialization*, especially in childhood through young adulthood. These influences are family, school, community, peers, and, of course, television.

The Agents of Early Socialization

Like psychologists, scholars of political socialization place great emphasis on early learning. Both groups point to two operating principles that characterize early learning:[8] the *primacy principle*, which holds that what is learned first is learned best, and the *structuring principle*, which maintains that what is learned first structures later learning.

Because most people learn first from their families, the family tends to be a very important agent of early socialization. The extent of family influence—and of the influence of other socializing agents—depends on the extent of our *exposure, communication*, and *receptivity* to these agents.[9]

Stop the Presses! Oops, Too Late . . .
As the 1948 election drew near, few people gave President Harry Truman a chance to defeat his Republican opponent, Thomas E. Dewey. Polling was still new, and virtually all the early polls showed Dewey far ahead. Most organizations simply stopped polling weeks before the election. The Chicago Daily Tribune *believed the polls and proclaimed Dewey's victory before the votes were counted. Here, the victorious Truman triumphantly displays the most embarrassing headline in American politics. Later it was revealed that the few polls taken closer to election day showed Truman catching up to Dewey, which demonstrates that polls estimate the vote only* at the time *they are taken.*

Family.   In most cases, exposure, communication, and receptivity are highest in family-child relationships, although parental influence has declined with the rise of single-parent families. Especially in two-parent homes, children learn a wide range of social, moral, religious, economic, and political values that help shape their opinions. It is not surprising, then, that most people link their earliest memories of politics with their families. Moreover, when parents are interested in politics, they influence their children to become more politically interested and informed.[10]

One of the most politically important things that many children learn from their parents is party identification. Overall, about one-half of young American voters identify with the political party of their parents. Parental influence on party identification is greater when both parents strongly identify with the same party.[11]

School.   According to some researchers, schools have an influence on political learning that is equal to or greater than that of parents.[12] Here, however, we have to distinguish between primary and secondary schools, on the one hand, and institutions of higher education, on the other. Primary schools introduce children to authority figures outside the family. They also teach the nation's slogans and symbols—the Pledge of Allegiance, the national anthem, national heroes and holidays. And they stress the norms of group behavior and democratic decision making. Much of this early learning—in the United States and elsewhere—is more indoctrination than education. Most children emerge from elementary school with a sense of nationalism and an idealized notion of American government.[13] By the end of the eighth grade, however, children begin to distinguish between government leaders and institutions. They become more aware of collective institutions, of Congress, and of elections.

Secondary schools typically continue to build "good citizens." They also offer more explicit political content in their curricula, including courses in recent U.S. history, civics, and American government. Better teachers challenge students to think critically about American government; others concentrate on teaching civic responsibilities. The end product is a greater awareness of the political process and of the people involved in that process.

Political learning at the college level can be very like that in high school or very different. The degree of difference is apt to increase if professors (or the texts they use) encourage their students to question authority. Questioning dominant political values does not necessarily mean rejecting them. For example, this text encourages you to recognize that freedom and equality—two idealized values in our culture—often conflict. It also invites you to think of democracy in terms of competing institutional models, one of which challenges the idealized notion of democracy. These alternative perspectives are meant to teach you about American political values, not to subvert those values.

Community and peers.   Your community and your peers are different but generally overlapping groups. Your *community* comprises the people of all ages with whom you come in contact because they live or work near you. Your *peers* are friends, classmates, and coworkers. Usually, they are your age and live within your community.

The makeup of the community has a lot to do with how political opinions are formed. *Homogeneous communities*—those with members similar in ethnicity, race, religion, or occupational status—can exert strong pressures on both children and adults to conform to the dominant attitude. For example, if all your neighbors talk up the candidates

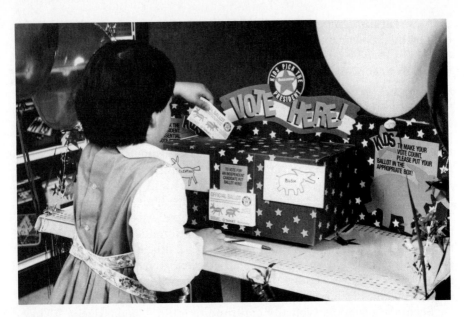

Voting is Child's Play
Political socialization begins early through many agents of socialization such as family, peers or school. In the weeks preceding the 1992 election, elementary school students in several states participated in an educational program in which they discussed both candidates and issues before casting their "ballots." Here a young California "voter" is making her choice.

of one party and criticize the candidates of the other, voicing or even holding a dissenting opinion is more difficult to do.[14]

Peer groups are sometimes used by children and adults as a defense against community pressures. In adolescence, children rely on their peers to defend their dress and lifestyle, not their politics. At the college level, however, peer group influence on politics can grow substantially, often fed by new learning that clashes with parental beliefs. A classic study of female students at Bennington College in the 1930s found that many became substantially more liberal than their affluent conservative parents. A follow-up study twenty-five years later showed that most retained their liberal attitudes, in part because their spouses and friends (peers) supported their views.[15]

Continuing Socialization

Political socialization continues throughout life. As parental and school influences wane, peer groups (neighbors, coworkers, club members) assume a greater importance in promoting political awareness and in developing political opinions.[16] Because adults usually learn about political events from the mass media—newspapers, magazines, television, and radio—the media themselves emerge as socialization agents.

Regardless of how people learn about politics, as they grow older, they gain perspective on government. They are apt to measure new candidates (and new ideas) against the old ones they remember. Their values may also change. Finally, political learning comes simply through exposure and familiarity. One example is the simple act of voting, which people do with increasing regularity as they grow older.

Social Groups and Political Values

No two people are influenced by precisely the same socialization agents in precisely the same way. Nevertheless, people with similar backgrounds do share learning experiences; this means they tend to develop similar political opinions. In this section, we examine the ties between people's social backgrounds and their political values. In the process, we look at two questions that appeared in a survey taken in 1990: Would you allow an admitted communist to teach in a college? Do you think that the government should reduce income differences between rich and poor?[17] Other questions might not produce identical results but would probably show the same general tendencies.

The first question is politically relevant because of the original dilemma of government, the conflict between freedom and order. Those who answered "no" to the question were willing to deny freedom of speech to a teacher who threatens the existing economic and political order. They apparently valued order over individual freedom. The second question, about the government reducing income differences, deals with the modern dilemma of government, the conflict between freedom and equality. Those who answered "yes" think that government should promote economic equality, even if that means taxing the rich more heavily (reducing their freedom to use their money as they want). These respondents apparently valued equality over freedom.

Overall, the responses to each of these questions were divided approximately equally. For the entire national sample, slightly more than one-half the respondents (52 percent) opposed firing a communist teacher. And more than one-half (also 52 percent) the respondents thought the government should reduce income differences. However, sharp differences in attitudes on both issues emerged when respondents were grouped by socioeconomic factors—education, income, region, ethnic origin, race, and religion. These differences are shown in Figure 4.2 as positive and negative deviations in percentage points from the national averages on the two questions. Bars that extend to the right identify groups that are more likely than most Americans to sacrifice freedom for a given value of government, either equality or order. Now

a. I should like to ask you some questions about a man who admits he is a communist. Suppose he is teaching in a college? Should he be fired or not?

b. Should the government in Washington D.C. reduce income differences between the rich and the poor, perhaps by raising taxes of wealthy families or by giving income assistance to the poor?

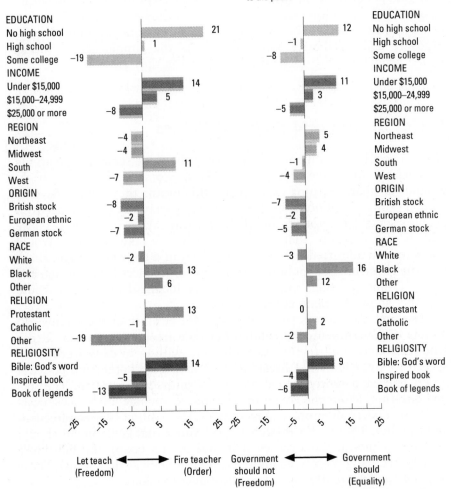

Let teach ←——→ Fire teacher   Government ←——→ Government
(Freedom)   (Order)   should not   should
                                   (Freedom)   (Equality)

FIGURE 4.2   Group Deviations from National Opinion on Two Questions
Two questions—one on the dilemma of freedom versus order and the other on the dilemma of freedom versus equality—were asked of a national sample in 1990. Public opinion for the nation as a whole was sharply divided on each question. These two graphs show how respondents in several social groups deviated from overall public opinion. The longer the bars next to each group are, the more its respondents deviated from the expression of opinion for the entire sample. Bars that extend to the left show group opinions that deviate toward freedom. Bars that extend to the right show deviations away from freedom and toward order (part a) or equality (part b). (Source: National Opinion Research Center, 1990 General Social Survey. These data were kindly furnished by Tom W. Smith, study director. Used by permission.)

we examine these opinion patterns more closely for each socioeconomic group.

Education

Education increases citizens' awareness and understanding of political issues. Higher education also underscores the value of free speech in a democratic society, increasing our tolerance for those who dissent. This result is clearly shown in Figure 4.2, where those with more education are more willing to let an admitted communist teach. When confronted with issues that involve a choice between personal freedom and social order, college-educated respondents tend to choose freedom.

With regard to the role of government in reducing income inequality, Figure 4.2 shows that more education produces opinions that favor freedom, this time over equality. The higher their level of education, the less respondents supported the redistribution of income. Educated people tend to be wealthier people, who would be more heavily taxed to help the poor. In this case at least, the effect of education on public opinion is overridden by the effect of income.

Income

In many countries, differences in social class—based on social background and occupational status—divide people in their politics.[18] In the United States, we have avoided the uglier aspects of class conflict, but here wealth sometimes substitutes for class. As shown in Figure 4.2, wealth is consistently related to opinions that limit the government's role in promoting order and equality. We find that wealth and education, then, have a similar impact on opinion here: In both cases, the groups with more education and higher income opt for freedom. But education has a stronger effect on opinions about order than about equality.[19]

Region

Early in our country's history, regional differences were politically important—important enough to spark a civil war between the North and South. For nearly a hundred years after the Civil War, regional differences continued to affect politics. The moneyed Northeast was thought to control the purse strings of capitalism. The Midwest was long regarded as the stronghold of "isolationism" in foreign affairs. The South was virtually a one-party region, almost completely Democratic. And the rustic West pioneered its own mixture of progressive politics.

In the past, cultural differences among regions were fed by differences in wealth. In recent decades, however, the movement of people and wealth away from the Northeast and Midwest to the Sunbelt states in the South and Southwest has equalized the per capita income of the regions. One product of this equalization is that the "Solid South" is no longer solid for the Democratic party. In fact, the South has become inclined toward voting for Republican candidates for president since the 1970s.

There are differences in public opinion among the four major regions of the United States, but not much. Figure 4.2 shows that people in the West are somewhat more likely to oppose government efforts to equalize income than are people in the Northeast. Regional differences are greater on the question of social order, particularly between the West, where respondents are more likely to support freedom of speech, and the South, where they are more likely to stop a communist from teaching. Despite these differences, regional effects on public opinion toward these issues are weaker than the effects of most other socioeconomic factors.

The "Old" Ethnicity: European Origin

At the turn of the century, the major ethnic groups in America were immigrants from Ireland, Italy, Germany, Poland, and other European countries who came to the United States in waves during the late 1800s and early 1900s. These immigrants entered a nation that had been founded by British settlers more than one hundred years earlier. They found themselves in a strange land, usually without money and unable to speak the language. Moreover, their religious backgrounds—mainly Catholic and Jewish—differed from the predominant Protestantism of the earlier settlers. Local politicians saw these newcomers, who were concentrated in urban areas in the Northeast and Midwest, as a new source of votes and soon mobilized them into politics. Holding jobs of lower status, these urban ethnics became part of the great coalition of Democratic voters that President Franklin Roosevelt forged in the 1930s. And for years after, studies of public opinion and voting behavior found consistent differences between their political preferences and those of the Anglo-Saxons.[20]

More recent studies of public opinion show these differences are disappearing. Figure 4.2 analyzes public opinion for three groups of white ethnics, who accounted for about one-half of the sample interviewed. Respondents who claimed English, Scottish, or Welsh ancestry ("British stock") and German, Austrian, or Swiss ancestry ("German stock") each comprised about 15 percent of the sample. "European ethnics" (primarily Catholics and Jews from Ireland, Italy, and Eastern Europe) comprised about 20 percent. The differences in opinions among these groups were not large. Americans of British stock—mostly "WASPs" (White Anglo-Saxon Protestants)—and German Americans were only slightly more opposed to government action on both issues of order and equality than were European ethnics, who are no longer very different from other white Americans in language, education, or occupation.[21] But if this "old" ethnicity (European origin) is disappearing, a **"new" ethnicity**—race—is taking its place.

The "New" Ethnicity: Race

With the rise of black consciousness and the grassroots civil rights demonstrations led by Dr. Martin Luther King, Jr., and others in the late 1950s and 1960s, blacks emerged as a political force. Through a series of civil rights laws backed by President Lyndon Johnson and northern Democrats in Congress, blacks secured genuine voting rights in the South and exercised those rights more vigorously in the North. Although they made up only about 12 percent of the total population, blacks comprised sizable voting blocs in southern states and in urban areas in northern states. Like the European ethnics before them, American blacks were being courted for their votes; suddenly their opinions were politically important.

Blacks presently constitute the largest racial minority in American politics but not the only significant one. Another 5 percent of the population is made up of Asians, American Indians (Native Americans), and other nonwhites. People of Spanish origin—Hispanics—are also commonly regarded as a racial group. According to the 1990 census, Hispanics make up about 9 percent of the nation's population; but they comprise up to 26 percent of the population in California and Texas and 38 percent in New Mexico.[22] Although they are politically strong in some communities, Hispanics have lagged behind blacks in mobilizing across the nation. However, Hispanics are being wooed by non-Hispanic candidates and are beginning to run more of their own candidates.

Blacks and members of other racial minorities display similar political attitudes. The reasons are twofold.[23] First, racial minorities (excepting second-generation Asians) tend to have low **socioeconomic status** (a combination of education, occupational status, and income). Second, all have been targets of racial prejudice and discrimination. Figure 4.2 clearly shows the effects of race on the freedom-equality issue: Blacks and other minority members (mostly Hispanics) strongly favor government action to equalize incomes and promote order.

Religion

Since the last major wave of European immigration in the 1930s and 1940s, the religious makeup of the United States has remained fairly stable. Almost 65 percent of those surveyed in 1990 were Protestant, about 25 percent identified themselves as Catholic, only 2 percent were Jewish, and about 10 percent denied any religious affiliation or chose some other.[24] For many years, analysts had found strong and consistent differences in the opinions of Protestants, Catholics, and Jews. Protestants were more conservative than Catholics, and Catholics tended to be more conservative than Jews.

Some differences remained in 1990, especially on the government's role in the question of freedom versus order (the communist teacher). Protestants, who constitute the religious majority in America, tended toward order, especially in comparison with the "other" religious grouping. Even greater differences emerged when respondents were classified by their "religiosity." As Figure 4.2 indicates, those who believed that the Bible is the word of God favored more government action in promoting both order and equality than those with more pragmatic interpretations. Political opinions in the U.S. can differ sharply according to religious beliefs.

From Values to Ideology

So far we have studied differences in groups' opinions on two survey questions. Although responses to these questions reflect value choices between freedom and order and between freedom and equality, we have not yet interpreted group opinions in the context of *political ideology* (the set of values and beliefs people hold about the purpose and scope of government). Political scientists generally agree that ideology enters into public opinion on specific issues but hold much less consensus on the extent to which people think in ideological terms.[25] They also agree that the public's ideological thinking cannot be categorized adequately in conventional liberal-conservative terms.

The Degree of Ideological Thinking in Public Opinion

In an early but important study, respondents were asked about the parties and candidates in the 1956 election.[26] Only about 12 percent of the sample volunteered responses that contained ideological terms (such as *liberal, conservative,* and *capitalism*). Most of the respondents (42 percent) evaluated the parties and candidates in terms of "benefits to groups" (farmers, workers, or businesspeople, for example). Others (24 percent) spoke more generally about "the nature of the times" (for example, inflation, unemployment, and the threat of war). Finally, a good portion of the sample (22 percent) displayed no classifiable issue content in their responses.

Subsequent research found somewhat greater ideological awareness within the electorate, especially during the 1964 presidential contest between Lyndon Johnson, a Democrat and ardent liberal, and Barry Goldwater, a Republican and archconservative.[27] But more recent research has questioned whether American voters have really changed in their ideological thinking.[28] The tendency to respond to questions by using ideological terms is strongly related to education, which helps people understand political issues and relate them to one another. Personal experiences in the socialization process can also lead people to think ideologically.

The Quality of Ideological Thinking in Public Opinion

It is not clear what people's ideological self-placement means in the 1990s. Originally, the liberal-conservative continuum represented a single dimension: attitudes toward the scope of government activity. Liberals were in favor of more government action to provide public goods, and conservatives were in favor of less. This simple distinction is not as useful today. Many people who call themselves "liberals" no longer favor government activism in general, and many self-styled "conservatives" no longer oppose it in principle.

In Chapter 1, we proposed an alternative ideological classification based on the relationships among the values of freedom, order, and equality. We described liberals as people who believe that government should promote equality, even if some freedom is lost in the process, but who oppose surrendering freedom to government-imposed order. Conservatives do not oppose equality in and of itself, but they do put a higher value on freedom than equality when the two conflict. Yet conservatives are not above restricting freedom when threatened with the loss of order. So both groups value freedom, but one is more willing to trade freedom for equality, and the other is more inclined to trade freedom for order.

If you have trouble thinking about these trade-offs on a single dimension, you are perfectly normal. The liberal-conservative continuum presented to survey respondents takes a two-dimensional concept and squeezes it into a one-dimensional format.[29] As a result, many people have difficulty deciding whether they are liberal or conservative, and others confidently choose the same point on the continuum for entirely different reasons. People describe themselves as liberal or conservative for the symbolic value of the terms as much as for ideological reasons.[30]

Studies of the public's ideological thinking find that two themes run through people's minds when they are asked to describe liberals and conservatives. One associates liberals with change and conservatives with traditional values. This theme corresponds to the distinction between liberals and conservatives on the exercise of freedom and the maintenance of order.[31]

The other theme has to do with equality. The conflict between freedom and equality was at the heart of President Roosevelt's New Deal economic policies (social security, minimum wage legislation, farm price supports) in the 1930s. These policies expanded the interventionist role of the national government. And government intervention in the economy served to distinguish liberals from conservatives for decades afterward.[32] Attitudes toward government interventionism still underlie contemporary opinions of domestic economic policies.[33] Liberals support intervention to promote their ideas of economic equality; conservatives favor less government intervention and more individual freedom in economic activities.

Ideological Types in the United States

Our ideological typology in Chapter 1 incorporates these two themes (see Figure 1.2). It classifies people as *liberals* if they favor freedom over order and equality over freedom. *Conservatives* favor the reverse set of values. *Libertarians* favor freedom over both equality and order—the opposite of *populists*. Respondents can also be classified according to their ideological *tendencies*, with their answers cross-tabulated to the two questions about order and equality. As shown in Figure 4.3, people's responses to the questions about firing a communist teacher and redistributing income are virtually unrelated, which indicates that people do not decide about government activity according to a one-dimensional ideological standard.

Figure 4.3 can also be used to classify the sample according to the two dimensions in our ideological typology. There is substantial room for error in using only two issues to classify people in an ideological framework. Moreover, the responses on each issue are forced into two categories for simplicity in presentation, and a "yes" response by some people is weaker than the same response by others. Nevertheless, if the typology is worthwhile, the results should be meaningful, and they are.

The respondents in the 1990 sample depicted in Figure 4.3 divide almost evenly in their ideological tendencies among the four categories of the typology. Surprisingly, the libertarian response pattern accounts for the largest portion of the sample.[34] Although pure conservatives are the smallest group, they still account for almost one-quarter of the public.

Populists are prominent among minorities and others with little education and low income, groups that tend to look favorably on the benefits of government in general. *Libertarians* are concentrated among respondents with more education and with higher income who live in the West. These groups tend to be suspicious of government interference in their lives. *Conservatives* are found mainly in the South, and *liberals* are concentrated in the Northeast.

This more refined analysis of political ideology explains why even some Americans who pay close attention to politics find it difficult to locate themselves on the liberal-conservative continuum. Their problem is that they are liberal on some issues and conservative on others. Forced to choose along just one dimension, they choose the middle category, "moderate." However, our analysis also indicates that many respondents who classify themselves as liberals and conservatives do conform to our typology. There is value, then, in the liberal-conservative distinction as long as we understand its limitations.

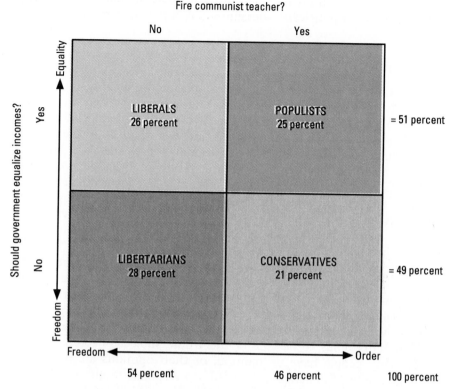

FIGURE 4.3   *Respondents Classified by Ideological Tendencies*
Choices between freedom and order and between freedom and equality were
represented by two survey questions that asked respondents whether a com-
munist should teach in college and whether the government should equalize
income differences. People's responses to the questions showed no correlation,
demonstrating that these value choices cannot be explained by a simple lib-
eral–conservative continuum. Instead, their responses conformed to four dif-
ferent ideological types. (Source: National Opinion Research Center, 1990 General
Social Survey. These data were kindly furnished by Tom W. Smith, study director.)

The Process of Forming Political Opinions

So far you have learned that people acquire their values through the
socialization process and that different social groups develop different
sets of political values. You have also learned that some people, but only
a minority, think about politics ideologically, holding a consistent set
of political attitudes and beliefs. However, we have not really discussed
how people form opinions on any particular issue. In particular, how do
those who are not ideologues—in other words, most citizens—form po-

litical opinions? Four factors—self-interest, political information, opinion schemas, and political leadership—play a part in the process.

Self-Interest

The **self-interest principle** states that people choose what benefits them personally.[35] This principle certainly explains how opinions are formed on government economic policies. Taxpayers tend to prefer low taxes to high taxes; farmers tend to favor candidates who promise more support rather than less. The self-interest principle also operates, but less clearly, for some noneconomic government policies. Members of minority groups tend to see more personal advantage in government policies that promote social equality than do members of majority groups; teenage males are more likely to oppose compulsory military service than are older people of either sex. Group leaders often "cue" group members, telling them what they should be for or against.[36]

When a citizen is not directly affected by a government policy, the self-interest principle has little explanatory power. Then people form opinions based on their underlying values.[37] When moral issues are not in question and when people do not benefit directly from a policy, they often have trouble relating to the policy and forming an opinion. This tends to be true of the whole subject of foreign policy. Here, many people have no opinion, or their opinions are not firmly held and are apt to change quite easily in response to almost any new information.

Political Information

In the United States today, the level of education is high, and media coverage of national and international events is extensive. Yet the average American displays an astonishing lack of political knowledge. After the 1988 election, for example, only 28 percent of a national sample could correctly identify even one of their candidates for the House of Representatives, and only 40 percent correctly named either of their candidates for the Senate.[38] In June 1990, the Supreme Court made news by overturning an act of Congress that outlawed flag burning as a protected means of expression. Despite the great publicity given the decision, 31 percent of a national sample incorrectly thought the Court had supported the anti-flag burning law, while 17 percent admitted that they did not know. Only 52 percent of the public knew (guessed?) what the Court had decided on this highly charged issue.[39]

But Americans do not let political ignorance stop them from expressing their opinions. They readily offer opinions on issues ranging from capital punishment, to nuclear power, to the government's handling of the economy. If opinions are based on little information, they change easily when new information becomes available. The result is a high degree of instability in public opinion poll results, depending on question wording and current events that bear on the issue.

Researchers use the term **political sophistication** to mean having a broad range of opinions, based on factual information, that are consistent and organized conceptually.[40] One study of political sophistication classified the American public into three broad groups of political sophistication. The least sophisticated (about 20 percent of the electorate) pay little attention to public affairs and seldom participate in politics. Most adults (about 75 percent) are only moderately sophisticated. "They half-attentively monitor the flow of political news, but they run for the most part on a psychological automatic pilot." Only a small portion of the electorate (about 5 percent) is politically sophisticated, sharing the knowledge and conceptualization of professional politicians, journalists, and political analysts. As expected, education is strongly related to political sophistication, but so are participation in groups and parents' interest in politics. The author likened the development of political sophistication to a "spiral process . . . a gradual process in which interest breeds knowledge, which, in turn, breeds further interest and knowledge over time."[41] Political events and the actions of political leaders can contribute to that spiraling process.

We should note that researchers have not found any meaningful relationship between political sophistication and self-placement on the liberal-conservative scale. That is, people with equal knowledge about public affairs and with similar levels of conceptualization are as likely to think of themselves as liberals as they are to consider themselves conservatives.[42] Equal levels of political understanding, then, may produce different political views as a result of individuals' unique patterns of political socialization.

Opinion Schemas

We have learned that only a minority of the population, about one person in five, can be classified as ideologues. These people regularly think about politics in ideological terms and come to new political issues with a set of political beliefs and values that helps them form opinions on these issues. But even people who do not approach politics with full-blown ideologies interpret political issues in terms of some pre-existing mental structure.

Psychologists refer to the packet of pre-existing beliefs that people apply to specific issues as an **opinion schema**—a network of organized knowledge and beliefs that guides the processing of information on a particular subject.[43] The schema concept is a sharper tool for analyzing public opinion than the blunter concept of ideology. Opinion schemas can pertain to any political figure and to any subject—race, economics, international relations.[44] For instance, one study found that

African-Americans' views on the importance of race in determining a person's chances in life could be analyzed according to five distinct schemas.[45]

Nevertheless, the more encompassing concept of ideology is hard to escape. Researchers have found that people tend to organize their personal schemas within a hierarchy of opinion that parallels broader ideological categories. A liberal's opinion schema about George Bush may not differ from a conservative's in the facts it contains, but the schema differs considerably in its evaluation of those facts.[46] In the liberal's schema, for example, anger may replace the conservative's praise for Bush's decision to invade Panama in 1989. The main value of schemas for understanding how opinions are formed is that they remind us that opinion questions trigger many different images, connections, and values in the mind of each respondent.

Some scholars argue that most citizens, in their attempt to make sense out of politics, pay less attention to the policies pursued by government than to their leaders' "style" in approaching political problems—whether they are seen as tough, compassionate, honest, or hard-working.[47] In this way, citizens can relate the complexities of politics to their own personal experiences. If many citizens view politics according to governing style, the role of political leadership becomes a more important determinant of public opinion than the leader's actual policies.

Political Leadership

Public opinion on specific issues is stimulated by political leaders, journalists, and policy experts. Because of the office and the media attention it receives, presidents are uniquely positioned to shape popular attitudes. Consider the issue of nuclear disarmament and Ronald Reagan. In late 1987, President Reagan and Mikhail Gorbachev signed a treaty banning intermediate-range nuclear forces (INF) from Europe and the Soviet Union. Soon afterward, a national survey found that 82 percent of the sample approved the treaty, while 18 percent opposed it. As might be expected, those hard-liners who viewed the Soviet Union as highly threatening were least enthusiastic about the INF treaty. Respondents were then asked to agree or disagree with this statement: "President Reagan is well known for his anticommunism, so if he thinks this is a good deal, it must be." Analysis of the responses showed that those hard-liners who agreed with the statement were nearly twice as likely to approve the treaty as those who were unmoved by his involvement. The researcher concluded that "a highly conciliatory move by a president known for long-standing opposition to just such an action" can override expected sources of opposition among the public.[48] The implication is that another president, such as Jimmy Carter or even Gerald Ford, could not have won over the hard-liners.

The role of political leaders in affecting public opinion has been enhanced enormously with the development of the broadcast media, especially television.[49] The majoritarian model of democracy assumes that government officials respond to public opinion, but there is substantial evidence that the causal sequence is reversed: that public opinion responds instead to the actions of government officials.[50] If this is true, how much potential is there for public opinion to be manipulated by political leaders through the mass media? We now examine the manipulative potential of the mass media.

The Nature of the Mass Media in America

"We never talk anymore" is a common lament among people who are living together but not getting along very well. In politics, too, citizens and their government need to communicate if they are to get along well. **Communication** is the process of transmitting information from one individual or group to another. **Mass communication** is the process by which individuals or groups transmit information to large, heterogeneous, and widely dispersed audiences. **Mass media** are the technical devices employed in mass communication. The mass media are commonly divided into two types. **Print media** (newspapers, magazines) communicate information through the publication of written words and pictures. **Broadcast media** (radio, television) communicate information electronically through sounds or sights.

In the United States, the mass media are in business to make money, which they do mainly by selling advertising through their major function, entertainment. We are more interested in the five specific functions the mass media serve for the political system: *reporting* the news, *interpreting* the news, *influencing* citizens' opinions, *setting the agenda* for government action, and *socializing* citizens about politics.

Our special focus is on the role of the mass media in promoting communication from a government to its citizens and from citizens to their government. In totalitarian governments, information flows more freely in one direction (from government to people) than in the other. In democratic governments, information must flow freely in both directions; a democratic government can be responsive to public opinion only if its citizens can make their opinions known. Moreover, the electorate can hold government officials accountable for their actions only if voters know what their government has done, is doing, and plans to do. Because the mass media provide the major channels for this two-way flow of information, they have the dual capability of reflecting and shaping political views.

Mass media are not the only means of communication between citizens and government. Agents of socialization (especially schools) function as "linkage mechanisms" that promote such communication. In the next three chapters, we discuss other major mechanisms for communication: voting, political parties, campaigning in elections, and interest groups.

Private Ownership of the Media

In the United States, private ownership of the media is an accepted fact. In other Western democratic countries, the print media (both newspapers and magazines) are privately owned, but the broadcast media often are not. Private ownership of both print and broadcast media gives the news industry in America more political freedom than any other in the world, but it also makes the media more dependent on advertising revenues. To make a profit, the news operations of mass media in America must appeal to the audiences they serve.

You might think that a story's political significance, educational value, or broad social importance determines whether it is covered in the media. The sad truth is that most potential news stories are not judged by such grand criteria. The primary criterion of a story's **newsworthiness** is usually its audience appeal, as judged by its *high impact* on readers or listeners; its *sensationalist* aspect (as exemplified by violence, conflict, disaster, or scandal); its treatment of *familiar* people or life situations; its *close-to-home* character; and its *timeliness*.[51]

Media owners can make more money either by increasing their audiences or by acquiring additional publications or stations. There is a decided trend toward concentrated ownership of the media, enhancing the possibility that a few major owners could control the news flow to promote their own political interests. In fact, the number of independent newspapers has declined as more papers have been acquired by newspaper chains (two or more newspapers in different cities under the same ownership). Only about four hundred dailies are still independent, and many of these papers are too small and unprofitable to invite acquisition.

Like newspapers, television stations in different cities are sometimes owned by the same group. In 1990, for example, the Capital Cities/ABC group owned outright eight television stations—in New York, Los Angeles, Chicago, Philadelphia, San Francisco, Houston, Fresno, and Raleigh-Durham—serving 24 percent of the television market.[52]

Ownership concentration can also occur across the media. Sometimes the same corporation owns a television station, a radio station, and a newspaper in the same area. For example, the Gannett Company, the largest newspaper chain, also operates ten television, nine FM, and seven AM broadcasting stations. Some people fear the concentration of media under a single owner, and government has addressed this fear by regulating media ownership as well as other aspects of media operation (see Feature 4.1).

Feature 4.1

Cross-Ownership–Cross-Censorship?

Is there good reason to fear the growing cross-media media ownership by a few giant corporations? Those who extoll the benefits of ownership deregulation contend that competition in the information marketplace will guarantee that the public gets a diversity of information sources. Critics argue that the information may be controlled by the governing corporation, regardless of whether it is owned by Americans or foreigners. Consider these examples.

Robert Hilliard, professor of mass communications at Boston's Emerson College, was invited by the *Boston Herald* in 1987 to review two new television programs, "Married . . . with Children" and "The Tracey Ullman Show," that launched the debut of the Fox Network. He initially refused because the network's creator, Rupert Murdoch, owned both the newspaper and the local Fox television channel. But Hilliard agreed to be one of the outside experts when told by the *Herald's* editors that they wanted an honest review. He did not like the programs, even calling "Married . . . with Children" one of the "worst sitcoms" he had even seen. None of his prepared remarks or those of any non-*Herald* employee who screened the programs, was published by the newspaper, which headlined a review by its regular critic "Fox Network Offers New, Lively Variety."

Peter Karl, an investigative reporter for Chicago's NBC affiliate, WMAQ-TV, prepared a story for the "Today" show in 1989 about the faulty nuts and bolts used in important construction projects such as bridges, airplane engines, nuclear missile silos, and the NASA space program. Karl also cited the General Electric Corporation, which builds airplane engines, as a user of shoddy nuts and bolts. The story was broadcast on November 30, 1989, but it was edited to delete all references to General Electric, which happens to own NBC.

When Matsushita Electric bought MCA in 1990, its president, Akio Tanii, held a news conference. He sought to quell American fears about Japanese censorship of motion pictures made by MCA's Universal Studios by announcing that he would keep MCA's American chair in his position. Then a reporter asked whether the new company would "be willing to produce a movie about the wartime role of the late Emperor Hirohito." Mr. Tanii seemed agitated and said, "I could never imagine such a case, so I cannot answer such a question." Would Matsushita permit the making of movies that criticized Japanese society or economic practices? Again he said, "I never dreamed of hearing such a question."

Sources: Paul Starobin, "Murdoch v. Murdoch," *Congressional Quarterly Weekly Report*, June 3, 1989, p. 1316; James Warren, "'Today' Edited GE from News Story," *Chicago Tribune*, December 2, 1989, p. 3; and David E. Sanger, "Politics and Multinational Movies," *New York Times*, November 27, 1990, p. C5.

Government Regulation of the Media

Although most of the mass media in the United States are privately owned, they are not free of government regulation. The broadcast media, however, operate under more regulations than the print media do.

The **Federal Communications Commission (FCC)**, is charged with regulating interstate and foreign communication by radio, television, telephone, telegraph, cable, and satellite. Its powers include granting licenses to operate, establishing technical regulations, and limiting the number of radio and television stations that may be owned by a single company.

The seven FCC commissioners, chosen by the president, serve overlapping terms—beginning and ending in different years—and can be removed from office only through impeachment conviction. Consequently, the FCC is considered an *independent regulatory commission*: It is insulated from political control by either the president or Congress. (We discuss independent regulatory commissions in Chapter 10.)

The First Amendment to the Constitution prohibits Congress from abridging the freedom of the press. Over time, the *press* has come to mean *all* the mass media. As might be expected, the press, particularly the print media, has broadly interpreted the Constitution's guarantee of "freedom of the press" to justify its right to print or broadcast what it wishes. Over the past two hundred years, the courts have decided numerous cases that define how far freedom of the press extends under the law. The most important of these cases, which are often quite complex, are discussed in Chapter 10. Usually the courts have struck down government attempts to restrain the press from publishing or broadcasting the information, events, or opinions that it finds newsworthy. One notable exception concerns strategic information during wartime: The courts have supported censorship in the publishing or broadcasting of such information as the sailing schedules of troop ships or the movements of troops in battle. Otherwise, the courts have recognized a strong constitutional case against press censorship. This stand has given the United States some of the freest, most vigorous news media in the world.

Because the broadcast media are licensed to use the public airwaves, they are subject to some regulation of the content of their news coverage that is not applied to the print media. The basis for the FCC's regulation of content lies in its charge to ensure that radio (and, later, television) stations would "serve the public interest, convenience, and necessity." For more than fifty years, broadcasters operated under three constraints rooted in the 1934 Federal Communications Act. In its **equal opportunities rule**, the FCC required that a broadcast station that gave or sold time to a candidate for any public office had to make an equal amount of time under the same conditions available to all other candidates for that office. The **reasonable access rule** required that stations make their facilities available for the expression of conflicting views or issues from all responsible elements in the community. Finally, the **fairness doctrine** obligated broadcasters to discuss public issues and to provide fair coverage to each side of those issues. The first two constraints are still in effect. The fairness doctrine was repealed in 1987 on the grounds that it denied the broadcast media free speech rights equal to those long enjoyed by the print media.

Political Effects of the Media

In this section we examine where citizens acquire their political knowledge, look at what people learn from the media, and probe the media's effects on public opinion, the political agenda, and political socialization.

Where the Public Gets Its News

Virtually all citizens rely on the mass media for their political news. Until the early 1960s, most people reported getting more of that news from newspapers than from any other source. In the early 1960s, television nudged out newspapers as the public's major source of news. By the end of the 1980s, about two-thirds of the public were citing television as their news source, compared with less than one-half who named newspapers and less than one-fifth who relied on radio. Not only is television the public's most important source of news; television news is also rated as more trustworthy than newspaper news—by a margin of nearly 2 to 1.[53] However, several studies indicate that these frequently cited data may overstate both people's reliance on television for news and their trust in the medium.[54]

As one would expect, level of education is strongly related to news attentiveness. So is age. One major study found that nearly one-half of the *news sophisticates*, who read specialized opinion magazines and listen to public radio and public television, were college graduates. Also, nearly one-half of those news sophisticates were age fifty or older.[55] Among other factors, race bears no relationship to news attentiveness,[56] but sex has a decided effect. Those who do not regularly read or watch any news are more likely to be female (60 percent), while news sophisticates are more likely to be male (56 percent).

What People Remember and Know

If 84 percent of the public read or heard the news the previous day, and if nearly 75 percent say they regularly watch the news on television, how much political information do they absorb? By all accounts, not much. In the first two months of 1990, respondents in two national surveys identified the political changes taking place in Eastern Europe as the most important news event. In February 1990, Vaclav Havel, the new president of Czechoslovakia, visited the United States and ad-

Compared with What? 4.1

Opinions on the Media

Americans are more likely to perceive the media as politically powerful than are citizens in four other Western democracies. This finding comes from sample surveys taken in Great Britain, France, West Germany, Spain, and the United States during the spring of 1987. Respondents in each country were asked, "Would you say that the influence exerted by the media on [name of institution] is very large, somewhat large, or not large at all?" The combined percentages of "very large" and "somewhat large" responses form the bars of the accompanying graph. Although most citizens in each country perceive the media as having a large influence on public opinion, only Americans think the media also influence the major branches of government.

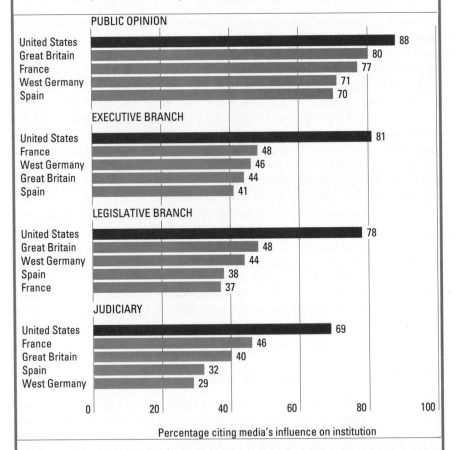

Source: Laurence Parisot, "Attitudes About the Media: A Five-Country Comparison," *Public Opinion* 10 (January-February 1988):60. Reprinted by permission.

dressed the U.S. Congress. In March, a national survey asked, "Do you happen to know who Vaclav Havel is?" and only 14 percent could identify him. The same survey asked, "Do you happen to know who Marla Maples is?" and 37 percent correctly identified her as New York multimillionaire Donald Trump's then-current girlfriend.[57]

When tested for political knowledge, people who are more attentive to news answer more questions correctly than those who are less attentive—as expected. Given the enormous improvements in television technology and the increasing reliance of the public on high-tech television news coverage, we might also expect that the public today knows more than it did twenty years ago.[58] Unfortunately, that is not so. Similar surveys in 1967 and in 1987 asked respondents to name their state governor, representative in the House, and head of the local school district. Only 9 percent failed to name a single official in 1967 compared with 17 percent in 1987. The author of this study attributed the lower performance in 1987 to greater reliance on television for news.[59]

Several studies have found that increased exposure to television news has a numbing effect on a person's capacity to discriminate among news messages.[60] Why should this be? We know that television tends to squeeze public policy issues into one-minute or, at most, two-minute fragments, which makes it difficult to explain candidates' positions. Television also tends to cast abstract issues in personal terms to enhance the visual image that the medium conveys.[61] Thus, viewers may become more adept at visually identifying the candidates and knowing their personal habits than at knowing their positions on issues. Finally, the television networks, whose content is regulated by the FCC, are concerned about being fair and equal in covering the candidates, which may result in equalizing candidates' positions as well. Whatever the explanation, the technological wonders of television seem to have contributed little to citizens' knowledge of public affairs. Indeed, electronic journalism may work against the citizen knowledge that democratic government requires.

There is also evidence that those people who rely on television coverage of politics are more confused and cynical than those who do not.[62] This problem may be even more acute where foreign affairs are concerned because most of the public has relatively little interest in foreign affairs, but the networks tend to "overreport" them.[63] The public witnesses conflict, criticism, and controversy in countries it knows little about. Not knowing what to think or whom to believe, the public responds "by becoming more cynical, more negative, and more critical of leadership and institutions."[64]

The Media's Effect on Public Opinion

Americans overwhelmingly believe that the media exert a strong influence on their political institutions, and almost nine out of ten Americans believe that the media strongly influence public opinion (see Compared with What? 4.1). However, it is not easy to determine the extent of media influence on public opinion. Because very few of us learn about political events except as they are reported through the media, it is arguable that the media create public opinion simply by reporting events. Consider the U.S.-led effort to reestablish order in Somalia in 1992. Surely the pictures of starving children being denied food by roving bands of armed men led American public opinion to support the use of U.S. forces there.

Broader studies of opinion change have found systematic, and in some cases dramatic, effects of television news. One study repeatedly polled the public on eighty issues in foreign and domestic affairs. In nearly one-half of these items, public opinion changed over time by about 6 percentage points. The researchers compared these changes with policy positions taken by ten different sources of information; including commentators on television network news, the president, members of the president's party, members of the opposition party, and members of interest groups. The study found the news commentators to have the most dramatic effect—a single commentary could be linked to more than 4 percentage points of opinion change.[65]

The Media's Power to Set the Political Agenda

Despite the media's potential for influencing public opinion, most scholars believe that the media's greatest impact on politics is found in their power to set the agenda. An *agenda* is a list of things to do or consider; a **political agenda** is a list of issues that need government attention. Those who set the political agenda define what issues should be discussed and debated by government decision makers. Like the tree that falls in the forest without anyone hearing it, an issue that does not get on the political agenda will not have anyone in government working on its behalf.

The mass media in the United States have traditionally played an important role in defining the political agenda. Television, which reaches daily into virtually every home, has especially great potential for setting the political agenda. A careful study designed to isolate and examine television's effects on public opinion concluded, "By attending to some problems and ignoring others, television news shapes the American public's political priorities."[66] Furthermore, "the more removed the viewer is from the world of public affairs, the stronger the agenda-setting power of television news."[67]

At the national level, the major news media help set the political agenda by what they report. One study of media coverage in newspapers, news magazines, and network television news found that what the public saw as "the most important problem facing this country today" correlated differently with the amount of media coverage, depending on the type of event. Public opinion was especially responsive to media

Seeing Is Believing (Sometimes)
On March 3, 1991, an amateur cameraman videotaped several Los Angeles
police officers beating Rodney King, a black motorist whom they had stopped
for a traffic violation. The now famous tape, which seemed to substantiate the
victim's charge of police brutality, was viewed by 80 percent of the country via
national and local newscasts prompted widespread scrutiny of the behavior of
law officers across the country. Later, a California's jury decision not to con-
vict the officers led to riots in Los Angeles and widespread public anger across
the U.S. In 1993, the four officers involved in the beating were charged with
depriving King of his civil rights and tried again in federal court. Two were
convicted.

coverage of recurring problems such as inflation and unemployment.[68]
The media's ability to influence public opinion by defining "the news"
makes politicians eager to influence media coverage.

Clearly, political leaders believe that the media are influential, and
these leaders act accordingly. Top government officials closely follow
the news reported in the major national news sources, and the president
receives a daily digest of news from many sources. Just as the president
tries to learn what the media think is happening in government and
politics, other political elites try to keep abreast of developments by
following news in the media.

In a curious sense, the mass media have become a network for communication among attentive elites, all trying to influence one another
or to assess others' weaknesses and strengths. Suppose the White House
is under pressure on some policy matter and is asked for a spokesperson
to appear for fifteen minutes of intensive questioning on the "MacNeil/

Lehrer Newshour." The White House complies not so much to influence opinions among the relatively few "news sophisticates" in the public as to influence the thinking of other elites that faithfully follow the program.

The Media's Influence on Socialization

We discussed the major agents of political socialization earlier in this chapter, but we did not include the mass media among them. However, the mass media do act as very important agents of political socialization. Young people who rarely follow the news by choice nevertheless acquire political values through the entertainment function of the broadcast media. Years ago, children learned from radio programs; now they learn from television.[69] What children learned from radio, however, was very different from what they are learning now. In the "golden days of radio," youngsters listening to popular radio dramas heard repeatedly that "crime does not pay." They were taught that law enforcement agencies inevitably caught criminals and put them behind bars. The message never varied: Criminals are bad; the police are good; criminals get caught and are severely punished for their crimes.

Television today does not portray the criminal justice system in the same way, even in police dramas. Consider programs such as "Cop Rock" and "Gabriel's Fire," which have portrayed police and prison guards as killers. These programs are not unique in their messages about institutional corruption. Other series, such as "Law and Order" and "Against the Law," also operate within a tainted criminal justice system.[70] Certainly, one cannot easily argue that television's entertainment programs help prepare law-abiding citizens.

So the media play contradictory roles in the process of political socialization. On one hand, they promote popular support for government by joining in the celebration of national holidays, heroes' birthdays, political anniversaries, and civic accomplishments. On the other hand, the media erode public confidence by publicizing citizens' grievances, airing investigative reports of agency malfeasance, and giving front-page and prime-time coverage to political critics, protestors, and even terrorists and assassins.

Evaluating the Media in Relation to Government

We have described the media's current status and how they report the news to their audiences. Are the media fair or biased in reporting the news? What contributions do the media make to democratic government? What effects do they have on freedom, order, and equality?

Fraternizing with the Enemy?
Although the news media and the government are sometimes viewed as adversaries, as this photo shows, they are also often very "close." In this picture, newsmen swarm around Bill Clinton in an effort to be the first to gain some new bit of information which will immediately be conveyed to the public.

Is Reporting Biased?

News professes to reflect reality, yet critics of modern journalism contend that this reality is colored by the way it is filtered through the ideological biases of media owners and editors (the gatekeepers) and of the reporters themselves.

The argument that news is politically biased has two sides. On one hand, news reporters are criticized for tilting their stories in a liberal direction, promoting social equality and undercutting social order. On the other hand, wealthy and conservative media owners are suspected of preserving inequalities and reinforcing the existing order by serving up a relentless round of entertainment that numbs the public's capacity for critical analysis.

Although the picture is far from clear, available evidence seems to confirm the charge of liberal bias among reporters in the major news media. Studies of the voting behavior of hundreds of reporters and broadcasters show that they voted overwhelmingly for Democratic candidates in presidential elections from 1964 through 1980.[71] Moreover, a 1989 survey of 1,200 news and editorial staffers on seventy-two papers found that 62 percent of the journalists described themselves as liberal/Democrat, versus 22 percent conservative/Republican.[72]

A study of television coverage during the summer of the 1992 presidential campaign found that the candidates alternated in the spotlight. In the weeks up to and including the Democratic convention, Clinton had 454 minutes on network news shows to Bush's 400. But between the Republican convention and Labor Day, Bush drew about 2.6 minutes per newscast versus Clinton's 1.6.[73] Of course, reporters can "spin" the news so that coverage is good or bad. When Bush chose Texas to announce that he would sell fighter jets to Taiwan to save jobs, ABC's Brit Hume reported that Bush was adjusting foreign policy to help his campaign in his home state. Nevertheless, the same study found that citizens and politicians who were chosen to appear on television during August made more favorable comments about Bush (43 percent) than about Clinton (32 percent).

Although most journalists classify themselves as liberal, more of them describe the newspapers for which they work as conservative (pro-Reagan and pro-business) rather than liberal (42 percent to 28 percent).[74] To some extent, working journalists are at odds with their own editors, who tend to be more conservative and therefore tone down the liberal biases of their reporters.[75]

If media owners and their editors are indeed conservative supporters of the status quo, we would expect them to support officeholders over challengers in elections. However, the campaign news that emerges from both print and broadcast media tends in the other direction. One researcher who found evidence of liberal bias in the 1984 presidential campaign had also studied the 1980 campaign, when Reagan was the challenger and Jimmy Carter the incumbent president.[76] In that campaign, the media covered Carter more negatively than his conservative challenger. Taking both election years into consideration, the researcher concluded that there was virtually no *continuing* ideological or partisan bias on the evening television news. Instead, what was seen as ideological or partisan bias in 1980 and 1984 was actually a bias against presidential *incumbents* and *frontrunners* for the presidency.[77]

According to this reasoning, if journalists have any pronounced bias, it is against politicians. When an incumbent runs for re-election, journalists may feel a special responsibility to counteract his or her advantage by putting the opposite partisan spin on the news.[78] Thus, whether the media coverage of campaigns is seen as pro-Democratic (and therefore liberal) or pro-Republican (and therefore conservative) depends on which party is in office at the time.

Of course, bias in reporting is not limited to campaigning for elections. For example, a study of stories on nuclear energy carried in the media over a period of ten years found that stories in the *New York Times* were well balanced between pronuclear and antinuclear sources. In contrast, the major newsmagazines and television tended to favor antinuclear sources and to slant their stories against nuclear energy.[79]

Contributions to Democracy

As noted earlier, the communication flow in a democracy must move in two directions: from government to citizens and from citizens to government. In fact, because the media are privately owned, political communication in the United States seldom goes directly from government to citizens without passing *through* the media. This is an important point because, as just discussed, news reporters tend to be highly critical of politicians; they instinctively search for inaccuracies in fact and weaknesses in argument. Some observers have characterized the news media and the government as adversaries—each mistrusting the other, locked in competition for popular favor. To the extent that this is true, the media serve both the majoritarian and the pluralist models of democracy well by improving the quality of information transmitted to people about their government.

Perhaps communication between citizens and their government was increased by the emergence in the 1992 presidential election of "talk-show politics" in which the candidates appeared on shows such as "Larry King Live" and responded directly to calls from listeners. However, some argue that by using that forum, the candidates may have avoided many of the probing questions that experienced journalists might have asked.

The mass media transmit information from citizens to government by reporting citizens' reactions to political events and government actions. The press has traditionally reflected public opinion (and often created it) by defining the news and suggesting courses of government action. But the media's role in reflecting public opinion has become much more refined in the information age. Before the widespread use of sample surveys, collections of newspaper stories from across the country were analyzed to assess public opinion on political affairs.[80] After commercial polls were established in the 1930s, newspapers began to report more reliable readings of public opinion. By the 1970s, survey research groups had become formal divisions of some news organizations. Occasionally, print and electronic media joined forces to conduct major national surveys.

The media now have the tools to do a better job of reporting mass opinion than ever before, and they use those tools extensively. The well-respected *New York Times*/CBS News poll conducts surveys that are aired first on the "CBS Evening News" and then analyzed at length in the *Times*. During the 1988 election campaign, the *Times* conducted

31 separate polls, most jointly with CBS News, which formed the basis of 35 articles and were cited in another 135 articles on the campaign.[81] The *Wall Street Journal* and NBC News are also allies in opinion polling, as are the *Washington Post* and ABC News. In fact, 40 percent of the daily newspapers are directly involved in polling.[82]

Although polls sometimes create opinions just by asking questions, their net effect has been to generate more accurate knowledge of public opinion and to report that knowledge back to the public. Although widespread knowledge of public opinion does not guarantee government responsiveness to popular demands, such knowledge is required if government is to function according to the majoritarian model of democracy.

Effects on Freedom, Order, and Equality

The media in the United States have played an important role in advancing equality, especially racial equality. Throughout the civil rights movement of the 1950s and 1960s, the media gave national coverage to conflict in the South, as black children tried to attend white schools or civil rights workers were beaten and even killed in the effort to register black voters. Partly because of the media coverage, civil rights moved up on the political agenda, and coalitions were formed in Congress to pass new laws promoting racial equality. Women's rights have also been advanced through the media, which focused attention on the National Organization for Women and other groups working for women's equality. In general, the mass media offer spokespersons for any disadvantaged group an opportunity to state their case before a national audience and to work for a place on the political agenda.

Although the media are willing to mobilize government action to infringe on personal freedom for equality's sake, they resist government's attempts to infringe on freedom of the press to promote order. The media, far more than the public, believe freedom of the press is sacrosanct. For example, 98 percent of 2,703 journalists surveyed by the *Los Angeles Times* opposed allowing a government official to prevent the publication of a story seen as inaccurate, compared with only 50 percent of the public. Whereas the public felt that certain types of news should never be published—"exit polls saying who will win an election, secret documents dealing with national security issues, the names of CIA spies, photographs that invade people's privacy"—journalists are more reluctant to draw the line anywhere.[83] Although reporters covering the Persian Gulf crisis chafed at restrictions imposed by the military, a survey during the war found that 57 percent of the public thought that the military "should exert more control" over reporting.[84]

The media, to protect their freedom, operate as an interest group in a pluralist democracy. They have an interest in reporting whatever they wish whenever they wish, which certainly erodes government's efforts to maintain order. Three examples illustrate this point.

- The media's sensational coverage of terrorist activities give terrorists exactly what they want, making it more difficult to reduce terrorist threats to order.

- The portrayal of brutal killings and rapes on television, often under the guise of entertainment, has produced "copycat" crimes, those admittedly committed "as seen on TV."

- The national publicity given to deaths from adulterated drugs (for instance, Tylenol capsules laced with cyanide) has prompted similar tampering with other products.

Freedom of the press is a noble value and one that has been important to our democratic government. But we should not ignore the fact that we sometimes pay a price for pursuing it without qualification.

Summary

Public opinion does not rule in America. On most issues, it merely sets general boundaries for government policy. Because most Americans' ideological opinions are normally distributed around the "moderate" category and have been so for decades, government policies can vary from left to right over time without provoking severe political conflict.

People form their values through the process of political socialization. The most important socialization agents in childhood and young adulthood are family, school, community, and peers. Members of the same social group tend to experience similar socialization processes and thus to adopt similar values. People in different social groups, who hold different values, often express vastly different opinions. Differences in education, race, and religion tend to produce sharper divisions of opinion today on questions of order and equality than do differences in income, region, and ethnicity.

Although most people do not think about politics in ideological terms, when asked to do so by pollsters, they readily classify themselves along a liberal-conservative continuum. Many respondents choose the middle category, "moderate," the safe choice. Others classify themselves as liberals or conservatives for vague or contradictory reasons. Our two-dimensional framework for analyzing ideology according to the values of order and equality produces four ideological types: liberals, conservatives, libertarians, and populists.

Responses to the survey questions used to establish our ideological typology divide the American electorate almost equally into these four ideological tendencies. The 25 percent of the public that gave liberal responses, opposing government action to impose order but not equality, was opposed by nearly as large a portion that gave the opposite conservative responses. Similarly, the group of populists, which wanted government to impose both order and equality, was opposed by a slightly larger group of libertarians, which wanted government to do neither.

In addition to ideological orientation, many other factors enter the process of forming political opinions. When individuals stand to benefit or suffer from proposed government policies, they usually base their opinions on self-interest. When citizens lack information on which to base their opinions, they usually respond anyway, which leads to substantial fluctuations in poll results depending on how questions are worded and what intervening events occur. The various factors that impinge on the process of forming political opinions can be mapped out within an opinion schema, a network of beliefs and attitudes about a particular topic. The schema imagery helps us visualize the complex process of forming opinions. This process, however, is not completely idiosyncratic: People tend to organize their schemas according to broader ideological thinking. In the absence of information, respondents are particularly susceptible to cues of support or opposition from political leaders as communicated through the mass media.

Which model of democracy, the majoritarian or the pluralist, is correct in its assumptions about public opinion? Sometimes the public shows clear and settled opinions on government policy, conforming to the majoritarian model. However, often public opinion is firmly grounded, not in knowledge, but in ideological bias. Moreover, powerful groups often divide on what they want government to do. This lack of consensus leaves politicians with a great deal of latitude in enacting specific policies, a finding that conforms to the pluralist model. Of course, politicians' actions are under close scrutiny by journalists reporting in the mass media.

The mass media transmit information to large, heterogeneous, and widely dispersed audiences through print and broadcasts. The main function of the mass media is entertainment, but the media also perform the political functions of reporting news, interpreting news, influencing citizens' opinions, setting the political agenda, and socializing citizens about politics.

The mass media in the United States are privately owned and in business to make money, which they do mainly by selling space or airtime to advertisers. Both print and electronic media determine which events are newsworthy, a determination made on the basis of audience appeal. In the media's aggressive competition for that audience, they often resort to sensationalism.

The broadcast media operate under technical, ownership, and content regulations set by the government, which tend to promote the equal treatment of political contests on radio and television more than in newspapers and news magazines.

Although more people today get more news from television than from newspapers, the latter usually do a more thorough job of informing the public about politics. Despite heavy exposure to news in the print and electronic media, most people have a shockingly low ability to retain much political information, and that ability is even less than it was in the mid-1960s. It appears that the problem is not with the media's inability to supply quality news coverage but with the lack of demand for it by the public.

The media's elite, including reporters from the major television networks, tend to be more liberal than the public, as judged by the journalists' tendency to vote for Democratic candidates and by their own self-descriptions. However, if the media systematically demonstrate pronounced bias in their news reporting, it is against incumbents and frontrunners, regardless of their party, rather than for liberal Democrats.

From the standpoint of majoritarian democracy, one of the most important effects of the media is to facilitate communication from the people to the government through the reporting of public opinion polls. The media zealously defend the freedom of the press, even to the point of encouraging disorder through criticism of the government and the granting of extensive publicity to violent protests, terrorist acts, and other threats to order.

Key Terms

public opinion
political socialization
"old" ethnicity
"new" ethnicity
socioeconomic status
self-interest principle
political sophistication
opinion schema
communication
mass communication

mass media
print media
broadcast media
newsworthiness
Federal Communications
  Commission (FCC)
equal opportunities rule
reasonable access rule
fairness doctrine
political agenda

Selected Readings

Asher, Herbert. *Polling and the Public: What Every Citizen Should Know.* Washington, D.C.: Congressional Quarterly Press, 1988. This concise text on polling methodology gives special attention to election polls.

Bozell, L. Brent, II, and Brent H. Baker, eds. *And That's the Way It Isn't.* Alexandria, Va.: Media Research Center, 1990. Prepared by a conservative research group, this study documents the liberal bias of the media. Contrast this book with that by Kellner.

Entman, Robert. *Democracy Without Citizens: Media and the Decay of American Politics.* New York: Oxford University Press, 1989. This penetrating study of the "supply" side of news reporting and the "demand" side of news consumption concludes that the media do not do a better job of reporting news because the public does not demand it.

Graber, Doris A. *Media Power and Politics.* 2d ed. Washington, D.C.: Congressional Quarterly Press, 1990. This is a collection of seminal essays on political journalism and empirical studies of media effects.

Ichilov, Orit. *Political Socialization, Citizenship Education, and Democracy.* New York: Teachers College Press, 1990. This collection of studies on how people acquire political attitudes draws special attention to childhood processes and includes examples from other cultures.

Iyengar, Shanto, and Donald R. Kinder. *News That Matters: Television and American Opinion.* Chicago: University of Chicago Press, 1987. The authors report fourteen experiments with townspeople in New Haven and Ann Arbor designed to assess the effects of television news on opinion.

Kellner, Douglas. *Television and the Crisis of Democracy.* Boulder, Colo.: Westview Press, 1990. This critical, leftist account of the role mass media play in controlling the limits of political discussion by extending the hegemony of the dominant culture serves as a counterpoint to the book by Bozell and Baker.

Lavrakas, Paul J., and Jack K. Holley, eds. *Polling and Presidential Election Coverage.* Newbury Park, Calif.: Sage Publications, 1991. This book contains studies of the media's use of public opinion in covering the 1988 presidential election.

Maddox, William S., and Stuart A. Lilie. *Beyond Liberal and Conservative: Reassessing the Political Spectrum.* Washington, D.C.: Cato Institute, 1984. Maddox and Lilie use an ideological typology similar to the one in this chapter to analyze surveys in presidential elections from 1952 through 1980.

Margolis, Michael, and Gary A. Mauser, eds. *Manipulating Public Opinion: Essays on Public Opinion as a Dependent Variable.* Pacific Grove, Calif.: Brooks/Cole, 1989. This book studies the abilities of political elites to manage public opinion in election campaigns, in the shaping of public policies, and in political socialization.

Niemi, Richard G., John Mueller, and Tom W. Smith. *Trends in Public Opinion: A Compendium of Survey Data.* Westport, Conn.: Greenwood Press, 1989. This handy volume collects some fifty years of polling data, with heavy concentration on annual data from the General Social Surveys, begun in 1972. The survey data are organized into fifteen chapters, each preceded by a useful descriptive essay.

Sanders, Arthur. *Making Sense of Politics.* Ames, Iowa State University Press, 1990. Sanders interviewed twenty-six citizens from Ithaca, New York, at length about their thoughts on politics. In contrast to the short responses gathered from many people in opinion polls, this study reports in depth on the thinking that average citizens devote to politics. The book concludes that more people try to make sense of politics by focusing on the style of decision making than on the content of government policies.

Serfaty, Simon, ed. *The Media and Foreign Policy.* New York: St. Martin's Press, 1990. This is a collection of short accounts, mostly anecdotal, by insiders who were in a position to observe the relationship of the media to the White House during foreign policy crises.

Wanniski, Jude, ed. *1990 Media Guide: A Critical Review of the Media's Recent Coverage of the World Political Economy.* Morristown, N.J.: Polyconomics, 1990. A handbook of the year's major stories and an assessment of the media coverage, this critical source evaluates the alternative press as well as the mainstream media.

Yeric, Jerry L., and John R. Todd. *Public Opinion: The Visible Politics.* 2d ed. Itasca, Ill.: F. E. Peacock, 1989. This basic textbook on public opinion is especially good on the development of individual opinions. It also contains useful case studies of public opinion as it developed on six national issues.

PARTICIPATION AND VOTING

5

Shouts of "No blood for oil! No war for Bush!" rang out from the Senate gallery. The eleven demonstrators who briefly interrupted Democratic Senator Sam Nunn's speech during the historic debate over war in the Persian Gulf were quickly removed by police officers.[1] Ironically, Nunn was speaking against the rush to use force, but neither his speech nor the protesters' shouts altered the outcome. The next day, on January 12, 1991, the Senate voted 52–47 to authorize the use of force to implement the UN resolution requiring Iraq to withdraw its troops from Kuwait. The House concurred in the joint resolution by a vote of 250–183. Within five days, the United States was at war with Iraq.

Unlike the antiwar movement of the 1960s, antiwar protesters in the 1990s were in disarray. From the beginning, vocal opposition to war over Kuwait came from some staunch conservatives, such as columnist Patrick Buchanan, who argued that the nation had no compelling interest in a conflict with Iraq.[2] These critics kept uneasy company with some former Vietnam antiwar protesters, but old partners in the Vietnam peace coalition were badly split over actions in the Persian Gulf.[3]

The congressional vote served to refine the antiwar coalition. Most right-wing critics, including Patrick Buchanan, quickly lined up behind the president. This imparted a left-wing flavor to the antiwar movement, evoking images of the Vietnam-era protests. New cries against "dying for U.S. oil profits" joined with the old slogan "Hell no, we won't go!" On the first Saturday after the war began, an antiwar rally in Washington, D.C., drew an estimated 75,000 people; another rally a week later drew 150,000.[4] Although these rallies represented a wide spectrum of America, polls taken the night war began showed that about 80 percent of the public supported Bush's actions.[5] As in the Vietnam era, antiwar protests were prominent on college campuses across the nation, but student opinion was more divided this time. At one rally, police had to separate antiwar demonstrators from about one hundred counterdemonstrators, mostly from the College Republican National Committee, who waved U.S. flags and chanted "U.S.A.!"[6] On many campuses, students demonstrated their support of the war by displaying flags or yellow ribbons.

Before the war with Iraq, many observers felt that today's college students were politically apathetic. Certainly they have not reflected the broad student activism of the 1960s, and it is not clear whether the war will have a lasting effect on their political involvement. Had anything happened during the 1970s and 1980s to change the political behavior of American youth? Or are we witnessing widespread political apathy among Americans of all ages? Are Americans today less active politically? How do they compare with citizens of other countries? And how much and what kind of participation are necessary to sustain the pluralist and majoritarian models of democracy?

In this chapter, we try to answer these and other important questions about popular participation in government. Although most people think of political participation primarily in terms of voting, there are other forms of political participation, which are sometimes more effective than voting. We begin by looking at the role of participation in democratic government, distinguishing between conventional and unconventional participation. Then we evaluate the nature and extent of both types of participation in American politics. Next, we study the expansion of voting rights and voting as the major mechanism for mass participation in politics. Finally, we examine the extent to which the various forms of political participation serve the values of freedom, equality, and order and the majoritarian and pluralist models of democracy.

Democracy and Political Participation

"Government ought to be run by the people." That is the democratic ideal in a nutshell. But how much and what kind of citizen participation are necessary for democratic government? Champions of direct democracy believe that if citizens do not participate directly in government affairs, making government decisions among themselves, they should give up all pretense of democracy. More practical observers contend that people can govern indirectly through their elected representa-

No Blood for Oil . . . No Tolerance for Tyranny
*Although the outset of the 1991 military action in the Persian Gulf provoked
some antiwar demonstrations on campuses, unlike their predecessors during
the Vietnam War, protesters did not draw broad support from American citizens. On some campuses more students participated in rallies that supported
the military effort than rallies that opposed it.*

tives and that choosing leaders through **elections**—formal procedures for
voting—is the only workable approach to democracy in a large, complex
nation.

Let us review the distinction between direct and indirect democracy
discussed in Chapter 1. In a direct democracy, citizens meet and make
decisions themselves. In an indirect democracy, citizens participate in
government by electing representatives to make decisions for them.
Voting is central to the majoritarian model of government, but it is not
the only means of political participation. In fact, the pluralist model of
democracy relies less on voting and more on other forms of participation.

Elections are a necessary condition of democracy, but they do not
guarantee democratic government. Even while it was still under communism, the Soviet Union regularly held elections in which more than
90 percent of the electorate turned out to vote, but it certainly did not
function as a democracy. Both the majoritarian and pluralist models of
democracy rely on voting to varying degrees, but both models expect
citizens to take part in other forms of political behavior as well. For

example, they expect citizens to discuss politics, form interest groups, contact public officials, campaign for political parties, run for office, and even protest government decisions.

We define **political participation** as "those actions of private citizens by which they seek to influence or to support government and politics."[7] This definition embraces both conventional and unconventional forms of political participation. **Conventional participation** is relatively routine behavior that uses the institutional channels of representative government, especially campaigning for candidates and voting in elections. **Unconventional participation** is relatively uncommon behavior that challenges or defies government channels or the dominant culture (and thus is personally stressful to participants and their opponents).

Voting and writing letters to public officials are examples of conventional political participation; staging sit-down strikes in public buildings and chanting slogans outside officials' windows are examples of unconventional participation. Demonstrations can be conventional (supporting Operation Desert Storm in the Persian Gulf) or unconventional (beating drums outside the White House to protest the war). Some forms of unconventional participation are used by powerless groups to gain political benefits while still working within the system.[8]

Unconventional Participation

On Sunday, March 7, 1965, a group of about six hundred people attempted to march 50 miles from Selma, Alabama, to the state capital at Montgomery. The marchers were demonstrating in favor of voting rights for blacks. (At the time, Selma had fewer than five hundred registered black voters, out of fifteen thousand who were eligible.)[9] Alabama Governor George Wallace declared the march illegal and sent state troopers to stop it. The two groups met at the Edmund Pettus Bridge over the Alabama River at the edge of Selma. The marchers were beaten and trampled by state troopers and deputy sheriffs (some on horseback) using clubs, bullwhips, and tear gas. The day became known as "Bloody Sunday."

The march from Selma was a form of unconventional political participation. Marching 50 miles in a political protest is certainly not common; moreover, the march challenged existing institutions, which had been preventing blacks from participating conventionally—voting in elections—for many decades.

Unlike some of the demonstrations against the Vietnam War somewhat later, this civil rights march posed no threat of violence. The brutal response to the marchers helped the rest of the nation realize the seriousness of the civil rights problem in the South. Unconventional participation is stressful and occasionally violent, but it is sometimes worth the risk.

Support for Unconventional Participation

Unconventional political participation has a long history in the United States. The Boston Tea Party in 1773 was only the first in a long line of violent protests against British rule that eventually led to revolution. Yet we know less about unconventional political participation than about conventional participation. The reasons are twofold. First, data on conventional means are easier to collect and so are more frequently studied. Second, political scientists are biased toward "institutionalized," or conventional, politics. In fact, some basic works on political participation explicitly exclude any behavior that is "outside the system."[10] One major study of unconventional political action asked people whether they had engaged in or approved of ten types of political participation outside of voting.[11] As shown in Figure 5.1, of the ten activities, only signing petitions was clearly regarded as conventional in the sense that the behavior is nearly universally approved and widely practiced.

There was a question about the conventionality of two other forms of behavior: lawful demonstrations and boycotts. The other political activities listed in Figure 5.1 are clearly unconventional. In fact, when political activities interfere with daily living (blocking traffic) or involve the destruction of property (painting slogans on walls, breaking windows) or physical violence, disapproval is nearly universal. Americans do not approve of unconventional political behavior. When protesters demonstrating against the Vietnam War disrupted the 1968 Democratic National Convention in Chicago, they were clubbed off the streets by the city's police. Although people saw graphic videotape of the confrontations, they condemned the demonstrators, not the police.

The Effectiveness of Unconventional Participation

Protests against war in the Persian Gulf did not prevent President Bush from ordering an attack against Iraq in 1991. Does unconventional participation ever work, especially when it provokes violence? Yes. For example, antiwar protesters discouraged President Lyndon Johnson from seeking re-election in 1968, and they heightened public concern over U.S. participation in the Vietnam War.

The unconventional activities of the civil rights workers also had notable success. Dr. Martin Luther King, Jr. led the 1955 Montgomery bus boycott that sparked the civil rights movement. He used **direct action**, assembling crowds to confront businesses and local governments, to demand equal treatment in public accommodations and government.

Denied opportunities for conventional political participation, members of the civil rights movement used unconventional politics to pressure Congress to pass a series of civil rights laws in 1957, 1960, 1964, and 1968—each one in some way extending federal protection against

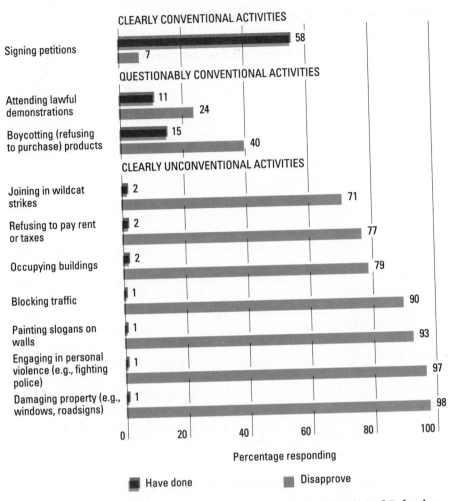

CLEARLY CONVENTIONAL ACTIVITIES

Signing petitions — 58 / 7

QUESTIONABLY CONVENTIONAL ACTIVITIES

Attending lawful demonstrations — 11 / 24

Boycotting (refusing to purchase) products — 15 / 40

CLEARLY UNCONVENTIONAL ACTIVITIES

Joining in wildcat strikes — 2 / 71

Refusing to pay rent or taxes — 2 / 77

Occupying buildings — 2 / 79

Blocking traffic — 1 / 90

Painting slogans on walls — 1 / 93

Engaging in personal violence (e.g., fighting police) — 1 / 97

Damaging property (e.g., windows, roadsigns) — 1 / 98

Percentage responding

■ Have done   ■ Disapprove

FIGURE 5.1 What Americans Think of as Unconventional Political Behavior
A survey of Americans asked whether they approved or disapproved of ten different forms of participation outside of the electoral process. The respondents disapproved of most of the ten forms, often overwhelmingly, although signing petitions was rarely disapproved of—and also widely done. But even attending lawful demonstrations (a right guaranteed in the Constitution) was disapproved of by 24 percent of the respondents and rarely practiced. Boycotting products was more objectionable but more widely practiced. Attending demonstrations and boycotting products are only marginally conventional. The other seven forms are clearly unconventional. From Political Action: Mass Participation in Five Western Democracies by Samuel H. Barnes and Max Kaase, eds. Reprinted by permission of Sage Publications.

discrimination by reason of race, color, religion, or national origin. (The 1964 act also prohibited discrimination in employment on the basis of sex.) In addition, the Voting Rights Act of 1965 put state electoral procedures under federal supervision, increasing the registration of black voters and the rate of black voter turnout, especially in the South. The history of the civil rights movement shows that social change can occur, even when it is violently opposed at first.

Although direct political action and the politics of confrontation can work, a special kind of commitment is needed to use them. Studies show that direct action appeals most to those who both (1) *distrust* the political system and (2) have a strong sense of political *efficacy*—the feeling that they can do something to affect political decisions.[12] Whether this combination of attitudes produces behavior that challenges the system depends on the extent of organized group activity.[13]

The decision to behave unconventionally also depends on the extent to which individuals develop a *group consciousness*—identification with the group and an awareness of its position in society, its objectives, and its intended course of action.[14] These factors were present among blacks and young people in the mid-1960s and are strongly present today among blacks and, to a lesser degree, among women.

Unconventional Participation in America

Although most Americans may disapprove of some forms of participation to protest government policies, our citizens are about as likely to take direct action in politics as are those in European democracies. Surveys in 1981 of citizens in Britain, Germany, and France found that Americans claim to "have done" as much or *more* in the way of unconventional behavior, such as participating in lawful demonstrations, joining in boycotts, and even engaging in personal violence.[15] Contrary to the popular view that Americans are apathetic about politics, a recent study suggested that they are more likely to engage in political protests of various sorts than are citizens in other democratic countries.[16]

Is there something wrong with our political system if citizens resort to unconventional, and widely disapproved, methods of political participation? To answer this question, we must first learn how much Americans use conventional methods of participation.

Conventional Participation

A practical test of the democratic nature of any government is whether citizens can affect its policies by acting through its institutions—meeting with public officials, supporting candidates, voting in elections, and so on. Citizens should not have to risk life and property to participate in politics, and they should not have to take direct action to force their views to be heard in government. The objective of democratic institutions is to make political participation *conventional*—to allow ordinary

L.A. Riots, 1992
At the extremes of unconventional political behavior are activities in which individuals with a group consciousness protest political actions through personal violence and the destruction of property. In at least some respects the 1992 riots in Los Angeles can be viewed as such behavior. In this photo two L.A. residents view the immediate results of that violence. Its long-term political results are yet to be determined.

citizens to engage in relatively routine, nonthreatening behavior to cause government to heed their opinions, interests, and needs.

The most visible form of conventional participation is voting to choose candidates. However, there are other important forms of conventional political participation. In fact, these other forms of participation are in many ways more important than voting, especially in the United States, where voter turnout is much lower than that in most other democratic nations. There are two major categories of conventional political behavior: actions that show support for government policies and actions that try to change or influence policies.

Supportive Behaviors

Supportive behaviors are actions that express allegiance to country and government. When we recite the Pledge of Allegiance or fly the American flag on holidays, we are showing support for the country and, by implication, its political system. These kinds of ceremonial activities usually require little initiative on the part of the citizen. The simple act of turning out to vote is in itself a show of support for the political system. Other supportive behaviors—for example, serving as an election judge in a nonpartisan election or organizing a holiday parade—demand greater initiative.

At times, people's perception of what constitutes patriotism moves them across the line from conventional to unconventional behavior. In their eagerness to support the American system, they break up a meeting or disrupt a rally of a group they believe is radical or somehow "un-American." Radical groups may threaten the political system with wrenching change, but superpatriots pose their own threat. Their misguided excess of allegiance denies nonviolent means of dissent to others.[17]

Influencing Behaviors

Influencing behaviors are used to modify or even reverse government policy to serve political interests. Some forms of influencing behavior seek particular benefits from government; other forms have broad policy objectives.

Particular benefits.   Some citizens try to influence government to obtain benefits for themselves, their immediate families, or their close friends. Serving one's own self-interest through the voting process is certainly acceptable to democratic theory. Each individual has only one vote, and no single voter can wangle particular benefits from government through voting unless a majority of voters agree.

Political actions that require considerable knowledge and initiative are another story, however. Individuals or small groups that influence government officials to advance their self-interests may benefit without others knowing about it. Those who quietly obtain particular benefits from government pose a serious challenge to a democracy. Pluralist theory holds that groups ought to be able to make government respond to their special problems and needs. Majoritarian theory, in contrast, holds that government should not do what a majority does not want it to do.

What might individual citizens or groups ask of their government, and how might they go about asking? Few people realize that using the court system is a form of political participation, a way for citizens to press their rights in a democratic society. Although most people use the courts to serve their particular interests, some also use them, as we discuss shortly, to meet broad objectives. Going to court demands high personal initiative,[18] a knowledge of the law, and the financial resources to hire a lawyer.

Some citizens ask for special services from their local government. Such requests may range from contacting the city forestry department to remove a dead tree in front of a house to calling the county animal control center to deal with a vicious dog in the neighborhood. Studies of such "contacting" behavior as a form of political participation find that it tends not to be related to other forms of political activity but is related to socioeconomic status: People of higher socioeconomic status are more likely to contact public officials.[19]

Americans demand much more of local government than of national government. Although many people value self-reliance and individualism in national politics, most people expect local government to solve a wide range of social problems. A study of residents of Kansas City, Missouri, found that more than 90 percent thought it was the city's responsibility to provide services in thirteen areas, including maintaining parks, setting standards for new home construction, demolishing vacant and unsafe buildings, ensuring that property owners clean up trash and weeds, and providing bus service. The researcher noted that "it is difficult to imagine a set of federal government activities about which there would necessarily be any more consensus—defense, environmental controls, and other areas."[20] Citizens can also mobilize against a project. The 1980s saw emergence of the "not in my back yard," or NIMBY, phenomenon, as citizens pressured local officials to stop undesirable projects from being located near their homes.

Finally, contributing money to a candidate's campaign is another form of influencing behavior. Here, too, the objective can be particular or broad benefits.

Several points emerge from this review of "particularized" forms of political participation. First, approaching government to serve one's particular interests is consistent with democratic theory because it encourages input from an active citizenry. Second, particularized contact may be a form of participation that is not necessarily related to other forms of participation. Third, such participation tends to be used more by citizens who are advantaged in terms of knowledge and resources. Fourth, particularized participation may serve private interests to the detriment of the majority.

Broad policy objectives. We come now to what many scholars have in mind when they talk about political participation: activities that influence the selection of government personnel and policies. Here, too, we find behaviors that require little initiative (such as voting) and high initiative (attending political meetings, persuading others how to vote). In the next section, we focus on elections as a mechanism for participation. For now, we simply note that voting to influence policy is usually a low-initiative activity. As we discuss later, it actually requires more initiative to *register* to vote in the United States than to cast a vote on election day.

Other types of participation to affect broad policies require high initiative. Running for office requires the most (see Chapter 6). Some high-initiative activities, such as attending party meetings and working in campaigns, are associated with the electoral process; others, such as attending legislative hearings and writing letters to Congress, are not. Studies of citizen contacts in the United States show that about two-thirds deal with broad social issues and only one-third are for private gain.[21]

As noted earlier, the courts can be used for both personal benefit and broad policy objectives. **Class-action suits** are brought by a person or group on behalf of other people in similar circumstances. Lawyers for the NAACP pioneered this form of litigation in the famous school desegregation case *Brown v. Board of Education* (1954).[22] They succeeded in getting the Supreme Court to outlaw segregation in public schools not just for Linda Brown, who brought suit in Topeka, Kansas, but also for all others "similarly situated"—that is, for all other black students who want to attend white schools. This form of participation has proved to be effective for organized groups, especially those that have been unable to gain their objectives through Congress or the president.

Individual citizens can also try to influence policies at the national level by direct participation in the legislative process. One way is to attend congressional hearings, which are public events occasionally held in various parts of the country. To facilitate citizen involvement, national government agencies are required to publish notices of regulations in the *Federal Register* (a list, published daily, of all proposed and approved regulations) and to make documents available to citizens on request.

Conventional Participation in America

How often do Americans contact government officials and engage in other forms of conventional political participation compared with citizens in other countries? The most common political behavior reported in a study of five countries was voting to choose candidates. Americans are *less* likely to vote than citizens in the other four countries. But Americans are as likely (or substantially more likely) to engage in all the other forms of conventional political participation, just as they are as likely or more likely to take part in unconventional behaviors. Americans, then, are more apt to engage in nearly all forms of unconventional *and* conventional political participation, *except* voting.

The researchers noted this paradox and wrote, "If, for example, we concentrate our attention on national elections we will find that the United States is the least participatory of our five nations." But looking at the other indicators, they found that "political apathy, by a wide margin, is lowest in the United States. Interestingly, the high levels of overall involvement reflect a rather balanced contribution of both . . . conventional and unconventional politics."[23] Clearly, low voter turnout in the United States constitutes something of a puzzle. We work at that puzzle, but first we focus on elections and electoral systems.

Participating Through Voting

The heart of democratic government lies in the electoral process. Whether a country holds elections and, if so, what kind constitute the critical differences between democratic and nondemocratic government. Elections are important to democracy for their potential to institutionalize mass participation in government according to the three normative principles for procedural democracy discussed in Chapter 1. Electoral rules specify (1) *who* is allowed to vote, (2) *how much* each person's vote counts, and (3) *how many* votes are needed to win.

Again, elections are formal procedures for making group decisions. **Voting** is the act that individuals perform when they choose among alternatives in an election. **Suffrage** and the **franchise** both mean "the right to vote." By formalizing political participation through rules for suffrage and counting ballots, electoral systems allow large numbers of people who individually have little political power to wield great power. Electoral systems decide collectively who governs and, in some instances, what government should do.

The simple fact of holding elections is less important than the specific rules and circumstances that govern voting. According to democratic theory, everyone should be able to vote. In practice, however, no nation grants universal suffrage. All countries have age requirements for voting, and all disqualify some inhabitants on various grounds: lack of citizenship, a criminal record, mental incompetence, and so forth. What is the record of enfranchisement in the United States?

Expansion of Suffrage

The United States was the first country to provide for general elections of representatives through "mass" suffrage, but the franchise was far from universal. When our Constitution was framed, the idea of full adult suffrage was too radical to be considered seriously, much less adopted. Instead, the framers left the issue of enfranchisement to the states, stipulating only that individuals who could vote for "the most numerous Branch of the State Legislature" could also vote for their representatives to the U.S. Congress (Article I, Section 2).

Initially, most states established taxpaying or property-holding requirements for voting, which limited political equality. Virginia, for example, required ownership of 25 acres of settled land or 500 acres of unsettled land. The original thirteen states began to lift these kinds of requirements after 1800. Expansion of the franchise accelerated after 1815, with the admission of new "western" states (Indiana, Illinois, Alabama), where land was more plentiful and widely owned. By the 1850s, virtually all taxpaying and property-holding requirements had been eliminated in all states, thereby allowing the working class to vote—at least its white male members. Extending the vote to blacks and women took more time.

The enfranchisement of blacks. The Fifteenth Amendment to the Constitution, adopted in 1870, prohibited the states from denying the right to vote "on account of race, color, or previous condition of servitude." However, the southern states of the old Confederacy worked around the amendment by re-establishing restrictive requirements (poll taxes, literacy tests) that worked against blacks. Also, the amendment said nothing about voting rights in private organizations, so blacks were denied the right to vote in the "private" Democratic primary elections held to choose the party's candidates for the general election. Because the Democratic party came to dominate politics in the South, the "white primary" effectively disenfranchised blacks despite the Fifteenth Amendment. Finally, in many areas of the South the threat of violence kept blacks from the polls.

The extension of full voting rights to blacks came in two phases separated by twenty years. In 1944, the Supreme Court decided in *Smith* v. *Allwright* that laws preventing blacks from voting in primary elections were unconstitutional, holding that party primaries were part of the continual process of electing public officials.[24] The Voting Rights Act of 1965, which followed Selma's Bloody Sunday by less than five months, suspended discriminatory voting tests against blacks. The act also authorized federal registrars to register voters in seven southern states, where fewer than one-half of the voting-age population had registered to vote in the 1964 election. For good measure, in 1966 the Supreme Court ruled in *Harper* v. *Virginia State Board of Elections* that state poll taxes are unconstitutional.[25] Although long in coming, these actions by the national government to enforce political equality within the states dramatically increased the registration of southern blacks.

The enfranchisement of women. Women also had to fight long and hard to win the right to vote. Until 1869, women could not vote anywhere—in the United States or in the rest of the world.[26] Women began to organize to obtain suffrage in the mid-1800s. Known then as suffragettes, these early feminists initially had a limited impact on politics. Their first victory did not come until 1869, when Wyoming, while still a territory, granted women the right to vote. No state followed suit until 1893, when Colorado enfranchised women.

Between 1896 and 1918, twelve other states gave women the vote. Most of these states were in the West, where pioneer women often departed from traditional women's roles. Nationally, the women's suffrage movement intensified, often resorting to unconventional political behaviors (marches, demonstrations), which occasionally invited violent attacks from men and even other women. In June 1919, Congress finally passed the Nineteenth Amendment to the Constitution, which prohibits states from denying the right to vote "on account of sex." The amendment was ratified in August 1920 in time for the November election.

The Fights for Women's Suffrage . . . and Against It
Young people and minorities are not the only groups who have resorted to unconventional means of political participation. In the late 1800s and early 1900s, women marched and demonstrated for equal voting rights, sometimes encountering strong opposition. Their gatherings were occasionally disrupted by men—and other women—who opposed extending the right to vote to women.

Evaluating the expansion of suffrage in America.   The last major expansion of suffrage in the United States took place in 1971, when the Twenty-sixth Amendment to the Constitution lowered the voting age to eighteen. For most of its history, then, the United States has been far from the democratic ideal of universal suffrage. However, compared with other countries, the United States looks pretty democratic.[27] Women did not gain the vote on equal terms with men until 1921 in Norway; 1922 in the Netherlands; 1944 in France; 1946 in Italy, Japan, and Venezuela; 1948 in Belgium; and 1971 in Switzerland. It is difficult to compare the enfranchisement of minority racial groups because most other democratic nations do not have this kind of racial division. We should, however, note that the indigenous Maori population in New Zealand won suffrage in 1867, but the aborigines in Australia were not fully enfranchised until 1961. And, of course, in notoriously undemocratic South Africa, blacks had no voting rights at all in national elections as late as 1993. With regard to voting age, nineteen of twenty-seven countries that allow free elections also have a minimum voting age of eighteen. None has a lower age.

Voting on Policies

Disenfranchised groups have struggled to gain voting rights because of the political power that comes with suffrage. Belief in the ability of ordinary citizens to make political decisions and to control government through the power of the ballot box was strongest in the United States during the Progressive Era, which began around 1900 and lasted until about 1925. **Progressivism** was a philosophy of political reform that trusted the goodness and wisdom of individual citizens and distrusted "special interests" (railroads, corporations) and political institutions (traditional political parties, legislatures).

The leaders of the Progressive movement were prominent politicians (former president Theodore Roosevelt, Senator Robert La Follette of Wisconsin) and eminent scholars (historian Frederick Jackson Turner, philosopher John Dewey). Not content to vote for candidates chosen by party leaders, the Progressives championed the **direct primary**—a preliminary election, run by the state government, in which the voters choose the party's candidates for the general election. Wanting a mechanism to remove elected candidates from office, the Progressives backed the **recall**—a special election initiated by a petition signed by a specified number of voters.

Progressives also relied on the voting power of the masses to propose and pass laws, thus approximating direct democracy—citizen participation in policymaking. They developed two voting mechanisms for policymaking that are still in use:

- A **referendum** is a direct vote by the people either on a proposed law or on an amendment to the state constitution. The issues subject to vote are known as **propositions**. About twenty-five states permit popular referenda on laws, and all but Delaware require a referendum on constitutional amendments. Most referenda are placed on the ballot by legislatures, not by voters.

- The **initiative** is a procedure by which voters can propose an issue to be decided by the legislature or by the people in a referendum. The procedure involves gathering a specified number of signatures from registered voters (usually 5 to 10 percent of the total in the state) and then submitting the petition to a designated state agency. About twenty states currently provide for some form of voter initiative.

One scholar estimates that there have been more than 17,000 referenda since 1898 and more than 2,300 between 1968 and 1978 alone.[28] There were almost 250 state issues on the ballots in each general election during the 1980s, although relatively few (usually less than 50) got there by the initiative.[29] In the 1992 election, however, citizens placed scores of initiatives on ballots in the 23 states that permit such direct lawmaking.[30]

What conclusion can we draw about the Progressives' legacy of mechanisms for direct participation in government? One scholar who studied the use of the initiative and referendum painted an unimpressive picture. He noted that an expensive "industry" developed in the 1980s that made money circulating petitions and then managing the large sums of money needed to run a campaign to approve (or defeat) a referendum.[31] In 1990, various industries conducted a $10 million campaign to defeat "Big Green," a sweeping environmental initiative that would have imposed restrictions on offshore drilling, pesticide use, and air pollutants.[32]

The money required to mount a statewide campaign has increased the involvement of special-interest groups in referendum politics. Moreover, most voters confess they do not know enough about most ballot propositions to vote intelligently on them. The 1990 election in California contained seventeen initiatives and constitutional amendments that were described in a ballot pamphlet more than 200 pages long.[33] Although another major study concluded that direct democracy devices "worked better at the state and local levels than most people realize," the study also proposed fourteen safeguards "to ensure that they serve the larger and longer-term public interest" at the state and local levels.[34] Noting that the United States was one of the few democracies that do not permit a national referendum, the study nevertheless opposed adopting the initiative and referendum at the national level.[35]

It is clear that citizens can exercise great power over government policy through the mechanisms of the initiative and referendum. What is not clear is whether these forms of direct democracy improve on the policies made by representatives elected for that purpose.

Voting for Candidates

We have saved for last the most visible form of political participation: voting to choose candidates for public office. Voting for candidates serves democratic government in two ways. First, it allows citizens to choose the candidates they think will best serve their interests. Second, voting allows the people to re-elect the officials about whom they guessed right and to kick out those about whom they guessed wrong. We look at the factors that underlie voting choice in Chapter 6. Here we examine Americans' reliance on the electoral process.

In national politics, voters seem content to elect just two executive officers—the president and vice president—and to trust the president to appoint a cabinet to round out his administration. But at the state and local levels, voters insist on selecting all kinds of officials. Every state elects a governor (and forty-two of them elect a lieutenant governor, too). Forty-three elect an attorney general; thirty-eight, a treasurer and

If It Moves in Office, Elect It

No other country requires its voters to make so many ballot decisions in a general election. Here is just a portion of the official ballot confronting voters in the city of Evanston at the 1990 election in Cook County, Illinois. It listed twenty-three different types of offices, from which voters were asked to choose forty-six separate candidates from 104 lines of names. In addition, voters were presented with the names of fifty-one lesser judges and asked to decide, yes or no, whether "each judge shall be retained in his present position." For good measure, the ballot also contained two countywide referenda and two city referenda. Most ballots in other states are comparably complex. If citizens feel unable to vote intelligently when facing such a ballot, they can hardly be blamed.

(continued)

a secretary of state; twenty-five, an auditor. The list goes on down through the superintendent of education, secretary of agriculture, controller, board of education, and public utilities commissioners.[36] Elected county officials commonly include a sheriff, a treasurer, a clerk, a superintendent of schools, and a judge (often several). Even at the local level, all but about 600 of 15,300 school boards across the nation are elected.[37] Instead of trusting state and local chief executives to appoint lesser administrators (as we do for more important offices at the national level), we expect voters to choose intelligently among scores of candidates they meet for the first time on a complex ballot in the polling booth (see Feature 5.1).

In the American version of democracy, our laws recognize no limit to voters' ability to make informed choices among candidates and thus to control government through voting. The reasoning seems to be that elections are good; therefore, more elections are better, and the most elections are best. By this thinking, the United States clearly has the best and most democratic government in the world because it is the undisputed champion at holding elections. The author of a study that compared elections in the United States with elections in twenty-six other democracies concluded:

> No country can approach the United States in the frequency and variety of elections, and thus in the amount of electoral participation to which its citizens have a right. No other country elects its lower house as often as every two years, or its president as frequently as every four years. No other country popularly elects its state governors and town mayors; no other has as wide a variety of nonrepresentative offices (judges, sheriffs, attorneys general, city treasurers, and so on) subject to election. . . .

Feature 5.1 (continued)

OFFICIAL BALLOT
GENERAL ELECTION
COOK COUNTY, ILLINOIS
TUESDAY, NOVEMBER 6, 1990

FOR UNITED STATES SENATOR			VOTE FOR ONE
REPUBLICAN	LYNN MARTIN	35	→
DEMOCRATIC	PAUL SIMON	36	→

FOR GOVERNOR AND LIEUTENANT GOVERNOR			VOTE FOR ONE GROUP
REPUBLICAN	GOVERNOR JIM EDGAR	LIEUTENANT GOVERNOR and BOB KUSTRA	38 →
DEMOCRATIC	GOVERNOR NEIL F. HARTIGAN	LIEUTENANT GOVERNOR and JAMES B. BURNS	39 →
ILLINOIS SOLIDARITY	GOVERNOR JESSIE FIELDS	LIEUTENANT GOVERNOR and MARISELLIS BROWN	40 →

FOR ATTORNEY GENERAL			VOTE FOR ONE
REPUBLICAN	JIM RYAN	42	→
DEMOCRATIC	ROLAND W. BURRIS	43	→

FOR SECRETARY OF STATE			VOTE FOR ONE
REPUBLICAN	GEORGE H. RYAN	45	→
DEMOCRATIC	JERRY COSENTINO	46	→

FOR COMPTROLLER			VOTE FOR ONE
REPUBLICAN	SUE SUTER	48	→
DEMOCRATIC	DAWN CLARK NETSCH	49	→

FOR TREASURER			VOTE FOR ONE
REPUBLICAN	GREG BAISE	51	→
DEMOCRATIC	PATRICK QUINN	52	→

VOTE FOR THREE	FOR TRUSTEES OF THE UNIVERSITY OF ILLINOIS	
← 27	REPUBLICAN	SUSAN LOVING GRAVENHORST
← 28	REPUBLICAN	RALPH CRANE HAHN
← 29	REPUBLICAN	JOHN G. HUFTALIN
← 30	DEMOCRATIC	GLORIA JACKSON BACON
← 31	DEMOCRATIC	TOM LAMONT
← 32	DEMOCRATIC	JOE LUCCO
← 33	ILLINOIS SOLIDARITY	MARTIN C. ORTEGA

FOR REPRESENTATIVE IN CONGRESS NINTH CONGRESSIONAL DISTRICT			VOTE FOR ONE
REPUBLICAN	HERBERT SOHN	60	→
DEMOCRATIC	SIDNEY R. YATES	61	→

VOTE FOR ONE	FOR STATE SENATOR SECOND LEGISLATIVE DISTRICT	
← 53	REPUBLICAN	BURLEIGH A. NETZKY
← 54	DEMOCRATIC	ARTHUR L. BERMAN

VOTE FOR ONE	FOR REPRESENTATIVE IN THE GENERAL ASSEMBLY FOURTH REPRESENTATIVE DISTRICT	
← 64	REPUBLICAN	JOAN W. BARR
← 65	DEMOCRATIC	JANICE D. (JAN) SCHAKOWSKY

VOTE FOR THREE	FOR COMMISSIONER OF THE METROPOLITAN WATER RECLAMATION DISTRICT (FULL 6 YEAR TERM)	
← 70	REPUBLICAN	KATHLEEN S. MICHAEL
← 71	REPUBLICAN	TERESA A. VALDES
← 72	REPUBLICAN	ESEQUIEL "ZEKE" IRACHETA
← 73	DEMOCRATIC	THOMAS S. FULLER
← 74	DEMOCRATIC	FRANK EDWARD GARDNER
← 75	DEMOCRATIC	KATHLEEN THERESE MEANY

FOR COUNTY CLERK OF COOK COUNTY			VOTE FOR ONE
REPUBLICAN	SAMUEL "SAM" PANAYOTOVICH	85	→
DEMOCRATIC	DAVID D. ORR	86	→
HAROLD WASHINGTON	HELDIA R. RICHARDSON	87	→

FOR TREASURER OF COOK COUNTY			VOTE FOR ONE
REPUBLICAN	THOMAS D. EILERS	91	→
DEMOCRATIC	EDWARD J. ROSEWELL	92	→
HAROLD WASHINGTON	CHARLES W. ALEXANDER	93	→

FOR SHERIFF OF COOK COUNTY			VOTE FOR ONE
REPUBLICAN	JAMES E. O'GRADY	100	→
DEMOCRATIC	MICHAEL F. SHEAHAN	101	→
ILLINOIS SOLIDARITY	WILLIAM M. PIECUCH, SR.	102	→
HAROLD WASHINGTON	TOMMY BREWER	103	→

VOTE FOR ONE	FOR SUPERINTENDENT OF EDUCATION SERVICE REGION	
← 82	REPUBLICAN	WILLIAM C. "BILL" MICELI
← 83	DEMOCRATIC	RICHARD J. MARTWICK
← 84	HAROLD WASHINGTON	DOROTHY C. HOGAN

VOTE FOR ONE	FOR ASSESSOR OF COOK COUNTY	
← 88	REPUBLICAN	RONALD BEAN
← 89	DEMOCRATIC	THOMAS C. HYNES
← 90	HAROLD WASHINGTON	DONALD PAMON

VOTE FOR TWO	FOR COMMISSIONER OF THE BOARD OF APPEALS OF COOK COUNTY	
← 94	REPUBLICAN	CHARLES A. WILSON
← 95	REPUBLICAN	GILBERT M. VEGA
← 96	DEMOCRATIC	WILSON FROST
← 97	DEMOCRATIC	JOSEPH BERRIOS
← 98	HAROLD WASHINGTON	WILL LAWRENCE
← 99	HAROLD WASHINGTON	KENNETH G. HOPKINS

FOR PRESIDENT OF THE COOK COUNTY BOARD			VOTE FOR ONE
REPUBLICAN	ALDO A. DeANGELIS	105	→
DEMOCRATIC	RICHARD J. PHELAN	106	→
HAROLD WASHINGTON	BARBARA J. NORMAN	107	→

FOR COUNTY COMMISSIONER OF COOK COUNTY			VOTE FOR SEVEN
REPUBLICAN	CARL R. HANSEN	111	→
REPUBLICAN	MARY M. McDONALD	112	→
REPUBLICAN	ALLAN C. CARR	113	→
REPUBLICAN	RICHARD A. SIEBEL	114	→
REPUBLICAN	ALDO A. DeANGELIS	115	→
REPUBLICAN	ANGELO "SKIP" SAVIANO	116	→
REPUBLICAN	HERBERT T. SCHUMANN, JR.	117	→
DEMOCRATIC	SHEILA H. SCHULTZ	118	→
DEMOCRATIC	THOMAS M. O'DONNELL	119	→
DEMOCRATIC	PATRICIA KANE McLAUGHLIN	120	→

The average American is entitled to do far more electing—probably by a factor of three or four—than the citizen of any other democracy.[38]

However, the United States ranks at the bottom of democratic countries in voter turnout![39] How do we square low voter turnout with Americans' devotion to elections as an instrument of democratic government? To complicate matters further, how do we square low voter turnout with the findings we talked about earlier, which establish the United States as the leader among five Western democratic nations in both conventional and unconventional political participation? Americans seem to participate at high levels in everything except elections.

Explaining Political Participation

As you have seen, political participation can be unconventional or conventional, can require little or much initiative, and can serve to support the government or influence its decisions. This section examines some factors that affect the more obvious forms of political participation, with particular emphasis on voting. Our first task is to determine how much variation there is in patterns of participation within the United States over time.

Patterns of Participation over Time

Have Americans become more politically apathetic? A study of several measures of participation from 1952 through 1988 showed a mixed pattern of participation over those years.[40] Participation was *stable* across time in the percentage of citizens who worked for candidates (3 to 6 percent), who attended party meetings (6 to 9 percent), and who persuaded people how to vote during presidential election years (29 to 35 percent). Interest in campaigns even *increased* across time by 8 to 10 percentage points. In spite of the sharp rise in voter turnout in 1992 (55 percent), participation has generally *decreased* over time when measured as voter turnout in presidential elections (dropping from 63 percent in 1952 to 50 percent in 1988). The plot has thickened. Not only is voter turnout low in the United States compared with that in other countries, but turnout has generally declined over time. Moreover, while voting has decreased, other forms of participation have increased. What is going on? Who votes? Who does not? Why? And does it really matter?

The Standard Socioeconomic Explanation

Researchers have found that socioeconomic status is a good indicator of most types of conventional political participation. People with more education, higher incomes, and white-collar or professional occupations tend to be more aware of the impact of politics on their lives, to know what can be done to influence government actions, and to have the necessary resources (time, money) to take action. So they are more likely to participate in politics than are people of lower socioeconomic status. This relationship between socioeconomic status and conventional political involvement is called the **standard socioeconomic model** of participation.[41]

Unconventional political behavior is less clearly related to socioeconomic status. Studies of unconventional participation in other countries have found that protest behavior is related to low socioeconomic status and especially to youth.[42] However, scattered studies of unconventional participation in the United States have found that protesters (especially blacks) are often higher in socioeconomic status than those who do not join in protests.[43]

Obviously, socioeconomic status does not account for all the differences in the ways people choose to participate in politics, even for conventional participation. Another important variable is age. As just noted, young people are more likely to take part in political protests, but they are less likely to participate in conventional politics. Voting rates tend to increase as people grow older until about age sixty-five, when physical infirmities begin to lower rates again.[44]

Two other variables—race and sex—have been related to participation in the past, but as times have changed, so have those relationships. Blacks, who had very low participation rates in the 1950s, now participate at rates comparable to whites when differences in socioeconomic status are taken into account.[45] Women also exhibited low participation rates in the past, but sex differences in political participation have virtually disappeared.[46] (The one exception is in attempting to persuade others how to vote, which women are less likely to do than men.)[47] Recent research on the social context of voting behavior has shown that married men and women are more likely to vote than those of either sex living without spouses.[48]

Of all the social and economic variables, education is the strongest single factor in explaining most types of conventional political participation. There is a striking relationship between level of formal education and various types of conventional political behaviors.[49] This strong link between education and electoral participation raises questions about low voter turnout in the United States both over time and relative to other democracies. The fact is that the proportion of individuals with college degrees is greater in the United States than in other countries. Moreover, that proportion has been increasing steadily. Why, then, is voter turnout in elections so low? And why is it dropping over time?

Low Voter Turnout in America

Voting is a low-initiative form of participation that can satisfy all three motives for political participation—showing allegiance to the nation, obtaining particularized benefits, and influencing broad policy. Yet with the exception of the 1992 election, voter turnout in the United States has steadily dropped since 1960, while other forms of participation have increased (see Figure 5.2). Americans participate as much or more than citizens of other countries in conventional and unconventional political behaviors. However, even with the sharp increase in turnout in the

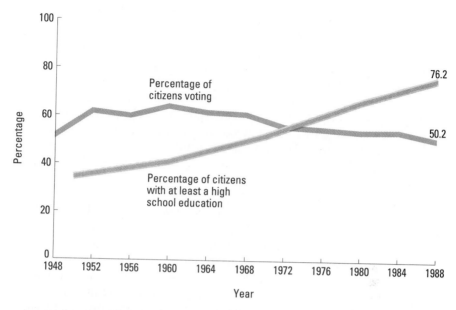

FIGURE 5.2   The Decline of Voting Turnout: An Unsolved Puzzle
Level of education is one of the strongest predictors of a person's likelihood of voting in the United States, and the percentage of citizens older than twenty-five with a high school education or more has grown steadily since the end of World War II. Nevertheless, the overall rate of voting turnout has gone down almost steadily in presidential elections since 1960. This phenomenon is recognized as an unsolved puzzle in American voting behavior. To be sure, voter turnout increased to 56 percent in 1992. Only time will tell whether that sharp rise was the beginning of a reversal of the trend. (Sources: "Percentage voting" data come from Michael Nelson, ed., Congressional Quarterly's Guide to the Presidency *[Washington, D.C.: Congressional Quarterly, 1989], p. 170; "percentage with four years of high school" data are for persons twenty-five years and older and come from the Bureau of the Census,* Statistical Abstract of the United States, 1990 *[Washington, D.C.: U.S. Government Printing Office, 1990], p. 133.)*

1992 election to 56 percent, Americans rank well below citizens of other countries in voter turnout. How do we explain the decline in voting within the United States over time and the low voter turnout in this country?

The decline in voting over time.   The sharpest drop in voter turnout (5 percentage points) occurred between the 1968 and 1972 elections.[50] It was during this period (in 1971, actually) that Congress proposed and the states ratified the Twenty-sixth Amendment to the Constitution, which expanded the electorate by lowering the voting age from twenty-one to eighteen. Because people under twenty-one are much less likely to vote, they actually reduced the overall national turnout rate (the percentage of those eligible to vote who actually vote). Some observers estimate that the enfranchisement of eighteen-year-olds accounts for about 1 or 2 percentage points in the total decline in turnout since 1952, but that still leaves more than 10 percentage points to be explained.[51]

Researchers have not been very successful in solving the puzzle of the decline in voting turnout since 1968.[52] Some scholars attribute most of the decline to changes in voters' attitudes toward politics. One major factor is the growing belief that government is not responsive to citizens and that voting does not do any good. Another is a change in attitude toward political parties, along with a decline in the sense of party identification.[53]

U.S. turnout versus turnout in other countries. Given the high level of education in the United States and the greater than usual participation in other forms of political activity, voter turnout is much lower than might be expected compared with that in other countries. Scholars cite two factors to explain the low percentage of voters in the United States. First, there are differences in voting laws and administrative machinery.[54] In a few countries, voting is compulsory, and, obviously, turnout is extremely high. But there are other ways to encourage voting— declaring election days to be public holidays, providing a two-day voting period, making it easy to cast absentee ballots. The United States does none of these things. Moreover, nearly every other democratic country places the burden of registration on the government rather than on the individual voter.

This is very important. Voting in the United States is a two-stage process, and the first stage—going to the proper officials to register—requires more initiative than the second stage—going to the polling booth to cast a ballot. In most American states, the registration process is separated from the voting process by both time (usually weeks in advance of the election) and geography (often at the county courthouse, not the polling place). Moreover, registration procedures are often obscure and require calling around to find out what to do. Furthermore, people who move (and roughly one-third of the U.S. population moves between presidential elections) must reregister. In short, although voting requires little initiative, registration usually requires high initiative. If we compute voter turnout on the basis of those who are registered to vote, then about 87 percent of Americans vote—a figure that moves the United States to the middle (but not the top) of all democratic nations.[55]

The second factor usually cited to explain low turnout in American elections is the lack of political parties that mobilize the vote of particular social groups, especially lower-class and less-educated people. American parties do make an effort to get out the vote, but neither party is as closely linked to specific groups as parties are in many other countries, where certain parties work hand in hand with ethnic, occupational, or religious groups. Research shows that strong party-group links can significantly increase turnout.[56]

To these explanations for low voter turnout in the United States—the burden of registration and the lack of strong party-group links—we add another. Although the act of voting requires low initiative, the process of learning about the scores of candidates on the ballot in American elections requires a great deal of initiative. Some people undoubtedly fail to vote simply because they feel inadequate to the task of deciding among candidates for the many offices on the ballot in U.S. elections.

Teachers, newspaper columnists, and public affairs groups tend to worry a great deal about low voter turnout in the United States, suggesting that it signifies some sort of political sickness—or at least that it gives us a bad mark for democracy. Others are less concerned.[57] Voter turnout is only one indicator of political participation, and Americans tend to do better according to most other indicators. Moreover, one scholar argued,

> Turnout rates do not indicate the amount of electing—the frequency of occasion, the range of offices and decisions, the "value" of the vote—to which a country's citizens are entitled. . . . Thus, although the turnout rate in the United States is below that of most other democracies, American citizens do not necessarily do less voting than other citizens; most probably, they do more.[58]

Participation and Freedom, Equality, and Order

As we have seen, Americans do participate in government in a variety of ways and to a reasonable extent, compared with citizens of other countries. What is the relationship of political participation to the values of freedom, equality, and order?

Participation and Freedom

From the standpoint of normative theory, the relationship between participation and freedom is clear. Individuals should be free to participate in government and politics the way they want and as much as they want. And they should be free *not* to participate as well. Ideally, all barriers to participation (such as restrictive voting registration and limitations on campaign expenditures) should be abolished, as should any schemes for compulsory voting.

In theory, freedom to participate also means that individuals should be able to use their wealth, connections, knowledge, organizational power (including sheer numbers in organized protests), or any other resource to influence government decisions, provided they do so legitimately. Of all these resources, the individual vote may be the weakest—and the least important—means of exerting political influence. Obviously, then, freedom as a value in political participation favors those with the resources to advance their own political self-interest.

America's Largest Civil Rights Demonstration
On August 28, 1963, more than 200,000 blacks and whites participated in a march on Washington, D.C., to rally for jobs and freedom. Martin Luther King, Jr., one of the march's leaders, delivered his electrifying "I Have a Dream" speech from the steps of the Lincoln Memorial. The demonstrators pressed for legislation ensuring full civil rights for blacks, and their leaders were welcomed at the White House by President John F. Kennedy.

Participation and Equality

The relationship between participation and equality is also clear. Each citizen's ability to influence government should be equal to that of every other citizen so that differences in personal resources do not work against the poor or otherwise disadvantaged. Elections, then, serve the ideal of equality better than any other means of political participation. Formal rules for counting ballots—in particular, one person, one vote—negate differences in resources among individuals.

At the same time, groups of people who have few individual resources can combine their votes to wield political power. This power was exercised in the late nineteenth and early twentieth centuries by various European ethnic groups whose votes won them entry into the sociopolitical system and allowed them to share in its benefits (see Chapter 4). More recently, blacks, Hispanics, homosexuals, and persons with handicaps have used their voting power to gain political recognition. However, minorities often have had to use unconventional forms of participation to win the right to vote. As two major scholars of political participation put it, "Protest is the great equalizer, the political action that weights intensity as well as sheer numbers."[59]

Participation and Order

The relationship between participation and order is complicated. Some types of participation (pledging allegiance, voting) promote order and so are encouraged by those who value order; other types promote disorder and so are discouraged. Even giving women the right to vote was resisted by many citizens (men and women alike) for fear of upsetting the social order, of altering the traditional roles of men and women.

Both conventional and unconventional participation can lead to the ouster of government officials, but the *regime*—the political system itself—is threatened more by unconventional participation. To maintain order, the government has a stake in converting unconventional participation into conventional participation whenever possible.

Think about the student unrest on college campuses during the Vietnam War, when thousands of protesting students stopped traffic, occupied buildings, destroyed property, and behaved in other unconventional ways. Confronted by such civil strife and disorder, Congress took action. On March 23, 1971, it passed and sent to the states the proposed Twenty-sixth Amendment, which would lower the voting age to eighteen. Three-quarters of the state legislatures had to ratify the amendment before it became part of the Constitution. Astonishingly, thirty-eight states (the required number) complied by July 1, establishing a new record for speedy ratification.[60]

Testimony by members of Congress before the Judiciary Committee stated that the eighteen-year-old vote was needed to "harness the energy of young people and direct it into useful and constructive channels," to keep students from becoming "more militant" and engaging "in destructive activities of a dangerous nature."[61] As one observer argued, the right to vote was extended to eighteen-year-olds, not because young people demanded it, but because "public officials believed suffrage expansion to be a means of institutionalizing youths' participation in politics, which would, in turn, curb disorder."[62]

Participation and the Models of Democracy

Ostensibly, elections are institutional mechanisms that implement democracy by allowing citizens to choose among candidates or issues. But elections also serve several other important purposes:[63]

- *Elections socialize political activity.* They transform what might otherwise consist of sporadic citizen-initiated acts into a routine public function. That is, the opportunity to vote for change encourages citizens to refrain from demonstrating in the streets. This helps preserve government stability by containing and channeling away potentially disruptive or dangerous forms of mass political activity.

- *Elections institutionalize access to political power.* They allow ordinary citizens to run for political office or to play an important role in selecting political leaders. Working to elect a candidate encourages the campaign worker to identify problems or propose solutions to the new official.

- *Elections bolster the state's power and authority.* The opportunity to participate in elections helps convince citizens that the government is responsive to their needs and wants, which increases its legitimacy.

Participation and Majoritarianism

Although the majoritarian model assumes that government responsiveness to popular demands comes through mass participation in politics, majoritarianism does not view participation broadly. It favors conventional, institutionalized behavior of a narrow form—primarily, voting in elections. Because majoritarianism relies on counting votes to determine what the majority wants, it is strongly biased toward the political equality of citizens in political participation. Favoring collective decisions formalized through elections, majoritarianism offers little opportunity for motivated, resourceful individuals to exercise private influence over government actions.

Majoritarianism also blunts individual freedom in another way. By focusing on voting as the major means of mass participation, majoritarianism narrows the scope of conventional political behavior. In this way, the mechanisms for participation in the majoritarian model restrict freedom by defining what political action is "orderly" and acceptable. By favoring equality and order in political participation, majoritarianism goes hand in hand with the ideological orientation of populism (see Chapter 1).

Participation and Pluralism

Resourceful citizens who want the government's help with problems find a haven in the pluralist model of democracy. A decentralized and organizationally complex form of government allows many points of access and is well suited to various forms of conventional participation aside from voting. For example, wealthy people and well-funded groups can afford to hire lobbyists to press their interests in Congress. In one view of pluralist democracy, citizens are free to ply and wheedle public officials to further selfish visions of the public good. From another viewpoint, pluralism offers citizens the opportunity to be treated as individuals when dealing with the government, to influence policymaking in special circumstances, and to fulfill (insofar as is possible in representative government) their social potential through participation in community affairs.

Summary

To have "government by the people," the people must participate in politics. Conventional forms of participation—contacting officials and voting in elections—come most quickly to mind. However, citizens can also participate in politics in unconventional ways—staging sit-down strikes in public buildings, blocking traffic, and so on. Most citizens disapprove of most forms of unconventional political behavior. Yet unconventional tactics have won blacks and women important political and legal rights, including the right to vote.

People are motivated to participate in politics for various reasons: to show support for their country, to obtain particularized benefits for themselves or their friends, or to influence broad public policy. Their political actions may require very little political knowledge or personal initiative, or a great deal of both.

The press often paints an unflattering picture of political participation in America. Clearly the proportion of the electorate that votes in general elections in the United States is dropping and is far below that in other nations. When compared with other nations on a broad range of conventional and unconventional political behavior, however, the United States tends to show as much or more citizen participation in politics. Voter turnout in the United States suffers by comparison with that in other nations because of differences in voter registration here and elsewhere. We also lack institutions (especially strong political parties) that increase voter registration and help bring those of lower socioeconomic status to the polls.

The tendency to participate in politics is strongly related to socioeconomic status. Education, one component of socioeconomic status, is the single strongest predictor of conventional political participation in the United States. Because of the strong effect of socioeconomic status on political participation, the political system is potentially biased toward the interests of higher-status people. Pluralist democracy, which provides many avenues for resourceful citizens to influence government decisions, tends to increase this potential bias.

Majoritarian democracy, which relies heavily on elections and the concept of one person, one vote, offers citizens without great personal resources the opportunity to control government decisions through elections. However, elections also serve to legitimize government simply by involving the masses in government through voting. Whether the vote means anything depends on the nature of the voters' choices in elections. The range of choice is a function of the nation's political parties, the topic of the next chapter.

Key Terms

elections
political participation
conventional participation

unconventional participation
direct action
supportive behaviors

influencing behaviors
class-action suits
voting
suffrage
franchise
progressivism

direct primary
recall
referendum
propositions
initiative
standard socioeconomic model

Selected Readings

Cloward, Richard, and Frances Fox Piven. *Why Americans Don't Vote.* New York: Pantheon, 1988. This is an in-depth analysis of voting and registration regulations that exclude citizens from voting.

Conway, M. Margaret. *Political Participation in the United States.* 2d ed. Washington, D.C.: Congressional Quarterly Press, 1990. Here is an excellent review of survey data on conventional political participation.

Cronin, Thomas E. *Direct Democracy: The Politics of Initiative, Referendum, and Recall.* Cambridge, Mass.: Harvard University Press, 1989. This sweeping study of three mechanisms of direct democracy uses data from a national survey of citizens commissioned specifically for this study.

Dalton, Russell J. *Citizen Politics in Western Democracies.* Chatham, N.J.: Chatham House, 1988. This book studies public opinion and behavior in the United States, Britain, Germany, and France. Two chapters compare conventional citizen action and protest politics in these countries.

Gant, Michael M., and Norman R. Luttbeg. *American Electoral Behavior: 1952–1988.* Itasca, Ill.: F. E. Peacock, 1991. Chapter 3 provides a concise, up-to-date analysis of trends in political participation in the United States.

Ginsberg, Benjamin. *Politics by Other Means: The Declining Importance of Elections in America.* New York: Basic Books, 1990. Ginsberg contends that a deadlock has occurred in the electoral arena and that political struggles have been waged outside of elections.

Jennings, M. Kent, Jan W. van Deth et al. *Continuities in Political Action: A Longitudinal Study of Political Orientations in Three Western Democracies.* New York: Walter de Gruyter, 1990. The three democracies are the United States, West Germany, and the Netherlands. This study also compares political participation across time, drawing on panel studies in the 1970s and the 1980s.

LeMay, Michael C. *The Struggle for Influence: The Impact of Minority Groups on Politics and Public Policy in the United States.* Lanham, Md.: University Press of America, 1985. The subtitle describes the book well; it discusses women and religious groups as well as virtually all racial and European ethnic groups.

Marone, James A. *The Democratic Wish: Popular Participation and the Limits of American Government.* New York: Basic Books, 1990. This reflective study argues that in the search for more direct democracy, Americans have built up a weaker but more bureaucratic and intrusive government.

Sharp, Elaine B. *Citizen Demand-Making in the Urban Context.* Huntsville: University of Alabama Press, 1986. The author interviewed thousands of residents of Kansas City, Missouri, about their contacts with local government.

Teixeira, Ruy A. *Why Americans Don't Vote: Turnout Decline in the United States, 1960–1984.* Westport, Conn.: Greenwood Press, 1987. This is a quantitative study of the demographic and political factors that explain voter turnout.

Verba, Sidney, and Norman H. Nie. *Participation in America: Political Democracy and Social Equality.* New York: Harper and Row, 1972. This classic study of political participation analyzes data from surveys of citizens and political leaders.

Zimmerman, Joseph F. *Participatory Democracy: Populism Revived.* New York: Praeger, 1986. This is a comprehensive review of the town meeting and the mechanisms (referendum, initiative, recall) that approximate direct democracy.

POLITICAL PARTIES, CAMPAIGNS, AND ELECTIONS

6

During the early summer of 1992, H. Ross Perot threw a scare into the Republican and Democratic parties. A prominent, successful, and outspoken businessman, Perot told talk-show host Larry King on CNN in February that he would run for president if his name was placed on the ballot in all fifty states. Perot's challenge struck a chord with citizens who did not like George Bush or any of the Democratic candidates seeking the nomination. Thousands of citizens called in to volunteer their assistance. By March 23, Perot volunteers had placed his name on the ballot in Tennessee. By May, he was on the ballot in five other states, and by June on several more. Perot volunteers had put his name on some thirty states by July and on all fifty by mid-September.

Perot's candidacy also enjoyed broad support among the general electorate. In a Gallup poll of voters' preferences taken in early June, Perot led with 39 percent, compared with 31 percent for Bush and 25 percent for Clinton.[1] At that time, many people believed that the race for the presidency would narrow into a two-way contest between Perot and Bush, leaving the Democratic candidate a dismal third. But most informed observers thought that Perot's candidacy would fade as the election approached and that Bush and Clinton between them would take most of the votes in the election.

The Populist Billionaire

H. Ross Perot promised to buy the presidency for the American people, and he made a valiant effort. Perot spent over $60 million and won nearly 20 percent of the popular vote, but he failed to carry a single state and won no electoral votes. Nevertheless, he profoundly affected the 1992 presidential campaign and the election outcome. His hard-hitting attacks on President Bush complemented Clinton's campaign, and Perot's snappy style played well on television and helped raise voting turnout to 55 percent, the highest level since 1972.

Given the boom for Perot in early summer, why did knowledgeable observers dismiss his ability to win? There are two reasons. First, there was the example of a similar independent candidacy more than a decade earlier. In the late spring of 1980, John Anderson, a Republican leader in Congress, ran for president as an independent. The country's mood was much like that in 1992. In announcing his candidacy, Anderson answered the charge that he would be only a spoiler: "What's to spoil? The chances of two men whom at least half of the country does not want?"[2] Like Perot, Anderson was very popular in early June, when he was favored by 26 percent of the voters.[3] Like Perot, Anderson's dedicated volunteers placed him on the ballot in all fifty states. But Anderson's support eroded as the election drew near, and he won less than 7 percent of the popular vote—failing to carry a single state.

The second reason is related to the first. Perot (like Anderson) was doomed to failure as an independent candidate because of the strength of America's two-party system. The Democratic and Republican parties have dominated national and state politics in the United States for more than 125 years. Their domination is more complete than that of any other pair of parties in any other democratic government. Indeed, very few democracies even have a two-party system (Britain and New Zealand being the most notable exceptions), although all have some form of multiparty politics. Why does the United States have political parties? What functions do they perform? How did the United States become a nation of Democrats and Republicans? Do these parties truly differ in their platforms and behavior? Are parties really necessary for democratic government, or do they just interfere in the relationship between citizens and government? In this chapter, we answer these questions with an examination of political parties, perhaps the most misunderstood element in American politics.

And what of the election campaigns conducted by the two major parties? In this chapter, we also consider how those campaigns have changed over time, how candidates get nominated in the United States, what factors are important in election campaigns, and why voters choose one candidate over another. Beyond that, we address these important questions: What roles do political parties play today in campaigns and nominations? Do election campaigns function more to inform or to discourage voters? How important is money in conducting a winning election campaign? What are the roles of party identification, issues, and candidate attributes in influencing voters' choices and thus election outcomes? How do campaigns, elections, and parties fit into the majoritarian and pluralist models of democracy?

Political Parties and Their Functions

According to democratic theory, the primary means by which citizens control their government is voting in free elections. Most Americans agree that voting is important: Of those surveyed after a recent presidential campaign, 86 percent felt that elections made the government "pay attention to what the people think."[4] However, Americans are not nearly as supportive of the role played by political parties in elections. An overwhelming majority (73 percent) surveyed in 1980 believed that "the best way to vote is to pick a candidate regardless of party label." A clear majority (56 percent) thought that "parties do more to confuse the issues than to provide a clear choice on issues." In fact, 49 percent took the extreme position: "It would be better if in all elections, we put no party labels on the ballot."[5]

Nevertheless, Americans are quick to condemn as "undemocratic" countries that do not hold elections contested by political parties. In truth, Americans have a love-hate relationship with political parties. They believe that parties are necessary for democratic government; at the same time, they think parties are somehow "obstructionist" and not to be trusted. This distrust is particularly strong among younger voters. To better appreciate the role of political parties in democratic government, we must understand exactly what parties are and what they do.

Definitions

A **political party** is an organization that sponsors candidates for political office *under the organization's name*. The italicized part of this definition is important. True political parties **nominate** candidates for election to public office by designating individuals as official candidates of the party. This function distinguishes the Democratic and Republican parties from interest groups. The AFL-CIO and the National Association of Manufacturers are interest groups. They often support candidates in various ways, but they do not nominate them to run as their avowed representatives. If they do, the interest groups become transformed into political parties. In short, it is the giving and accepting of a political label by organization and candidate that defines an organization as a party.

Most democratic theorists agree that a modern nation-state could not practice democracy without at least two political parties that regularly contest elections. In fact, the link between democracy and political parties is so close that many people define democratic government in terms of competitive party politics.

Party Functions

Parties contribute to democratic government through the functions they perform for the **political system**—the set of interrelated institutions that links people with government. Four of the most important party functions are nominating candidates for election to public office, structuring the voting choice in elections, proposing alternative government programs, and coordinating the actions of government officials.

Nominating candidates. Political parties contribute to democratic government simply by nominating candidates for election to public office. In the absence of parties, voters would be confronted with a bewildering array of self-nominated candidates, each seeking a narrow victory over others on the basis of personal friendships, celebrity status, or name. Parties can provide a form of quality control for their nominees through the process of *peer review*. Party insiders, the nominees' peers, usually know potential candidates much better than the average voter does, and candidates are judged by their peers for acceptability as the party's representatives.

In nominating candidates, parties often do more than pass judgment on potential office seekers; sometimes they go so far as to recruit talented individuals to become party candidates. In this way, parties help not only to ensure a minimum level of quality among candidates who run for office but also to raise the quality of those candidates.

Structuring the voting choice.   Political parties also help democratic government by structuring the voting choice—reducing the number of candidates on the ballot to those who have a realistic chance of winning. Established parties—those that have contested elections in the past—acquire a following of loyal voters who guarantee the party's candidates a predictable base of votes. This has the effect of discouraging nonparty candidates from running for office and new parties from forming. Consequently, the realistic choice is between candidates offered by the major parties. This choice focuses the election on the contest between parties and on candidates with established records, which reduces the amount of new information that voters need to make a rational decision.

Proposing alternative government programs.   Parties also help voters choose candidates by proposing alternative programs of government action—general policies that party candidates will pursue if they win control of government. Even if voters know nothing about the qualities of the parties' candidates, they can vote rationally for candidates of the party that stands closest to the policies they favor. The specific policies advocated in an election campaign vary from candidate to candidate and from election to election. However, candidates of the same party tend to favor policies that fit their party's underlying political philosophy, or ideology. In many countries, party labels, such as "conservative" and "socialist," reflect their political stance.

Although the Democrats and Republicans have issue-neutral names, many minor parties in the United States have used their names to advertise their policies: the Prohibition party, the Farmer-Labor party, and the Socialist party, for example. The neutrality of the names of the two major parties suggests that they are also undifferentiated in their policies. This is not true. They regularly adopt very different policies in their platforms, a fact discussed at length later.

Coordinating the actions of government officials.   Finally, party organizations help coordinate the actions of public officials. A government based on the separation of powers, like that of the United States, divides responsibilities for making public policy. The president and the leaders of the House and Senate are not required to cooperate with one another. Political party organizations are the major means for bridging the separation of powers, for producing coordinated policies that can govern the country effectively.

A History of U.S. Party Politics

The two major U.S. parties are among the oldest in the world. In fact, the Democratic party, founded in 1828 but with roots reaching back into the late 1700s, has a strong claim to being the oldest party in existence. Its closest rival is the British Conservative party, formed in 1832, two decades before the Republican party was organized, in 1854. Both the Democratic and Republican parties have been supported by several generations of citizens and are part of American history. They have become *institutionalized* in our political process.

The Emergence of the Party System

Today we think of party activities as normal, even essential, to American politics. It was not always so. The Constitution makes no mention of political parties, and none existed when the Constitution was written in 1787. Instead, it was common to refer to groups pursuing some common political interest as *factions*. Although factions were seen as inevitable in politics, they were also considered dangerous. One argument for adopting the Constitution—proposed in "Federalist No. 10" (see Chapter 2)—was that its federal system would prevent factional influences from controlling the government.

The debate over ratification of the Constitution produced two factions. Those who backed the Constitution were loosely known as "federalists"; their opponents, as "antifederalists." At this stage, the groups could not be called parties because they did not sponsor candidates for election. We can classify George Washington as a federalist because he supported the Constitution, but he was not a factional leader and actually opposed factional politics. During Washington's administration, however, the political cleavage sharpened between those who favored a stronger national government and those who wanted a less powerful, more decentralized national government.

The first group, led by Alexander Hamilton, proclaimed themselves *Federalists*. The second group, led by Thomas Jefferson, called themselves *Republicans*.* Disheartened by the political split in his administration, Washington spoke out against "the baneful effects" of parties in his farewell address in 1796. However, the party concept was already firmly entrenched in the political system. For the most part, two major political parties have competed for political power from that time to the present.

---

* Although they used the same name, they were not Republicans as we know them today. Indeed, Jefferson's followers were later known as Democratic Republicans, and in 1828 a wing of that party became the Democratic party.

The Present Party System: Democrats and Republicans

By the 1820s, the Federalists were no more. In 1828, the Democratic Republican party split in two. One wing, led by Andrew Jackson, became the Democratic party; the other later joined forces with several minor parties and formed the Whig party, which lasted for two decades.

In the early 1850s, antislavery forces (including Whigs, Free Soilers, and antislavery Democrats) began to organize. They formed a new party, the Republican party, to oppose the extension of slavery into the Kansas and Nebraska territories. It is this party, founded in 1854, that continues as today's Republican party.

The Republican party contested its first presidential election in 1856. Although it was an entirely new party, it took 33 percent of the vote. Moreover, its candidate (John Fremont) carried eleven states—all in the North. Then, in 1860, the Republicans nominated Abraham Lincoln and successfully confronted a Democratic party that was deeply divided over the slavery issue.

Lincoln's victory in 1860 is considered the first of three critical elections during the present party system.[6] A **critical election** produces a sharp change in the existing patterns of party loyalties among groups of voters. Moreover, this change in voting patterns, which is called an **electoral realignment**, lasts through several subsequent elections.[7] When one party in a two-party system regularly enjoys support from most of the voters, it is called the **majority party**; the other is called the **minority party**.

The election of 1860 divided the country between the Northern states, which mainly voted Republican, and the Southern states, which were overwhelmingly Democratic. The victory of the North over the South in the Civil War cemented Democratic loyalties in the South, particularly following the withdrawal of federal troops after the 1876 election. For forty years, from 1880 to 1920, no Republican presidential candidate won even one of the eleven states of the Confederacy.

A second critical election, in 1896, transformed the Republican party into a true majority party when, in opposition to the Democrats' inflationary free silver platform, a link was forged between the Republican party and business. Voters in the heavily populated Northeast and Midwest surged toward the Republican party—many of them permanently.[8]

A third critical election occurred in 1932 when Franklin Delano Roosevelt led the Democratic party to majority party status by uniting southern Democrats, northern urban workers, middle-class liberals, Catholics, Jews, and white ethnic minorities in the "Roosevelt coalition." (The relatively few blacks who voted at that time tended to remain loyal to the Republicans—the "party of Lincoln.") Democrats have maintained virtually continuous control of Congress since that time.

However, today there are strong signs that the coalition of Democratic voters forged by Roosevelt in the 1930s has cracked. Certainly the

South is no longer solidly for the Democrats. Since 1952, in fact, it has voted more consistently for Republican presidential candidates than for Democrats. The party system in the United States does not seem to be undergoing another realignment; rather, it seems to be in a period of **electoral dealignment**, in which party loyalties have become less important in the decisions of voters when they cast their ballots. We examine the influence of party loyalty on voting later in this chapter.

The American Two-Party System

The critical election of 1860 established the Democratic and Republican parties as the major parties in our two-party system. In a **two-party system**, most voters are so loyal to one or the other of the major parties that candidates from a third party—which means any minor party— have little chance of winning office. Certainly that is true in presidential elections, as H. Ross Perot found out. When third-party candidates do win, they are most likely to win offices at the local or state level. Since the present two-party system was established, relatively few minor-party candidates have won election to the U.S. House, very few have won election to the Senate, and *none* has won the presidency. However, we should not ignore the special contributions of certain minor parties, among them the Anti-Masonic party, the Populists, and the Progressives of 1912. In this section, we study the fortunes of third parties in American politics. We also look at why the United States has just two major parties, explain how federalism helps the parties survive, and describe voters' loyalties toward the major parties today.

Minor Parties in America

Minor parties have always figured in party politics in America. The National Unity campaign that promoted John Anderson's candidacy in 1980 and the United We Stand organization that backed Perot in 1992 should not be regarded as parties, for both candidates ran as independents in most states. Most of the true minor parties in our political history have been one of four types: bolter parties, farmer-labor parties, parties of ideological protest, and single-issue parties.[9]

- **Bolter parties** are formed from factions that have split off from one of the major parties. Six times in thirty presidential elections since the Civil War, disgruntled leaders, such as Teddy Roosevelt in 1912 and George Wallace in 1968, have "bolted the ticket" and challenged their former parties.

- **Farmer-labor parties** represent farmers and urban workers who believe that they, the working class, are not getting their share of society's wealth. The People's party, founded in 1892 and nicknamed the Populist party, was a prime example of a farmer-labor party.

- **Parties of ideological protest** go further than farmer-labor parties in criticizing the established system. These parties reject prevailing doctrines and propose radically different principles, often favoring more government activism. The Socialist party has been the most successful party of ideological protest. However, in recent years the sound of ideological protest has been heard more from rightist parties arguing for the radical disengagement of government from society. Such is the program of the Libertarian party, which stresses freedom over order and equality.

- **Single-issue parties** are formed to promote one principle, not a general philosophy of government. The Prohibition party, the most durable example of a single-issue party, opposed the consumption of alcoholic beverages. The party has run candidates in every presidential election since 1884.

Third parties, then, have been formed primarily to express discontent with the choices offered by the major parties and to work for their own objectives within the electoral system.[10] How have they fared? As *vote getters*, minor parties have not performed well, with two exceptions. First, bolter parties have twice won more than 10 percent of the vote; no other type has ever won as much. Second, the Republican party originated in 1854 as a single-issue third party opposed to slavery in new territories; in its first election, in 1856, the party came in second, displacing the Whigs. (Undoubtedly, the Republican exception to the rule has inspired the formation of other hopeful third parties.)

As *policy advocates*, minor parties have a slightly better record. At times, they have had a real effect on the policies adopted by the major parties. Women's suffrage, the graduated income tax, and the direct election of senators all originated in third parties.[11]

Most important, minor parties function as *safety valves*. They allow those who are unhappy with the status quo to present their policies within the system, to contribute to the political dialogue. Although not representing a third party, Ross Perot's candidacy and his 19 percent of the vote also allowed many voters to blow off steam in 1992. If minor parties indicate discontent, what should we make of the numerous minor parties—including the Libertarian, Workers', and Prohibition parties—in the 1992 election? Not much. Minor parties collected less than 1 percent of the vote. The number of third parties that contest elections is much less important than the total number of votes they receive.

Why a Two-Party System?

The history of party politics in the United States is essentially the story of two parties alternating control of the government. With relatively few exceptions, elections for national office and for most state and local offices are conducted within the two-party system. This pattern is unusual in democratic countries, where multiparty systems are more common. Why does the United States have only two major parties? The two most convincing answers to this question stem from the electoral system in the United States and the process of political socialization here.

In the typical U.S. election, one office is contested by two or more candidates and is won by the single candidate who collects the most votes. When these two principles of (1) *single winners* chosen by (2) a *simple plurality* of votes are used to elect the members of a legislature, the system is known as **majority representation**. Think about the way the states choose representatives to Congress. If a state is entitled to ten representatives, the state is divided into ten congressional districts, and one representative is elected by a majority of voters in each district. Majority representation of voters through *single-member districts* is also employed in most state legislatures. Alternatively, a legislature might be chosen through a system of **proportional representation**, which awards legislative seats to a party in proportion to the vote it won in elections. Under this system, the state might have a single statewide election for all ten seats, with each party presenting a list of ten candidates. Voters could vote for the entire party list they preferred, and candidates would be elected from the top of each list, according to the proportion of votes won by the party.

Although this form of election may seem strange, it is used in many democratic countries. Proportional representation tends to produce (or to perpetuate) several parties, each of which has enough voting strength nationwide to elect some minimum number of candidates on its party list. In contrast, the U.S. system of single winners by simple plurality vote forces groups in society to work within one of the only two parties with any realistic chance of winning an election. Therefore, the system tends to produce only two parties.

The rules of the U.S. electoral system may explain why only two parties tend to form in specific election districts. But why do the *same* two parties (Democratic and Republican) operate within each state? The contest for the presidency is the key to this question. The presidential election can be won only by the single candidate who wins a majority of electoral votes across the entire nation. Presidential candidates must win votes under the same label in each state so that they can pool their states' electoral votes to win in the electoral college. The presidency is a big enough prize to produce uncomfortable coalitions of voters (southern white Protestants allied with northern Jews and blacks in the Democratic party, for example) just to win the electoral vote and the presidential election.

The American electoral system may force party politics into a two-party mold, but why must the same parties *reappear* from election to election? Why do the Democrats and Republicans persist? This is where *political socialization* comes into play. These two parties persist simply because they have persisted. After more than one hundred years of political socialization, the two parties today have such a head start

The Democratic Party of Virginia

Wild about Wilder

In November 1989, Democrat L. Douglas Wilder was elected governor of Virginia by a margin of less than one-half of 1 percent of the vote. He became the nation's first elected black governor. Wilder's victory demonstrates the federal structure of the party system: One party may win executive office at the national level, while another party wins executive offices at the state level. Currently, approximately 60 percent of the nation's governors are Democrats.

in structuring the vote that they discourage challenges from new parties.

The Federal Basis of the Party System

Studying the history of American parties by focusing on contests for the presidency is convenient and informative. It also oversimplifies party politics to the point of distortion. In a party's darkest defeats for the presidency, it can still claim many victories for state offices. These victories outside the arena of presidential politics give each party a base of support that keeps its machinery oiled and running for the next contest.

The Republican victory in the 1984 presidential election helps illustrate how the states serve as a refuge for parties defeated for the presidency. Ronald Reagan swept forty-nine states in 1984—winning in every state but Minnesota, the home of his opponent, Walter Mondale.

Even in the wake of Reagan's stunning victory, however, the Democrats kept control of the House of Representatives. They wound up with thirty-four state governorships to the Republicans' sixteen (unchanged from before the election) and 65 percent of the state legislatures. They controlled the governorship, the upper house, and the lower house in eighteen states, compared to only four states for the Republicans.[12]

Reagan's victory in 1980, his 1984 landslide, and Bush's win in 1988 suggested that the Democrats might have been doomed to extinction in presidential politics. Perhaps in an earlier time, when the existing parties were not so well institutionalized, that would have been so. However, the Democratic party was able to remain alive and thrive within most states in our federal system. The separation of state politics from national trends affords each party a chance to lick its wounds after a presidential election debacle, return to campaign optimistically in the next election, and even win—as Bill Clinton did in 1992.

Party Identification in America

The concept of **party identification** is one of the most important in political science. It refers to the voter's sense of psychological attachment to a party, which is not the same thing as voting for the party in any given election. Scholars measure party identification simply by asking, "Do you usually think of yourself as a Republican, a Democrat, an independent, or what?"[13] Voting is a behavior; identification is a state of mind. For example, millions of southerners voted for Dwight Eisenhower for president in 1952 and 1956, although they still considered themselves Democrats.

The proportions of self-identified Republicans, Democrats, and independents (no party attachment) in the electorate since 1952 are shown in Figure 6.1. Three significant points stand out.

- The proportion of Republicans and Democrats combined far exceeds the proportion of independents in every year.
- The proportion of Democrats consistently exceeds that of Republicans.
- The proportion of Democrats has shrunk somewhat over time, to the benefit of both Republicans and independents.

Although a sense of party identification predisposes citizens to vote for their favorite party, other factors may cause voters to choose the opposition candidate. If they vote against their party often enough, they may rethink their party identification and eventually switch. Apparently, this rethinking has gone on in the minds of many southern Democrats over time. In 1952, about 70 percent of white southerners thought of themselves as Democrats, and fewer than 20 percent thought of themselves as Republicans. In 1988, white southerners were only 37 percent Democratic, 25 percent Republican, and 38 percent independ-

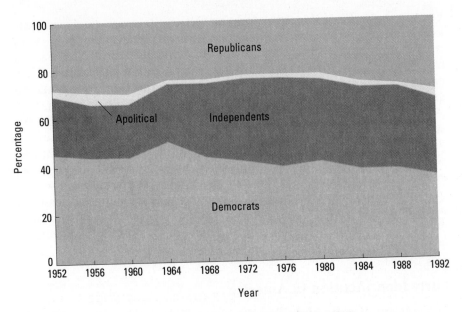

FIGURE 6.1   *Distribution of Party Identification, 1952–1992*
*In every presidential election since 1952, voters across the nation have been
asked, "Generally speaking, do you usually think of yourself as a Republican,
a Democrat, an independent, or what?" Most voters readily admit to thinking
of themselves as either Republicans or Democrats, but the proportion of those
who think of themselves as independents has increased over time. The Democrats' status as the majority party has also lessened over time. Nevertheless,
most Americans today still identify with one of the two major parties, and
there are still more Democrats than Republicans. (Sources: Warren E. Miller, Arthur H. Miller, and Edward J. Schneider,* American National Election Studies Data
Sourcebook, 1952–1978 *[Cambridge, Mass.: Harvard University Press, 1980, 1981].
Supplemented by data from the 1980 and 1984 National Election Studies conducted at
the Center for Political Studies, University of Michigan, and distributed by the Inter-
University Consortium for Political and Social Research. Data for 1988 come from the
General Social Survey, provided by Dr. Tom W. Smith, National Opinion Research Cen-
ter, and the 1992 data come from the September survey by Times Mirror.)*

ent. Much of the nationwide growth in the proportion of Republicans
and independents (and the parallel drop in the number of Democrats)
stems from party switches among white southerners.

Who are the self-identified Democrats and Republicans in the electorate? According to a 1988 survey, the effects of socioeconomic factors
are clear. People who have lower incomes, less education, and less pres-
tigious occupations and who live in union households tend to think of
themselves as Democrats more than as Republicans. But the cultural
factors of religion and race produce even sharper differences between the
parties. Jews are strongly Democratic compared with other religious
groups. Members of minority groups (especially blacks) are also over-

whelmingly Democratic. Differences between the sexes have opened a "gender gap" in American politics: Women tend to be more Democratic than men.[14]

The influence of region on party identification has altered over time. The South is now only slightly more Democratic than the other regions, while the West has become predominantly Republican. Despite the erosion of Democratic support in the South, we still see elements of Roosevelt's old Democratic coalition in the socioeconomic groups. Perhaps the major change in that coalition has been the replacement of white European ethnic groups by blacks attracted by the Democrats' backing of civil rights legislation in the 1960s.

Studies show that about one-half the citizens in the United States adopt their parents' party. But it often takes time for party identification to develop. The youngest group of voters is most likely to be independent, but these voters also identified more with Republicans during the Reagan years. The oldest group shows the most partisan commitments. Also, the youngest and oldest age groups are most evenly divided between the parties. Some analysts believe this division of party identification among the young will continue as they age, contributing to further erosion of the Democratic majority and perhaps greater electoral dealignment.

Nevertheless, citizens find their political niche, and they tend to stay there.[15] The widespread enduring sense of party loyalty among American voters tends to structure the vote even before the election is held, even before the candidates are chosen. Later we examine the extent to which party identification determines voting choice. But first, we look to see if there are any significant differences between the Democratic and the Republican parties.

Party Ideology and Organization

George Wallace, a disgruntled Democrat who ran for president on the American Independent party ticket, complained, "There isn't a dime's worth of difference" between the Democrats and Republicans. Humorist Will Rogers said, "I am not a member of any organized political party—I am a Democrat." Wallace's comment was made in disgust; Rogers's, in jest. Wallace was wrong; Rogers was close to being right. Here we try to dispel the myth that the parties do not differ significantly on issues and explain how they are organized to coordinate the activities of party candidates and officials in government.

Differences in Party Ideology

George Wallace notwithstanding, there is more than a dime's worth of difference between the two parties. In fact, the difference amounts to many billions of dollars, the cost of the different government programs

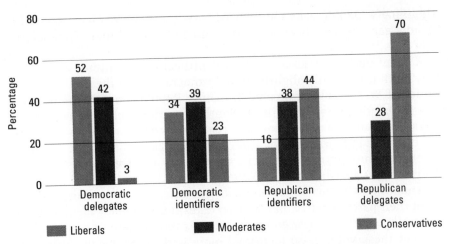

FIGURE 6.2 *Ideologies of Party Identifiers and Delegates in 1992*
*Contrary to what many people think, the Democratic and Republican parties
differ substantially in their ideological centers of gravity. When citizens were
asked to classify themselves on an ideological scale, more Republican than
Democratic identifiers described themselves as conservative. When delegates
to the parties' national conventions were asked to classify themselves, even
greater ideological differences appeared. (Sources: "Who Are the Delegates?" Washington Post, July 12, 1992, p. A13; and "Delegates: Who They Are," Washington Post,
August 16, 1992, p. A19.*

supported by each party. Democrats are more disposed to government
spending to advance social welfare (and hence to promote equality) than
are Republicans. And social welfare programs cost money, a lot of
money. Meanwhile, Republicans are not averse to spending billions of
dollars for the projects they consider important, among them, national
defense.

Ronald Reagan portrayed the Democrats as big spenders, but the defense buildup during just his first administration cost the country over
$1 trillion—more precisely, $1,007,900,000,000.[16] And Reagan's Strategic Defense Initiative (the "Star Wars" space defense), which Bush supported, cost many billions more. These differences in spending patterns
reflect some real philosophical differences between the parties.

Voters and activists. One way to examine these differences is to compare party identifiers (those who identify themselves as Democrats or
Republicans) among the voters with those who are active in the party
at election time. As shown in Figure 6.2, 23 percent of those who identified themselves as Democrats in 1992 described themselves as conservatives, compared with 44 percent of those who identified themselves as
Republicans. As we discuss in Chapter 4, many ordinary voters do not
think about politics in ideological terms, but party activists often do.

The ideological gap between the parties looms even larger when we focus on the party activists. Only 3 percent of the delegates to the 1992 Democratic convention considered themselves conservatives, compared with 70 percent of the delegates to the Republican convention.

Platforms: Freedom, order, and equality.   For another test of party philosophies, we can look to the **party platforms**—the statements of policies—adopted at party conventions. Although many people feel that party platforms do not matter very much, several scholars using different approaches have demonstrated that winning parties tend to carry out much of their platforms when in office.[17]

Party platforms also matter a great deal to delegates at conventions. The wording of a platform plank often means the difference between victory and defeat for factions within the party. Platforms, then, give a good indication of policy preferences among party activists.

The platforms adopted by the Democratic and Republican conventions in 1992 were strikingly different in style and substance. The Democrats, who met first, produced a rather short document of about 9,000 words that reflected Bill Clinton's moderate philosophy and shifted toward the center of the ideological spectrum compared with previous Democratic platforms. Whereas the party's 1988 platform led with this principle: "We believe that all Americans have a fundamental right to economic justice" (a phrase usually interpreted as a commitment to equality), the 1992 platform was "about restoring America's economic greatness." Whereas four years earlier the party had pledged "equal access" to education, government services, employment, housing, business, and so on for all citizens, the Democrats now said, "Our party's first priority is opportunity—broad based, non-inflationary economic growth and the opportunity that flows from it. Democrats in 1992 hold nothing more important for America than an economy that offers growth and jobs for all."

Meanwhile, the Republicans moved further right than perhaps President Bush wanted in their lengthy platform of 35,000 words. In the preamble, the Republicans quoted Lincoln that "government ought not to interfere" in things that people could individually do well for themselves, and it offered other expressions of traditional Republican philosophy: "Republicans have always believed that economic prosperity comes from individual enterprise, not government programs. . . . We believe that individual freedom, hard work and personal responsibility—basic to free society—are also basic to effective government."

The differences between the two 1992 party platforms emerged more clearly in their specific proposals. On abortion, the Democrats supported a woman's right to an abortion without exception, whereas the Republicans would outlaw abortion through a constitutional amendment. On gun control, the Democrats favored it; the Republicans opposed it. Democrats defended homosexual rights; Republicans opposed treating homosexuals as a protected minority. As for medical care, the

Democrats favored using government to guarantee universal access to health care; the Republicans opposed more government control.

These statements of values clearly separate the two parties on the values of freedom, order, and equality that underlie the dilemmas of government discussed in Chapter 1. According to the typology presented there, the Republicans' 1992 platform placed their party firmly in the conservative category, whereas the Democrats' platform put their party squarely into the liberal category—despite downplaying the rhetoric of equality.

Different but similar.   The Democrats and the Republicans have very different ideological orientations. Yet many observers claim that the parties are really quite similar in ideology, especially when compared with other countries' parties. They are similar in that both support capitalism; that is, both reject government ownership of the means of production (see Chapter 1). A study of Democratic and Republican positions on four economic issues—ownership of the means of production, role in economic planning, redistribution of wealth, and provision of social welfare—found that Republicans consistently opposed increased government activity. Comparing these findings with data on party positions in thirteen other democracies, the researchers found about as much difference between the American parties as was usual within two-party systems. However, both American parties tended to be more conservative on economic matters than did parties in other two-party systems. In most multiparty systems, the presence of strong socialist and antisocialist parties ensured a much greater range of ideological choice than our system, despite genuine differences between Democrats and Republicans.[18]

National Party Organization

American parties parallel the U.S. federal system: They have separate national and state organizations (and virtually separate local organizations, in many cases). At the national level, each major party has four main organizational components:

- *National convention.* Every four years, each party assembles thousands of delegates from the states and other entities (such as Puerto Rico and Guam) in a **national convention** for the purpose of nominating a candidate for president. This presidential nominating convention is also the supreme governing body of the party. It determines party policy through the platform, formulates rules to govern party operations, and designates a national committee, which is empowered to govern the party until the next convention.

- *National committee.* The **national committee** of each party is composed of party officials representing the states and territories and including the chairpersons of their party organizations. Prior to the

Leading Man
*Ronald Brown, the first African-American to head a major political party, be-
came the Democratic National Committee chairman in 1989, after managing
Jesse Jackson's presidential campaign in 1988. Following the Clinton victory in
1992, Brown was appointed Secretary of Commerce.*

1992 presidential campaign, the Republican National Committee
(RNC) had 162 members, and the Democratic National Committee
(DNC) had 403 members.[19] The chairperson of each national committee is chosen by the party's presidential nominee and is then
duly elected by the committee. If the nominee loses the election, the
national committee usually replaces the nominee's chairperson.

- *Congressional party conferences.* At the beginning of each session of
  Congress, the Republicans and Democrats in each chamber hold separate **party conferences** (the House Democrats call theirs a "caucus")
  to select their party leaders and to decide committee assignments.
  Each party conference is autonomous and concerned only with the
  party's legislative activities within each chamber.

- *Congressional campaign committees.* Democrats and Republicans
  in the House and Senate also maintain separate **congressional campaign committees**, each of which raises its own funds to support its
  candidates in congressional elections. That these are separate organizations tells us that the national party structure is loose; the na-

tional committee seldom gets involved with the election of any individual member of Congress. Moreover, even the congressional campaign organizations merely supplement the funds that senators and representatives raise on their own to win re-election.

It is tempting to think of the national party chairperson sitting at the top of a hierarchical party organization that not only controls its members in Congress but also runs through the state committees to the local level. Few ideas could be more wrong.[20] There is virtually no national committee control of congressional activity and very little national direction of and even less national control over state and local campaigns. The main role of a national committee is to cooperate with its candidate's personal campaign staff in the hope of winning the election.

For many years, the role of the national committees was essentially limited to planning for the next party convention. The committee would select the site, issue the call to state parties to attend, plan the program, and so on. In the 1970s, however, the roles of the DNC and RNC began to expand—but in different ways.

In response to street rioting during the 1968 Democratic convention, the Democrats created a special commission to introduce party reforms. The McGovern-Fraser Commission formulated guidelines for the selection of delegates to the 1972 Democratic convention. Included in these guidelines was the requirement that state parties take "affirmative action"—that is, do something to see to it that women, blacks, and young people were included among their delegates "in reasonable relationship to the group's presence in the population of the state."[21]

Never before had a national party committee imposed such rules on a state party organization, but it worked. Although the party has since reduced its emphasis on quotas, the gains by women and blacks have held up fairly well. The representation of young people, however, has declined substantially.

While the Democrats were busy with *procedural* reforms, the Republicans were making *organizational* reforms.[22] Republicans were not inclined to impose quotas on state parties through the national committee. Instead, the RNC strengthened its fund-raising, research, and service roles. Republicans acquired their own building and their own computer, and in 1976 they hired the first full-time chairperson of either national party. As RNC chair, William Brock expanded the party's staff, launched new publications, started seminars, conducted election analyses, advised candidates, and did most of the things that national party committees had done routinely in other countries for years.

The vast difference between the Democratic and Republican approaches to reforming the national committees shows in the funds raised by the DNC and RNC during election campaigns. Since Brock's tenure as chair of the RNC, the Republicans have used direct-mail solicitation to raise three to four times the money raised by the Democrats, with the larger portion of their funds from smaller contributors (of less than $100). In short, the RNC has raised far more money than the DNC from many more citizens in a long-term commitment to improving its organizational services. Evidence of its efforts has appeared at the level of state party organizations.

State and Local Party Organizations

At one time, both major parties were firmly anchored in strong state and local party organizations. Big-city party organizations, such as the Democrats' Tammany Hall in New York City and the Cook County Central Committee in Chicago, were prototypes of the party machine. The **party machine** was a centralized organization that dominated local politics by controlling elections—sometimes by illegal means, often by providing jobs and social services to urban workers in return for their votes. The patronage and social service functions of party machines were undercut as government expanded its role in providing unemployment compensation, aid to families with dependent children, and other social services. As a result, most local party organizations lost their ability to deliver votes and thus to determine the outcome of elections.

The state organizations of both parties vary widely in strength, but Republican state organizations tend to be stronger than Democratic organizations. The Republicans are likely to have larger budgets and staffs and tend to recruit candidates for more offices. Republicans also provide more financial and educational support from the national organization to the state organizations than do Democrats. However, the dominant pattern in both parties is for the national organization *not* to intervene in state activities unless asked and then only to supply services. But the national-state-county linkages are not as weak as some believe; and they may be growing stronger.[23]

Decentralized But Growing Stronger

The absence of centralized power has always been the most distinguishing characteristic of American political parties. Only a few years ago, scholars wrote that these weak parties were in further decline.[24] But there is evidence that our political parties today are enjoying a period of resurgence. As shown in Figure 6.3, fewer voters fail to see any differences between the parties in election years now than during the previous three decades, and more votes in Congress are being decided along party lines. A specialist in congressional politics concluded, "When compared to its predecessors of the last half-century, the current majority party leadership is more involved and more decisive in organizing the party and the chamber, setting the policy agenda, shaping legislation, and determining legislative outcomes."[25] However, American par-

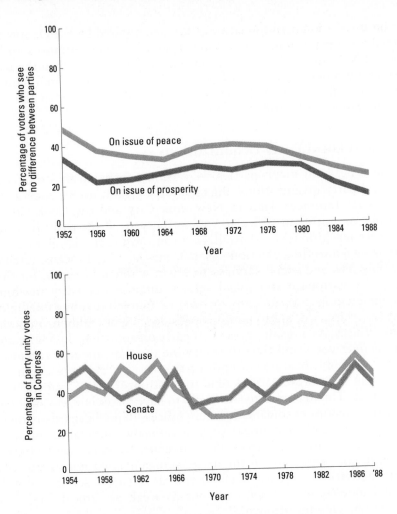

FIGURE 6.3 *Evidence of Party Resurgence*

*These graphs provide two different types of evidence for the resurgence of po-
litical parties since the 1970s. The first graph shows the percentage of registered voters who say that they see "no difference" between the Democrats and
Republicans when asked which party "will do a better job" either in keeping
the country prosperous or in keeping it out of war. Note that this percentage
has declined substantially since the 1970s and was lower in 1988 than in any
time since the 1950s. The second graph plots the percentage of "party unity"
votes taken in the House and the Senate in even-numbered years. A party
unity vote pits a majority of Democrats against a majority of Republicans on
issues before the chamber. It shows that the amount of party voting in Congress has risen almost steadily since its low point around 1970 and that the
parties divide in their voting patterns about as much as or more than they did
in the 1950s. (Sources: Data for the first graph come from* The Gallup Poll Monthly
*[September 1990], p. 32. Data for the second graph come from Harold W. Stanley and
Richard G. Niemi,* Vital Statistics on American Politics, *2d ed. [Washington, D.C.: Congressional Quarterly Press, 1990], p. 192.)*

ties have traditionally been so weak that these positive trends have not altered their basic character. American political parties are still so organizationally diffuse and decentralized that they raise questions about how well they link voters to government.

The Model of Responsible Party Government

According to the majoritarian model of democracy, parties are essential to making the government responsive to public opinion. In fact, the ideal role of parties in majoritarian democracy has been formalized in the four principles of **responsible party government**:[26]

1. Parties should present clear and coherent programs to voters.
2. Voters should choose candidates according to the party programs.
3. The winning party should carry out its program once in office.
4. Voters should hold the governing party responsible at the next election for having executed the program.

How well are these principles being met in American politics? You have learned that the Democratic and Republican platforms are different from each other and that each one is much more ideologically consistent than many people believe. So the first principle is being met fairly well. So is the third principle: Once parties gain power, they usually do what they said they would do. From the standpoint of democratic theory, the real questions lie in the second and fourth principles: Do voters really pay attention to party platforms and policies when they cast their ballots? If so, do voters hold the governing party responsible at the next election for having delivered, or failed to deliver, on its pledges? To answer these questions, we must consider in greater detail the parties' role in nominating candidates and in structuring the voters' choice in elections. At the conclusion of this chapter, we return to evaluating the role of political parties in democratic government.

Evolution of Campaigning

An **election campaign** is an organized effort to persuade voters to choose one candidate over others competing for the same office. An effective campaign requires sufficient resources to identify and acquire information about voters' interests, to develop a strategy and matching tactics for appealing to these interests, to deliver the candidate's message to the voters, and to get them to cast their ballots.[27]

Historically, political parties have played a central role in all phases of the election campaign. Today, however, candidates seldom rely much on political parties to do what they did even in the 1950s. Candidates learn about voters' interests today by contracting for public opinion polls, not by asking the party. Candidates plan their campaign strategy and tactics now by hiring political consultants to devise clever "sound bites" (brief, catchy phrases) that capture voters' attention, not by consulting party headquarters. Candidates deliver their messages to voters by conducting a media campaign, not by counting on party leaders to canvass the neighborhoods.

Increasingly, election campaigns have evolved from being party centered to being candidate centered.[28] The parties' roles have been substantially altered from one of production to one of support. Whereas parties virtually conducted or produced election campaigns in the past, now they exist mainly to support campaigns by ensuring democratic procedures or by providing services or funds to party candidates. Although candidates often avoid publicizing their party affiliation, the party label is usually a candidate's most important attribute at election time.

Perhaps the most important change in electoral campaigning is that candidates do not campaign anymore just to get elected. They must now campaign to get nominated as well, a function once controlled by the party organizations. However, for most important offices today, candidates are no longer nominated *by* the party organization but *within* the party. That is, party leaders seldom choose candidates themselves; they organize and supervise the election process by which party *voters* choose the candidates. Because almost all individuals who aspire to be a party candidate for a major office must first win an election to gain the party's nomination, those who would campaign for election must first campaign for the nomination.

Nominations

The most important feature of the nomination process in American party politics is that it usually involves an election by party voters. Virtually no other political parties in the world nominate candidates to the national legislature through party elections.[29] In more than one-half the world's parties, legislative candidates are chosen by local party leaders, and in most of those cases, even these choices must be approved the national organization. In fact, in more than one-third of the world's parties, the national organization itself selects the party candidates for the national legislature (see Compared with What? 6.1).[30]

Democrats and Republicans nominate their candidates for national and statewide offices somewhat differently across the country because each state is entitled to make its own laws governing the nomination process. (This is significant in itself, for political parties in most other countries are largely free of laws stating how they must select their candidates.) Their nomination practices can be summarized according to the types of party elections and the level of office sought.

Compared with What? 6.1

Choosing Legislative Candidates

In the United States, we believe that the nomination of party candidates through primary elections is the normal way to select candidates. Compared with the practice in other countries, however, it is not "normal" at all. Most competitive political parties in Western democracies exercise far more control over who is allowed to represent the party in elections. As shown in this graph, the most common method of selection, used by thirty-two parties in nine European countries, is to have a group of party activists interview the candidates and then select among them in committees or conventions. A few parties allow all enrolled party members to hear the candidates and then vote on them in party meetings, but more parties exercise even greater control, having national executive committees choose the candidates. This is evidence of how weak our parties are compared with those elsewhere.

Source: Data are tabulated from Table 11.1 in Michael Gallagher, "Conclusion," in Michael Gallagher and Michael Marsh, eds., *Candidate Selection in Comparative Perspective: The Secret Garden of Politics* (London: Sage Publications, 1988), p. 237. Some parties use a combination of methods and are thus counted twice in the tabulation.

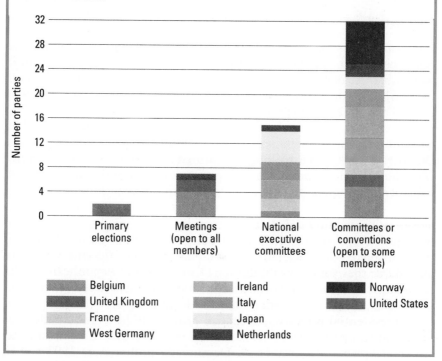

For Congress and State Offices

In the United States, most aspiring candidates for major offices are nominated through a **primary election**, a preliminary election conducted within the party to select candidates who will run for office in a subsequent election. In thirty-seven states, primary elections alone are used to nominate candidates for all state and national offices, and primaries figure in the nomination process in important ways in all other states.[31] The nomination process, then, is highly decentralized, resting on the decisions of thousands, perhaps millions, of the party rank and file who participate in primary elections.

There are different types of primary elections for state and congressional offices, depending on the state in which they are held. The most common type (used by about forty states) is the **closed primary**, in which voters must declare their party affiliation before they are given the primary ballot, which lists the party's potential nominees. A handful of states use the **open primary**, in which voters need not declare a party affiliation but must choose one party's ballot to take into the polling booth. In a **blanket primary**, currently used in only two or three states, voters receive a ballot listing both parties' potential nominees and can participate in nominating candidates for all offices.

For President

Party candidates for president are nominated by delegates attending national conventions held the summer before the presidential election in November. At one time, the nomination was decided right at the convention, sometimes after repeated balloting over several candidates who divided the vote and kept anyone from getting the majority needed to nominate. However, the last time that either party needed more than one ballot to nominate its presidential candidate was in 1952, when the Democrats took three ballots to nominate Adlai E. Stevenson. Since 1968, both parties' nominating conventions have simply ratified the results of the complex process for selecting the convention delegates.

Selecting convention delegates.   There is no national legislation specifying how state parties must select delegates to their national conventions. Instead, state legislatures have enacted a bewildering variety of procedures that sometimes differ for Democrats and Republicans in the same state. The most important distinction in delegate selection is between the presidential primary and the local caucus.

A **presidential primary** is a special primary used to select delegates to attend the party's national nominating convention. In *presidential preference primaries* (used in all Democratic primaries in 1992 and in thirty-four Republican primaries), party supporters vote directly for the person they favor as their party's nominee for president, and delegates are won accordingly through a variety of formulas. In *delegate selection primaries* (used only by Republicans in five states in 1992), party voters directly elect convention delegates, who may or may not have declared for a presidential candidate.

The **local caucus** method of delegate selection has several stages. It begins with a *caucus*, a local meeting of party supporters to choose delegates to attend a subsequent meeting, usually at the county level. Most delegates selected in the local caucus openly back one of the presidential candidates. The county meetings, in turn, select delegates to a higher level. The process culminates in a state *convention*, which actually selects the delegates to the national convention. About fifteen states used the caucus process in 1992 (a few states combined caucuses with primaries), and caucuses were employed more by Democrats than by Republicans.

Primary elections were first used to select delegates to nominating conventions in 1912. Now parties in nearly forty states rely on presidential primaries, which generate more than 80 percent of the delegates.

Campaigning for the nomination.   The process of nominating party candidates for president in the United States is a complex, drawn-out affair that has no parallel in party politics in any other nation. Would-be presidents announce their candidacies and begin campaigning many months before the first convention delegates are selected. The selection process in 1992 began in early February with the Iowa caucuses, closely followed by the New Hampshire primary. By historical accident, these two small states have become the first tests of candidates' popularity with party voters. Accordingly, each basks in the media spotlight once every four years.

The Iowa caucuses and the New Hampshire primary have served different functions in the presidential nominating process.[32] The contest in Iowa tends to winnow out candidates who are rejected by the party faithful. The New Hampshire primary, held one week after the Iowa caucuses, tests the Iowa frontrunners' appeal to ordinary party voters, which foreshadows their likely strength in the general election.

Almost 35 million citizens voted in both parties' presidential primaries in 1992, and another half-million participated in party caucuses. Requiring prospective presidential candidates to campaign before many millions of party voters in primaries and hundreds of thousands of party activists in caucus states has several consequences:

- The uncertainty of the nomination process attracts a half-dozen or so plausible candidates, especially when the party does not have a president seeking re-election.

- Candidates usually cannot win the nomination unless they are favored by most party identifiers. There have been only two exceptions to this rule since 1936, when poll data first became available:

Political Campaigning: The Inside Story
Actually, it's not all that exciting. Conducting a successful campaign usually involves a careful statistical analysis of voting trends and various social and economic characteristics of the electorate. The sign in Republican strategist Karl Rove's office in Austin, Texas, says a lot: These days, computers may be everything.

Adlai E. Stevenson in 1952 and George McGovern in 1972.[33] Both were Democrats; both lost impressively in the general election.

- Candidates who win the nomination do it mainly on their own and owe little or nothing to the national party organization, which usually does not promote a candidate. In fact, Jimmy Carter won the nomination in 1976 against a field of nationally prominent Democrats, even though he was a party outsider with few strong connections in the national party leadership.

Campaigns

Barbara and Stephen Salmore developed a framework of analysis that emphasizes the political context of election campaigns, the financial resources available for conducting campaigns, and the strategies and tactics that underlie the dissemination of information about the candidate.

Political Context

The two most important structural factors that face each candidate planning a campaign are the office the candidate is seeking and whether he or she is the **incumbent** (the current officeholder running for re-election) or the **challenger** (the person who seeks to replace the incumbent). Alternatively, the candidate can be running in an **open election**, which lacks an incumbent because of resignation or death. Incumbents usually enjoy great advantages over challengers, especially in elections to Congress.

Every candidate organizing a campaign must also examine the characteristics of the electorate in the territory that votes for the office. These include its physical size, its voting population, and its sociological makeup. In general, the larger, more populous, and more diverse the electorate is, the more complicated and costly the campaign is.

The political tendency of the electorate is a very important factor in the context of a campaign. Not only is it easier for a candidate to get elected when his or her party matches the electorate's preference, but it is also easier to raise the funds needed to conduct a winning campaign. Finally, significant political issues—such as economic recession, personal scandals, and war—can affect a campaign or even dominate it and negate positive factors such as incumbency and the normal inclinations of the electorate.

Financing

Former House Speaker Thomas ("Tip") O'Neill once said, "As it is now, there are four parts to any campaign. The candidate, the issues of the candidate, the campaign organization, and the money to run the campaign with. Without money you can forget the other three."[34] Money will buy the best campaign managers, equipment, transportation, research, and consultants—making the quality of the organization only a function of money. Although the equation is not quite as strong, when ample campaign funds are available, so are good candidates.

It is difficult to generalize about raising funds for political campaigns. Campaign financing is now heavily regulated by national and state governments, and regulations vary according to the level of the office—national, state, or local. Even at the national level, there are major differences in financing laws for presidential and congressional elections.

Regulating campaign financing.   Strict campaign financing laws are relatively new to American politics. Early laws to limit campaign contributions and to control campaign spending were flawed in one way or another, and none clearly provided for administration and enforcement.

In 1971, during the period of party reform, Congress passed the *Federal Election Campaign Act (FECA)*, which imposed stringent new rules for full reporting of campaign contributions and expenditures. The weakness of the old legislation soon became apparent. In 1968, before the FECA was passed, House and Senate candidates reported spending $8.5 million for their campaigns. With the FECA in force, the same number of candidates confessed to spending $88.9 million in 1972.[35]

The FECA has been amended several times since 1971, but the amendments have for the most part strengthened the law. The 1974 amendment created the **Federal Election Commission (FEC)** to implement the law. The FEC now enforces limits on financial contributions to national campaigns and requires full disclosure of campaign spending. The FEC also administers the public financing of presidential campaigns, which began with the 1976 election.

Financing presidential campaigns.   Presidential campaigns have always been expensive, and at times the methods of raising funds to support them were open to question. In the presidential election of 1972, the last election before the FEC took over the funding of presidential campaigns and the regulating of campaign expenditures, President Richard Nixon's campaign committee spent more than $65 million, some of it obtained illegally (for which campaign officials went to jail). In 1974, a new campaign finance law made public funds available to presidential primary and general election candidates under certain conditions.

Candidates for the nomination for president can qualify for federal funding by raising $5,000 (in private contributions no greater than $250 each) in each of twenty states. The FEC then matches these contributions up to one-half of the spending limit. Originally, under the 1974 law, the FEC limited spending in presidential primary elections to $10 million. But cost-of-living provisions had raised the limit in the 1992 primaries to $27.6 million (plus $5.5 million for fund-raising activities).

The presidential nominees of the Democratic and Republican parties receive twice the primary election limit in public funds for the general election campaign ($55.2 million in 1992) provided that they spend only the public funds. Each of the two major parties also receives funds for its nominating convention ($11 million in 1992). Every major candidate since 1976 has accepted public funding, holding the costs of presidential campaigns well below Nixon's record expenditures in 1972.

Public funds are given directly to each candidate's campaign committee, not to the national committee of either party. But the FEC also limits what the national committees can spend on behalf of the nominees. In 1992, that limit was $10.3 million. And the FEC limits the amount individuals ($1,000) and organizations ($5,000) can contribute to candidates per election. They are not limited, however, in the amount of expenses they can incur to promote candidates of their choice.*

Public funding has had several effects on campaign financing. Obviously, it has limited campaign costs. Also, it has helped equalize the amounts spent by major candidates in general elections. And it has strengthened the trend toward "personalized" campaigns since federal funds are given to the presidential candidate of each party, not to the party organization that the candidate represents. Finally, public funding has forced candidates to spend a great deal of time seeking thousand-dollar contributions—a limit that has not changed since 1974, despite the inflation that has more than doubled the FEC's spending limits.

In the 1980s, however, both parties began to exploit a loophole in the law that allowed them to raise virtually unlimited funds from individuals and organizations—provided the money was spent on party mailings, voter registration, and get-out-the-vote campaigns for the entire ticket. The Democratic and Republican National Committees raised this so-called soft money, which they channeled to state and local party committees for registration drives and other activities that were not exclusively devoted to the presidential candidates but helped them nevertheless.[36] The net effect of these "coordinated campaigns" was to increase the organization role of both the national and state parties in the campaigns.

You might think that a party's presidential campaign would be closely coordinated with the campaigns of the party's candidates for Congress. But remember that campaign funds go to the presidential candidate, not to the party, and that the national party organization does not run the presidential campaign. Presidential candidates may join congressional candidates in public appearances for mutual benefit, but presidential campaigns are usually isolated—financially and otherwise—from congressional campaigns.

Strategies and Tactics

In an election campaign, *strategy* refers to the overall approach used to persuade citizens to vote for the candidate; *tactics*, to the content of the messages and the way they are delivered. Salmore and Salmore identified three basic strategies, which campaigns may blend in different mixes: (1) a *party-centered* strategy, which relies heavily on voters' par-

---

* The distinction between contributions and expenses hinges on whether funds are spent as part of a coordinated campaign (a contribution) or spent independently of the candidate's campaign (an expense). The 1974 amendment to the FECA established limits on both campaign contributions and independent expenditures by interested citizens. In *Buckley* v. *Valeo* (1976), the Supreme Court struck down the limits on citizens' expenditures as an infringement on the freedom of speech, protected under the First Amendment.

tisan identification as well as on the party's organization to provide the resources necessary to wage the campaign; (2) an *issue-oriented* strategy, which seeks support from groups that feel strongly about various policies; and (3) an *image-oriented* strategy, which depends on the candidate's perceived personal qualities, such as experience, leadership ability, integrity, independence, and trustworthiness.[37]

The campaign strategy must be tailored to the political context of the election. Research suggests that a party-centered strategy is more suited to voters with less political information than to those with more.[38] How does the candidate learn what the electorate knows and thinks about politics, and how can he or she use this information? Candidates today usually turn to pollsters and political consultants, of whom there are hundreds.[39] Using information from such sources, professional campaign managers can settle on a strategy that mixes party, issues, and images in its messages. In major campaigns, these messages are disseminated to voters via the mass media through news coverage and advertising.[40]

Making the news. Campaigns value news coverage by the media for two reasons: The coverage is free, and it seems objective to the audience. Efforts are made to attract reporters by various means, such as holding a news conference on a slow news day (such as Sunday) or linking a candidate's statement to ongoing news stories. Getting free news coverage is yet another advantage that incumbents enjoy over challengers, for incumbents can command attention simply by announcing political decisions.

Paid advertising. Television news contains little information about the issues in the campaign. In fact, a study of television news and television advertising in the last weeks of the 1984 campaign found that "voters got the overwhelming majority of their campaign information from political ads, rather than from television coverage."[41] The first objective of such paid advertising is to gain name recognition. The next is to promote the candidate by extolling his or her virtues. Finally, campaign advertising can have a negative objective, attacking the opponent to promote the candidate. But name recognition is the most important. Studies show that many voters cannot recall the names of their U.S. senators or representative, but they can recognize their names on a list—as on the ballot. Researchers attribute the high re-election rate for members of Congress mainly to high levels of name recognition (see Chapter 8).

At one time, candidates for national office relied heavily on newspaper advertising in their campaigns; today, they overwhelmingly use the electronic media.[42] This emphasis on the electronic media, particularly television, has raised concern about the promotion of candidates by developing a "videostyle" in which consultant and candidate arrive at a theme, based on anticipated audience reactions, to be conveyed in thirty-second commercials. The trend in recent years, however, has been away from promoting candidates through slick ads to attacking them in slick ads. Although such negative campaigns may turn some people away from politics, they often work.

Elections

By national law, all seats in the House of Representatives and one-third of the seats in the Senate are filled in a **general election** held on the first Tuesday after the first Monday in November in even-numbered years. Every state takes advantage of the national election to fill some of nearly 500,000 state and local offices across the country, which makes the election even more "general."[43] When the president is chosen every fourth year, the election year is identified as a *presidential election*. The intervening years are known as *congressional, midterm,* or *off-year elections.*

Presidential Elections

Unlike elections for almost all other offices in the United States, the office of president does not go automatically to the candidate who wins the most votes. Instead, elections for president are decided by a two-stage procedure specified in the Constitution that requires the president to be chosen by a group (college) of electors representing the states.

The electoral college.   Voters choose the president only indirectly; they actually vote for a little-known slate of electors (their names are usually not even on the ballot) pledged to one of the candidates. Occasionally, electors break their pledges when they cast their written ballots at their state capitols in December. This last happened in 1988, when Margaret Leach, chosen as a Democratic elector in West Virginia, abandoned Michael Dukakis and voted for his running mate, Senator Lloyd Bentsen.[44] But usually the electors are faithful. The more important issue surrounding the electoral college is the match between the outcome of the popular vote and the outcome of the electoral vote. Whether a candidate wins a state by 5 or 500,000 votes, he wins all that state's electoral votes.*

In the electoral college, each state is accorded 1 vote for each of its senators (100 votes total) and representatives (435 votes total), adding up to 535 votes. In addition, the Twenty-third Amendment to the Consti-

---

* The two exceptions are in Maine and Nebraska, where 2 and 3 of the state electoral votes, respectively, are awarded by congressional district. The presidential candidate who carries each district wins 1 electoral vote, and the statewide winner gets 2 votes.

tution awarded 3 electoral votes to the District of Columbia, even though it elects no voting members of Congress. So the total number of electoral votes is 538, and a majority of 270 electoral votes is needed to win the presidency.* Because of population changes recorded by the 1990 census, there were important changes in the distribution of electoral votes among the states between the 1988 and 1992 presidential elections (see Figure 6.4).

The most troubling aspect of the electoral college is the possibility that despite winning a plurality or even a majority of popular votes, a candidate could lose the election in the electoral college. This could happen if one candidate won some states by a very large amount, while the other candidate won some states by a slim margin. Indeed, it has happened in three elections, but all were over one hundred years ago.

Abolish the electoral college?   Reformers argue that it is simply wrong to have a system that allows a candidate who receives the most popular votes to lose the election. Reforms that call for the direct election of the president would institute a purely majoritarian means of choosing the president. Defenders of the electoral college point out that the present system, warts and all, has been a stable one. It might be riskier to replace it with a new arrangement that could alter the party system or the way presidential campaigns are conducted. Also, some scholars argue that the electoral college's tendency to magnify the winner's victory margin increases the legitimacy of the president-elect. For example, Bill Clinton won only 43 percent of the popular vote but 69 percent of the electoral college vote in 1992. In any case, recent proposals for fundamental reform have not come close to adoption.

Congressional Elections

The candidates for the presidency are listed at the top of the ballot in a presidential election, followed by candidates for other national, state, and local offices. A voter is said to vote a **straight ticket** when he or she chooses only one party's candidates for all the offices. A voter who switches parties when choosing candidates for different offices is said to vote a **split ticket**. About one-half the voters admit to splitting their tickets between the parties for state and local offices, and the proportion of voters who choose a presidential candidate from one party and a congressional candidate from the other has increased from about 13 percent in 1952 to 25 percent in 1988.[45] The net effect in recent decades has

---

* If no candidate receives a majority when the electoral college votes, the election is thrown into the House of Representatives. The House votes by state, with each state casting 1 vote for a single presidential candidate. The top three finishers in the general election are the candidates in the House election. A presidential election has gone to the House only twice in American history, the first time in 1800 and the second in 1824. Both cases occurred before a stable two-party system had developed.

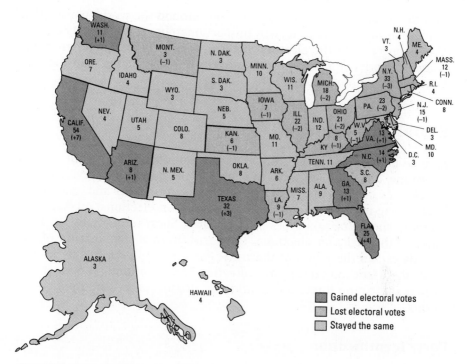

FIGURE 6.4   *Distribution of Electoral Votes in 1992*
*The 1990 census produced some major changes in congressional reapportion-
ment with implications for presidential elections. Remember that each state
has as many electoral votes as its combined representation in the Senate (always 2) and in the House (which depends on population). As shown on the
map, states in the South and West gained population and thus picked up seats
in the House of Representatives, mainly at the expense of the Northeast. Thus,
California, with two senators and fifty-two representatives, now has 54 electoral votes—or more than 10 percent of the total of 538. (Washington, D.C.,
has 3 electoral votes—equal to the smallest state—although it has no representation in Congress.) From* Congressional Quarterly Weekly Report, *March 23, 1991, p.
765. Copyright 1991. Used by permission.*

been to produce a divided government in which Republicans control the
presidency and Democrats control the Congress (see Chapter 9).

If the electoral college provides Republicans with an advantage in
winning the presidency, Democrats seem to have a lock on congressional elections. Not only have they won a majority of House elections
every year since 1955; they have also controlled the Senate for all but
six years during that period. Since 1954, Republicans have won a lower
percentage of seats than votes (on average, 6.8 percent) in every House
election. Election specialists point out that this is the inevitable consequence of **first-past-the-post** elections—a British term for elections conducted in single-member districts that award victory to the candidate

with the most votes. In all such elections around the world, parties that win the most votes tend to win proportionately more seats. The same process operates in the electoral college, which, as discussed, produces a larger majority in the electoral vote over the fifty states than the candidate won nationwide.*

Explaining Voting Choice

Why do people choose one candidate over another? That is not easy to determine, but there are ways to approach the question. Individual voting choices can be analyzed as products of *long-term* and *short-term* forces. Long-term forces operate over a series of elections, predisposing voters to choose certain types of candidates. Short-term forces are associated with particular elections; they arise from a combination of the candidates and the issues of the time. *Party identification* is by far the most important long-term force affecting U.S. elections. The most important short-term forces are *candidates' attributes* and their *policy positions*.

Party Identification

Most research on voting in presidential elections stems from a series of studies that originated at the University of Michigan. Comparable surveys have been conducted for every presidential election and most congressional elections since 1952. When voters in 1988 were asked at what point they had decided how to vote for president, nearly one-half (49 percent) said that they "knew all along" or had decided before the conventions.[46] In 1992, many voters changed their choices after Ross Perot withdrew in July—and changed again when he re-entered in October. In other presidential elections since 1952, about 40 percent of the voters reported making up their minds before the candidates squared off in the general election campaign. And voters who make an early voting decision generally vote according to their party identification.

Despite frequent comments in the media about the decline of partisanship in voting behavior, party identification had a substantial effect on the presidential vote in 1992. Avowed Democrats voted 77 percent for Clinton, while Republicans voted 73 percent for Bush. Thirty-eight percent of the independents also voted for Clinton. This is a common pattern in presidential elections.

---

* If you have trouble understanding this phenomenon, think of a basketball team that scores, on average, 51 percent of the total points in all games it plays during the season. Such a team usually wins far more than one-half its games, for it wins systematically and tends to win the close ones.

Because there are more Democrats than Republicans, the Democrats should benefit. Why, then, have Republican candidates won seven out of eleven presidential elections since 1952? For one thing, Democrats do not turn out to vote as consistently as Republicans do. For another, Democrats defect more easily from their party. Defections are sparked by the candidates' attributes and the issues, which have favored Republican presidential candidates since 1952.

Candidates' Attributes

Candidates' attributes are especially important to voters who lack good information about a candidate's past behavior and policy stands—which means most of us. Without this kind of information, voters search for clues about the candidates to try to predict their behavior in office.[47] Some fall back on their firsthand knowledge of religion, gender, and race in making political judgments. Such stereotypic thinking accounts for patterns of opposition and support met by a Catholic candidate for president (John Kennedy), a woman candidate for vice president (Geraldine Ferraro in 1984), and a black contender for a presidential nomination (Jesse Jackson in 1984 and 1988).

Apart from candidates' sociological attributes, voters say that candidates' personal qualifications are very important. Two election surveys in 1988 asked, "What must the winner of the election have within himself, and bring to the job, in order to be a good president?" In both surveys, about 55 percent of the voters cited character traits, with the overwhelming majority of those emphasizing "trustworthiness." About 40 percent believed that competence traits, spread across "leadership," "knowledge," and "experience," were very important. Only about 33 percent linked policy positions to being a good president, and about 50 percent of those mentioned "concern for needs of all the people" or some kind of fairness.[48]

Nevertheless, when the same survey asked for factors "most important to you in terms of deciding who to support for president," respondents listed policy positions and competence first (about 40 percent for each)—substantially above personal traits (about 15 percent) and party identification (6 percent).[49] Moreover, when voters were asked just before the election, "What is the most important reason for choosing (Bush/Dukakis) over his opponent?" party identification emerged next to experience at the top of the list (16 percent each).[50]

Issues and Policies

Choosing among candidates according to personal attributes may be understandable, but it is not rational voting according to democratic theory. That theory specifies that citizens should vote according to the candidates' past performance and proposed policies. Voters who choose between candidates on the basis of their policies are voting "on the issues," which fits the idealized conception of democratic theory. However, issues, candidates' attributes, and party identification all figure in the voting decision. Although it is difficult to sort out their relative influence, their effects can be estimated using multivariate statistical models. Some scholars contend that issues played a more important role in the voting decision in the 1980s than in the 1950s.[51] Unfortunately for democratic theory, most studies of presidential elections show that issues are less important than either party identification or the candidate's image when people cast their ballots. Only in 1972, when voters perceived George McGovern as too liberal, did issue voting exceed party identification in importance.[52]

Although there has been some decline in party voting since the 1950s, there is a closer alignment now between voters' positions on the issues and their party identification. The more closely party identification is aligned with ideological orientation, the more sense it makes to vote by party. In the absence of detailed information about candidates' positions on the issues, party labels are a handy indicator of those positions.[53]

Campaign Effects

If party identification is both the most important factor in the voting decision *and* also resistant to short-term changes, then there are definite limits to the effects of an election campaign on the outcome of elections.[54] In a close election, however, just changing a few votes means the difference between victory and defeat, so a campaign can be decisive even if it has little overall effect. One major limitation to the capacity of image makers and campaign consultants to control elections, however, is that they regularly offset one another by working on opposite sides in an election. Moreover, specialists in the new campaign technology argue that

> no one has even a vague idea of what percentage of the vote a consultant or a piece of new campaign technology can or does add to a candidate under any given circumstances. Campaign observers rarely even have a precise idea of what event or series of events produced the election result. Campaigning remains complex, unpredictable, and very unscientific, and one may expect and be grateful that it always will be.[55]

Another school of thought holds that campaigns for the presidency and other major offices are overridden by salient political issues, especially economic conditions such as unemployment and inflation. Additional factors outside the control of campaign managers, such as war and incumbency, also have powerful effects on voting behavior and can be incorporated into rather successful models for forecasting presidential elections in advance of the campaign.[56]

Campaigns, Elections, and Parties

Election campaigns in contemporary American politics tend to be highly personalized, centered on the candidates, and conducted outside the control of party organizations. The increased use of electronic media, especially television, has encouraged candidates to personalize their campaign messages, while the decline of party identification has decreased the power of party-related appeals. Although the party affiliation of the candidates and the party identification of the voters work together to explain a good deal of electoral behavior, party organizations are not central to elections in America. This fact has implications for democratic government.

Parties and the Majoritarian Model

According to the majoritarian model of democracy, parties are essential in linking people with their government by making government responsive to public opinion. And Republican and Democratic parties do follow this model to the extent that they do formulate different platforms and do tend to pursue their announced policies when in office. The stumbling blocks to this model of responsible party government lie more with the linkage of candidates to voters through campaigns and elections.

You have not read much about the role of the party platform in nominating candidates, in conducting campaigns, or in explaining voter choice. The fact of the matter is that voters do not choose between candidates according to party programs, and they do not hold the governing party responsible at the next election for having executed its program. In large part, it has been impossible for them to hold the governing party responsible because there is no "governing party" when the president is of one party and Congress is controlled by the other, which has occurred most of the time since the end of World War II (and in ten of thirteen congresses since 1969). When voters elect presidents of one party and congresses of another, there is little hope for the majoritarian model of party government.

Parties and the Pluralist Model

The way parties in the United States operate is more in keeping with the pluralist model of democracy than with the majoritarian model. Our parties are not the basic mechanism through which citizens control their government; instead, they function as two giant interest groups. The parties' interests are in electing and re-electing party candidates to enjoy the benefits of public office. Except in extreme cases, the parties care little about the issues or ideologies favored by candidates for Congress and statewide offices.

Some scholars believe that stronger parties would contribute more to democratic government, even if they could not meet all the requirements of the responsible party model. Although our parties perform valuable functions in structuring the vote along partisan lines and in proposing alternative government policies, stronger parties might be able to play a more important role in coordinating government policies after elections. At present, the decentralized nature of the nominating process and campaigning for election offers many opportunities for organized groups outside the party to identify and back candidates who favor their interests when elected to government. This is in keeping with pluralist theory, although it is certain to frustrate majority interests on occasion.

Summary

Political parties perform four important functions in a political system: nominating candidates, structuring the voting choice, proposing alternative government programs, and coordinating the activities of government officials. Political parties have been performing these functions longer in the United States than in any other country. The Democratic party, founded in 1828, is the world's oldest political party. When the Republican party emerged as a major party after the 1856 election, it joined the Democrats to produce our present two-party system—the oldest party system in the world.

America's two-party system has experienced three critical elections, each of which realigned the electorate for years and affected the party balance in government. The election of 1860 established the Republicans as the major party in the North and the Democrats as the dominant party in the South. The critical election of 1896 strengthened the link between the Republican party and business interests in the heavily populated Northeast and Midwest and produced a surge in voter support that made the Republicans the majority party nationally for more than three decades. The Great Depression produced conditions for the critical election of 1932, which transformed the Democrats into the majority party, giving them almost uninterrupted control of Congress since then.

Minor parties have not enjoyed much electoral success in America, although they have contributed ideas to the Democratic and Republican platforms. The two-party system is perpetuated in the United States because of the nature of our electoral system and of the political socialization process, which results in most Americans identifying with either the Democratic or the Republican party. The federal system of government has also helped the Democrats and Republicans survive major national defeats by sustaining them with electoral victories at the state level. The pattern of party identification has been changing in recent years: As more people are becoming independents and Republicans, the number of Democratic identifiers is dropping. Nevertheless, the proportion of Democrats consistently exceeds that of Republicans, and together both far outnumber the independents.

Party identifiers, party activists, and party platforms show consistent differences in ideological orientations between the two major parties. Democratic identifiers and activists are more likely to describe themselves as liberal; Republican identifiers and activists tend to be conservative. The 1992 Democratic party platform also showed a more liberal orientation by stressing equality over freedom; the Republican platform was more conservative, concentrating on freedom but also emphasizing the importance of restoring social order. Organizationally, the Republicans have recently become the stronger party at both national and state levels, and both parties are showing signs of resurgence. Nevertheless, both parties are very decentralized compared with parties in other countries.

Campaigning for elections has evolved from a party-centered to a candidate-centered process. The successful candidate for public office usually must campaign first to win the party nomination and then to win the general election. A major factor in the decentralization of American parties is their reliance on primary elections to nominate candidates. Democratic and Republican nominations for president are no longer actually decided in the party's national conventions but are determined in advance of the convention through the complex process of selecting delegates pledged to those seeking the nomination. Although candidates cannot win the nomination unless they have broad support within the party, the winners can legitimately say that they captured the nomination through their own efforts and that they owe little to the party organization.

Candidates usually retain the staffs that got them the nomination to help them win the general election. The dynamics of campaign financing also force candidates to rely mainly on their own resources or—in the case of presidential elections—on public funds. Party organizations contribute

relatively little toward campaign expenses, and candidates must raise most of the money themselves. Money is essential in conducting a modern campaign for a major office. Funds are needed to conduct polls that disclose the voters' interests and to advertise the candidate's name, qualifications, and policy positions through the media. Free news coverage is sought whenever possible, but most candidates must rely on paid advertising to get across their messages. Ironically, voters also get most of their campaign information from advertisements. There has been a trend in recent years toward negative advertising, which seems to work, although it contributes to voters' distaste for politics.

Presidential elections are structured by the need to win a majority of votes in the electoral college. Although it is possible for a candidate to win a majority of the popular vote but lose in the electoral college, that has not happened in more than one hundred years. The electoral college operates to magnify the victory margin of the winning candidate. Since World War II, Republicans have generally been successful in winning the presidency, while Democrats seem to have a lock on Congress, certainly on the House of Representatives.

Voting choice can be analyzed in terms of party identification, candidates' attributes, and policy positions. Party identification is still the most important long-term factor in shaping the voting decision, but few candidates rely on party in their campaigns. Most candidates today run personalized campaigns that stress their attributes or their policies. There is evidence that presidential campaigns do increase people's knowledge about issues, but there is some disagreement about how important campaigns are in affecting election outcomes.

As demanded by the model of responsible party government, American parties do tend to enact their platform positions into government policy if elected to power. However, the way that nominations, campaigns, and elections are conducted in America makes it difficult for parties to fulfill the ideals of responsible party government that fit the majoritarian model of democracy. In particular, there is a problem in linking parties to voters through campaigns and elections. American parties are better suited to the pluralist model of democracy, which sees them as major interest groups competing with lesser groups to further their own interests. At least political parties aspire to the noble goal of representing the needs and wants of most of the people. As we see in the next chapter, interest groups do not even pretend as much.

Key Terms

political party
nominate
political system
critical election
electoral realignment
majority party
minority party
electoral dealignment
two-party system
bolter parties
farmer-labor parties
parties of ideological protest
single-issue parties
majority representation
proportional representation
party identification
party platforms
national convention
national committee
party conferences

congressional campaign
  committees
party machine
responsible party government
election campaign
primary election
closed primary
open primary
blanket primary
presidential primary
local caucus
incumbent
challenger
open election
Federal Election Commission
  (FEC)
general election
straight ticket
split ticket
first-past-the-post elections

Selected Readings

Advisory Commission on Intergovernmental Relations. *The Transformation of American Politics: Implications for Federalism.* Report A–106. Washington, D.C.: August 1986. This general study of American political parties is especially useful for its data on state party organizations.

Buchanan, Bruce. *Electing a President: The Report on the Markle Commission on the Media and the Electorate.* Austin: University of Texas Press, 1991. This book analyzes the 1988 presidential election using a special set of surveys designed to measure media effects.

Frantzich, Stephen E. *Political Parties in the Technological Age.* New York: Longman, 1989. This text on political parties discusses the impact of technological change on parties and evaluates proposals for party reform.

Jewell, Malcolm E., and David M. Olson. *Political Parties and Elections in American States.* 3d ed. Chicago: Dorsey Press, 1988. Jewell and Olson compare the political party and electoral systems in the fifty states drawing on generalizations backed by empirical research and years of experience.

Kern, Montague. *30-Second Politics: Political Advertising in the Eighties.* New York: Praeger, 1989. This book surveys the scene in campaign advertising and uses some original data analysis to support its contentions.

Lichtman, Allan J., and Ken DeCell. *The Thirteen Keys to the Presidency.* Lanham, Md.: Madison Books, 1990. The authors argue that presidents are elected or defeated on the basis of the record of the incumbent administration and that campaigns have little effect on the outcome.

Mableby, David B., and Candice J. Nelson. *The Money Chase: Congressional Campaign Finance Reform.* Washington, D.C.: Brookings Institution, 1990. This book reviews problems in campaign finance and issues in reform and also provides valuable data on campaign receipts and expenditures.

Maisel, L. Sandy, ed. *The Parties Respond: Changes in the American Party System.* Boulder, Colo.: West-view Press, 1990. Here are essays on state party organization, parties in the electoral arena, the relationship between parties and voters, and parties in government.

Orren, Gary R., and Nelson W. Polsby, eds. *Media and Momentum: The New Hampshire Primary and Nomination Politics.* Chatham, N.J.: Chatham House, 1987. This book contains a series of studies of media coverage of early campaigning for the presidential nomination mainly in New Hampshire, but also in Iowa.

Rosenstone, Steven J., Roy L. Behr, and Edward H. Lazarus. *Third Parties in America: Citizen Response to Major Party Failure.* Princeton, N.J.: Princeton University Press, 1984. The authors not only provide an excellent review of the history of third-party movements in American politics but also analyze the factors that lead third-party voters and candidates to abandon the two major parties. The authors conclude that third-party efforts improve the performance of the party system.

Salmore, Barbara G., and Stephen A. Salmore. *Candidates, Parties, and Campaigns: Electoral Politics in America.* 2d ed. Washington, D.C.: Congressional Quarterly Press, 1989. This is the best textbook treatment of election campaigning.

Schattschneider, E. E. *Party Government.* New York: Holt, 1942. This classic book in political science offers a clear and powerful argument for the central role of political parties in a democracy according to the model of responsible party government.

Shafer, Byron E. *Bifurcated Politics: Evolution and Reform in the National Party Convention.* Cambridge, Mass.: Harvard University Press, 1988. Shafer argues that the national conventions lost the function to nominate candidates in the 1950s and now are used to launch a campaign and to politic for other causes. The convention is bifurcated because delegates experience one convention, while television viewers see another.

Sorauf, Frank J. *Money in American Elections.* Glenview, Ill.: Scott, Foresman, 1988. This book surveys receipts and expenditures in presidential and congressional campaigns, including financing by individuals, political action committees, parties, and government.

INTEREST GROUPS

7

There are things in this life that are easier than getting a clean air bill out of the Congress. The reason is simple: So many interest groups push Congress in so many different directions. No single group can get everything that it wants, and the resulting struggle for an acceptable compromise is inevitably difficult and protracted.

In 1989, despite many recent abortive efforts (the last successful attempt had been in 1977), Congress again took up clean air legislation. The Senate succeeded in passing a bill in the spring of 1990—but not without a lot of squabbling over who would get exemptions and special privileges. One observer described the conflict over clean air as "the Super Bowl of lobbying."[1] In principle, everybody is for clean air—as long as the law does not require them to do anything to pay for it. Power plants in North Dakota didn't want to spend the money to reduce their pollution and managed to get an exemption from the requirements of the bill. Utility plants in Florida got an exemption, too, and could save as much as $400 million in pollution-control costs. Automobile manufacturers were successful in fighting off the efforts of environmental groups to mandate an increase in gasoline mileage. Corn farmers won a big battle when a provision was put into the bill requiring the nine smoggiest cities in the country to sell less polluting gasoline made of ethanol, a corn-distilled alcohol.

There were some big losers, too. Coal miners from West Virginia and the Midwest, who saw themselves being sacrificed on the altar of clean air, asked for financial aid because the bill would likely reduce the use of coal and thus put many miners out of work. On the floor of the Senate, they lost by a single vote, 50–49. Steel manufacturers wanted less stringent standards regulating the volume of toxic emissions at their plants. They lost also. Overall, however, the Senate's version of the Clean Air Act was an amalgam of deals cut with various interest groups. One environmentalist described the process as a "special-interest feeding frenzy." He added, "It was not a pretty sight watching this happen to the bill."[2]

A clean air bill containing its own set of deals and compromises between lawmakers and interest groups was subsequently passed in the House. Many of its provisions differed from the Senate bill, but after more horse trading in a conference committee, those differences were worked out, and a clean air bill was sent to President George Bush, who signed it into law.

The history of the Clean Air Act illustrates some of the basic dynamics of interest group politics. At the heart of pluralist democracy are groups fighting for their own narrow interests. Here, various manufacturers, unions, and farm groups fought environmentalists (and sometimes each other) over different provisions in the legislation. The majoritarian interest is clean air, but clean air politics cannot simply be described as a process whereby interest groups work to weaken majority control over public policy. The American public surely does want less pollution, but it also wants cheap electricity, inexpensive gasoline, a growing economy, and low inflation. The interest groups that worked for special provisions in the Senate bill used these public preferences—sometimes quite effectively—to convince lawmakers to reduce proposed standards for clean air.

In analyzing the process by which interest groups and lobbyists come to speak on behalf of different groups, we focus on a number of questions. How do interest groups form? Whom do they represent? What tactics do they use to convince policymakers that their views are best for the nation? Why has the number of interest groups grown so rapidly in recent years? And what is the impact of that growth?

Interest Groups and the American Political Tradition

An **interest group** is an organized body of individuals who share some political goals and try to influence public policy decisions.[3] Among the most prominent interest groups in the United States are the AFL-CIO (representing labor union members), the American Farm Bureau Federation (representing farmers), the Business Roundtable (representing big business), and Common Cause (representing citizens concerned with reforming government). Interest groups are also called **lobbies**, and their representatives are referred to as **lobbyists**.

Interest Groups: Good or Evil?

A recurring debate in American politics concerns the role of interest groups in a democratic society. Are interest groups a threat to the well-being of the political system, or do they contribute to its proper functioning? Alexis de Tocqueville, a French visitor to the United States in the early nineteenth century, marveled at the array of organizations he found and later wrote that "Americans of all ages, all conditions, and all dispositions, constantly form associations."[4] Tocqueville was suggesting that the ease with which we form organizations reflects a strong democratic culture.

James Madison offered a different perspective. Writing in the *Federalist Papers*, he warned of the dangers of "factions," the major divisions in American society. In "Federalist No. 10," written in 1787, Madison said that it was inevitable that substantial differences would develop between factions and that each faction would try to persuade government to adopt policies that favored it at the expense of others.

But Madison argued against trying to suppress factions. He concluded that factions could be eliminated only by removing our freedoms: "Liberty is to faction what air is to fire." Instead, Madison suggested that "relief" from the self-interested advocacy of factions should come only through controlling the *effects* of that advocacy. This relief would be provided by a democratic republic in which government would mediate between opposing factions. The size and diversity of the nation as well as the structure of government would also ensure that even a majority faction could never come to suppress the rights of others.[5]

How we judge interest groups—"good" or "evil"—may depend on how strongly we are committed to freedom or equality (see Chapter 1). Most Americans are generally supportive of citizen groups representing a range of ideological causes (see Figure 7.1). Giving people the freedom to organize lobbies, however, does not guarantee that they will all end up with equally powerful interest groups acting on their behalf. Judgment is also influenced by whether we believe democracy works best if it abides by majoritarian or by pluralist principles (see Chapter 1). We return to these broader questions of democratic theory after looking at the operation of interest groups more closely.

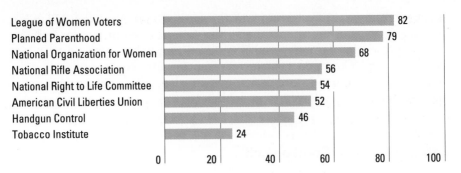

Percentage of respondents with favorable opinion

FIGURE 7.1 *Special Interest Groups: We Just Love 'Em*
Despite some anxiety over the power of special interest groups, the results of this Gallup poll show that Americans applaud the work of most individual lobbying organizations. Nevertheless, there is substantial variation in the approval ratings, and the low score for the Tobacco Institute indicates that some organizations are seen in a less-than-positive light. (Source: Gallup Report, May 1989, pp. 25–27. Used by permission.)

The Roles of Interest Groups

The "evil" side of interest group politics is all too apparent. Each group pushes its own selfish interests, which, despite the group's claims to the contrary, are not always in the best interest of other Americans. The "good" side of interest group advocacy may not be as clear. How do the actions of interest groups benefit our political system?[6]

Representation. Interest groups represent people before their government. Just as a member of Congress represents a particular constituency, so does a lobbyist. A lobbyist for the National Association of Broadcasters, for example, speaks for the interests of radio and television broadcasters when Congress or a government agency is considering a relevant policy decision.

Whatever the political interest—the cement industry, social security, endangered species—it is helpful to have an active lobby operating in Washington. Members of Congress represent a multitude of interests —some of them conflicting—from their own districts and states. Government administrators, too, are pulled in different directions and have their own policy preferences. Interest groups articulate their members' concerns, presenting them directly and forcefully in the political forum.

Participation. Interest groups are also vehicles for political *participation.* They provide a means by which like-minded citizens can pool their resources and channel their energies into collective political action. One farmer fighting for more generous price supports probably will not get very far, but thousands of farmers united in an organization stand a much better chance of getting policymakers to consider their needs.

Education. As part of their efforts at lobbying and increasing their membership, interest groups help *educate* their members, the public at large, and government officials. Although they give only their side of the "facts," they do bring more information out into the open to be digested and evaluated by the public.

Agenda building. In a related role, interest groups bring new issues into the political limelight through a process called **agenda building.** There are many problem areas in American society, but not all of them are being addressed by public officials. Interest groups, through their advocacy, make the government aware of problems and then press for solutions. For example, after videocassette recorders (VCRs) became popular in the United States, competing lobbies raised a number of questions about copyright law and royalty payments to movie studios. The Motion Picture Association of America and the Electronic Industries Association (the trade group for VCR manufacturers) brought these issues to the fore by pressing Congress for action.[7]

Program monitoring. Finally, interest groups engage in **program monitoring.** In other words, they follow government programs important to their constituents, keeping abreast of developments in Washington and in the local communities where policies are implemented. When problems emerge, interest groups push administrators to resolve them in ways that promote the groups' goals. They draw attention to agency officials' transgressions and even file suit to stop actions they consider unlawful.

Interest groups do, then, play some positive roles in their pursuit of self-interest. But it is too soon to assume that the positive side of interest groups neatly balances the negative. Questions remain to be answered about the overall impact of interest groups on public policymaking. Most important, are the effects of interest group advocacy being controlled, as Madison believed they should be?

How Interest Groups Form

Do some people form interest groups more easily than others? Are some factions represented, while others are not? Pluralists assume that when a political issue arises, interest groups with relevant policy concerns begin to lobby. Policy conflicts are ultimately resolved through bargaining and negotiation between the involved organizations and government. Unlike Madison, who dwelt on the potential for harm by factions, pluralists believe interest groups are a good thing, that they further democracy by broadening representation within the system.

An important part of pluralism is the belief that new interest groups form as a matter of course when the need arises. David Truman outlined this idea in his classic work, *The Governmental Process.*[8] He said that when individuals are threatened by change, they band together in an interest group. For example, if government threatens to regulate a particular industry, the firms making up that industry will start a trade association to protect their financial well-being. Truman saw a direct cause-and-effect relationship in all of this: Existing groups stand in equilibrium until some type of disturbance (such as falling wages or declining farm prices) forces new groups to form.

Truman's disturbance theory paints an idealized portrait of interest group politics in America. In real life, people do not automatically organize when they are adversely affected by some disturbance. A good example of this "nonorganization" can be found in Herbert Gans's book *The Urban Villagers.*[9] Gans, a sociologist, moved into the West End, a low-income neighborhood in Boston, during the late 1950s. The neighborhood had been targeted for urban redevelopment; the city was planning to replace existing buildings with modern ones. This meant that the people living there—primarily poor Italian-Americans who very much liked their neighborhood—would have to move. The people of the West End barely put up a fight to save their neighborhood. An organization was started but attracted little support. Residents remained unorganized; soon they were moved and buildings were demolished.

Disturbance theory clearly fails to explain what happened in Boston's West End. An adverse condition or change does not automatically mean that an interest group will form. What, then, is the missing ingredient? According to political scientist Robert Salisbury, the quality of interest group leadership may be the crucial factor.[10]

Interest Group Entrepreneurs

Salisbury likens the role of an interest group leader to that of an entrepreneur in the business world. An entrepreneur is someone who starts new enterprises, usually at considerable personal financial risk. Salisbury maintains that an **interest group entrepreneur** or organizer succeeds or fails for many of the same reasons a business entrepreneur does. The interest group entrepreneur must have something attractive to "market" in order to convince members to join.[11] Potential members must be persuaded that the benefits of joining outweigh the costs.

The development of the United Farm Workers Union shows the importance of leadership in the formation of an interest group. This union is made up of men and women who pick crops in California and other parts of the Southwest. The pickers are predominantly poor, uneducated Mexican-Americans.

Throughout the twentieth century, there had been efforts to organize the pickers. Yet for many reasons, including distrust of union organizers, intimidation by employers, and lack of money to pay union dues, all had failed. Then in 1962, Cesar Chavez, a poor Mexican-American, began to crisscross the central valley of California, talking to workers and planting the idea of a union.

At first, Chavez tried to build a stronger union by recruiting a larger membership. After a strike against grape growers failed in 1965, he changed his tactics. Copying the black civil rights movement, Chavez and his followers marched 250 miles to the state capitol in Sacramento to demand help from the governor. This march and other nonviolent tactics began to draw sympathy from people who had no direct involvement in farming.

With his stature increased by that support, Chavez called for a boycott. A small but significant number of Americans stopped buying grapes. The growers, who had bitterly fought the union, were finally hurt in their wallets. Under other economic pressure, they eventually agreed to recognize and bargain with the United Farm Workers Union. The union, in turn, helped its members through the wage and benefit agreements it was able to negotiate.

Who Is Being Organized?

The case of the late Cesar Chavez is a good example of the importance of leadership in the formation of a new interest group. Despite many years of adverse conditions, efforts to organize the farm workers had failed. The dynamic leadership of Cesar Chavez is what seems to have made the difference.

But another important element is at work in the formation of interest groups. The residents of Boston's West End and the farm workers in California were poor, uneducated or undereducated, and politically inexperienced—factors that made it extremely difficult to organize them into interest groups. If they had been well-to-do, educated, and politically experienced, they probably would have banded together immediately. People who have money, are educated, and know how the system operates are more confident that their actions can make a difference.

Every existing interest group has its own unique history, but the three variables just discussed help explain why groups may or may not become fully organized. First, an adverse change or disturbance can contribute to people's awareness that they need political representation. However, change alone does not ensure that an organization will form, and organizations have formed in the absence of disturbance. Second, the quality of leadership is critical in the organization of interest groups. Finally, the higher the socioeconomic level of potential members is, the more likely they are to know the value of interest groups and to participate in politics by joining them.

A question remains: It is not *whether* various opposing interests are represented but *how well* they are represented. Or, in terms of Madison's premise in "Federalist No. 10," are the effects of faction—in this case, the advantages of the wealthy and well educated—being controlled? Before we can answer this question, we need to turn our attention to the resources available to interest groups.

Interest Group Resources

The strengths, capabilities, and effects of an interest group depend in large part on its *resources*. A group's most significant resources are its members, lobbyists, and money, including funds that can be contributed to political candidates. The sheer quantity of a group's resources is important, and so is the wisdom with which these resources are used.

Members

One of the most valuable resources an interest group can have is a large, politically active membership. If a lobbyist is trying to convince a legislator to support a particular bill, it is tremendously helpful to have a large group of members living in the legislator's home district or state. The National Rifle Association is an effective interest group on Capitol Hill because members of Congress know that the NRA keeps its 2.6 million members informed on how each senator and each representative votes on proposed gun control bills, and many of those members might be influenced by that information when they go to the polls.

Members give an organization not only the political muscle to influence policy but also financial resources. The more money an organization can collect through dues and contributions, the more people it can hire to lobby government officials and monitor the policymaking process. Greater resources also allow the organization to communicate with its members more and inform them better. And funding helps the group maintain its membership and attract new members.

Maintaining membership. To keep the members it already has, an organization must persuade them that it is doing a good job in its advocacy efforts. A major tool for shoring up support among members is a newsletter or magazine. Through publications, members are informed and reminded about the organization's activities.

Business, professional, and labor associations generally have an easier time holding onto members than do **citizen groups**—groups whose basis of organization is a concern for issues that are not related to the members' jobs. In many corporations, membership in a trade group constitutes only a minor business expense. Labor unions are helped in states where workers are required to belong to the union that is the bargaining agent with their employer. Citizen groups, in contrast, base their appeal on members' ideological sentiments. These groups face a difficult challenge: Issues can blow hot and cold, and a particularly hot issue one year may not hold the same interest to citizens the next.

Attracting new members. All interest groups are constantly looking for new members to expand resources and clout. Groups that rely on ideological appeals have a special problem because the competition in most policy areas is intense. People concerned about the environment, for example, can join a seemingly infinite number of local, state, and national groups that lobby on environmental issues.

One method of attracting new members that is being used more and more is **direct mail**—letters sent to a selected audience to promote the organization and appeal for contributions. The main drawbacks to direct mail are its expense and low rate of return.

The free-rider problem. The need for aggressive marketing by interest groups suggests that it is not easy to get people who sympathize with a group's goals actually to join and support it with their contributions. Economists call this difficulty the **free-rider problem**, but we might call it, more colloquially, the "let George do it" problem.[12] The funding for public television stations illustrates this dilemma. Almost all agree that public television, which survives in large part through viewers' contributions, is of great value. But only a fraction of those who watch public television contribute on a regular basis because the free rider has the same access to public television as the contributor.

The same problem crops up for interest groups. When a lobbying group wins benefits, those benefits are not restricted to members of the organization. Therefore, many individuals do not join an interest group even though they might benefit from its efforts; they prefer instead to let others shoulder the financial burden.

The free-rider problem increases the difficulty of attracting paying members. Nevertheless, as we discuss later in this chapter, the number of interest groups has grown significantly in recent years. Millions of Americans contribute to interest groups because they are concerned about an issue or feel a responsibility to help organizations that work on their behalf.[13] Also, many organizations offer membership benefits that have nothing to do with politics or lobbying. Business trade associations, for example, are a source of information about industry trends and effective management practices; and they organize conventions where members can learn, socialize, and occasionally find new customers or suppliers.

Lobbyists

Part of the money raised by interest groups is used to pay lobbyists, who represent the organizations before government. Lobbyists make sure that people in government know what their members want and that

Feature 7.1

His Client: Japan, Inc.

When a Japanese company runs into a problem with the United States government, one person it is likely to call on for help is Stanton Anderson. Part lawyer, part troubleshooter, and part lobbyist, Anderson is very successful at all he does.

After graduating from college, Anderson became a Washington lobbyist for an aviation trade group. He also worked in Republican politics before pursuing a law degree. Later he gained invaluable experience working for the Commerce Department, where he held a high-ranking job doing congressional liaison.

In addition to being a senior partner in a law firm that he founded, Anderson is also head of Global USA, a lobbying firm. His Japanese clients include All Nippon Airways and high-tech companies such as Fanuc Ltd. and Kyocera Corp. When clients such as Japanese telecommunications companies are threatened with tariffs, Anderson devises strategies to convince members of Congress that a likely consequence of such a law would be retaliation by the Japanese government that would hurt American companies doing business in Japan.

Anderson stresses that his job is not just lobbying the U.S. government; he also explains America to his foreign clients. Says Anderson, "I interpret things for my clients. They tend to want to solicit as much information as they can. . . . I just happen to be a source."

Sources: Clyde H. Farnsworth, "Japan's Top U.S. Lobbyist." *New York Times,* June 2, 1985, p. F6; Kathryn Johnson, "How Foreign Powers Play for Status in Washington," *U.S. News & World Report,* June 17, 1985, pp. 35–40; and Eduardo Lachica, "Japanese Are Lobbying Hard in U.S. to Offset Big Protectionist Push," *Wall Street Journal,* August 23, 1985, p. 1.

their organizations know what government is doing (see Features 7.1 and 7.2).

Lobbyists can be full-time employees of the organization or employees of public relations or law firms who are hired on retainer. When hiring a lobbyist, an interest group looks for someone who knows his or her way around Washington. Lobbyists are valued for their experience and knowledge of how government operates. Often they are people who have served in the legislative or executive branches, where they have had firsthand experience with government.

Lobbying is a lucrative profession. One study of Washington representatives from a variety of organizations found that the average yearly salary was just over $90,000.[14] The financial rewards are such that many former members of Congress are part of the profession. As one old Washington saying has it, "They come to govern, they stay to lobby."[15] In order to prevent former members of Congress from earning large sala-

Her Client: Poor Children

Marian Wright Edelman's constituents do not pay dues to her organization. They do not read newsletters that explain what her organization is doing for them. Indeed, precious few of this country's poor youth have ever heard of an organization called the Children's Foundation.

The Children's Foundation lobbies on behalf of a variety of health and social service issues, including family planning to prevent teenage pregnancy. Edelman knows the numbing statistics all too well: Every year 1.1 million teenage girls get pregnant. This figure includes 125,000 girls fifteen years old or younger. The poorest girls are the most likely to get pregnant.

The daughter of a small-town Baptist minister in South Carolina, Edelman went to Spelman College and Yale Law School. She worked as a civil rights lawyer for the NAACP Legal Defense Fund in Mississippi before coming to Washington. She founded the Children's Defense Fund in 1973 and has built it into a respected organization with an annual budget of $4.4 million and a staff of sixty-seven.

One focus of Edelman's lobbying is to make government officials understand that helping poor children is not only a humane thing to do but also a way of saving resources in the long run. Says Edelman, "Our goal is to educate the nation about the needs of children and encourage preventive investment in children before they get sick, drop out of school, or get into trouble."

Edelman's message should gain a sympathetic hearing in the Clinton White House. Her close friend, Hillary Rodham Clinton, has been involved with the Children's Defense Fund for two decades as a lawyer and as a member of the board. Another friend, Donna Shalala, serves as Clinton's Secretary of Health and Human Services. Edelman was herself considered for a cabinet-level appointment, but she prefers to remain an independent, outside voice.

Sources: *Public Interest Profiles* (Washington, D.C.: Foundation for Public Affairs, 1986), p. 13; Lena Williams, "She Whose Constituents Are 61 Million Children," *New York Times*, February 27, 1986, p. B10; Katherine Bouton, "Marian Wright Edelman," *Ms.* (July-August 1987); 98ff; Marian Wright Edelman, "How to Prevent Teenage Pregnancy," *Ebony* (July 1987); 62–66. Thomas Toch, "Hillary Clinton, Directing a Sweeping Children's Crusade," *U.S. News & World Report*, December 28, 1992, p. 46; and "Power and the Glory," *Newsweek*, December 28, 1992, pp. 12–19.

ries lobbying on behalf of the very legislation they worked on while there, since 1991, such individuals cannot lobby the House or Senate for a year after leaving office.[16]

Bill Clinton imposed even more stringent requirements on the highest ranking appointed officials in his administration. They may not lobby any agency "with respect to which they had substantial personal responsibility" for a period of five years after they leave office. In addition, they are banned for life from representing any foreign government.[17]

By the nature of their location, many Washington law firms are drawn into lobbying. Corporations without their own Washington offices rely heavily on law firms to lobby for them before the national government. Over time, lawyer-lobbyists tend to develop expertise in particular policy areas.

The most common image of a lobbyist is that of an "arm twister," someone who spends most of the time trying to convince a legislator or administrator to back a certain policy. But lobbying is more subtle than that. Lobbyists' primary job is to pass on information to policymakers. Lobbyists provide government officials and their staffs with a constant flow of data that support their organizations' policy goals. Lobbyists also try to build a compelling case for their goals, showing that the "facts" dictate that a change be made. What lobbyists are really trying to do, of course, is to convince policymakers that their data deserve more attention and are more accurate than those presented by other lobbyists.

Political Action Committees

One of the organizational resources that can make a lobbyist's job easier is a **political action committee (PAC)**. PACs pool campaign contributions from group members and donate those funds to candidates for political office. Under federal law, a PAC can give up to $5,000 for each separate election to a candidate for Congress. A change in campaign finance law in 1974 led to a rapid increase in the number of PACs. The greatest growth came from corporations, most of which had been legally prohibited from operating political action committees. There was also rapid growth in the number of **nonconnected PACs**, largely ideological groups that have no parent lobbying organization and are formed solely for the purpose of raising and channeling campaign funds. (A PAC can be the campaign-wing affiliate of an existing interest group or a wholly independent, unaffiliated group.)

Why do interest groups form PACs? One businessman said his company formed a PAC because "talking to politicians is fine, but with a little money they hear you better."[18] Members of Congress and their staffers generally are eager to meet with representatives of their constituencies, but their time is limited. However, a member of Congress or an assistant would find it difficult to turn down a request for a meeting with a lobbyist from a company if its PAC had made a campaign contribution in the last election.

Typically, PACs, like most other interest groups, are highly pragmatic organizations; pushing a particular political philosophy takes second place to achieving immediate policy goals. As a group, corporate PACs gave 83 percent of their contributions to incumbent members of

Congress—many of them liberal and moderate Democrats—during the two years preceding the 1990 election.[19] Citizen-group PACs tend to be moved more by ideology; they give a higher proportion of their funds to challengers than do business, labor, or trade-group PACs. For most PACs, donations are a means of gaining access, and that access is seen as critical to gaining influence with congressional offices.[20]

The growing role of PACs in financing congressional campaigns has become the most controversial aspect of interest group politics. Close to one-half the members of the House of Representatives receive 50 percent or more of all their campaign contributions from political action committees.[21] Critics charge that PAC money can lead to favoritism and corruption; they point to the savings and loan (S&L) scandal, which will cost taxpayers hundreds of billions of dollars, as an example. The savings and loan industry gave more than $11 million in donations to members of Congress during the 1980s.[22] Some of the influential legislators who were recipients of these funds intervened with federal regulators and asked administrators to go easy on some S&Ls that were in financial difficulty.

It should come as no surprise that corporate PACs contribute more to congressional candidates than any other PACs. But in a democracy, influence should not be a function of money; some citizens have little to give, yet their rights need to be protected. From this perspective, the issue is political equality. In the words of Republican Senator Robert Dole, "There aren't any Poor PACs or Food Stamp PACs or Nutrition PACs or Medicare PACs."[23]

Nevertheless, strong arguments can be made for retaining PACs. They offer a means for people to participate in the political system. They allow small givers to pool their resources and to fight the feeling that one person cannot make a difference. PAC defenders also point out that prohibiting PACs would amount to restricting freedom of political expression.

Lobbying Tactics

Keep in mind that lobbying extends beyond the legislative branch. Groups can seek help from the courts and administrative agencies as well as from Congress. Moreover, interest groups may shift their focus from one branch of government to another. After a bill becomes a law, for example, a group that lobbied for the legislation will probably try to influence the administrative agency responsible for implementing the new law. Some policy decisions are left unresolved by legislation and are settled through regulations. The lobby wants to make sure regulatory decisions are as close as possible to the group's preferences.

We discuss three types of lobbying tactics here: those aimed at policymakers and implemented through interest group representatives (direct lobbying); those that involve group members (grassroots lobbying);

and those directed toward the public (information campaigns). We also examine the cooperative efforts of interest groups to influence government through coalitions.

Direct Lobbying

Direct lobbying relies on personal contact with policymakers. One survey of Washington lobbyists showed that 98 percent used direct contact with government officials to express their groups' views.[24] This interaction takes place when a lobbyist meets with a member of Congress, an agency official, or a staff member. In these meetings, lobbyists usually convey their arguments in the form of data about a specific issue. If a lobbyist from, for example, the Chamber of Commerce meets with a member of Congress about a bill the organization backs, the lobbyist does not say (or even suggest), "Vote for this bill, or our people in the district will vote against you in the next election." Instead, the lobbyist might say, "If this bill is passed, we're going to see hundreds of new jobs created back home." The representative has no trouble at all figuring out that a vote for the bill can help in the next election.

Personal lobbying is a day-in, day-out process. Lobbyists must maintain contact with congressional and agency staffers, constantly providing them with pertinent data. Lobbyists for the American Gas Association, for instance, keep a list of 1,200 agency personnel who are "called frequently to share informally in association intelligence." The director of the group's lobbying efforts has a shorter list of 104 key administrators with whom he has met personally and who can "be counted on to provide information on agency decisionmaking."[25]

A tactic related to direct lobbying is *testifying* at committee hearings when a bill is before Congress. This tactic allows the interest group to put its views on record and make them widely known when the hearing testimony is published. Although testifying is one of the most visible parts of lobbying, it is generally considered window dressing. Most lobbyists believe that testimony usually does little by itself to persuade members of Congress.

Another direct but somewhat different approach is *legal advocacy*. Using this tactic, a group tries to achieve its policy goals through litigation. During the Reagan years, the Department of the Interior had little sympathy for environmental groups. When the department tried to open more ocean land for offshore drilling, the National Resources Defense Council and other environmental groups used litigation in an effort to stop the policy from being implemented.[26]

Grassroots Lobbying

Grassroots lobbying involves an interest group's rank-and-file members and may also include people outside the organization who sympathize with its goals. Grassroots tactics, such as letter-writing campaigns and

May We Have Your Attention?
One technique used by interest groups to influence policymakers is the mass
demonstration. Here the National Organization for Women sponsored a rally
which, in 1992, attracted thousands of pro-choice demonstrators to an area
very near the White House.

protests, are often used in conjunction with direct lobbying by Washington representatives. Policymakers are more concerned about what a lobbyist says when they know that constituents are really watching their decisions.

If people in government seem unresponsive to conventional lobbying tactics, a group may resort to some form of *political protest*. A protest or demonstration, such as picketing or marching, is designed to attract media attention to an issue. When three thousand farmers from the American Agriculture Movement drove tractors from their homes to Washington to show their disappointment with Carter administration farm policies, the spectacle attracted considerable publicity. Their unconventional approach increased the public's awareness of falling produce prices and stimulated the government to take some limited action.[27]

The main drawback to protest activity is that policymaking is a long-term, incremental process, whereas a demonstration is short-lived. It is difficult to sustain the anger and activism of group supporters—to keep large numbers of people involved in protest after protest—simply to keep the group's demands in the public eye. A notable exception was the civil rights demonstrations of the 1960s, which were sustained over a long period. The protests were a major factor in public opinion, which, in turn, hastened the passage of the Civil Rights Act of 1964 and the Voting Rights Act of 1965.[28]

Information Campaigns

Interest groups generally feel that public backing adds strength to their lobbying efforts. They believe that they will get that backing if they make the public aware of their positions and the evidence that supports them. To this end, interest groups launch **information campaigns**, organized efforts to gain public backing by bringing group views to the public's attention. Various means are used. Some are directed at the larger public; others, at smaller audiences with longstanding interest in an issue.

Public relations is one information tactic. A public relations campaign may involve sending speakers to meetings in various parts of the country or producing pamphlets and handouts. A highly visible form of political public relations is newspaper and magazine advertising. But it has one major drawback: It is extremely expensive. Consequently, few groups rely on newspaper and magazine advertising as their primary weapon.

Sponsoring *research* is another way interest groups press their cases. When a group believes that evidence has not been fully developed in a certain area, it may commission research on the subject. For example, groups working for the rights of the disabled have protected programs from would-be budget cutters by, for example, providing "lawmakers with abundant research findings demonstrating that it costs much more to keep people in institutions . . . than it does to utilize home and community living programs."[29]

Some groups believe that publicizing *voting records* of members of Congress is an effective means of influencing public opinion. These interest groups simply publish in their newsletters a record of how all members of Congress voted on issues of particular concern to the organization. Other groups prepare statistical indexes that compare the voting records of all members of Congress on selected key issues. Each member is graded (from 0 to 100 percent) according to how often he or she voted in agreement with the group's views.

Coalition Building

A final aspect of lobbying strategy is **coalition building**, in which several organizations band together for the purpose of lobbying. This joint effort conserves or makes more effective use of the resources of groups with similar views. Coalitions form most often among groups that work in the same policy area and are similar in their political outlook.[30] On feminist issues, for example, the National Organization for Women, the National Women's Political Caucus, the League of Women Voters, the American Association of University Women, and the Women's Equity Action League usually work with one another.[31] Most coalitions are informal, ad hoc arrangements.

The Growth of Interest Group Politics

The growing number of active interest groups is one of the most important trends in American politics. One survey of Washington-based lobbies showed that fully 30 percent of existing groups were formed between 1960 and 1980.[32] The greatest growth occurred in three types of interest groups: PACs (which we discussed earlier), citizen groups, and business lobbies.

The Public Interest Movement

Many recently formed citizen groups are commonly known as *public interest groups*. A **public interest group** is generally considered to have no economic self-interest in the policies it pursues.[33] For example, the members of the environmental groups fighting for stricter pollution-control requirements in the bill described at the opening of this chapter receive no financial gain from the institution of such standards. The benefits to members are largely ideological and aesthetic. In contrast, corporations fighting against the same stringent standards are trying to protect profits. The motives of these two sets of groups are different. The environmental lobby is a public interest group; the corporation is not.

Many public interest groups have become major players in national politics. Common Cause, one of the best-known "good government" groups, works for campaign finance reform, codes of ethics in government, and open congressional and administrative proceedings.[34]

Origins of the movement.   Traditionally, public interest lobbies have not been a major factor in Washington politics. Yet the upsurge of these groups that began in the late 1960s did not prove to be as short-lived a phenomenon as many had expected. At first, most new groups were on the liberal side of the political spectrum. However, many new conservative groups have recently formed. Groups on both the Left and the Right have become more politically prominent.

Why have so many public interest groups formed in the last two decades? The movement grew from the civil rights and anti–Vietnam War activism of the 1960s.[35] In both cases, citizens with passionate beliefs about a cause felt that political parties and the electoral process were not producing change; collective citizen action had to be used instead.

The late 1960s and early 1970s were also a time when Americans were becoming increasingly cynical about government. Loyalty to political parties was declining, too. If neither government nor political parties could be trusted to provide adequate representation in the nation's capital on such issues as preserving the environment or protecting consumers, then the obvious alternative was membership in an ideological interest group.

Conservative reaction.   Why conservatives were slower than liberals to mobilize is not altogether clear, but the new right-of-center groups appear, in part, to be a reaction to the perceived success of liberal groups. Conservative groups, like their liberal counterparts, cover a wide variety of policy areas. Most stand in direct opposition to causes espoused by liberal organizations. Phyllis Schlafly's Eagle Forum, for example, fought long and hard against the Equal Rights Amendment and other positions favored by feminist groups.

But conservative groups are not merely mirror images of liberal citizen lobbies.[36] A distinctive feature of the "New Right" is the active participation of religious organizations. Groups such as the Religious Roundtable and Christian Voice actively promote policies that they feel are in line with Christian teachings, such as permitting prayer in school and restricting abortions.[37] Some Americans who believe that the country is best served by a complete separation of church and state strongly criticize the lobbying of the religious Right. But the religious Right believes that its moral duty is to see that Christian principles are embodied in government policy.

During the Reagan presidency, conservative citizen groups enjoyed substantial access to the White House, their lobbyists meeting frequently with White House aides.[38] They did not have the same degree of success with Congress, however, where many of their most cherished goals—including a constitutional amendment allowing school prayer—were not realized. Conservative groups were not as enthusiastic about George Bush, whom many considered a "closet moderate," or Bill Clinton, whose positions on several issues they found, and still find, unacceptable.

Business Lobbies

The number of business lobbies in Washington has also increased. Offices of individual corporations and of business trade associations are more in evidence than ever before. A **trade association**, such as the Mortgage Bankers Association or the National Electrical Manufacturers Association, is an organization that represents companies within the same industry. At one point during the 1970s when the boom in business lobbying began, trade associations were moving their headquarters to Washington at an average of one every week.[39] Corporations that

The Tax Lobbyist

Charls Walker is one of the most skilled business lobbyists in Washington. He holds a Ph.D. in economics and was a high-ranking official in the U.S. Treasury Department. Because of Walker's expertise and political skills, many large corporations hire him to lobby Congress on tax policy.

already had offices in Washington typically upgraded them by adding staff.

The vast increase in business representation in Washington was in large part a response to the expanded scope of national government activities during the 1960s and 1970s. Ironically, that expansion followed directly from the success of liberal public interest groups that strongly supported regulation to protect the environment and consumers. As the Environmental Protection Agency, the Consumer Product Safety Commission, and other regulatory agencies were created, many more companies found themselves affected by federal regulations. And those located outside of Washington often found themselves *reacting* to policies already made rather than *participating* in their making. They saw a move to Washington—where the policymakers are—as necessary if they were to obtain information on pending government actions in enough time to act on them.

The increase in business advocacy in Washington was also fueled by the competitive nature of business lobbying. For example, in recent years insurance companies, brokerage houses, investment banks, and retail banks have all made efforts to encroach on one another's turf. So many new players have entered the picture that policymaking has become even more complex. A member of the House Banking Committee said of the change, "When I first came to Congress there were five major financial trade groups, but now there are at least five times that. Now if you're trying to satisfy all the trade groups, it's pretty hard to do."[40]

The growth of business lobbies has reinforced and possibly expanded the overrepresentation of business in national politics. As Figure 7.2 shows, approximately one-half of all interest groups with a Washington office are either corporations or business trade associations. And because business lobbies are able to draw on the institutional resources of corporations, they can fund their lobbying operations more easily than can groups that depend on the voluntary contributions of individuals.

Interest Groups: An Evaluation

The pluralist scholars who wrote during the 1950s and 1960s were right on one important point but wrong on another. They argued that interest groups are at the center of the policymaking process. Certainly, the growing number of groups in recent years seems to reflect a broad acceptance of this view by various sectors of American society. Although pluralists never predicted perfect representation of affected interests, they did assume that representation would be more balanced than it is. What the country has instead is a political system increasingly centered on interest group advocacy but one in which some interests—most notably, those of business—are much better represented than others. What are the consequences of this condition?

One consequence is that the large and growing number of interest groups works against a strengthening of our party system. Many activists find narrowly based interest groups more appealing than parties. The lobbies that these activists support work intensely on the few issues they care about most; parties often dilute issue stands to appeal to as broad a segment of the electorate as possible. Thus, many people who care deeply about public policy questions work to influence government through particular lobbies rather than through political parties. This surely contributes to Americans' lack of concern for revitalizing the parties, for making them more responsive policymaking bodies.

This lack of concern is unfortunate. Interest groups can do no more than supplement the functions of parties. Most interest groups are small bodies concerned with only a few issues. Parties, however, can be instruments of majoritarian democracy. They can bring together broad coalitions of people and translate their concerns into large-scale social and economic change. Parties are particularly important because they can represent those who are not well represented by interest groups. As political scientist Walter Dean Burnham put it, parties "can generate countervailing collective power on behalf of the many individually

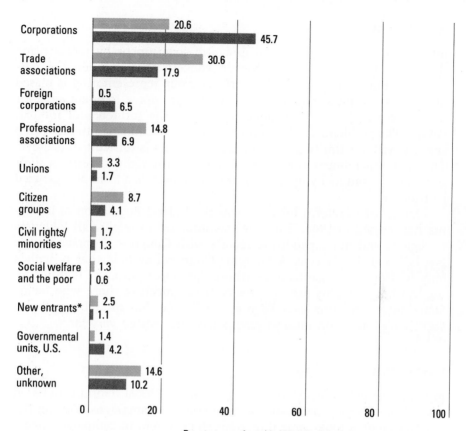

Percentage of total in Washington, D.C.

■ Office in Washington, D.C.
■ Retains lobbyist in Washington, D.C., or has office there.

FIGURE 7.2   *The Washington Interest Group Community*
Although the interest group community is highly diverse, business organiza-
tions form the biggest part of that community. Corporations and trade associ-
ations are the most prevalent interest group actors in terms of having an office
in Washington or, at the very least, employing a lobbyist there. From Organized
Interests and American Democracy *by Kay Lehman Schlozman and John T. Tierney.*
(Copyright © 1986 by Kay Lehman Schlozman and John T. Tierney. Reprinted by permis-
sion of HarperCollins Publishers, Inc. Adapted from the Encyclopedia of Associations,
ed. Denise S. Akey. Gale Research.)

powerless against the relatively few who are individually—or organizationally—powerful."[41] Unfortunately, few people seem interested in re-
viving the parties at the cost of their own interest group's influence. If
our party system is revitalized, then it will be because the parties make
themselves more appealing, not because people turn away from their
interest groups.

Regulation

Interest groups contribute to democratic government by representing their supporters' interests. However, concern that individual groups have too much influence or that interest group representation is biased in favor of certain segments of society has prompted frequent calls for reform. Yet little has been done to weaken the influence of interest groups. The problem, as Madison foresaw, is that limiting interest group activity without limiting fundamental freedoms is difficult to achieve. The First Amendment guarantees Americans the right to petition their government, and lobbying, at its most basic level, is a form of organized petitioning.

One effort to reform lobbying was the Federal Regulation of Lobbying Act, passed in 1946. This law was intended to require all lobbyists to register and file expenditure reports with Congress. In practice, the law has been ineffective. A Supreme Court ruling held that it applies only to people or organizations whose "principal purpose" is influencing legislation.[42] This exempts many, if not most, of those who lobby. Some modest reforms have been enacted since that time, but calls for stricter regulation on interest groups have not gotten very far.[43]

Campaign Financing

Much of the debate over interest groups and political reform centers on the role PACs play in financing congressional campaigns. During the 1970s, Congress took some important steps to reform campaign financing practices. Strong disclosure requirements now exist so that the source of all significant contributions to candidates for national office is part of the public record. Public financing of presidential campaigns is also provided for; taxpayer money is given in equal amounts to the presidential nominees of the major parties.

Reformers have also sought to reduce the alleged influence of PACs in Congress by calling for public financing and other schemes designed to reduce the percentage of campaign funds supplied by PACs. But incumbents usually find it easier to raise money from PACs than their electoral challengers do, so there is a strong incentive to leave the status quo intact. Strong public criticism of current campaign financing has, however, pushed Congress to take up reform legislation. Nevertheless, sharp partisan differences between Republicans and Democrats have kept a reform bill from being enacted.

The debate over PACs is another manifestation of the sharp tension between the principles of freedom and equality. For many, restrictions on PACs represent restrictions on their personal freedom. Shouldn't people have the right to join others who think as they do and contribute to the candidates of their choice? Others argue that the consequence of PAC giving is to reinforce, if not expand, the inequities between rich and poor.[44]

Summary

Interest groups play many important roles in our political process. They are a means by which citizens can participate in politics, and they communicate their members' views to those in government. Interest groups differ greatly in the resources at their disposal and in the tactics they use to influence government. The number of interest groups has grown sharply in recent years.

Despite the growth and change in the nature of interest groups, the fundamental problem identified by Madison over two hundred years ago endures. In a free and open society, groups form to pursue policies that favor themselves at the expense of the broader national interest. Madison hoped that the solution to this problem would come through the diversity of the population and the structure of our government.

To a certain extent, Madison's expectations have been borne out. The natural differences between groups have prevented the tyranny of any one faction. Yet the interest group system remains unbalanced, with some segments of society (particularly business, the wealthy, and the educated) considerably better organized than others. The growth of citizen groups has reduced this disparity somewhat, but there are still significant inequities in how well different interests are represented in Washington.

These inequities have led most contemporary scholars to reject two key propositions of the early pluralists: that the freedom to form lobbies produces a healthy competition among opposing groups and that the compromises emerging from that competition lead to policies that fairly represent the divisions in society. Instead, business and professional groups have an advantage because of their ability to organize more readily and their greater resources. The interest group system clearly compromises the principle of political equality as stated in the maxim "one person, one vote." Formal political equality is certainly more likely to occur outside of interest group politics in elections between candidates from competing political parties, a circumstance that better fits the majoritarian model of democracy.

Despite the inequities of the interest group system, little general effort has been made to restrict interest group activity. Madison's dictum that suppressing political freedoms must be avoided, even at the expense of permitting interest group activity that promotes the selfish interests of narrow segments of the population, has generally guided public policy. Yet as the problem of PACs demonstrates, government has had to set some restrictions on interest groups. Permitting PACs to give unlimited contributions to political candidates would undermine confidence in the system. Where to draw the limit on PAC activity remains a thorny problem because there is little consensus on how to balance the conflicting needs of our society.

Key Terms

interest group
lobbies
lobbyists

agenda building
program monitoring
interest group entrepreneur

citizen groups
direct mail
free-rider problem
political action committee
  (PAC)
nonconnected PACs

direct lobbying
grassroots lobbying
information campaigns
coalition building
public interest group
trade association

Selected Readings

Berry, Jeffrey M. *The Interest Group Society.* 2d ed. Glenview, Ill.: Scott, Foresman/Little, Brown, 1989. An analysis of the growth of interest group politics.

Berry, Jeffrey M. *Lobbying for the People.* Princeton, N.J.: Princeton University Press, 1977. This is a study of eighty-three public interest groups active in national politics.

Cigler, Allan J., and Burdett A. Loomis, eds. *Interest Group Politics.* 3d ed. Washington, D.C.: Congressional Quarterly, 1991. This reader includes eighteen separate essays on lobbying groups.

Lowi, Theodore J. *The End of Liberalism.* 2d ed. New York: Norton, 1979. This is a critical analysis of the role of interest groups in our society.

Olson, Mancur, Jr. *The Logic of Collective Action.* New York: Schocken, 1968. Olson, an economist, looks at the free-rider problem and the rationale for joining lobbying organizations.

Schlozman, Kay Lehman, and John T. Tierney. *Organized Interests and American Democracy.* New York: Harper and Row, 1986. This valuable and comprehensive study draws on an original survey of Washington lobbyists.

Vogel, David. *Fluctuating Fortunes.* New York: Basic Books, 1989. This book traces the rise and fall and rise of American corporate power.

CONGRESS

8

When Louise Slaughter decided to enter the race for Congress in 1986, she was definitely an underdog. Slaughter, a Democrat, ran against a sitting member of the House of Representatives, Republican Fred Eckert. It is extremely difficult to defeat sitting members (incumbents), although Eckert had first won election to Congress in 1984 and was a little less secure than most incumbents. Before Eckert, another Republican had served this suburban Rochester, New York, district for twenty years.

Despite the odds, the New York state assemblywoman plunged ahead. With some early campaign contributions from labor PACs, Slaughter began to build a campaign organization. She proved effective at raising money, which gave her campaign credibility and made it easier to raise additional funds from those cautious about donating funds to the challenger of an incumbent. Eventually, hundreds of thousands of dollars from PACs would flow into Slaughter's and Eckert's campaign war chests, and overall campaign spending in this one district topped $1 million.

During his term in Washington, Eckert voted in line with President Reagan's positions more than any other single member of Congress. His rock-ribbed conservative ideology led him to cast a number of votes that offended various constituencies back home, such as a vote to reduce social security payments, a vote against the student loan program, a vote against funding for toxic waste cleanup, and a vote against imposing sanctions on the apartheid government of South Africa. Slaughter exploited those votes with TV ads.

Slaughter did a far better job of developing a campaign organization than did Eckert. She had an energized troop of volunteers who went door to door in the district; Eckert recruited few people to work on his behalf. Eckert also was an erratic campaigner, while Slaughter aggressively attacked him for his unpopular votes. Despite these disadvantages, the power of incumbency almost pulled Eckert through— Slaughter won by just 3,300 votes.[1] Eckert was one of only six incumbents who lost that fall.

The Slaughter-Eckert race illustrates one of the basic dynamics of American democracy: the conflict between local politics and national politics. Eckert went to Washington wanting to promote the ideological, conservative agenda so powerfully articulated by Ronald Reagan. If he thought he had a mandate to vote this way from his constituents, he was wrong. Different constituency groups within the district were strongly opposed to parts of the Reagan program, and when Eckert voted against the interests of senior citizens, environmentalists, and so on, he was inadvertently building Slaughter's electoral base. Eckert wanted to be an instrument of majoritarian democracy; he was undone, instead, by the forces of pluralist democracy.

In this chapter and in Chapters 9, 10, and 11, we emphasize the tension between pluralist and majoritarian visions of democracy. In democracies this conflict is evident in the way legislators act as representatives of their constituencies. Thus, two central questions emerge in studying Congress. First, when members of Congress vote on policy issues, whom *do* they actually represent? And second, whom *should* they represent? We try to answer the first question here, leaving you to think about the second.

The Origin and Powers of Congress

The framers of the Constitution wanted to keep power from being concentrated in the hands of a few, but they were also concerned with creating a union strong enough to overcome the weaknesses of the government that had operated under the Articles of Confederation. They argued passionately about the structure of the new government. In the end, they produced a legislative body that was as much an experiment as was the new nation's democracy.

The Great Compromise

The U.S. Congress has two separate and powerful chambers: the House of Representatives and the Senate. A bill cannot become law unless it is passed in identical form by both chambers. When the Constitution was being drafted, "the fiercest struggle for power" centered on representation in the legislature.[2] The small states wanted all states to have equal representation. The more populous states wanted representation based on population; they did not want their power diluted. The Great Compromise broke the deadlock: The small states received equal representation in the Senate, but the House, where the number of each state's representatives would be based on population, retained the sole right to originate money bills.

According to the Constitution, each state is represented by two senators, each of whom serves for six years. Terms of office are staggered, so that one-third of the Senate is elected every two years. When it was ratified, the Constitution directed that senators be chosen by the state legislatures. However, the Seventeenth Amendment, adopted in 1913, provided for the election of senators by popular vote. From the beginning, members of the House of Representatives have been elected by the people. They serve two-year terms, and all House seats are up for election at the same time.

Because each state's representation in the House is in proportion to its population, the Constitution provides for a national census every ten years. Until the first census, the Constitution fixed the number of representatives at 65. As the nation's population grew and new states joined the Union, new seats were added to the House. At some point, however, a legislative body becomes too unwieldy to be efficient, and in 1929, the House decided to fix its membership at 435. Population shifts are handled by the **reapportionment** (redistribution) of representatives among the states after each census is taken. Reapportionment following the 1990 census gave California, the nation's largest state, a gain of 7 seats, giving it 52 representatives overall. Michigan, Ohio, Illinois, and Pennsylvania each lost 2 representatives, and New York lost 3.

Representatives are elected from a particular congressional district within their state. The number of districts in a state is equal to the number of representatives the state sends to the House. Since a series of Supreme Court rulings in the 1960s, the states have been required to draw the boundaries of their districts in such a way that the districts have approximately equal populations.[3]

Duties of the House and the Senate

Although the Great Compromise provided considerably different schemes of representation for the House and the Senate, the Constitution gives them essentially similar legislative tasks. They share many important powers, among them the powers to declare war, raise an army and a navy, borrow and coin money, regulate interstate commerce, create federal courts, establish rules for the naturalization of immigrants, and "make all Laws which shall be necessary and proper for carrying into Execution the foregoing Powers."

Of course, there are at least a few important differences in the constitutional duties of the two chambers. As noted earlier, the House alone has the right to originate revenue bills, which apparently was coveted at the Constitutional Convention. In practice, this function is of limited consequence because all bills—including revenue bills—must be approved by both the House and Senate. The House also has the power of **impeachment**, the power formally to charge the president, vice president, or other "civil Officers" of the national government with "Treason, Bribery, or other high Crimes and Misdemeanors." The Senate is empowered to act as a court to try impeachments; a two-thirds vote of the senators present is necessary for conviction. Only one president—Andrew Johnson—has ever been impeached, and in 1868 the Senate came within a single vote of finding him guilty. More recently, the House Judiciary Committee voted to impeach President Richard Nixon for his role in the Watergate scandal, but he resigned in August 1974 before the full House could vote. A small number of federal judges, however, have been impeached, convicted, and removed from the bench.

The Constitution gives the Senate the power to approve major presidential appointments (such as to federal judgeships, ambassadorships, and Cabinet posts) and treaties with foreign nations. The president is empowered to *make* treaties, but then they must be submitted to the Senate for approval by a two-thirds majority. Because of this requirement, the executive branch generally considers the Senate's sentiments when it negotiates a treaty.

Despite the long list of congressional powers in the Constitution, the question of what powers are appropriate to the Congress has generated substantial controversy. For example, although the Constitution gives Congress the sole power to declare war, many presidents have initiated military action on their own. And at times, the courts have found that congressional actions have usurped the rights of the states.

Electing The Congress

If Americans are not happy with the job Congress is doing, they can use their votes to say so. With a congressional election every two years, the voters have frequent opportunities to express themselves.

The Incumbency Effect

Congressional elections offer voters a chance to show their approval of Congress's performance by re-electing incumbents or "throwing the rascals out." The voters seem to do more re-electing than rascal throwing. The re-election rate is astonishingly high; in the majority of elections since 1950, more than 90 percent of all House incumbents have held their seats (see Figure 8.1). (In 1992, however, less than 90 percent of all

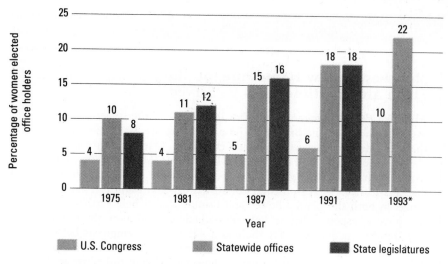

FIGURE 8.1   *Congress: Still the Men's Club*
*In recent years, women have made considerable progress in winning election
to state legislatures and statewide offices. Women have not been as successful
at the congressional level, but 1992 was a major step forward, with more
women than ever before elected to the House and Senate. (Sources: Paula Ries
and Anne J. Stone,* The American Woman, *1992–93 [New York: Norton, 1992], p. 409;*
Election Supplement, *New York Times, November 5, 1992, pp. B1–B13; and Center for
the American Woman and Politics, Eagleton Institute of Politics, Rutgers University.)*

House incumbents running for re-election won.) Most House elections
are not even close; in recent elections most House incumbents have
won at least 60 percent of the vote.[4]

These findings may seem surprising. Congress as a whole is not held
in particularly high esteem. Polls show that only about one-third of the
public expresses a good deal of confidence in the Congress.[5] And in
1992, voters in many states passed initiatives setting limits on the number of terms their members of Congress could serve. (However, these
term limits are of dubious constitutionality.)* People appear to distinguish between the institution of Congress and their own representatives
and senators. Why is it that incumbents do so well? (Because most research on the incumbency effect has focused on House elections, our
discussion concentrates on that body.)

---

* The reason that term limits may be unconstitutional is that the Supreme Court ruled some
years ago that the qualifications for election to Congress are those specified in the Constitution. In 1992, voters passed congressional term limits in all fourteen states where this reform
was on the ballot. (Colorado had passed term limits in 1990.) Limits on terms in the state legislature were also passed through initiatives in many states, and the Supreme Court has already ruled state legislative term limits constitutional.

Manchester, New Hampshire, or Manchester, England, There Are Constituents to Be Served

Although there are some important differences in the structure of the U.S. Congress and the British Parliament, there are many similarities in the way members of both bodies do their jobs. One similarity is that U.S. representatives and members of Parliament (MPs) work extremely hard at cultivating the grassroots. They frequently travel back to their districts to hear what's on their constituents' minds and to offer assistance. In both the United States and Britain, voters believe that legislators have a responsibility to help individuals and promote the economic welfare of their districts. Yet there is a difference in emphasis between the two countries. The figure on the next page charts the results of a poll of American and British citizens who were asked to choose which legislative role was the most important.

In Britain, local concerns seemed paramount. Americans, in contrast, were more likely to cite policy concerns ("policymaking" and "oversight"). The weaker committee system and stronger party system in Britain make it more difficult for rank-and-file legislators to influence policy outcomes. The British responses to the interview questions might have reflected this reality.

Legislators place such importance on their work in the constituency because they want to be re-elected and they believe that the help they offer constituents wins them loyal voters. This is not wishful thinking. Research shows that American and British legislators who more actively promote service to constituents are better known, more highly rated, and more successful at the ballot box than legislators who do not work as hard in the constituency. In addition, American representatives have large staffs—typically, four or five full-time caseworkers—to tackle constituents' problems. British MPs have little or no help handling casework; they have to do it the old-fashioned way—by themselves.

(continued)

Redistricting. One explanation of the incumbency effect centers on **redistricting**, the way House districts are redrawn after a census-based reapportionment. It is entirely possible for state legislatures to draw new districts to benefit the incumbents of one or both parties. Altering district lines for partisan advantage is commonly called **gerrymandering**.

But redistricting does not explain the incumbency effect in the House as a whole. Statistics show that after a reapportionment, redistricted and unredistricted seats end up approximately the same in terms of competitiveness.[6] Nevertheless, politicians regard gerrymandering as very important, and the political parties put considerable effort into trying to make sure that new boundaries are drawn in the most advantageous way.

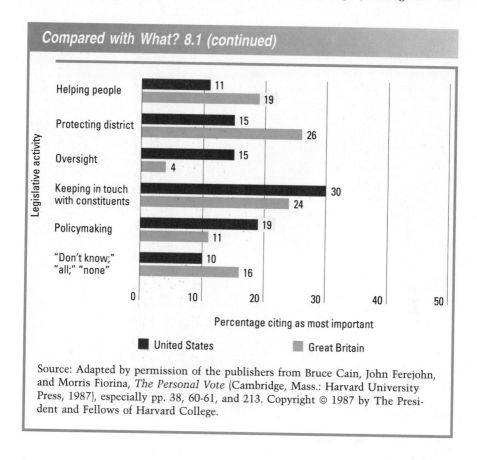

Compared with What? 8.1 (continued)

Source: Adapted by permission of the publishers from Bruce Cain, John Ferejohn, and Morris Fiorina, *The Personal Vote* (Cambridge, Mass.: Harvard University Press, 1987), especially pp. 38, 60-61, and 213. Copyright © 1987 by The President and Fellows of Harvard College.

Name recognition.   Holding office brings with it some important advantages. First, incumbents develop significant name recognition among voters simply by being members of Congress. The name recognition advantage is helped along by congressional press secretaries' efforts to get publicity for the activities and speeches of their bosses. The primary focus of such publicity seeking is with the local media back in the district—that is where the votes are.[7] The local press, in turn, is eager to cover what members of Congress are saying about the issues of the day.

Another resource available to members of Congress is the **franking privilege**—the right to send mail free of charge. Mailings see to it that constituents are aware of legislators' names, activities, and accomplishments. Periodic newsletters, for example, almost always highlight success at winning funds and projects for the district.

The large staff that works for a member of Congress is able to do **casework**, providing services for constituents—perhaps tracking down a social security check or directing the owner of a small business to the appropriate federal agency. Constituents who are helped in this way usually remember who assisted them (see Compared with What? 8.1).

The Year of the Woman
*Although it is very difficult for a challenger to unseat an incumbent in either
house of Congress, in 1992 California Senator Dianne Feinstein (left) did just
that. Fellow California Democrat Barbara Boxer also won a seat in that body
as the number of women in the U.S. Senate rose from two to six.*

Campaign financing. It should be clear that anyone who wants to
challenge an incumbent needs solid financial backing. But here, too, the
incumbent has the advantage. Challengers face great difficulty in raising
campaign funds because they have to overcome contributors' doubts
about whether they can win. Political action committees show a strong
preference for incumbents (see Chapter 7). They tend not to want to risk
offending an incumbent by giving money to a long-shot challenger. For
example, during the 1989–1990 election cycle, PACs contributed $116.6
million to incumbents but only slightly more than $15.8 million to
challengers.[8]

Successful challengers. Although defeating an incumbent (particularly
a member of the House) is difficult, it is not impossible. The opposing
party and unsympathetic PACs may target incumbents who seem vulnerable because of age, lack of seniority, or unfavorable redistricting.

The result is a flow of campaign contributions to the challenger, increasing the chance of victory. Incumbents can also be the victims of general dissatisfaction with their party. Popular disaffection with a president can translate into popular disaffection with House and Senate incumbents who belong to the president's party.

Nineteen ninety-two shaped up as a year in which incumbents would fare poorly, for three reasons. First, a major scandal erupted when it was revealed that a House "bank" allowed members to overdraw their accounts without penalty. Close to 250 current members of the House were identified as "check bouncers," and some had overdrawn their accounts hundreds of times. Second, reapportionment after the 1990 census meant that some states lost House seats, that some districts were radically altered, and that some incumbents had to run against other incumbents. Third, poor economic conditions made incumbents vulnerable, especially Republicans since they controlled the White House.

In the Senate, one incumbent lost in the primaries, three lost in the general election, and one lost in a runoff election. In the House, nineteen representatives lost their seats in the primaries, and another two dozen lost in the general election, for a total of forty-three defeated House incumbents. This is a significant number, but given the level of anger expressed by the public toward Congress, many observers had expected a much higher turnover in the House. The GOP gained ten House seats and retained the same representation in the Senate.

For proponents of majoritarian democracy, the success rate of incumbents running for re-election, especially in the House, is disconcerting. Surveys show that voters are more likely to vote on the basis of candidates' personal characteristics or experience than on national issues.[9] The tendency toward noncompetitive House elections means that it is difficult to translate the votes cast into a meaningful policy mandate that the winning candidates should follow.[10]

Whom Do We Elect?

The people we elect (and then re-elect) to Congress are not a cross-section of American society. Most members of Congress are professionals—primarily lawyers and businesspeople.[11] Although nearly one-third of the American labor force works in blue-collar jobs, it is close to impossible for someone currently employed as a blue-collar worker to win a congressional nomination.

Women and minorities have long been underrepresented in Congress. Amendments in 1982 to the Voting Rights Act forced changes in redistricting that led to the creation of many new districts with a majority or near majority of African-Americans or Hispanics.[12] After the 1992 elections, the number of African-Americans in the House increased from 25 to 38, and the number of Hispanics increased from 10 to 17. Native American Ben Nighthorse Campbell, a Democrat from Colorado, was elected to the Senate. Nineteen ninety-two was touted as the "year of the woman," and a record 106 women won nomination for a House seat. Nineteen new women were elected, bringing the total in the House to 47. Four new women were elected to the Senate, tripling their number from just 2 to 6.[13] Among the new women senators was Carol Moseley-Braun, the first African-American woman to serve in that body.

Despite their gains, minorities and women have not yet achieved proportional representation in either house, and, as noted, blue-collar workers remain outsiders when it comes to party nominations for Congress. If a representative legislative body is supposed to mirror the electorate, then Congress does not qualify as one. Yet the correspondence between social characteristics of the population and the membership of Congress is only one way to look at the question of representation. A more crucial measure may be how well the members of Congress represent their constituents' views as policy is made. After examining the legislative process, we return to the subject of representation.

How Issues Get on the Congressional Agenda

The formal legislative process begins when a member of Congress introduces a **bill**, a proposal for a new law. In the House, members drop new bills in the "hopper," a mahogany box near the rostrum where the speaker presides. Senators give their bills to one of the Senate clerks or introduce them from the floor.[14] But before a bill can be introduced to solve a problem, someone must perceive that a problem exists or that an issue needs to be resolved. In other words, the problem or issue somehow must find its way onto the congressional agenda. **Agenda** actually has two meanings in the vocabulary of political scientists. The first is that of a narrow, formal agenda, such as a calendar of bills to be voted on. The second meaning refers to the broad, imprecise, and unwritten agenda that consists of all the issues an institution is considering. Here we use the term in the second, broader sense.

Many of the issues Congress is working on at any one time seem to have been around forever, yet all issues begin at some point in time. For example, a dozen years ago few Americans outside the medical profession knew anything of Alzheimer's disease, a form of dementia that causes memory loss, a decrease in cognitive ability, and personality disorders. After advances in science helped define Alzheimer's as a particular pathology, some of those who had a family member diagnosed with Alzheimer's organized an interest group, the Alzheimer's Association. Recently, the Alzheimer's Association opened a Washington office to help with its lobbying efforts. The group's current goal is to get Congress to double the amount of federal funds devoted to Alzheimer's research.[15]

Advances in science are just one means by which new issues reach the congressional agenda. Sometimes a highly visible event focuses national attention on a problem. When an explosion in a West Virginia mine in 1968 killed seventy-eight miners, Congress promptly went to work on laws to promote miners' safety.[16] Presidential support can also move an issue onto the agenda quickly. The media attention paid to the president gives him enormous opportunity to draw the nation's attention to problems he believes need some form of governmental action. Within Congress, party leaders and committee chairs have the best opportunity to influence the political agenda.

The Dance of Legislation: An Overview

The process of writing bills and getting them passed is relatively simple in the sense that it follows a series of specific steps. What complicates the process is the many different ways legislation can be treated at each step. Here we examine the straightforward process by which laws are made. In the next few sections, we discuss some of the complexities of that process.

After a bill is introduced in either house, it is assigned to the appropriate committee of that chamber for study (see Figure 8.2). A banking bill, for example, would be assigned to the Banking, Finance, and Urban Affairs Committee in the House or to the Banking, Housing, and Urban Affairs Committee in the Senate, depending on where it was introduced. When a committee actively considers a piece of legislation assigned to it, the bill is usually referred to a specialized subcommittee. The subcommittee may hold hearings, and legislative staffers may do research on the bill. The original bill is usually modified or revised; then, if passed in some form by the subcommittee, it is sent back to the full committee. A bill that is approved by the full committee is *reported* (that is, sent) to the entire membership of the chamber, where it may be debated, amended, and either passed or defeated.

Bills coming out of House committees go to the Rules Committee before going before the full House membership. The Rules Committee attaches a "rule" to the bill that governs the coming floor debate, typically specifying the length of the debate and the types of amendments that can be offered. The Senate does not have a comparable committee, although restrictions on the length of floor debate can be reached through unanimous consent agreements.

Even if a bill on the same subject is passed by both houses of Congress, the Senate and House versions are typically different from each other. In that case, a conference committee, composed of legislators from both houses, works out the differences and develops a compromise version. This version is sent back to both houses for another floor vote. If the bill passes in both chambers, it is then sent to the president for his signature or veto.

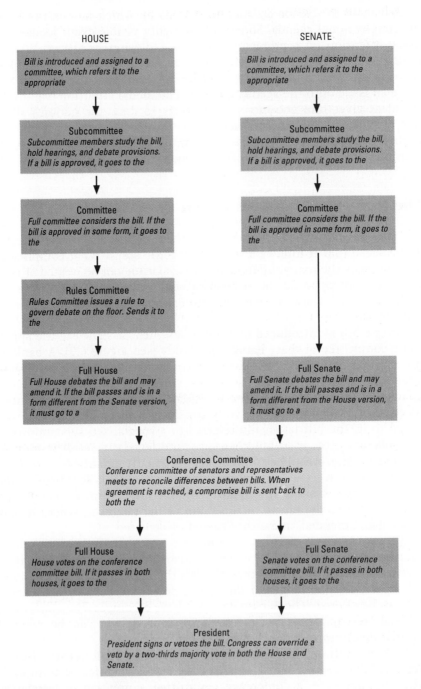

FIGURE 8.2   The Legislative Process
The process by which a bill becomes law is subject to much variation. This diagram depicts the typical process a bill might follow. It is important to remember that a bill can fail at any stage because of lack of support.

When the president signs a bill, it becomes law. If the president **vetoes** (disapproves) the bill, it is sent back to Congress with his reasons for rejecting it. The bill then becomes law only if Congress overrides the president's veto by a two-thirds vote of each house. If the president neither signs nor vetoes the bill within ten days (Sundays excepted) of receiving it, the bill becomes law. There is an exception here: If Congress adjourns within the ten days, the president can let the bill die through a **pocket veto**, by not signing it.

The content of a bill can be changed at any stage of the process, in either house. Lawmaking (and thus policymaking) in Congress has many access points for those who want to influence legislation. This openness tends to fit within the pluralist model of democracy. As a bill moves through the "dance of legislation,"[17] it is amended again and again in a search for a consensus that will get it passed and signed into law. The process can be tortuously slow and often fruitless. Derailing legislation is much easier than enacting it. The process gives groups frequent opportunities to voice their preferences and, if necessary, to thwart their opponents.

In recent years, one variation of this general process that has become very important is **omnibus legislation**. An omnibus proposal is a package of a number of different bills that are brought to the floor of the House and the Senate for consideration as a single entity. Omnibus proposals are often used for budget bills appropriating money for various functions of government. A major advantage of omnibus legislation is that it gives Congress more leverage over the president, who is sometimes handed an omnibus appropriations bill passed at the last moment. If such a bill was vetoed, it would force much of the government to shut down for lack of funds. Omnibus appropriations bills are also advantageous to Congress because they can be brought to the floor under a rule or agreement mandating an up-or-down vote with no amendments. Thus, members can tell constituents or lobbying groups that they were presented with a take-it-or-leave-it situation. As one analyst put it, omnibus bills "provide political cover to members."[18]

Committees: The Workhorses of Congress

Woodrow Wilson once observed, "Congress in session is Congress on public exhibition, whilst Congress in its committee-rooms is Congress at work."[19] The real nuts-and-bolts of lawmaking goes on in the congressional committees.

The Division of Labor Among Committees

The House and Senate are divided into committees for the same reason that other large organizations are broken into departments or divisions—to develop and use expertise in specific areas. For example, congressional decisions on weapons systems require a special knowledge that is of little relevance to decisions on reimbursement formulas for health insurance. It makes sense for some members of Congress to spend more time examining defense issues, becoming increasingly expert as they do so, while others concentrate on health matters.

Eventually, however, all members of Congress have to vote on each bill that emerges from the committees. Those who are not on a particular committee depend on committee members to examine the issues thoroughly, to make compromises as necessary, and to bring forward a sound piece of legislation that has a good chance of being passed. Each member decides individually on the bill's merits. But once it reaches the House or Senate floor, members may get to vote on only a handful of amendments (if any at all) before they must cast their yeas and nays for the entire bill.

Standing committees.   There are several different kinds of congressional committee, but the standing committee is predominant. **Standing committees** are permanent committees that specialize in a particular area of legislation—for example, the House Judiciary Committee or the Senate Environment and Public Works Committee. Most of the day-to-day work of drafting legislation takes place in the sixteen standing Senate committees and the twenty-two standing House committees (see Table 8.1). There are typically fifteen to twenty senators on each standing Senate committee and thirty to forty members on each standing House committee. The proportions of Democrats and Republicans on a standing committee generally reflect party proportions in the full Senate or House, and each member of Congress serves on only a small number of committees.

With a few exceptions, standing committees are further broken down into subcommittees. The House Agriculture Committee, for example, has eight separate subcommittees, among them one on wheat, soybeans, and feed grains and another on livestock, dairy, and poultry. Subcommittee members acquire expertise by continually working within the same fairly narrow policy area.

Other congressional committees.   Members of Congress can also serve on joint, select, and conference committees. **Joint committees** are made up of members of both the House and Senate. Like standing committees, the small number of joint committees is concerned with particular policy areas. The Joint Economic Committee, for instance, analyzes the country's economic policies. Joint committees operate in much the same way as standing committees, but they are almost always restricted from reporting bills to the House or Senate.

A **select committee** is a temporary committee created for a specific purpose. Select committees are established to deal with special circumstances or with issues that either overlap or are not included in the

Table 8.1   Standing Committees of Congress

Standing Committees of the Senate

Agriculture, Nutrition, and Forestry	Finance
Appropriations	Foreign Relations
Armed Services	Governmental Affairs
Banking, Housing, and Urban Affairs	Judiciary
Budget	Labor and Human Resources
Commerce, Science, and Transportation	Rules and Administration
Energy and Natural Resources	Small Business
Environment and Public Works	Veterans' Affairs

Standing Committees of the House

Agriculture	Interior and Insular Affairs
Appropriations	Judiciary
Armed Services	Merchant Marine and Fisheries
Banking, Finance, and Urban Affairs	Post Office and Civil Service
Budget	Public Works and Transportation
District of Columbia	Rules
Education and Labor	Science, Space, and Technology
Energy and Commerce	Small Business
Foreign Affairs	Standards of Official Conduct
Government Operations	Veterans' Affairs
House Administration	Ways and Means

Source: *Committees and Subcommittees of the 99th Congress*, supplement to *Congressional Quarterly Weekly Report*, 2 May 1987. Copyrighted material reprinted with permission, Congressional Quarterly Inc.

areas of expertise of standing committees. The Senate committee that investigated the Watergate scandal was a select committee created for that purpose only.

A **conference committee** is also a temporary committee, created to work out differences between the House and Senate versions of a specific piece of legislation. Its members are appointed from the standing committees or subcommittees that originally handled and reported the legislation to each house. Depending on the nature of the differences and the importance of the legislation, a conference committee may meet for hours or for weeks on end. When the conference committee agrees on a compromise, the bill is reported to both houses of Congress. Each house may either approve or disapprove the compromise; neither house can amend or change the compromise bill in any way. Only about 15 to 25 percent of all bills that eventually pass Congress go to a conference committee (although virtually all important or controversial bills do).[20] Differences are reconciled in other bills through informal negotiating by committee or subcommittee leaders.

Congressional Expertise and Seniority

Once appointed to a committee, a representative or senator has great incentive to remain on it to gain increasing expertise and influence in Congress. Influence also grows in a more formal way with **seniority**, or years of consecutive service on a committee. In the quest for expertise and seniority, members tend to stay on the same committees. Sometimes, however, they switch places when they are offered the opportunity to move to one of the high-prestige committees (such as Ways and Means or Appropriations in the House) or to a committee that handles legislation of vital importance to their constituents.

In a committee, the member of the majority party with the most seniority usually becomes the committee chair. (The majority party in each house controls committee leadership.) Other high-seniority members of the majority party become subcommittee chairs, while their counterparts from the minority party gain influence as *ranking minority members*. With about 140 subcommittees in the House and 90 in the Senate, there is a great deal of power and status available to the members of Congress.

Committee Reform

The committee system and the seniority system that determines the leadership of committees were sharply attacked during the 1970s. The push for reform came primarily from liberal and junior members of the House who "chafed under the restrictions on their participation and policy influence that the old, committee-dominated regime imposed. The committee chair, often in collaboration with the ranking minority member, dominated the panel."[21]

A number of select committees were established to study the organization of the House and Senate. Although not all their reforms were adopted, many significant changes were made. The power of the subcommittees in relation to their parent committees and their number were increased; and House Democrats (the majority party) prohibited their members from serving as chairs of more than one subcommittee. Also in the House, the seniority system was weakened by new rules that held that seniority did not have to be followed in the selection of committee chairs. In 1975, House Democrats voted out three aging, unpopular committee chairs, serving notice to all committee chairs that autocratic rule would not be tolerated. An earlier change by House Democrats had eliminated the committee chairs' power to appoint subcommittee chairs. The general thrust of these changes was to make subcommittees more autonomous and powerful.[22]

There was considerably less reform in the Senate. The smaller number of members in that body guarantees virtually all senators in the majority party at least one subcommittee chair. Moreover, the Senate's greater national visibility makes its members less dependent on their committee activities or seniority to gain recognition and influence. As one study concluded, "Committees are simply less crucial to the pursuit of personal goals in the Senate than in the House."[23]

The Lawmaking Process

The way in which committees and subcommittees are organized within Congress is ultimately significant because much public policy decision making takes place there. The first step in drafting legislation is to collect information on the issue. Committee staffers research the problem, and hearings may be held to take testimony from witnesses who have some special knowledge on the subject.

The meetings at which subcommittees or committees actually debate and amend legislation are called *markup sessions*. The process by which committees reach decisions varies. In many committees, there is a strong tradition of decision by consensus. The chair, the ranking minority member, and others in these committees work hard, in formal committee sessions and in informal negotiations, to find a middle ground on issues that divide committee members. In other committees, members exhibit strong ideological and partisan sentiments. Committee and subcommittee leaders prefer, however, to find ways of overcoming the inherent ideological and partisan divisions so that they can build compromise solutions that will appeal to the broader membership of their house.

Committees: The Majoritarian and Pluralist Views

It makes sense to bring as much expertise as possible to the policymaking process, and the committee system does just that. But government by committee vests a tremendous amount of power in the committees and subcommittees of Congress, especially in their leaders. This is particularly true of the House, which is more decentralized in its patterns of influence and more restrictive in the degree to which legislation can be amended on the floor. Committee members can bury a bill by not reporting it to the full House or Senate. The influence of committee members extends even further to the floor debate. And many of them make up the conference committee that is charged with developing a compromise version of the bill.

This vesting of policy-area power in many committees and subcommittees tends to remove that power from the majority party and thus to operate against majoritarianism. At the same time, the committee system enhances the force of pluralism in American politics. Representatives and senators are elected by the voters in particular districts and states and tend to seek membership on the committees whose decisions are most important to their constituents. Members from farm areas, for example, want membership on the House or Senate Agriculture Committee. Urban liberals like the committees that handle social programs. As a result, the various committees are predisposed to writing legislation favorable to those who are most affected by their actions.

A meeting of the entire House or Senate to vote a bill up or down may seem to be an example of majoritarianism at work. The views of the collective membership of each body may reasonably approximate the diverse mix of interests in the United States.[24] Committee decision making also anticipates what is acceptable to the entire membership. Nevertheless, by the time the broader membership begins to debate legislation on the floor, many crucial decisions have already been made in committees with a much narrower constituency in mind. Clearly, the internal structure of Congress gives small groups of members with intense interests in particular policy areas a disproportionate amount of influence over those areas.[25]

Leaders and Followers in Congress

Above the committee chairs is another layer of authority in the organization of the House and Senate. The Democratic and Republican leaders in each house work to maximize the influence of their own party while at the same time trying to keep their chamber functioning smoothly and efficiently. The operation of the two houses is also influenced by the rules and norms that each chamber has developed over the years.

The Leadership Task

Each of the two parties in each of the two houses elects leaders. In the House of Representatives, the majority-party leader is the **Speaker of the House**, who, gavel in hand, chairs sessions from the ornate rostrum at the front of the chamber. The counterpart in the opposing party is the *minority leader*. The majority party chooses the Speaker at its **caucus**, a closed-door meeting of the party. The majority and minority parties then "slate" their candidates for Speaker at the opening session of Congress. The official election follows strict party lines, affirming the majority party's caucus decision. The minority-party candidate becomes the minority leader. The Speaker is a constitutional officer, but the Constitution does not list the Speaker's duties. The minority leader is not mentioned in the Constitution, but that post has evolved into an important party position in the House.

The Constitution makes the vice president of the United States the president of the Senate. But the vice president usually does not come to the Senate chamber unless there is a possibility of a tie vote, in which case he can break the tie. The *president pro tempore* (president "for the time"), elected by the majority party, is supposed to chair the Senate in the vice president's absence, but by custom this constitutional position is entirely honorary.

The real power in the Senate resides in the **majority leader**. As in the House, the top position in the opposing party is that of *minority leader*. Technically, the majority leader does not preside (members rotate in the president pro tempore's chair); but the majority leader does schedule legislation in consultation with the minority leader. More broadly, party leaders play a critical role in getting bills through Congress. The most significant function that leaders play is steering the bargaining and negotiating over the content of legislation. When an issue divides their party, their house, the two houses, or their house and the White House, the leaders must take the initiative to work out a compromise solution.

Party leaders are coalition builders, not kingmakers. As recently as the 1950s, strong leaders dominated the legislative process. However, in today's Congress, rank-and-file representatives and senators would not stand for this kind of leadership. But there is no doubt that contemporary leaders have an impact on policy outcomes in Congress. As one expert concluded, "Although leadership contributions may be marginal, most important political choices are made at the margins."[26]

Rules of Procedure

The operation of the House and the Senate is structured by both formal *rules of procedure* and informal *norms of behavior*. Rules in each chamber are mostly matters of parliamentary procedure. For example, they govern the scheduling of legislation, outlining when and how certain types of legislation can be brought to the floor.

As noted earlier, an important difference between the two chambers is the House's use of its Rules Committee to govern floor debate. Without a similar committee to act as a "traffic cop" for legislation approaching the floor, the Senate relies on *unanimous consent agreements* to set the starting time and length of debate. If one senator objects to an agreement, it does not take effect. Senators do not routinely object to unanimous consent agreements, however, because they need them when a bill of their own awaits scheduling by the leadership.

If a senator wants to stop a bill badly enough, he or she may start a **filibuster**, trying to talk the bill to death. By historical tradition, the Senate gives its members the right of unlimited debate. The record for holding the floor belongs to Republican Senator Strom Thurmond of South Carolina for a twenty-four-hour, eighteen-minute marathon.[27] In the House, no member is allowed to speak for more than an hour without unanimous consent.

After a 1917 filibuster, the Senate adopted **cloture**, a means of limiting debate. A petition signed by sixteen senators initiates a cloture vote. It now takes the votes of sixty senators to invoke cloture.[28]

Norms of Behavior

Both houses have codes of behavior that help keep them running. These codes are largely unwritten norms, although some have been formally adopted as rules. Members of Congress recognize that personal conflict must be eliminated (or minimized), lest Congress dissolve into bickering factions unable to work together. One of the most celebrated norms is that members show respect for their colleagues in public deliberations. During floor debate, bitter opponents still refer to one another in such terms as "my good friend, the senior senator from . . . ," or "my distinguished colleague."

Probably the most important norm of behavior in Congress is that individual members should be willing to bargain with one another. Policymaking is a process of give and take; it demands compromise. However, members of Congress are not expected to violate their consciences on policy issues simply to strike a deal. Rather, they are expected to listen to what others have to say and to make every effort to reach a reasonable compromise. Obviously, if each of them sticks rigidly to his or her views, they will never agree on anything. Moreover, few policy matters are so clear-cut that compromise destroys one's position.

In recent years, an important evolution in some of these norms of behavior has occurred. Junior members have become much more assertive and now refuse to spend a long time as apprentices gaining experience before playing a major role in the development of legislation. As one scholar noted, "The apprenticeship norm . . . has disappeared in both chambers."[29]

There is also less respect for the primacy of committees. Committees continue to be a dominant force in Congress, but members not serving on a committee are no longer content to grant it autonomy over its policy area. Today, members not serving on committees offer more amendments on the floor to try changing the policy thrust of a committee's bill.[30]

The Legislative Environment

After legislation emerges from committee, it is scheduled for floor debate. How do legislators make up their minds on how to vote? In this section, we examine the broader legislative environment that affects decision making in Congress. More specifically, we look at the influence of political parties, interest groups, colleagues, staff, the president, and constituents on legislators.[31]

Political Parties

The national political parties have limited influence over lawmakers. They do not control the nominations of House and Senate candidates. Candidates receive the bulk of their funds from individual contributors and political action committees, not from the national parties. The party leadership in each house, however, does try to influence the rank and file. Individual members may, for example, need their party leaders'

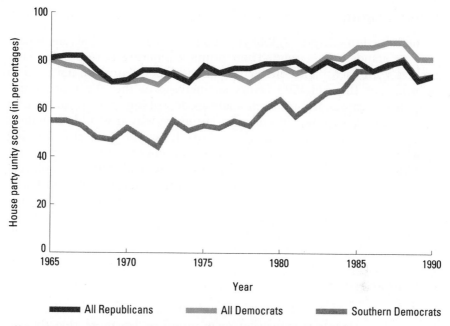

FIGURE 8.3   *Southern Democrats Come Back to the Party*
*The civil rights movement of the 1960s badly divided the Democratic party in
Congress. These House of Representatives party unity scores demonstrate how
that division has gradually healed, spurred on by the enfranchisement of
blacks after the Voting Rights Act was passed in 1965. The figures here show
the percentage of House members who voted with a majority of their party on
party unity votes. (Party unity votes are those in which a majority of one party
votes one way and the majority of the second party votes the other way.)*
(Sources: Norman J. Ornstein, Thomas E. Mann, and Michael J. Malbin, Vital Statistics
on Congress, 1989–1990 [Washington, D.C.: Congressional Quarterly Inc., 1990], p. 199;
"For the Record," Congressional Quarterly Weekly Report, 22 December 1990, p. 4212.
Used by permission.)

assistance on specific legislation; members therefore have an incentive
to cooperate with those leaders.

One important trend is the greater party loyalty of southern Democrats. Although they are still less likely to vote with the majority of
their Democratic colleagues than are the party's northern members,
their loyalty has risen significantly (see Figure 8.3). A primary reason for
this increased party loyalty is that the issue of race no longer dominates
southern politics or the national agenda the way it once did. Since the
Voting Rights Act of 1965 was passed, blacks have registered in large
numbers. They make up a large share of the Democratic coalition in the
South and act as a moderating influence on the traditionally conservative southern Democratic party.[32]

Interest Groups

As discussed in Chapter 7, lobbyists do more than tell legislators where a group stands on an issue. Their primary function is to provide lawmakers with useful and reliable information. Legislators do not need to be told that the AFL-CIO favors an increase in the minimum wage. They need reports and research analyses describing why an increase in the minimum wage would not be inflationary, why it would not reduce competitiveness in world markets, how it would raise the working poor's standard of living, and why it would reduce welfare payments.

Critics often refer to lobbies as "pressure groups." Although political scientists would choose a more neutral term, interest groups do try to pressure Congress. One of the most effective forms of pressure is having constituents contact their legislators with their version of the facts. Members of Congress are not re-elected by Washington lobbyists; the people back home cast the ballots.

Colleagues

Lobbyists and interest groups are a good source of information, but their facts and arguments support their own interests. For more objective information, a legislator may very well turn to a fellow representative or senator. One reason for doing so is the expertise that comes with committee specialization. A second reason is that representatives and senators form a peer group, and strong bonds of trust, friendship, and professional respect develop over time within that peer group.

Consultation with colleagues also comes through various formal groupings of legislators. Many of the state delegations in the House meet regularly to discuss issues of mutual concern. There are many other groups, or caucuses, that work together on issues that particularly concern them or their constituents. In the House, for example, there are bipartisan caucuses for steel, coal, and Irish affairs. The Hispanic caucus is another such group; it has taken an active leadership role on issues such as immigration and bilingual education.[33] Finally, there are partisan groups of legislators, like the Democratic Study Group and the Republican's Conservative Opportunity Society, both in the House.

Staff

The number of congressional staff members has risen dramatically in the last several decades, although it has now leveled off. In the mid-1950s, House members had about two thousand five hundred personal staffers; by 1981, the figure had grown to about seven thousand five hundred. Over the same period, Senate personal staffs grew from around one thousand to about four thousand people, which is where it is today. The number of staff members assigned to congressional committees grew significantly during this time as well.[34]

These larger staffs have helped members of Congress handle an increasing workload. (See the discussion on oversight in the next section.) Staffers reliably represent their bosses' interests during the day-to-day negotiations over legislation.[35] Staffers are particularly helpful in involving their bosses in new issues that will increase their influence both with constituents and within Congress. More broadly, one scholar noted, "The increased use of personalized, entrepreneurial staffs has helped Congress retain its position as a key initiator of federal policy, despite the growing power of the executive branch."[36]

The President

Unlike members of Congress, who are elected by voters in individual states and districts, the president is elected by voters across the entire nation. The president has a better claim, then, to representing the nation than does any single member of Congress. But it can also be argued that Congress as a whole has a better claim than the president to representing the majority of voters. In any case, presidents capitalize on their popular election and usually act as though they are speaking for the majority.

During the twentieth century, the public's expectations of what a president can accomplish in office have grown enormously. We now expect the president to be our chief legislator: to introduce legislation on major issues and to use his influence to push bills through Congress. This is much different from our early history, when presidents felt constrained by the constitutional doctrine of separation of powers and had to have members of Congress work confidentially for them.[37]

Today the White House is openly involved not only in the writing of bills but also in their development as they wind their way through the legislative process. If the White House does not like a bill, it tries to work out a compromise with key legislators to have the legislation amended. On issues of the greatest importance, the president himself may meet with individual legislators to persuade them to vote a certain way. To monitor daily congressional activities and lobby for the broad range of administration policies, there are hundreds of legislative liaison personnel working for the executive branch.

Although members of Congress grant presidents a leadership role in proposing legislation, they jealously guard their power to debate, shape, pass, or defeat any legislation the president proposes. Congress often clashes sharply with the president when his proposals are seen as ill-advised.

Constituents

Constituents are the people who live and vote in a legislator's district or state. As much as members of Congress want to please the party

The State of the Union
The Constitution requires that the president "shall from time to time give to the Congress Information of the State of the Union, and recommend to their Consideration such Measures as he shall judge necessary." Here President Clinton fulfills that requirement in his first State of the Union Address.

leadership or the president by going along with their preferences, legislators have to think about what the voters back home want. If legislators displease enough people by the way they vote, they might lose their seats in the next election.

In considering the influence of all these factors in the legislator's environment, it is important to keep in mind that legislators also have strong views of their own. They come to Congress deeply committed to working on some key issues and do not need to be pressured into acting on them or into voting a certain way. In fact, their strong views on certain policy questions can conflict with what their constituents want, a problem discussed in detail later in this chapter.

Of all the possible sources of influence, which are the most important? Unfortunately, there is no one way of measuring. However, in an interesting and straightforward study, political scientist John Kingdon asked a sample of House members how they made up their minds on a variety of issues. He found that colleagues and constituency were more likely to have an impact than the other factors we are discussing here. Kingdon cautioned, however, that the decision-making process in Congress is complex and that no single factor "is important enough that one could conclude that congressmen vote as they do" because of its influence.[38]

Oversight: Following Through on Legislation

It is often said in Washington that "knowledge is power." For Congress to retain influence over the programs it creates, it must be aware of how they are being administered by the agencies responsible for them. To that end, legislators and their committees engage in **oversight**, the process of reviewing agency operations to determine whether the agency is carrying out policies as Congress intended.

Congress performs its oversight function in a number of different ways. The most visible is the hearing. Hearings may be part of a routine review or the by-product of information that reveals a major problem with a program or with an agency's administrative practices. Another way Congress keeps track of what departments and agencies are doing is to request reports on specific agency practices and operations. A good deal of congressional oversight also takes place in an informal manner. There is ongoing contact between committee/subcommittee leaders and agency administrators and between committee staffers and top agency staffers.[39]

Congressional oversight of the executive branch has sharply increased since the early 1970s. A primary reason for this increase was that Congress gave itself the necessary staff to watch over the growing federal government. In addition to the personal and committee staffs mentioned earlier, Congress created two new specialized offices in the 1970s—the Congressional Budget Office and the Office of Technology Assessment—to do sophisticated analyses of agency operations and proposals. The longer-standing Government Accounting Office (GAO) and the Congressional Research Service of the Library of Congress also do in-depth studies for Congress.

Congress was long criticized for doing too little oversight. Today, critics charge that Congress is going too far, that Congress is engaged in **micromanagement** through its constant intervention in administrative policymaking. These critics argue that Congress is violating the spirit of the separation of powers by not giving agencies the flexibility to administer programs as they see fit.

Particularly interesting is the increasing aggressiveness of the Congress in the area of foreign policy, long the preserve of the presidency. In 1970, the Nixon administration refused to reveal its negotiating position to Congress until just before the start of arms limitation talks with the Soviet Union. However, when the United States was developing an arms proposal in 1983, Senators William Cohen and Sam Nunn went to the White House to hammer out a proposal with Chief of Staff James Baker.[40]

The Dilemma of Representation

When candidates for the House and Senate campaign for office, they routinely promise to work hard for their district's or state's interests. When they get to Washington, however, they all face the troubling dilemma with which we began this chapter: What their constituents want may not be what the people across the nation want.

Presidents and Shopping Bags

In doing the research for his book *Home Style*, political scientist Richard Fenno accompanied several representatives on trips back to their home districts. On one trip, he was in an airport with a congressional aide, waiting for the representative's plane from Washington to land. When the congressman arrived, he said, "I spent fifteen minutes on the telephone with the president this afternoon. He had a plaintive tone in his voice and he pleaded with me." The congressman had prevailed over the president and was elated by the victory. When the three men reached the aide's car, the congressman saw the back seat piled high with campaign paraphernalia: shopping bags printed with the representative's name and picture. "Back to this again," he sighed.[41]

Every member of Congress lives in two worlds: the world of presidents and the world of personalized shopping bags. A typical week in the life of a representative means working in Washington, then boarding a plane and flying back to the district. There the representative spends time meeting with individual constituents and talking to civic groups, church gatherings, business associations, labor unions, and the like. A survey of House members during a nonelection year showed that each made an average of thirty-five trips back to his or her district, spending an average of 138 days there.[42]

Members of Congress are often criticized for being out of touch with the people they are supposed to represent. This charge does not seem justified. Legislators work extraordinarily hard at keeping in touch with voters, at finding out what is on constituents' minds. The difficult problem is how to act on that knowledge.

Trustees or Delegates?

Are members of Congress bound to vote the way their constituents want them to vote, even if it means voting against their conscience? Some say no. They argue that legislators must be free to vote in line with what they think is best. This view has long been associated with the eighteenth-century English political philosopher Edmund Burke (1729–1797). Burke, who served in Parliament, told his constituents in Bristol that "you choose a member, indeed; but when you have chosen him, he is not a member of Bristol, but he is a member of *Parliament*."[43]

Burke reasoned that representatives are sent by their constituents to vote as they think best. As **trustees**, representatives are obligated to consider the views of constituents but not to vote according to those views when they appear misguided.

Others hold that legislators are dutybound to represent the majority view of their constituents, that they are **delegates** with instructions from the people at home on how to vote on critical issues. And delegates, unlike trustees, must be prepared to vote against their own policy preferences.

Members of Congress are subject to two opposing forces, then. While the interests of the district push them toward the role of delegates, the larger national interest calls on them to be trustees. Given these conflicting role definitions, it is not surprising that Congress is not clearly a body of delegates or of trustees. Research has shown, however, that members of Congress are more apt to take the delegate role on issues that are of great concern to constituents.[44] But much of the time, what the constituency really wants is not clear. Many issues are not highly visible back home, they cut across the constituency to affect it in different ways, or they are only partially understood. Mail from constituents may represent the sentiment of activists and may not be representative of the broader population in the district.

Pluralism, Majoritarianism, and Democracy

The dilemma that individual members of Congress face in adopting the role of either delegate or trustee has broad implications for the way our country is governed. When legislators act as delegates, congressional policymaking is more pluralistic, and policies reflect the bargaining that goes on among lawmakers who speak for different constituents. When legislators act as trustees and vote their consciences, policymaking becomes less tied to the narrower interests of districts and states. But even here there is no guarantee that congressional decision making reflects majority interests.

We end this chapter with a short discussion of the pluralist nature of Congress. But first, to establish a frame of reference, we need to take a quick look at a more majoritarian type of legislature—the parliament.

Parliamentary Government

In our legislative system, the executive and legislative functions are divided between a president and a congress, each elected separately. Most other democracies—for example, Britain and Japan—have parliamentary governments. In a **parliamentary system**, the chief executive is the legislative leader whose party holds the most seats in the legislature after an election or whose party forms a major part of the ruling coalition. For instance, in Great Britain, voters do not cast a ballot for prime minister. They vote only for their member of Parliament and thus must influence the choice of prime minister indirectly by voting in the local district election for the party they favor.

In a parliamentary system, government power is highly concentrated in the legislature because the leader of the majority party is also the head of government. Moreover, parliamentary legislatures are usually composed of only one chamber or have a second one that is much weaker than the other. (In the British Parliament, the House of Commons makes the decisions of government; the other chamber, the House of Lords, is largely an honorary debating club for distinguished members of society.) And parliamentary governments usually do not have a court that can invalidate acts of parliament. Under such a system, the government is in the hands of the party that controls the parliament. With no separation of government powers, there are few checks on government action. The net effect is that parliamentary governments fit the majoritarian model of democracy to a much greater extent than do congressional governments.

Pluralism Versus Majoritarianism in Congress

Nowadays, the U.S. Congress is often criticized for being too pluralist and not majoritarian enough. The federal budget deficit is a case in point. Americans are deeply concerned about the large deficits that have plagued our national budgets in recent years. And both Democrats and Republicans in Congress repeatedly call for reductions in those deficits. But when spending bills come before Congress, legislators' concern turns to what the bills will or will not do for their districts or states. A $604 million spending bill passed by Congress in 1988 included numerous examples of individual members winning some "pork barrel" project that benefited their district or state and added further to the deficit. Republican Senator James McClure won inclusion of a $6.4 million grant to build a ski resort in Kellogg, Idaho. Democratic Representative Daniel Akaka got a $250,000 appropriation for pig and plant control at the Haleakala National Park in Hawaii. And Republican Senator Ted Stevens delivered $2.6 million to the Fisheries Promotional Fund in Alaska.[45]

Projects such as these get into the budget through bargaining among members; as you saw earlier in the chapter, congressional norms encourage it. Members of Congress try to win projects and programs that will not only benefit their constituents but also help members at election time. To win approval of something helpful to one's own constituents, a member must be willing to vote for other legislators' projects. This type of system obviously promotes pluralism.

Some feel that Congress has to be less pluralistic if it is going to attack such serious problems as the national deficit. Yet those who favor pluralism are quick to point out Congress's merits. For example, many different constituencies are well served by the spending deliberations just described. For Alaska's fishermen, an appropriation to promote new markets for their industry is not frivolous spending; it is vital to their livelihood. They pay taxes to fund the government, and they have a right to expect the government to care about their problems and try to help them.

Proponents of pluralism also argue that the makeup of Congress generally reflects that of the nation, that different members of Congress represent farm areas, oil and gas areas, low-income inner cities, industrial areas. These proponents point out that America itself is pluralistic, with a rich diversity of economic, social, religious, and racial groups, and that even if our own representatives and senators do not represent our particular viewpoint, it is likely that someone else in Congress does.[46]

An alternative to our pluralistic legislature would operate on strictly majoritarian principles. For this kind of system to work, we would need strong parties—as described by the principles of responsible party government (see Chapter 6). That is, congressional candidates for each party would have to stand relatively united on the major issues. Then the majority party in Congress would act on a clear mandate from the voters—at least on the major issues discussed in the preceding election campaign. This would be very different from the pluralist system we now have, which furthers the influence of interest groups and local constituencies in national policymaking. But which is better?

Summary

Congress plays a central role in our government through its lawmaking function. It writes the laws of the land and attempts to oversee their implementation. It helps educate us about new issues as they appear on the political agenda. Most important, members of Congress represent us, working to see to it that interests from home and from around the country are heard throughout the policymaking process.

We count on Congress to do so much that criticism about how well it does some things is inevitable. But certain strengths are clear. The committee system fosters expertise; representatives and senators who know the most about particular issues have the most influence over them. And the structure of our electoral system keeps legislators in close touch with their constituents.

Bargaining and compromise play important roles in the congressional policymaking process. Some people find this disquieting. They want less deal making and more adherence to principle. This thinking is in line with the desire for a more majoritarian democracy. Others defend the current system, arguing that the United States is a large, complex nation and the policies that govern it should be developed through bargaining among various interests.

There is no clear-cut answer on whether a majoritarian or a pluralist legislative system provides better representation for voters. Our system is pluralistic. It serves minority interests that might otherwise be neglected or even harmed by an unthinking or uncaring majority. But there is validity to the argument that responsiveness to special interests comes at the expense of the majority of Americans.

Key Terms

reapportionment
impeachment
redistricting
gerrymandering
franking privilege
casework
bill
agenda
veto
pocket veto
omnibus legislation
standing committee
joint committee
select committee

conference committee
seniority
speaker of the House
caucus
majority leader
filibuster
cloture
constituents
oversight
micromanagement
trustees
delegates
parliamentary system

Selected Readings

Aberbach, Joel D. *Keeping a Watchful Eye*. Washington, D.C.: Brookings Institution, 1990. This is a careful analysis of the growth of congressional oversight.

Cain, Bruce, John Ferejohn, and Morris Fiorina. *The Personal Vote*. Cambridge, Mass.: Harvard University Press, 1987. The authors provide a detailed comparison of the services offered constituents by American and British legislators.

Dodd, Lawrence C., and Bruce I. Oppenheimer. *Congress Reconsidered*. 4th ed. Washington, D.C.: Congressional Quarterly Press, 1989. This collection of essays pulls together much of the latest research on Congress.

Fenno, Richard F., Jr. *Home Style*. Boston: Little, Brown, 1978. This is a classic analysis of how House members interact with constituents during visits to home districts.

Fowler, Linda L., and Robert D. McClure. *Political Ambition*. New Haven, Conn.: Yale University Press, 1989. This is an engaging, highly readable study of the recruitment of congressional candidates.

Loomis, Burdett. *The New American Politician*. New York: Basic Books, 1988. Loomis studies how the ambition and entrepreneurship of legislators are changing Congress.

THE PRESIDENCY

9

"Read my lips: No new taxes." When George Bush uttered these words in his acceptance speech at the 1988 Republican convention in New Orleans, he announced to the world that he was now the keeper of his party's most precious imagery: The GOP was against taxes. Ronald Reagan had successfully labeled the Democrats as the party of "tax and spend," and taxes had been cut substantially during his administration. Nevertheless, Bush felt that standing for "no new taxes" was not enough. During the presidential campaign, he proposed a cut in taxes on capital gains. (Capital gains are profits from the sale of assets such as stocks and real estate.) Such a cut would be popular with people who had money to invest. A special capital gains rate was not, however, of great relevance to most Americans, who lived from week to week on their paychecks.

Bush almost made good on his campaign promise. In the fall of 1989, the House of Representatives passed a bill that set lower taxes for capital gains than for income earned from a salary. Such a two-tiered tax system had existed before but had been eliminated in a tax reform bill a few years earlier. There was majority support for the capital gains cut in the Senate, too, but liberal Democrats threatened a filibuster, so the Republicans threw in the towel and vowed to come back the following year with a similar proposal.

The capital gains fight reflects a traditional division in our party system. The Republicans emphasized that a capital gains cut would spur economic growth by giving people more incentive to put their money into long-term investments. Democrats claimed that it was just a tax cut for the wealthy.

Bush tried again in 1990. A major change in the equation came when the huge federal deficit and lack of cooperation between Republicans and Democrats over the budget led Bush to go back on his no new taxes pledge. He hoped that in exchange for his support for some tax increases he could get some concessions, including a capital gains tax cut. Nevertheless, the Democrats stood firm against the capital gains cut. Bush conceded again, agreeing to a budget deal with congressional leaders that contained enough tax increases and budget cuts to reduce the deficit by $500 billion over five years.

The budget deal soon fell apart, however. Republicans in Congress revolted because it raised taxes and contained no spurs to investment (such as a capital gains cut). Democrats revolted because the tax increases hit the working class the hardest. Bush made a nationally televised speech asking the American people for their support, saying, "If we fail to enact this agreement, our economy will falter. Markets may tumble. And recession will follow."[1] The speech was a bomb. Americans wrote and called their congressional representatives in large numbers to tell them to vote against the package. The House voted down the budget bill, giving Bush a stinging defeat.

And then it got worse for Bush. Emboldened by the rejection of Bush's plea for the budget bill, the Democrats started hammering away at the Republicans, calling them the party of the rich. This maneuver struck a responsive chord with the American public, and Bush and the Republicans were put in a defensive position. The Democrats introduced legislation that substantially raised taxes on the wealthy and reduced the amount the middle class would pay. Republicans quickly realized that higher taxes on the rich were inevitable. But if Bush was going to give in on a big tax increase for the rich, then perhaps he should get something back in return—such as capital gains.

Yet it was hard to figure out what Bush would settle for. After saying he would accept higher taxes in exchange for a capital gains cut, Bush changed his mind the very same day. Then he changed his mind again the next day. This indecisiveness weakened his bargaining position further. The budget bill that was finally passed contained only minor adjustments in the way capital gains were taxed. The Democrats won a clear victory.

What the Democrats had done, of course, was to play majoritarian politics. If politics and elections can be turned into referenda on what is best for Americans with modest incomes versus what is best for the wealthy, the party aligned with the less affluent has a distinct advantage.

As we analyze the various facets of the presidency, bear in mind one recurring question: Is the presidency primarily an instrument of pluralist democracy, serving small but vocal constituencies, or does the office promote majoritarian democracy by responding primarily to public opinion? In addition to examining this question, we focus in this chapter on a number of other important aspects of the presidency. What are the powers of the presidency? How is the president's advisory system organized? How does the separation of powers between the executive and the legislative branches affect public policymaking? Finally, what are the particular issues and problems that presidents face in foreign affairs?

The Constitutional Basis of Presidential Power

When the presidency was created, the colonies had just fought a war of independence; their reaction to British domination had focused on the autocratic rule of King George III. Thus, the delegates to the Constitutional Convention were extremely wary of unchecked power and were determined not to create an all-powerful, dictatorial presidency.

The delegates' fear of a powerful presidency was counterbalanced by their desire for strong leadership. The Articles of Confederation—which did not provide for a single head of state—had failed to bind the states together into a unified nation (see Chapter 2). With the failed confederation in mind, John Jay wrote to George Washington, asking him, "Shall we have a king?"[2]

Although the idea of establishing an American royalty was far from popular among the delegates, they knew that some type of executive office had to be created. Their task was to provide national leadership without allowing any opportunity for tyranny.

Initial Conceptions of the Presidency

Debates over the nature of the office began. Should there be one president or a presidential council or committee? Should the president be chosen by Congress and remain largely subservient to that body?

The final structure of the presidency reflected the checks and balances philosophy that shaped the entire Constitution. Important limits were imposed on the presidency through the powers specifically delegated to Congress and the courts. Those counterbalancing powers would act as checks, or controls, on presidents who might try to expand the office beyond its proper bounds. (The separation of the executive from the legislative branch has had an effect on the type of experience our presidential candidates have; see Compared with What? 9.1.)

What Kind of Experience Counts?

Candidates nominated for the presidency of the United States are an impressive lot in terms of their accomplishments and political experience. Nevertheless, their European counterparts are actually better seasoned in jobs providing valuable experience in government. Excellent campaign skills are critical to winning a presidential nomination in the United States. It is no small feat to conduct a lengthy campaign, putting together a winning coalition by convincing large numbers of voters that one would be a better nominee than the many other capable candidates competing in the primaries. Experience in office is hardly irrelevant in a candidate's ultimate appeal to American voters—they need to be convinced he can do the job. Nevertheless, candidates who have spent relatively modest amounts of time in governmental service and have limited ranges of experience, such as Jimmy Carter and Ronald Reagan, are able to win their party's nomination.

In European democracies, a considerably different pattern emerges. Party activists who aim for the post of prime minister in a parliamentary system must win the backing of their legislative party. As they rise in their party's hierarchy, aspiring leaders typically head major departments of state when their party is in control of the government. In Great Britain, for example, an aspiring prime minister typically has served an average of twelve years as a minister of a governmental department before he or she became a party leader in Parliament. In contrast, U.S. presidential candidates typically do not have Cabinet experience, although they may have had executive experience as a governor. As the graph indicates, American candidates are considerably less experienced in government than European political leaders.

(continued)

The Powers of the President

The requirements for the presidency are set forth in Article II of the Constitution: A president must be a natural-born citizen, at least thirty-five years old, who has lived in the United States for a minimum of fourteen years. The responsibilities of presidents are also set forth in this article. In view of the importance of the office, the constitutional description of the president's duties is surprisingly brief and vague. This vagueness has led to repeated conflict over the limits of presidential power.

The major presidential duties and powers listed in the Constitution can be summarized as follows:

- *Serve as administrative head of the nation.* The Constitution gives little guidance on the president's administrative duties. It states merely that "the executive power shall be vested in a President of

Compared with What? 9.1 (Continued)

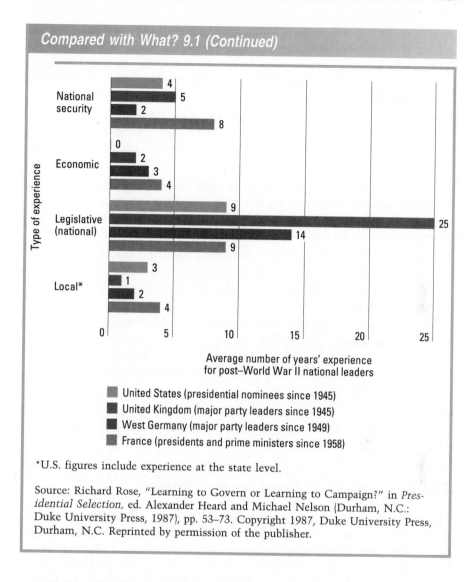

Average number of years' experience
for post–World War II national leaders

■ United States (presidential nominees since 1945)
■ United Kingdom (major party leaders since 1945)
■ West Germany (major party leaders since 1949)
■ France (presidents and prime ministers since 1958)

*U.S. figures include experience at the state level.

Source: Richard Rose, "Learning to Govern or Learning to Campaign?" in *Presidential Selection*, ed. Alexander Heard and Michael Nelson (Durham, N.C.: Duke University Press, 1987), pp. 53–73. Copyright 1987, Duke University Press, Durham, N.C. Reprinted by permission of the publisher.

the United States of America" and that "he shall take care that the laws be faithfully executed." These imprecise directives have been interpreted to mean that the president is to supervise and offer leadership to various departments, agencies, and programs created by Congress. In practice, a chief executive spends much more time making policy decisions for his Cabinet departments and agencies than trying to enforce existing policies.

- *Act as commander in chief of the military.* In essence, the Constitution names the president as the highest-ranking officer in the armed forces. But it gives Congress the power to declare war. The framers no doubt intended Congress to control the president's military power; nevertheless, presidents have initiated military action without the approval of Congress. The entire Vietnam War was fought without a congressional declaration of war. (The Congress did pass a resolution authorizing the use of force in the Persian Gulf before the American-led coalition began its military campaign.)

- *Convene Congress.* The president can call Congress into special session on "extraordinary occasions," although this has rarely been done. He must also periodically inform Congress of "the state of the Union."

- *Veto legislation.* The president can **veto** (disapprove) any bill or resolution passed by Congress, with the exception of joint resolutions that propose constitutional amendments. Congress can override a presidential veto with a two-thirds vote in each house.

- *Appoint various officials.* The president has the authority to appoint federal court judges, ambassadors, Cabinet members, other key policymakers, and many lesser officials. Many appointments are subject to Senate confirmation.

- *Make treaties.* With the "advice and consent" of at least two-thirds of those senators voting at the time, the president can make treaties with foreign powers. The president is also to "receive ambassadors," a phrase that presidents have interpreted as the right to recognize other nations.

- *Grant pardons.* The president can grant pardons to individuals who have committed "offenses against the United States, except in cases of impeachment."

The Expansion of Presidential Power

The framers' limited conception of the president's role has given way to a considerably more powerful interpretation. In this section, we look beyond the presidential responsibilities explicitly listed in the Constitution and examine the additional sources of power that presidents have used to expand the authority of the office. First, we look at the claims that presidents make about "inherent" powers implicit in the Constitution. Second, we turn to congressional grants of power to the executive branch. Third, we discuss the influence that comes from a president's political skills. Fourth, we analyze how a president's popular support affects his political power.

The Inherent Powers

Several presidents have expanded their power by taking actions that exceeded commonly held notions of the president's proper authority. These men justified what they had done by saying that their actions fell within the **inherent powers** of the office. From this broad perspective, presidential power derives not only from those duties clearly outlined in Article II but also from inferences that may be drawn from the Constitution.

When a president claims a power that has not been considered part of the chief executive's authority, he forces Congress and the courts to acquiesce to his claim or to restrict it. In doing so, he runs the risk of suffering a politically damaging rebuff by either body. However, when presidents succeed in claiming a new power, they leave to their successors the legacy of a permanent expansion of presidential authority. One early use of the inherent power of the presidency occurred during George Washington's tenure in office. The British and the French were at war, and Washington issued a proclamation of strict neutrality, angering many who harbored anti-British sentiments; the ensuing controversy provoked a constitutional debate. Washington's critics noted that the Constitution does not include a presidential power to declare neutrality. His defenders said that the president had inherent powers to conduct diplomatic relations. In the end, Washington's decision was not overturned by Congress or the courts and thus set a precedent in the area of foreign affairs.[3]

Claims of inherent powers often come at critical points in the nation's history. During the Civil War, for example, Abraham Lincoln issued a number of orders that exceeded the accepted limits of presidential authority and usurped powers constitutionally conferred on Congress. Lincoln said the urgent nature of the South's challenge to the Union forced him to act without waiting for congressional approval. His rationale was simple: "Was it possible to lose the nation and yet preserve the Constitution?"[4] In other words, Lincoln circumvented the Constitution to save the nation. Subsequently, Congress and the Supreme Court approved Lincoln's actions. That approval gave added legitimacy to the theory of inherent powers—a theory that over time has transformed the presidency.

Congressional Delegation of Power

Presidential power grows when presidents successfully challenge Congress, but in many instances Congress willingly delegates power to the executive branch. As the American public pressures the national government to solve various problems, Congress, through a process called **delegation of powers**, gives the executive branch more responsibility to administer programs that address those problems. One example of delegation of legislative power occurred in the 1930s, during the Great Depression, when Congress gave Franklin Roosevelt's administration wide latitude to do what it thought was necessary to solve the nation's economic ills.

When Congress concludes that the government needs flexibility in its approach to a problem, the president is often given great freedom in how or when to implement policies. Richard Nixon, for example, was given discretionary authority to impose a freeze on wages and prices in an effort to combat escalating inflation. If Congress had been forced to debate the timing of this freeze, merchants and manufacturers would surely have raised their prices in anticipation of the event. Instead, Nixon was able to act suddenly, and the freeze was imposed without warning. (Congressional delegation of authority to the executive branch is discussed in more detail in Chapter 10.)

At other times, however, Congress believes that too much power is accumulating in the executive branch, and it passes legislation reasserting congressional authority. During the 1970s, many representatives and senators agreed that Congress's role in the American political system was declining, that presidents were exercising power that rightfully belonged to the legislative branch. The most notable reaction was the passage of the War Powers Resolution (1973), which was directed toward ending the president's ability to pursue armed conflict without explicit congressional approval. More recently, Congress has demanded a much greater role in foreign policymaking and (as noted in Chapter 8) has successfully pushed the president to consult with it on arms control issues.[5]

The President's Power to Persuade

A president's influence in office comes not only from his assigned responsibilities but also from his political skills and how effectively he uses the resources of his office. A classic analysis of the use of presidential resources was offered by Richard Neustadt in his book *Presidential Power*, which discussed how presidents gained, lost, or maintained their influence. Neustadt's initial premise was simple: "Presidential *power* is the power to persuade."[6] Presidents, for all their resources—a skilled staff, extensive media coverage of presidential actions, the great respect for the office—must depend on others' cooperation to get things done. Harry Truman echoed Neustadt's premise when he said, "I sit here all day trying to persuade people to do the things they ought to have sense enough to do without my persuading them. . . . That's all the powers of the President amount to."[7]

The abilities displayed in bargaining, dealing with adversaries, and choosing priorities, according to Neustadt, separate above-average presidents from mediocre ones. A president must make wise choices about which policies to push and which to put aside until more support can be found. He must decide when to accept compromises and when to stand on principles. He must know when to go public and when to work behind the scenes.

A president's political skills can be important in affecting outcomes in Congress. The chief executive cannot intervene in every legislative struggle. He must choose his battles carefully and then try to use the force of his personality and the prestige of his office to forge an agreement among differing factions. In terms of getting members to vote a

It's a Matter of Priorities

In 1992 Bill Clinton assumed the presidency of the world's only remaining superpower. However, the U.S. was plagued by a huge federal deficit and continuing unemployment. By reducing military spending the president sought to satisfy the public demand that the deficit be reduced. Unfortunately, defense cuts require that additional workers join the ranks of the unemployed. California, the state with the largest number of defense-related industries and military bases, also had the highest unemployment rate. Here several workers at the Long Beach Naval Shipyard celebrate the news that their facility would not be among those to be closed.

certain way, presidential influence is best described as taking place "at the margins." That is, presidents do not have the power to consistently move large numbers of votes one way or the other. They can, however, affect some votes—possibly enough to affect the outcome of a closely fought piece of legislation.[8]

Neustadt stressed that a president's influence is related to his professional reputation and prestige. When a president pushes hard for a bill that Congress eventually defeats or eviscerates, the president's reputation is hurt. The public perceives him as weak or showing poor judgment, and Congress becomes even less likely to cooperate with him in the future. Jimmy Carter damaged his prestige by backing bills that proposed welfare reform, hospital cost containment, and an agency for consumer protection—none of which passed. Yet the other side of this coin is that presidents cannot easily avoid controversial bills, especially if campaign promises were made. If a president backs only sure things, he will be credited with little initiative and perceived as too cautious.

The President and the Public

Neustadt's analysis suggests that a popular president is more persuasive than an unpopular one. A popular president has more power to persuade because he can use his public support as a resource in the bargaining process.[9] Members of Congress who know that the president is highly popular back home have more incentive to cooperate with the administration.

A familiar aspect of the modern presidency is the effort of its incumbents to mobilize public support for their programs. A president uses televised addresses and the press coverage that surrounds his speeches, remarks to reporters, and public appearances to speak directly to the American people and convince them of the wisdom of his policies. Although today it is common for a president to seek popular endorsement of particular bills or broad initiatives, as George Bush did with the tax proposal discussed in the chapter opening, public appeals have not always been a part of the presidency. The founders' fear that the executive office might be used to inflame popular passions led early presidents to be reserved in their communications.[10] Our first fifteen presidents averaged fewer than ten speeches a year.

Since then, presidents have increased their direct communication with the American people. The number of presidential public appearances has grown sharply since World War II. Obviously, modern technology has contributed to this growth. Nonetheless, the increase in public appearances represents something more than increased visibility for the president and his views. There has also been a fundamental change in the power of the presidency. The decline of party and congressional leadership has hastened the rise of the public president; at the same time, the president's direct communication with the American people has made it more difficult for political parties and Congress to reinvigorate themselves.[11]

Presidential popularity is typically at its highest during a president's first year in office. This "honeymoon" period affords the president a particularly good opportunity to use public support to get some of his programs through Congress. During Ronald Reagan's first year in office, when he made a televised appeal for support for a legislative proposal, some congressional offices received calls and letters that ran 10 to 1 in favor of the president. At the beginning of his second term, typical congressional offices received an equal number of negative and positive responses after a Reagan appeal.[12] Clearly, Reagan had lost some of his ability to mobilize public opinion.

The rise and fall in presidential popularity can generally be explained by several factors. First, public approval of the job done by a president is affected by economic conditions, such as inflation and unemployment.[13] Second, a president is affected by unanticipated events of all types that occur during his administration. When U.S. Embassy personnel were taken hostage in Tehran by militantly anti-American Ira-

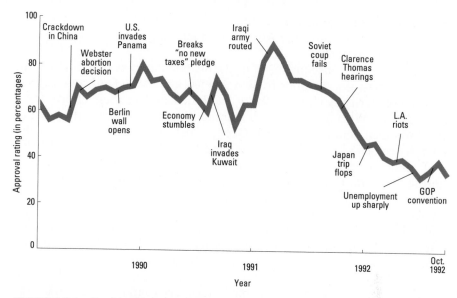

FIGURE 9.1 *Bush's Slippery Slope*

Since the Truman years, each month the Gallup poll has asked, "Do you ap-
prove or disapprove of the way [the present officeholder] is handling his job as
president?" After the American-led coalition inflicted a punishing defeat on
Saddam Hussein's army, Bush's popularity rose to 89 percent, the highest score
ever recorded by Gallup's surveys of presidential performance. Bush's popular-
ity fell so precipitously, however, that only Jimmy Carter ran for re-election
with a lower score. (Source: Gallup poll data compiled from various issues of Ameri-
can Enterprise *and the* Gallup Poll Monthly. *The most recent data provided directly to*
the authors by the Gallup poll, Princeton, New Jersey. Labels added.)

nians, Carter's popularity soared. This "rally 'round the flag" support for
the president eventually gave way to frustration with his inability to
gain the hostages' release, and Carter's popularity plummeted. Third,
presidential popularity is affected by American involvement in a war,
which can alter public approval. Johnson, for example, suffered a loss of
popularity during his escalation of the American effort in Vietnam.[14]

Politicians and journalists have a good "feel" for how well a president is doing, but objective evidence comes from a steady stream of
national opinion surveys (see Chapter 4). Figure 9.1 depicts the Gallup
poll's monthly measurement of George Bush's popularity from his first
days in office through the month before the 1992 election. With the
economy continuing to be strong, Bush had a prolonged honeymoon
with very strong poll ratings during his first year. He declined modestly
in his second year, hurt by a softer economy and the reversal of his "no
new taxes" pledge. His popularity went sky high after the American-led
coalition drove the Iraqi army from Kuwait. However, his popularity
plummeted after the glow of victory had worn off. The third year in a

row of weak economic performance drove the Bush ratings down further, with only one in three Americans approving of his performance at some points in 1992.

The ultimate consequence of declining popularity is that a first-term president may not be able to win re-election. Both Ford and Carter, whose popularity declined sharply, were defeated in their efforts for a second term. With his popularity waning, Lyndon Johnson pulled out of the 1968 Democratic primaries. George Bush was unable to regain the confidence of the American public, and his defeat showed the electorate's desire to punish him for the economy's lackluster performance during his term. Decline, however, is not inherently irreversible. When the economy recovered after the 1981–1982 recession, Reagan's popularity recovered, too. After it was revealed that the Reagan administration had sold arms to Iran and had used some of the profits to fund rebel forces in Nicaragua, Reagan's popularity plunged. By the end of his term, however, his popularity had moved up again.[15] Presidents who develop a strong residue of respect and approval for the basic thrust of their presidency seem more capable of recovery from adverse conditions or events.

The Electoral Connection

In his farewell address to the nation, Jimmy Carter lashed out at the interest groups that had bedeviled his presidency. Interest groups, he said, "distort our purposes because the national interest is not always the sum of all our single or special interests." Carter noted the president's singular responsibility: "The president is the only elected official charged with representing all the people."[16] Carter, like all other presidents, quickly recognized the dilemma of majoritarianism versus pluralism after he took office. The president must try to please countless separate constituencies while trying to do what is best for the whole country.

It is easy to stand on the sidelines and say that presidents should always try to follow a majoritarian path—pursuing policies that reflect the preferences of most citizens. Simply by running for office, however, candidates align themselves with particular segments of the population. As a result of their electoral strategy, their identification with activists in their party, and their own political views, candidates come into office with an interest in pleasing some constituencies more than others.

Each candidate attempts to put together an electoral coalition that will provide at least the minimum 270 (out of 538) electoral votes needed for election. As the campaign proceeds, the candidate tries to win votes from different groups of voters through his stand on various issues. Because issue stands can cut both ways—attracting some voters and driving others away—candidates may try to finesse an issue by being deliberately vague.

Candidates cannot, however, be deliberately vague about all issues. A candidate who is noncommittal on too many issues appears wishy-washy. And future presidents do not build their political careers without working strongly for and becoming associated with important issues and constituencies. As a result, presidents enter office with both a majority of voters on their side and a close identification with particular issues.

Elections and Mandates

Candidates who win the presidency inevitably claim that they have been given a **mandate**, or endorsement, to carry out the policies they campaigned on. Newly chosen presidents make a majoritarian interpretation of the electoral process, claiming that their selection is an expression of the direct will of the people and they are a superior embodiment of national sentiment when compared to the 535 individual members of Congress, who are elected from much smaller constituencies.

More dispassionate observers usually have difficulty finding concrete evidence of broad public support for the range of specific policies a winning candidate wants to pursue. Even a landslide at the polls does not give a president a crystal-clear mandate. Lyndon Johnson crushed his Republican opponent, Barry Goldwater, in the 1964 election, winning all but six states in the electoral college. Nevertheless, Johnson misread the public's willingness to endure a ground war in Southeast Asia, and his popularity went into a steep decline. The social programs of his Great Society, which seemed so popular at the beginning of his presidency, produced a backlash by middle-class whites.

Divided Government

A major problem the president faces in translating whatever mandate he perceives into actual policies is that the separation of powers makes Congress independent of the executive branch. Not only are the branches separate, but a president also has no guarantee that members of his party will be in control of the two houses of Congress. Indeed, in recent years there has been a pattern of **divided control of government**, with the Republicans controlling the White House and the Democrats controlling Congress. Between 1968 and 1992, the Republicans won five of the seven presidential elections. Only for six years of that time did they control a single house of the Congress. Although partisan identification remains important, American voters have become less loyal to political parties and today vote more on the basis of candidate appeal and issues.

Voters appear to use quite different criteria when choosing a president than they do when choosing congressional representatives. As one scholar has noted, "Presidential candidates are evaluated according to their views on national issues and their competence in dealing with national problems. Congressional candidates are evaluated on their personal character and experience and on their devotion to district services and local issues."[17] This congressional independence is another reason contemporary presidents work so hard to gain public support for their policies. Without a strong base of representatives and senators who feel their election was tied to his, a president often feels that he needs to win in the court of public opinion.

The Executive Branch Establishment

As a president tries to maintain the support of his electoral coalition for the policies he pursues, he draws on the great resources of the executive branch of government. The president has a White House staff that helps him formulate policy. The vice president is another resource; his duties within the administration vary according to his relationship with the president. The president's Cabinet secretaries—the heads of the major departments of the national government—play a number of roles, including the critical function of administering the programs that fall within their jurisdiction. Finally, within the departments and agencies, operating at a level below that of the president's appointees are the career bureaucrats. These bureaucrats (who are discussed in Chapter 10) offer great expertise in program operations.

The White House Staff

A president depends heavily on his key aides. They advise him on crucial political choices, devise the general strategies the administration follows in pursuing congressional and public support, and control access to the president to ensure that he has enough time for his most important tasks. Consequently, he needs to trust and respect these top staffers; many of a president's inner circle of assistants are long-time associates.

Presidents typically have a chief of staff, who may be a "first among equals," or, in some administrations, the unquestioned leader of the staff. There is also a national security adviser to provide daily briefings on foreign and military affairs and longer-range analyses of issues confronting the administration. A council of economic advisers is also located in the White House. Senior domestic policy advisers help determine the administration's basic approach to such areas as health, education, and social services.

Below these top aides are the large staffs that serve them and the president. These staffs are organized around certain specialties. Some staff members work on "political" matters, such as liaison with interest groups, relations with ethnic and religious minorities, and party affairs. One staff deals exclusively with the press, and a legislative liaison staff lobbies Congress for the administration. The large Office of Management and Budget (OMB) analyzes budget requests, is involved in the policymaking process, and also examines agency management practices. This extended White House executive establishment is known as the **Executive Office of the President**. Under George Bush, the Executive Office employed approximately sixteen hundred individuals and had an annual budget of about $100 million.[18] A few weeks after assuming office, President Clinton announced plans to reduce the size of the White House staff by 25 percent as a demonstration that government should make sacrifices before asking the taxpayer to do so. However, under Clinton, that staff remains larger than it had been under President Reagan, Carter, Ford, or Nixon.[19]

There is no agreed-on "right way" for a president to organize his White House staff. Each president creates the structure that works best for him.[20] Dwight Eisenhower, for example, a former general, wanted clear lines of authority and a hierarchical structure that mirrored a military command. One factor that influences how a president uses his senior staff is the degree to which he delegates authority to them. Carter immersed himself in the policymaking process to ensure that he made all the significant decisions. Ronald Reagan was the opposite: He saw his role as setting a general direction for the administration but delegated wide-ranging authority to his staff to act on his behalf. Bill Clinton's style is to appoint top-level officials who provide him with a variety of often conflicting views on issues and then "resolve nearly all the conflicts" himself.[21]

Despite the formal organization of the White House staff, it suffers from the same "turf wars" that plague other large organizations. These struggles over authority stem not only from personal ambition and political differences but also from overlapping jurisdictions. For example, conflict frequently arises between a secretary of state (a member of the Cabinet) and a president's national security adviser; each wants primacy in shaping the administration's foreign policy.

The Vice President

The vice president's primary function is to serve as standby equipment, only a heartbeat away from the presidency itself (see Feature 9.1). Traditionally, vice presidents have not been used in any important advisory capacity. Instead, presidents tend to give them political chores—campaigning, fund raising, and "stroking" the party faithful. This is often the case because vice-presidential candidates are chosen for reasons that have more to do with the political campaign than with governing the nation.

Dan Quayle illustrated this common pattern. In 1988, Quayle was a youthful second-term senator from Indiana who had served twelve years in the Congress, but he was widely regarded as a "lightweight."[22] Nobody really believed that he was the best-suited person to step in as president should something happen to Bush. Bush emphasized that he chose Quayle because he wanted to reach out to younger generations.

Who's President When the President Can't Be?

What happens when a president dies in office? The vice president, of course, becomes the new president. But what happens if the vice president has died or left office for some reason? What happens if the president becomes senile or is disabled by illness? These are questions that the authors of the Constitution failed to resolve.

The nuclear age has made these questions more troubling. When Woodrow Wilson suffered a stroke in 1919, the country was without effective leadership for a time, but the lack of an active president during that period did not endanger the lives of all Americans. Today, with the possibility of nuclear attack, national security dictates that the nation have a commander in chief at all times. The Twenty-fifth Amendment, which was ratified in 1967, specifies a mechanism for replacing a living president in case he cannot carry out the duties of his office. A president can declare himself unable to carry on, or the vice president and the Cabinet can decide collectively that the president is incapacitated. In either case, the vice president becomes acting president and assumes all powers of the office.

In 1981, when Ronald Reagan was seriously wounded in an assassination attempt and had to undergo emergency surgery, the Twenty-fifth Amendment was not invoked by the vice president and the Cabinet. Four years later, when Reagan underwent cancer surgery, he sent a letter to Vice President George Bush transferring the power of the office to him at the moment the president was anesthetized. Eight hours later, Reagan reclaimed his authority. Under the Twenty-fifth Amendment, if the president and the Cabinet disagree about whether he is able to resume his duties, Congress must ultimately decide.

The Twenty-fifth Amendment also provides that the president select a new vice president in the event that office becomes vacant; the president's choice must be approved by a majority of both houses of Congress. In 1973, Gerald Ford became vice president in this manner when Spiro Agnew resigned after pleading no contest to charges of income tax evasion and accepting bribes. Later, when Richard Nixon resigned and Ford became president, he chose Nelson Rockefeller as his vice president.

As President Clinton's running mate, Al Gore contributed to their successful 1992 campaign in several ways. As a young, liberal southerner, he both reinforced an image of youth and change and helped lure back to the Democratic party many southern voters who had strayed during the Reagan and Bush years. Clinton also no doubt recognized that Gore's years of experience in the House and Senate would be useful to a president who had never served in either.

Table 9.1   The Cabinet ▬▬▬▬▬▬

Department	Created	Number of Employees
State	1789	25,288
Treasury	1789	158,655
Defense[*]	1789	1,034,152
Justice[†]	1789	83,932
Interior	1849	77,679
Agriculture	1862	122,594
Commerce	1913	69,920
Labor	1913	17,727
Health and Human Services[††]	1953	123,957
Housing and Urban Development	1965	13,596
Transportation	1966	67,364
Energy	1977	17,731
Education	1979	4,771
Veterans Affairs	1988	248,174

[*]The War Department was created in 1789. The Defense Department was created in 1949. Employment figure is for civilian employees only.

[†]The attorney general was a member of the first Cabinet. The Justice Department was established in 1870.

[††]The Department of Health, Education, and Welfare became the Department of Health and Human Services in 1979 when an independent Department of Education was established.

Source: Bureau of the Census, *Statistical Abstract of the United States*, 1992 (Washington, D.C.: U.S. Government Printing Office, 1992), p. 330.

The Cabinet

The president's **Cabinet** is composed of the heads of the departments in the executive branch and a small number of other key officials, such as the head of the OMB and the ambassador to the United Nations. The Cabinet has expanded greatly since George Washington formed his first Cabinet, which included an attorney general and the secretaries of state, treasury, and war. Clearly, the growth of the Cabinet to fourteen departments reflects the growth of government responsibility and intervention in areas such as energy, housing, and transportation (see Table 9.1).

In theory, the members of the Cabinet constitute an advisory body that meets with the president to debate major policy decisions. In practice, however, Cabinet meetings have been described as "vapid non-events in which there has been a deliberate non-exchange of information as part of a process of mutual nonconsultation."[23] Why is this so? First, the Cabinet has become rather large. Counting department heads, other officials of Cabinet rank, and presidential aides, it is a body of at least twenty people—a size that many presidents find unwieldy for the give-and-take of political decision making. Second, most Cabinet members have limited areas of expertise and simply cannot contribute much to deliberations on areas they know little about. The secretary of defense, for example, would probably be a poor choice to help decide important issues of agricultural policy. Third, although Cabinet members have impressive backgrounds, they may not be personally close to the president or easy for him to work with. The president often chooses Cabinet members because of their reputations, or he may be guided by a need to give his Cabinet some racial, ethnic, geographic, sexual, or religious balance.

Finally, modern presidents do not rely on the Cabinet to make policy because they have such large White House staffs, which offer most of the needed advisory support. In contrast to Cabinet secretaries, who may be pulled in different directions by the wishes of the president and the wishes of their departments' clientele groups, White House staffers are likely to see themselves as responsible to the president alone. Thus, despite periodic calls for the Cabinet to be a collective decision-making body, Cabinet meetings seem doomed to be little more than academic exercises. In practice, presidents prefer the flexibility of ad hoc groups, specialized White House staffs, and the advisers and Cabinet secretaries with whom they feel most comfortable.

More broadly, presidents use their personal staffs and the large Executive Office of the President to centralize control over the entire executive branch. The vast size of the executive branch and the number and complexity of decisions that must be made each day pose a challenge for the White House. In sum, to fulfill more of their political goals and policy preferences, modern presidents have encouraged their various staffs to play increasingly important roles in executive branch decision making.[24]

The President as National Leader

With an election behind him and the resources of his office at hand, a president is ready to lead the nation. Each president enters office with a general vision of how government should approach policy issues. During his term, a president spends much of his time trying to get Congress to enact legislation that reflects his general philosophy and specific policy preferences.

From Political Values . . .

Presidents differ greatly in their views of the role of government. Lyndon Johnson had a strong liberal ideology concerning domestic affairs. He believed that government had a responsibility to help disadvantaged Americans. Johnson described his vision of justice in his inaugural address:

> Justice was the promise that all who made the journey would share in the fruits of the land. In a land of wealth, families must not live in hopeless poverty. In a land rich in harvest, children just must not go

hungry. In a land of healing miracles, neighbors must not suffer and die untended. In a great land of learning and scholars, young people must be taught to read and write.

For more than thirty years that I have served this nation, I have believed that this injustice to our people, this waste of our resources, was our real enemy. For thirty years or more, with the resources I have had, I have vigilantly fought against it.[25]

Johnson used *justice* and *injustice* as code words for *equality* and *inequality*. These words were used six times in his speech; *freedom* was used only twice. Johnson used his popularity, his skills, and the resources of his office to press for a "just" America, which he termed the *Great Society.*

To achieve his Great Society, Johnson sent Congress an unprecedented package of liberal legislation. He launched such projects as the Job Corps (which created centers and camps offering vocational training and work experience to youths aged sixteen to twenty-one), Medicare (which provided medical care for the elderly), and the National Teacher Corps (which funded teachers to work in impoverished neighborhoods). Supported by huge Democratic majorities in Congress during 1965 and 1966, he had tremendous success in getting his proposals through. Liberalism was in full swing.

Exactly twenty years after Johnson's inaugural speech, Ronald Reagan took his oath of office for the second time and then addressed the nation. Reagan reasserted his conservative philosophy. He emphasized *freedom*, using the term fourteen times, and failed to mention justice or equality once. He turned Johnson's philosophy on its head, declaring that "government is not the solution to our problem. Government is the problem."[26] During his presidency, Reagan worked to undo many welfare and social service programs, and funding was reduced for such programs as the Job Corps and food stamps. By the end of his term, there had been a fundamental shift in federal spending, with sharp increases in defense spending and "decreases in federal social programs [which] served to defund Democratic interests and constituencies"[27] (see Figure 9.2).

. . . To Policy Agendas

The roots of particular policy proposals, then, can be traced to the more general political ideology of the president. A presidential candidate outlines that philosophy of government during his campaign for the White House. But when the hot rhetoric of the presidential campaign meets the cold reality of what is possible in Washington, the newly elected president must make some hard choices about what he will push for during the coming term. These choices are reflected in the bills the president submits to Congress as well as in the degree to which he works for their passage. The president's bills, introduced by his allies in the House and Senate, always receive a good deal of initial attention. In

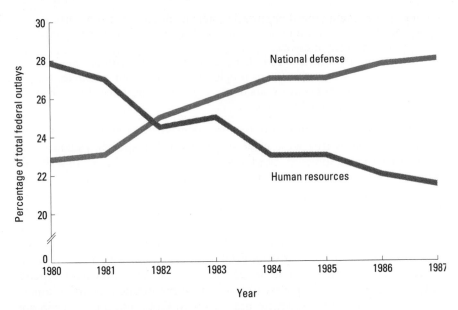

FIGURE 9.2   *The Reagan Impact on Budget Priorities*
Ronald Reagan was particularly effective in persuading Congress to shift spending priorities. Although he was not able to dismantle the welfare state, he was able to reduce funding for social programs significantly. (These figures exclude social security and Medicare from spending for human resources.)
(Source: From The Politics of Rich and Poor *by Kevin Phillips. Copyright © 1990 by Kevin Phillips. Reprinted by permission of Random House, Inc.)*

the words of one Washington lobbyist, "When a president sends up a bill, it takes first place in the queue. All other bills take second place."[28]

The president's role in legislative leadership is largely a twentieth-century phenomenon. Not until the Budget and Accounting Act (1921) did executive branch departments and agencies have to clear their proposed budget bills with the White House. Before this, the president did not even coordinate proposals for how much the executive branch would spend on all the programs it administered. Later, Franklin Roosevelt required that all major legislative proposals by an agency or a department be cleared by the White House. No longer could a department submit a bill without White House support.[29]

Roosevelt's impact on the relationship between the president and Congress went far beyond this new administrative arrangement. With the nation in the midst of the Great Depression, Roosevelt began his first term in 1933 with an ambitious array of legislative proposals. During the first hundred days Congress was in session, it enacted fifteen significant laws, including the Agricultural Adjustment Act, the Civilian Conservation Corps, and the National Industrial Recovery Act.

Never had a president demanded—and received—so much from Congress. Roosevelt's legacy was that the president would henceforth provide aggressive leadership for Congress through his own legislative program.

Chief Lobbyist

When Franklin Roosevelt and Harry Truman first became heavily involved in preparing legislative packages, political scientists typically described the process as one in which "the president proposes and the Congress disposes." In other words, once the president sent his legislation to Capitol Hill, Congress decided what to do with it. Over time, however, presidents have become increasingly active in all stages of the legislative process. The president is expected not only to propose legislation but also to make sure that it passes.

The president's efforts to influence Congress are reinforced by the work of his legislative liaison staff. All departments and major agencies have legislative specialists as well. These department and agency people work with the White House liaison staff to coordinate the administration's lobbying on major issues.

The **legislative liaison staff** is the communications link between the White House and Congress. As a bill slowly makes its way through Congress, liaison staffers advise the president or a Cabinet secretary on the problems that emerge. They specify what parts of a bill are in trouble and may have to be modified or dropped. They tell their boss what amendments are likely to be offered, which members of Congress need lobbying, and what the chances are for the passage of the bill with or without certain provisions. Decisions on how the administration will respond to such developments must then be reached. For example, when the Reagan White House realized that it was still a few votes short of victory on a budget bill in the House, it reversed its opposition to a sugar price-support bill. This attracted the votes of representatives from Louisiana and Florida, two sugar-growing states, for the budget bill. The White House would not call what happened a "deal" but noted that "adjustments and considerations" had been made.[30]

A certain amount of the president's job is stereotypical "arm-twisting"—pushing reluctant legislators to vote a certain way. Yet most day-in, day-out interactions tend to be more subtle as the liaison staff tries to build consensus by working cooperatively with members of Congress. Liaison people talk to committee members individually to see what concerns they have and to help fashion a compromise if some members differ with the president's position.

The White House also works directly with interest groups in its efforts to build support for legislation. Presidential aides hope key lobbyists will activate the most effective lobbyists of all: the voters back home. Interest groups can quickly reach the constituents who are most concerned about a bill. One White House aide said with admiration,

"The Realtors can send out half a million Mailgrams within 24 hours."[31]

Although much of the liaison staff's work with Congress is done in a cooperative spirit, agreement cannot always be reached. When Congress passes a bill the president opposes, he may veto it and send it back to Congress; as noted earlier, Congress can override a veto with a two-thirds majority of those voting in each house. Presidents use their veto power sparingly, but the threat that a president will veto an unacceptable bill increases his bargaining leverage with members of Congress. A president's leverage with Congress is also related to his standing with the American people. The ability of the president and his liaison staff to bargain with members of Congress is enhanced when he is riding high in the popularity polls.

Party Leader

Part of the president's job is to lead his party. This is very much an informal duty with no prescribed tasks. In this respect, American presidents are considerably different from European prime ministers, who are the formal leaders of their parties in the national legislatures as well as the heads of government. Since political parties in Europe tend to have strong national organizations, there is more reason for prime ministers to lead the party organization.

The simple fact is that presidents can operate effectively without the help of a national party apparatus. Lyndon Johnson, for example, was contemptuous of the Democratic National Committee. He saw to it that the committee's budget was cut and refused some advisers' request that he replace its ineffectual head. Johnson thought a weak national committee would allow him to control party affairs out of the White House. Like other modern presidents, Johnson believed he would be most effective communicating directly with the American people and did not see the need for national, state, or local party officials to be intermediaries in the process of coalition building.[32]

Work with the party may be more important for gaining the presidency than actually governing. George Bush worked tirelessly on the "rubber chicken" circuit while he was vice president and built up a hefty billfold of IOUs by campaigning for Republican candidates and appearing at their fund-raising dinners. When he and his main competitor for the 1988 Republican nomination, Senator Robert Dole, faced each other in the critical Super Tuesday primaries in 1988, Bush had enormous strength among state and local party leaders; those individuals formed the backbone of his campaign organization.

The President as World Leader

The president's leadership responsibilities extend beyond Congress and the nation into the international arena. Each administration tries to further what it sees as the country's best interests in relations with allies, adversaries, and the developing countries of the world. In this role, the president must be ready to act as diplomat and crisis manager.

Foreign Relations

Since the end of World War II, presidents have been preoccupied with containing communist expansion around the globe. Now, with the collapse of communism in the former Soviet Union and Eastern Europe, American presidents are entering a new era in international relations. The new presidential job description places much more emphasis on managing economic relations with the rest of the world, especially with Europe and Japan. Trade relations are a particularly difficult problem because presidents must balance the conflicting interests of foreign countries (many of whom are our allies), the interests of particular American industries, the overall needs of the American economy, and the demands of the legislative branch.

The decline of communism has not, however, enabled the president to ignore security issues. The world remains a dangerous place, and regional conflicts can still embroil the United States. When Iraq invaded and quickly conquered Kuwait in August 1990, President Bush felt he had no choice but to respond firmly to protect our economic interests and to stand beside our Arab allies in the area. Bush worked the phones hard to get both Western and Arab leaders to join the United States in a coordinated military buildup in the area surrounding Kuwait. It was, said one journalist, a "dazzling performance. In roughly four days, Bush organized the world against Saddam Hussein."[33]

Crisis Management

Periodically the president faces a grave situation in which conflict is imminent or a small conflict threatens to explode into a larger war. Handling such episodes is a critical part of the president's job. Today, we must put enormous trust in the person who has the power to pull the nuclear trigger; voters may make the candidates' personal judgment and intelligence primary considerations in how they cast their ballots. A major reason for Barry Goldwater's crushing defeat in the 1964 election was his warlike image. Goldwater's bellicose rhetoric scared many Americans, who, fearing that he would be too quick to resort to nuclear weapons, voted for Lyndon Johnson instead.

A president must be able to exercise good judgment and remain cool in crisis situations. John Kennedy's behavior during the Cuban missile crisis of 1962 has become a model of effective crisis management. When it was discovered that the Soviet Union had placed missiles containing nuclear warheads in Cuba, Kennedy sought the advice of a group of senior aides. An armed invasion of Cuba and air strikes against the missiles

A Friend in Need . . .

In the international arena, the president serves as America's chief diplomat and crisis manager. In this picture President Clinton performs both tasks as he meets with Russian president Boris Yeltsin at a 1992 summit conference in Vancouver, Canada. The meeting occurred shortly after Mr. Yeltsin had weathered a crisis in which the Russian parliament had sought his impeachment, and just weeks before the Russian people were to vote on whether he should continue in office. President Clinton provided the Russian president with assurances of U.S. support and economic assistance to his embattled reform program.

were two options considered. In the end, Kennedy decided on a less dangerous response: implementing a naval blockade of Cuba. The Soviet Union thought better of prolonging its challenge to the United States and soon agreed to remove the missiles. For a short time, however, the world held its breath over the very real possibility of a nuclear war.

Are there guidelines for what a president should do in times of crisis or at other important decision-making junctures? Drawing on a range of advisers and opinions is certainly one.[34] Not acting in unnecessary haste is another. A third is having a well-designed, formal review process that promotes thorough analysis and open debate.[35] A fourth guideline is rigorously examining the chain of reasoning that has led to the chosen option, ensuring that presumptions have not been subconsciously equated with what is actually known to be true. When Kennedy decided to back a CIA plan to sponsor a rebel invasion of Cuba by expatriates hostile to Fidel Castro, he never really understood that its chances for success were based on unfounded assumptions of immediate uprisings by the Cuban population.[36]

Nevertheless, these are rather general rules and provide no assurance that mistakes will not be made. Almost by definition, each crisis is a unique event. Sometimes all the alternatives carry substantial risks. And almost always, time is of the essence.

Presidential Character

How does the public assess which presidential candidate has the best judgment and a character suitable to the office? Americans must make a broad evaluation, considering the candidates' personalities and leadership styles. In 1988, questions about Gary Hart's character forced him out of the race for the Democratic presidential nomination. The public was disturbed not only by the allegations of adultery that followed the Democratic candidate but also by his recklessness. As one journalist noted, "Why would any man in his right mind defy a New York *Times* reporter who asked about his alleged womanizing to 'put a tail on me,' then cancel his weekend campaign appearances and arrange a tryst at his Washington town house with a Miami party girl?"[37]

Character also emerged in 1992 when the Bush campaign harshly attacked Bill Clinton because Clinton had been evasive about how he had avoided the Vietnam draft. Although the negative campaign run against Clinton did raise doubts about his character, the economy weighed far more heavily on voters' minds.

A candidate's character is clearly a valid campaign issue. A president's actions in office reflect something more than ideology and politics; they also reflect the moral, ethical, and psychological forces that comprise his character.

Candidates do not come neatly labeled as having healthy or unhealthy presidential characters. Although voters make their own estimations of how presidents will behave in office, there is no guarantee that those evaluations will turn out to be accurate. And a candidate's character must still be weighed along with other factors, including ideology, party affiliation, and stances on specific issues.

A Difference in Character
The personalities of Calvin Coolidge and John F. Kennedy led to considerably different styles of presidential leadership. Coolidge's motto, "Let well enough alone," says much about his approach to the presidency. "Vigorous" was the term commonly used to describe Kennedy, and it's an apt description of his presidency as well. Historian Arthur Schlesinger, Jr., said of Kennedy, "His presidential life was instinct with action."

Summary

When the delegates to the Constitutional Convention met to design the government of this new nation, they had trouble shaping the office of the president. They struggled to find a balance between an office that was powerful enough to provide unified leadership but not so strong that presidents could use their powers to become tyrants or dictators. The initial conceptions of the presidency have slowly been transformed over time as presidents have adapted the office to meet the nation's changing needs. The trend has been to expand presidential power. Some of this expansion has come from presidential actions under claims of inherent powers. Congress has also delegated a great deal of power to the executive branch, further expanding the role of the president.

Because the president is elected by the entire nation, when proposing policy he can claim to represent all citizens. This broad electoral base equips the presidency to be an institution of majoritarian democracy—compared with Congress's structural tendencies toward pluralist democracy. Whether the presidency actually operates in a majoritarian manner depends on several factors—the individual president's perception of public opinion on political issues, the relationship between public opinion and the president's political ideology, and the extent to which the president is committed to pursuing his values through his office.

The executive branch establishment has grown rapidly, and the White House has become a sizable bureaucracy. New responsibilities of the twentieth-century presidency are particularly noticeable in the area of legislative leadership. Now a president is expected to be a policy initiator for Congress as well as a lobbyist who guides his bills through the legislative process.

The presidential "job description" for foreign policy has changed considerably. Post–World War II presidents were preoccupied with containing the spread of communism, but with the collapse of communism in the former Soviet Union and Eastern Europe, international economic relations now loom even larger as a priority for presidents. National security issues still remain, however, as regional conflicts can directly involve the interests of the United States.

Key Terms

veto
inherent powers
delegation of powers
mandate
divided control of government

Executive Office of the
  President
Cabinet
legislative liaison staff

Selected Readings

Burke, John P., and Fred I. Greenstein. *How Presidents Test Reality.* New York: Russell Sage, 1989. This is a study of the way Eisenhower and Johnson considered intervening in Southeast Asia.

Edwards, George C. *At the Margins.* New Haven, Conn.: Yale University Press, 1989. This is a systematic analysis of the impact of presidential leadership on congressional voting.

Jones, Charles O., ed. *The Reagan Legacy.* Chatham, N.J.: Chatham House, 1988. Here is an excellent collection of essays that covers different aspects of the Reagan presidency.

Kernell, Samuel. *Going Public.* Washington, D.C.: Congressional Quarterly Press, 1986. This book investigates how modern presidents, to expand their influence, rely more and more on direct communication with the American people.

Lowi, Theodore J. *The Personal President.* Ithaca, N.Y.: Cornell University Press, 1985. In Lowi's eyes, the decline of our party system has helped give rise to a direct relationship between contemporary presidents and the people.

Neustadt, Richard E. *Presidential Power.* Rev. ed. New York: John Wiley, 1980. Neustadt's classic study examines the president's power to persuade.

Neustadt, Richard E., and Earnest R. May. *Thinking in Time.* New York: Free Press, 1986. Neustadt and May offer an analytical framework that presidents can use to try minimizing errors that lead to faulty decisions.

THE BUREAUCRACY

10

The question was not whether Andres Serrano's photograph, "Piss Christ," was art—some said it was; others said it was an obscenity. Rather the question was whether taxpayers' money should have been spent to support his work. (Serrano had been given a federal grant of $15,000 in 1987.) His photograph of a thirteen-inch crucifix submerged in a small tank of his urine would ignite a firestorm of criticism and provoke a national debate over the role of the National Endowment for the Arts (NEA), a government agency that provides support for the arts.

After a Richmond, Virginia, art museum showed Serrano's photograph as part of an exhibition, an incensed Reverend Donald Wildmon, head of the American Family Association, a conservative advocacy group, sent a reproduction of a newspaper clipping about it to every member of Congress. Republican Senator Jesse Helms of North Carolina quickly responded, "He [Serrano] was trying to create indignation. That is all right for him to be a jerk, but let him be a jerk on his own time and with his own resources."

Helms struck a chord. Many hard-working taxpayers wondered why a portion of their federal income taxes was going to support art that satirized the most sacred symbol of Christianity. The controversy over "Piss Christ" led to a broader examination of other grants by the NEA,

Your Tax Dollars at Work
Controversial artist Andres Serrano received a grant from the National Endow-
ment for the Arts in support of his work. Here he appears with his photograph
Piss Christ, *which provoked a national debate over the role of that government*
agency.

such as an exhibit by photographer Robert Mapplethorpe that included
pictures of men in homoerotic and sadomasochistic poses (see Chapter 12).

Inevitably, legislation was introduced to restrict NEA funding; there
were even proposals to eliminate the agency. Critics charged that the
NEA was out of control, that it was an all too typical case of a government bureaucracy doing whatever it wanted to do with little concern
for what the public wanted.

A spirited counterattack was mounted on behalf of the NEA. Not
surprisingly, much of this support came from artists, who would be
most directly affected by restrictions on the NEA. They made a powerful argument that limiting NEA funding would constitute an assault on
the freedom of artistic expression.

Congress responded to controversy as it usually does—with a compromise. Both the House and the Senate passed bills requiring artists to

return their grants if convicted of obscenity. Congress left it to the courts, not the NEA, to determine if a work of art is obscene. Although obscenity convictions are hard to obtain, many people worry that the NEA may now be much more cautious about the kind of art it chooses to support with federal grants.[1]

The fight over the NEA illustrates the continuing tension between freedom and order in American society. Wildmon, Helms, and other critics of the NEA believed that they were trying to preserve decency and religion in American life. On the other side were those who believed that what is best about America is its unswerving devotion to freedom, including freedom of expression. This episode also reflects the virtues and shortcomings of both the majoritarian and pluralist views of government. The artists who were clients of the NEA had considerable influence over its policymaking—some say too much—and the public was not well informed about this rather narrow area of federal activity. When people were aroused, it was by a few unrepresentative and sensationalistic pieces of art. Nevertheless, the opinions of ordinary citizens should not be discounted just because they have less sophisticated views of what constitutes art that is worth supporting.

Like the NEA, many government organizations are accused of being powers unto themselves, independent of democratic controls. In this chapter, we try to determine who controls the bureaucracy in our government. We also analyze why people are so dissatisfied with bureaucracy and examine reforms that might make government work better.

Organization Matters

A nation's laws and policies are administered, or put into effect, by a variety of departments, agencies, bureaus, offices, and other government units, which together are known as its *bureaucracy*. **Bureaucracy** actually means any large, complex organization in which employees have very specific job responsibilities and work within a hierarchy of authority. The employees of these government units have become known somewhat derisively as **bureaucrats.** We study bureaucracies because they play a central role in the governments of postindustrial societies. Yet organizations are a crucial part of any society, no matter how elementary. For example, the organization of a preindustrial tribe is not merely a quaint aspect of its evolution but is critical to the survival of its members.

The organization of modern governmental bureaucracies also reflects their need to survive. Preindustrial tribes often had to struggle to survive in hostile environments; the environment of modern bureaucracies, filled with conflicting political demands and the ever-present threat of budget cuts, can be no less hostile. The way government bureaucracies are organized also reflects the needs of their clients. The bottom line, however, is that the manner in which any bureaucracy is organized affects how well it is able to accomplish its tasks.

Unfortunately, "if organization matters, it is also the case that there is no one best way of organizing."[2] For example, although greater autonomy may improve the performance of public schools, it may not be a good solution for improving a state social welfare agency, where a primary goal is treating its clients equally and providing the same benefits to people with the same needs and circumstances.

The Development of the Bureaucratic State

The study of bureaucracy, then, centers on finding solutions to the many different kinds of problems faced by large governmental organizations. A common complaint voiced by Americans is that the bureaucracy is too big and tries to accomplish too much. To the average citizen, the federal government may seem like an octopus—its long arms reach just about everywhere.

The Growth of American Government

American government seems to have grown without limit during this century. As one observer noted wryly, "The assistant administrator for water and hazardous materials of the Environmental Protection Agency presided over a staff larger than Washington's entire first administration."[3] Yet even during Washington's time, bureaucracies were necessary. No one argued then about the need for a postal service to deliver mail or a department of the treasury to maintain a system of currency. However, government at all levels (national, state, and local) has grown enormously in the twentieth century. There are a number of major reasons why our government has grown the way it has.

Science and technology.   One reason government has grown so much is the increasing complexity of society. George Washington did not have an assistant administrator for water and hazardous materials because there was no need for one. A National Aeronautics and Space Administration (NASA) was not necessary until rockets were invented.

Even longstanding departments have had to expand the scope of their activities to keep up with technological and societal changes. Consider the changes brought about by genetic engineering, for example. The Patent Office in the U.S. Department of Commerce has had to respond to requests that new life forms be patented to protect manufacturers' interests. Under a new policy, the creators of new animals—like the geep, a species derived from the fusion of goat and sheep embryos—must receive royalties for each animal raised by a farmer.[4]

Business regulation.   Another reason government has grown is that the public's attitude toward business has changed. Throughout most of the nineteenth century, business was generally autonomous, and any government intervention in the economy that might limit that autonomy was considered inappropriate. This attitude began to change toward the end of the nineteenth century as more Americans became aware that the end product of this laissez-faire approach was not always highly competitive markets that benefited consumers. Gradually, government intervention came to be accepted as necessary to protect the integrity of business markets. And if government was to police unfair business practices effectively, then it needed administrative agencies. Over the course of the twentieth century, new bureaucracies were organized to regulate specific industries. Among them are the Securities and Exchange Commission (SEC), which oversees securities trading; the Food and Drug Administration (FDA), which tries to protect consumers from unsafe food, drugs, and cosmetics; and the Federal Communications Commission (FCC), which oversees the television, radio, and telephone industries.

Through bureaucracies like these, government has become a referee in the marketplace, developing standards of fair trade, setting rates, and licensing individual businesses for operation. As new problem areas have emerged, government has added new agencies, further expanding the scope of its activities. As we discuss later in this chapter, however, there has been significant movement in recent years toward lessening the government's role in the marketplace.

Social welfare.   General attitudes about government's responsibilities in the area of social welfare have changed, too. An enduring part of American culture has been a belief in self-reliance. In years past, those who could not take care of themselves had to hope that their families or primitive local programs would help them.

People in this country were slow to accept government in the role of "brother's keeper." Only in the wake of the Great Depression did the national government begin to take steps to provide income security. In 1935, the Social Security Act became law, creating the social security fund that workers pay into and then collect income from during old age. A small part of that act was a provision for impoverished families, which evolved into Aid to Families with Dependent Children, the nation's basic welfare program.

A belief in progress.   A larger, stronger central government can also be traced to Americans' firm belief in the idea of progress. Another thread that runs through the fabric of American culture is faith in our ability to solve problems. This attitude was typified by President John F. Kennedy's commitment in 1961 to put a man on the moon by 1970. As difficult as the task seemed when Kennedy made the pledge, a man walked on the moon on July 20, 1969. This same spirit leads politicians to declare war on poverty or war on cancer through massive programs of coordinated, well-funded activities.

Ambitious administrators. Finally, government has grown because agency officials have expanded their organizations and staffs to take on added responsibilities. Imaginative, ambitious agency administrators look for ways to serve their clients. Each new program that is developed leads to new authority. Larger budgets and staffs, in turn, are necessary to support that authority. When, for example, the collapse of communism in the Soviet bloc threatened the budgets of the defense and security bureaucracies, the Department of Defense started to think about taking on research tasks relating to serious worldwide environmental problems.[5]

Can We Reduce the Size of Government?

When Ronald Reagan campaigned for the presidency in 1980, he promised to cut bureaucracies, which he said were wasteful, and to get government "off the back" of the American people. Reagan was preaching the traditional conservative Republican sermon: Government is too big; only Republicans are committed to shrinking the government. As Figure 10.1 shows, however, Reagan expanded government (as measured by the federal work force) at a greater rate than his liberal predecessor, Jimmy Carter. Although Reagan was very successful in influencing spending priorities and reducing some agencies in scope, he actually made big government even bigger.

Presidents and members of Congress face a tough job when they try to reduce the size of the bureaucracy. Each government agency performs a service of value to some sector of society. Farmers need the price supports of the U.S. Department of Agriculture. Builders profit from programs offered by the U.S. Department of Housing and Urban Development (HUD). And labor unions want a vigorous Occupational Safety and Health Administration (OSHA). Efforts to cut an agency's scope, then, are almost always resisted by interest groups that have a stake in the agency. Also, although the American public says it wants spending restrained and government cut back, when asked about specific programs or functions of government, citizens tend to be highly supportive of the activities of government.[6]

Despite their political support, agencies are not immune to change. Although it is rare for a department or an agency to be completely abolished, it is not uncommon for one to undergo a major reorganization in which programs are consolidated and the size and scope of activities are reduced.[7] Programs can lose support if they are perceived to be working poorly. And as funds are cut, bureaucratic positions are eliminated.

The tendency for big government to endure reflects the tension between majoritarianism and pluralism. Even when the public wants a

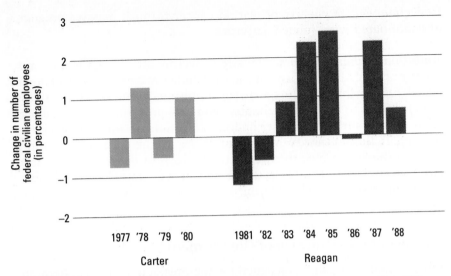

FIGURE 10.1 *Conservatives Battle Big Government, Big Government Wins*
According to U.S. Census Bureau statistics, despite Ronald Reagan's vow to
shrink the government, the number of bureaucrats working for the national
government grew significantly during his time in office. Surprisingly, the rate
of increase was greater under Reagan than under the Democratic administra-
tion that had preceded him. (Source: "A Dubious Reagan Achievement," New York
Times, *January 4, 1990, p. A22. Copyright © 1990 by The New York Times Company.*
Reprinted by permission.)

smaller national government, that sentiment can be undermined by the
strong preferences of different segments of society for government to
perform some valuable function for them. Lobbies that represent these
segments work strenuously to convince Congress and the administration that their agency's particular part of the budget is vital and that any
cuts ought to come out of some other agency's hide.

Bureaus and Bureaucrats

We often think of the bureaucracy as a huge monolith. In reality, the
bureaucracy in Washington is a disjointed collection of departments,
agencies, bureaus, offices, and commissions—each a bureaucracy in its
own right.

The Organization of Government

By examining the basic types of government organizations, we can better understand how the executive branch operates. This discussion pays
particular attention to the relative degree of independence of these organizations and their relationship to the White House.

Departments. **Departments** are the largest units of the executive branch, covering broad areas of government responsibility. As noted in Chapter 9, the secretaries (heads) of these departments, along with a few other key officials, form the president's Cabinet. The current Cabinet departments are State, Treasury, Defense, Interior, Agriculture, Justice, Commerce, Labor, Health and Human Services, Housing and Urban Development, Transportation, Energy, Education, and Veterans Affairs. Each of these massive organizations is broken down into subsidiary agencies, bureaus, offices, and services.

Independent agencies. Within the executive branch, there are also many **independent agencies,** agencies that are not a part of any Cabinet department. Instead, they stand alone and are controlled in varying degrees by the president. Some, among them the Central Intelligence Agency (CIA), are directly under the president's control. Others, like the FCC, are structured as **regulatory commissions.** Each commission is run by a small number of commissioners appointed to fixed terms by the president. Some commissions were formed to guard against unfair business practices. Others were formed to police the side effects, or *externalities,* of business operations, such as polluted air emitted by a factory. Still others were formed to protect the public from unsafe products.

Regulatory commissions are outside the direct control of the White House, so they are freer from the pressures of the political process and the partisan considerations that influence other agencies. Nevertheless, regulatory commissions are not immune to political pressure. They are lobbied fervently by client groups and must take the demands of those groups into account when they make policy. Also, the president exerts influence on these agencies through his power to appoint new commissioners when terms expire or when resignations create openings.

Government corporations. Finally, Congress has also created a small number of **government corporations**. The services that these executive branch agencies perform could theoretically be provided by the private sector, but Congress has decided that the public will be better served if these organizations have some link with the government. For example, the national government maintains a postal service because it feels that Americans need low-cost, door-to-door service for all kinds of mail, not just for mail on profitable routes or mail that requires special services. In some instances, there is not enough of a financial incentive for the private sector to provide an essential service. This is the case with the financially troubled Amtrak train line.[8]

The Civil Service

The national bureaucracy is staffed by around 3 million civilian employees, who account for about 2.5 percent of the U.S. work force.[9] Government workers include forest rangers, FBI agents, typists, foreign

Up in Smoke
As illustrated by this picture of typical big-city rush hour traffic, motor vehicles are a major source of air pollution. The Environmental Protection Agency is responsible for issuing regulations to enforce national automobile emissions standards.

service officers, computer programmers, engineers, plumbers, and people from hundreds of other occupations.

An important feature of the national bureaucracy is that most of its workers are hired under the requirements of the **civil service.** The civil service was created by the Pendleton Act (1883). The objective of that act was to reduce *patronage*—the practice of filling government positions with the president's political allies or cronies. The civil service fills jobs on the basis of merit and sees to it that workers are not fired for political reasons. Over the years, job qualifications and selection procedures have been developed for most government positions.

Studies of the social composition of the civil service as a whole indicate that it mirrors the American population on such important characteristics as father's occupation and worker's education, income, and age.[10] There is also substantial representation of minorities (27 percent) within the federal government's work force. However, at the highest-level policymaking positions, minorities are woefully underrepresented, and in recent years there has been little progress in placing more blacks, Hispanics, and other minorities into top career positions in the government.[11]

Bill Clinton came to Washington promising to make his Cabinet "look like America" and promptly selected four blacks, two Hispanics, and three women as Cabinet secretaries. To be sure, such appointees are not part of the civil service. However, those and other high-level appointments, such as that of Laura D'Andrea Tyson to head the Council of Economic Advisers and Carol Browner to head the Environmental Protection Agency (EPA) seem to indicate at least some movement toward increased representation of women and minorities in high-level policymaking positions.

Presidential Control over the Bureaucracy

Civil service and other reforms have effectively insulated the vast majority of government workers from party politics. An incoming president can appoint fewer than 1 percent of all executive branch employees. Nevertheless, presidential appointees fill the top policymaking positions in government. Each new president, then, establishes an extensive personnel review process to find appointees who are both politically compatible and qualified in their field. Although the president selects some people from his campaign staff, Cabinet secretaries, assistant secretaries, agency heads, and the like tend to be drawn directly from business, universities, and government itself.

Because so few of a president's own people are in each department and agency, he often believes that he does not have enough control over the bureaucracy. There have been repeated efforts by recent presidents to centralize power by tightening the reins over the rest of the executive branch.[12]

Those who believe that presidents should be able to make more political appointments to staff the national government argue that presidents might be able to fulfill more of their campaign promises if they had greater control over the bureaucracy. But others point out the value of a stable, experienced work force that implements policy in a consistent fashion. There is also legitimate concern about the presidency becoming too powerful. Despite the frustration of recent presidents with the bureaucracy, presidents are hardly helpless, pitiful giants. They can have a substantial impact on agencies.

Administrative Policymaking: The Formal Processes

Bureaucratic actions and policies often appear irrational to ordinary citizens, who know little about how government officials reach their decisions. Many Americans wonder why agencies sometimes actually make policy rather than merely carry it out. Administrative agencies are, in fact, authoritative policymaking bodies, and their decisions on substantive issues are legally binding on the citizens of this country.

Administrative Discretion

What are executive agencies set up to do? First, Cabinet departments, independent agencies, and government corporations are creatures of Congress. Congress creates a new department or agency by passing a law that describes each organization's *mandate,* or mission. As part of that mandate, Congress grants to the agency the authority to make certain policy decisions. Congress long ago recognized that it has neither the time nor the technical expertise to make all policy decisions. Ideally, it sets general guidelines for policy, and agencies are expected to act within those guidelines. The latitude that Congress gives agencies to make policy in the spirit of their legislative mandate is called **administrative discretion**.

Congress is often vague about its intent when setting up a new agency or program. At times, a problem is clear-cut, but the solution is not; yet Congress is under pressure to act. So it creates an agency or program to demonstrate congressional concern and responsiveness and leaves the agency's administrators to develop specific solutions. For example, the enabling legislation in 1934 that established the FCC recognized a need for regulation in the burgeoning radio industry. But Congress avoided tackling several sticky issues by leaving the FCC with the ambiguous directive that broadcasters should "serve the public interest, convenience, and necessity."[13] In other cases, a number of "obvious" solutions to a problem may be available, but lawmakers cannot agree on which one is best. Compromise wording is thus often ambiguous, papering over differences and assuring conflict over the administrative regulations that try to settle the lingering policy disputes.

The wide latitude Congress gives bureaucratic agencies often leads to charges that government is out of control, a power unto itself. But these claims are frequently exaggerated. If Congress is unhappy with an agency's actions, it can pass laws invalidating specific policies. This method of control may seem cumbersome, but Congress does have periodic opportunities to amend the original legislation that created an agency or program. Over time, Congress makes increasingly detailed policy decisions, often affirming or modifying agency decisions.[14]

Informal contacts with members of Congress also influence administrators. Through these communications, legislators can clarify exactly which actions they want administrators to take. And administrators listen because they are wary of offending members of the committees and subcommittees that oversee their programs and, particularly, their budgets. In addition to getting a better idea of congressional intent, contacts with legislators allow administrators to explain the problems their agencies are facing, justify their decisions, and negotiate compromises on unresolved issues.

In general, then, the bureaucracy is not out of control. But there is one area in which Congress has chosen to limit its oversight—that of domestic and international security. Both the FBI and CIA have had a great deal of freedom from formal and informal congressional constraints because of the legitimate need for secrecy in their operations. (For an example of how security needs were met in communist East Germany, see Compared with What? 10.1.). During the years that the legendary J. Edgar Hoover ran the FBI (1924–1972), it was something of a rogue elephant, independent of both Congress and presidents. Over the years, the CIA has also abused its need for privacy by engaging in covert operations that should never have been carried out. Congress, however, has increased its oversight over the agency and has passed legislation designed to force the administration to share more information with it.

Rule Making

The policymaking discretion that Congress gives to agencies is exercised through formal administrative procedures, usually either *rule making* or *adjudication*. **Rule making** is the administrative process that results in regulations. **Regulations** are rules that govern the operation of government programs. When the FCC develops policies necessary to serve the public interest, it uses its broad discretionary authority to promulgate those policies in the form of regulations.

Because regulations are authorized by congressional statutes, they have the effect of law. In theory, the policy content of regulations follows from the intent of enabling legislation. As already noted, however, Congress does not always express its intent clearly. The administrative discretion available to agencies often produces political conflict when regulations are in the process of being made.

When agencies issue regulations, they are first published as proposals so that all interested parties have an opportunity to comment on them and try persuading the agency to make them final, alter them, or withdraw them. When the EPA issued a proposal to regulate pollution from incinerators in 1989, environmentalists were pleased to see that it required incinerator operators to recycle one-quarter of their incoming garbage. A White House committee on competitiveness, however, disliked this component of the regulation because it placed financial burdens on the solid waste management industry. The White House forced the EPA to retreat and drop the recycling provision, although the other pollution-control provisions were finalized.[15]

The regulatory process is controversial because regulations require individuals and corporations to act in prescribed ways, often against their own self-interest. In the foregoing case, both environmental groups and the waste management industry believed that they knew what was truly in the public interest. Government, however, must balance society's need for clean air with the need of industry to make a profit. When the EPA writes regulations that specify the details of that balance, it becomes the object of criticism from both those who would like government to do more and from those who would like it to do less. The EPA

No Tears for the Staatsicherheit

Every society needs to maintain order, but in many countries of the world the bureaucratic apparatus designed to maintain order is really a mechanism for ensuring the survival of an autocratic regime. Nowhere was this more vividly illustrated than in the former communist regimes in Eastern Europe. The state security agencies there were instruments of terror, enforcing control by making any kind of opposition to these governments extremely dangerous.

The East German secret police, the Staatsicherheit (or Stasi), was an enormous bureaucracy that reached into every part of that society. It had 85,000 full-time employees, including 6,000 people whose sole task was to listen in on phone conversations. Another 2,000 steamed open mail, read it, resealed the letters, and then sent them on to the intended recipients. The Stasi also employed 150,000 active informers and hundreds of thousands of part-time snitches. Files were kept on an estimated 4 to 5 million people in a country that had a total population, including children, of just 17 million. And although there was a large standing army in East Germany, the Stasi kept its own arsenal of 250,000 weapons.

The Stasi infiltrated the top echelons of government, business, and universities in East Germany, placing two thousand of its agents in positions of importance in these institutions. The Stasi's primary job was to make East Germans too scared to threaten the communist dictatorship that ran the country. Eventually, of course, the East German government did fall as a largely peaceful revolution swept through the East bloc countries. After a democratic transition government was installed, angry East Germans ransacked the Stasi building, piling up old uniforms that would later be sold and smashing glass and office equipment. Protestors said that they were worried that the Stasi was trying to find a role for itself in the new government.

It is understandable that East Germans were appalled at the idea of a secret police in a unified, democratic Germany. But democracies do have legitimate security needs, and these interests require that the bureaucracies in charge of security be allowed to operate largely in private. The United States has a sizable internal security establishment, including the FBI and the Secret Service. However, the internal security bureaucracies of this country have at times acted in a highly irresponsible manner. A society's need for police powers to help it maintain order must be balanced by mechanisms of accountability. Accountability in a democracy should involve some elected representatives being fully informed of all the major activities of the state's secret police.

Sources: Steven Emerson, "Keeping Watch on the Stasi Machine," *San Francisco Chronicle,* August 15, 1990, p. Br.1; Serge Schemann, "East Berlin Faults Opposition on Raid," *New York Times,* January 17, 1990, p. A9; and Craig R. Whitney, "East Europeans Are Making Big Brother Smaller," *New York Times,* January 22, 1991, p. A1.

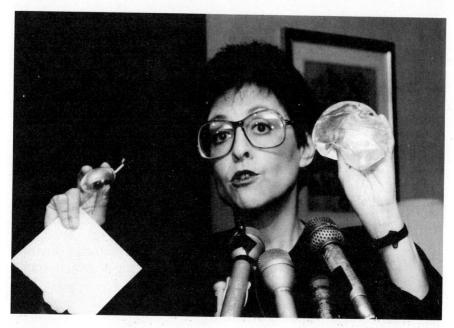

Weighing the Evidence
As it oversees the safety of food, drugs, cosmetics, and medical devices, the Food and Drug Administration must weigh the benefits of each against any possible health risk. Here, author Karen Berger, who wrote a book about women deciding to use breast implants, testifies at an FDA hearing considering the banning of silicone gel implants due to health fears.

is in many ways taking the "heat" for Congress because Congress has the ultimate responsibility for pollution policy—a responsibility it has delegated, in part, to the EPA.

Adjudication

Rule making is a quasi-legislative process because it develops *general* rules, just as Congress does when it passes a law. **Adjudication** is a quasi-judicial process; it is used to resolve *individual* conflicts, much as trials are used in a court of law. Adjudicatory proceedings in an agency determine whether a person or business is failing to comply with the law or with agency rules.

Congress delegates adjudicatory authority to certain agencies because it anticipates conflicts over the interpretation of laws and regulations and because it does not have the time to settle all the fine points of law when writing statutes. The National Labor Relations Board (NLRB), which acts as a mediator in business-labor disputes, is an example of an agency that relies heavily on adjudication.

Adjudicatory decisions are made by administrative law judges, who are technically their agencies' employees. Yet they are strictly independent; they cannot be removed except for gross misconduct. Adjudicatory proceedings are somewhat less formal than a court trial, but the proceedings are still adversarial in nature. In NLRB cases, the party that loses may appeal to the board, which has set up three-member panels to review decisions.[16]

Administrative Policymaking: Informal Politics

When a new regulation is being considered and the evidence and arguments on all sides have been presented, how does an administrator reach a decision? Few important policy decisions can be calculated with the efficiency of a computer solving mathematical problems. Instead, policy decisions emerge from the weighing and judging of complex problems that often have no single satisfactory solution.

The Science of Muddling Through

Administrative decisions are subject to many influences and constraints. In a classic analysis of policymaking, "The Science of Muddling Through," Charles Lindblom compared the way policy ideally should be made with the way it is formulated in the real world.[17] The ideal "rational" decision-making process, according to Lindblom, begins with an administrator tackling a problem by ranking values and objectives. After the objectives are clarified, all possible solutions to the problem are given thorough consideration. Alternative solutions are analyzed comprehensively, taking all relevant factors into account. Finally, the alternative that is seen as the most effective means of achieving the desired goal and solving the problem is chosen.

Lindblom claimed that this "rational-comprehensive" model is unrealistic. To begin with, policymakers have great difficulty defining precise values and goals. Administrators at the U.S. Department of Energy, for example, want to be sure that supplies of home heating oil are sufficient each winter. At the same time, they want to reduce dependence on foreign oil. Obviously, these two goals are not fully compatible. How do administrators decide which is more important? And how do they relate them to the other goals of the nation's energy policy?

Real-world decision making parts company with the ideal in another way: The policy selected is not always the most effective means to the desired end. Even if a tax at the pump is the most effective way of reducing gasoline consumption during a shortage, motorists' anger would make this theoretically "right" decision politically difficult. So the "best" policy is often the one on which most people can agree. However, political compromise may mean that the government is able to solve only part of a problem.

A final point critics of the rational-comprehensive model raise is that policymaking can never be based on truly comprehensive analysis. Time is of the essence, and problems often are too pressing to wait for a complete study.

In short, policymaking tends to be *incremental*, with policies and programs changing bit by bit, step by step. Decision makers are constrained by competing policy objectives, opposing political forces, incomplete information, and the pressures of time. They choose from a limited number of feasible options that are almost always modifications of existing policies rather than wholesale departures from those policies.

The Culture of Bureaucracy

How an organization makes decisions and performs its tasks is greatly affected by the people who work there—the bureaucrats. Americans often find that their interactions with bureaucrats are frustrating because bureaucrats are inflexible ("go by the book") or lack the authority to get things done. Top administrators can also become frustrated with the bureaucrats who work for them.

Why do people act "bureaucratically"? Individuals who work for large organizations cannot help but be affected by the "culture of bureaucracy." Modern bureaucracies develop explicit rules and standards to make operations more efficient and treat their clients fairly. But within each organization, *norms* (informal, unwritten rules of behavior) also develop and influence the way people act on the job.

Bureaucracies are often influenced in their selection of policy options by the prevailing customs, attitudes, and expectations of the people working within them. Departments and agencies commonly develop a sense of mission where a particular objective or a means for achieving it is emphasized. The Army Corps of Engineers, for example, is dominated by engineers who define the bureaucracy's objective as protecting citizens from floods by means of building dams. Certainly there could be other objectives, and certainly there are other methods of achieving this one, but the engineers promote the solutions that fit their conception of what the agency should be doing.

At first glance, bureaucrats seem to be completely negative sorts of creatures. They do have their positive side, however. Those agencies with a clear sense of mission are likely to have a strong *esprit de corps* that adds to the bureaucrats' motivation. Also, bureaucrats' caution and close adherence to agency rules offer a measure of consistency. It would be unsettling if government employees interpreted rules as they pleased. Simply put, bureaucrats "go by the book" because the "book" is composed of the laws and regulations of this country as well as the internal rules and norms of a particular agency. Americans expect to be treated equally before the law, and bureaucrats work with that expectation in mind.

Policymaking: Issue Networks

Within each policy area there are a number—often a very large number—of interest groups trying to influence decisions. Representatives from these organizations interact with each other and with government officials on a recurring basis. This ongoing interaction produces both conflict and cooperation.

Government by Policy Area

Policy formulation takes place across different institutions and involves many different participants, all of whom have an interest in the policy. What these participants have in common is membership in an **issue network**, "a shared-knowledge group having to do with some aspect . . . of public policy."[18] The boundaries of an issue network are fuzzy, but in general terms they are made up of members of Congress, committee staffers, agency officials, lawyers, lobbyists, consultants, scholars, and public relations specialists who interact on an ongoing basis as they work to influence policies in a particular issue area. This makes for a large number of participants—the number of interest group organizations alone in a broad policy area is usually in the dozens.[19]

Not all participants in an issue network have a working relationship with all others. Indeed, some may be chronic antagonists. Others tend to be allies. For example, environmental groups working together to influence antipollution programs are likely to place themselves in opposition to business groups. The common denominator that ties friends and foes together in an issue network is technical mastery of a particular policy area.

Iron Triangles

The idea of examining politics in Washington by looking at policy areas, rather than at individual institutions, is not new. Research by an earlier generation of political scientists and journalists described a system of *subgovernments*, tightly knit groups that dominated policymaking in an issue area. For example, journalist Douglass Cater wrote about the sugar subgovernment of the late 1950s:

> Political power within the sugar subgovernment is largely vested in the Chairman of the House Agricultural Committee who works out the schedule of quotas. It is shared by a veteran civil servant, the director of the Sugar Division of the U.S. Department of Agriculture, who provides the necessary "expert" advice for such a complex marketing arrangement. Further advice is provided by Washington representatives of the domestic beet and cane sugar growers, the sugar refineries, and the foreign producers.[20]

According to Cater, this subgovernment had three components:

- Key members of the congressional committees and subcomittees responsible for the policy area (in this case, the chair of the House Agriculture Committee)
- Officials from the agency or bureau that administered the policy (the director of a division of the U.S. Department of Agriculture)
- Lobbyists who represented the agency's clients (growers, refineries, and foreign producers)

These policymaking communities were called **iron triangles.** The word *iron* describes a very important property of these subgovernments: They were largely autonomous and closed; outsiders had a great deal of difficulty penetrating them. Even presidents had difficulty influencing iron triangles, which endured over time and changed little when new administrations came into power. And job changes did not usually affect them. An individual who left one component of the triangle would often move to another. Iron triangles worked because participants shared similar policy views and tried to reach a consensus that would be mutually beneficial.[21]

The iron triangle model was very popular with political scientists.[22] Although some used different terms *(subgovernments, cozy little triangles)* and some developed more sophisticated frameworks than the simplified version offered here, the basic ideas were the same: Typically, a small group of individuals dominated policymaking in their issue area, these policy communities were largely autonomous, and they favored those who were well organized. The model was used not only to explain how American politics operated but also to show what was wrong with our policymaking system.[23]

The Case of Telecommunications

In recent years, it has become increasingly clear that iron triangles are not typical policymaking systems. The telecommunications industry provides a useful illustration of the changing nature of politics in Washington. Once an iron triangle, telecommunications today is a large issue network filled with conflict.

Until fairly recently, the telecommunications industry was dominated by AT&T. Customers generally had no choice but to use the phone lines and equipment of "Ma Bell." Within the telecommunications iron triangle—a policymaking community made up of some key members of Congress, the FCC, and AT&T—policymaking was usually consensual and uncontroversial.

In 1974, the U.S. Department of Justice brought a lawsuit against the corporation, charging it with illegal monopolistic behavior in the telecommunications industry. The eventual outcome of the suit was an out-of-court settlement that stipulated that AT&T had to divest itself of control over local operating service. The Bell System was broken up into seven regional phone companies, each independent of AT&T. AT&T was allowed to retain its long-distance service, but it would have to compete against other long-distance carriers.[24] The giant telephone company fell victim to a growing belief among academics and policymakers that government regulation was hampering the economy by restricting competition and lessening the incentives for innovation as well as limiting the price and product choices available to consumers. Thus, telecommunications was deregulated.[25]

Today, policymaking in telecommunications bears no resemblance to an iron triangle.[26] As Figure 10.2 shows, a large and varied group participates in this issue network. Although there is no single way to draw an issue network, in this representation the most important policymaking bodies lie within the inner ring. In the middle ring are the most frequent interest group participants and a secondary policymaking body in the U.S. Department of Commerce. Organizations that have a more limited focus on the telecommunications issues they work on are in the outer ring.

Conflict within the network is chronic. Alliances change rapidly as coalition partners on one issue become opponents on the next. The different lobbying organizations fight to protect their market share while trying to encroach on that of others. No one controls telecommunications policymaking, but a large array of organizations and individuals have a say in it.[27]

Not all policymaking communities in Washington have evolved into issue networks.[28] Some are still better described as iron triangles or subgovernments. For example, the Sea Grant Program, which offers grants to colleges to promote the study of marine resources, is closer to being an iron triangle than an issue network. There are just a small number of participants, and policymaking is consensual. The only groups interested in the program outside of government are the colleges, and they are all on the same side of the issue—there are no groups trying to stop the program. It is likely that this is true of many other small, uncontroversial programs that just distribute grants or benefits of some type.[29]

Broader policy areas, such as health and agriculture, are distinguished by large numbers of participants and high degrees of conflict.[30] Why have so many iron triangles rusted through and larger, more conflicted issue networks evolved? A primary force behind this change has been the rapid growth in the number of interest groups. As more and more new groups set up shop in Washington, they demanded the attention of policymakers. These new groups brought with them new concerns, and their interests were usually at odds with at least some of the groups active in the policy area. Change also came to Congress. As indicated earlier, the number of subcommittees expanded signficantly; this resulted in many overlapping jurisdictions over programs.

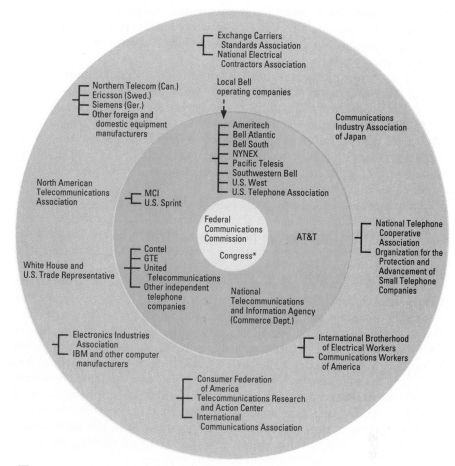

Indicates primary interest group alliance.

*Primary congressional actors are the House Committee on Energy and Commerce, Subcommittee on Telecommunications and Finance, and the Senate Committee on Commerce, Science, and Transportation, Subcommittee on Communications.

FIGURE 10.2   The Telecommunications Issue Network
Policymaking in telecommunications is characterized by a multitude of actors and a great deal of conflict. Among the interest group participants are AT&T, the regional phone companies, long distance carriers, equipment manufacturers, labor unions, consumer groups, and foreign corporations and trade associations. From THE INTEREST GROUP SOCIETY *by Jeffrey M. Berry. (Copyright © 1989 by Scott, Foresman and Company. Reprinted by permission of HarperCollins Publishers.)*

Problems in Implementing Policy

The development of policy in Washington is the end of one part of the policymaking cycle but the beginning of another. After policies have been developed, they must be implemented. **Implementation** is the process of putting specific policies into operation. It is important to study implementation because policies do not always do what they were designed to do.

One reason implementation may be difficult is that the policy to be carried out is not always clearly stated. Policy directives to bureaucrats in the field sometimes lack clarity and leave lower-level officials with too much discretion. The source of vague regulations is often vague legislation. Congress, for example, included in the Elementary and Secondary School Act (1965) a program of grants to meet the "special needs of educationally deprived children." But the act did not spell out who qualified as educationally deprived.

Another reason for implementation failures is faulty coordination. Programs frequently cut across the jurisdictions of a number of agencies, and in our federal system programs must often be coordinated between national officials and state or local officials implementing the program out in the field.

Policymakers can create implementation difficulties by ignoring the administrative capabilities of an agency they have chosen to carry out a program. This happened in 1981 when the Reagan administration and Congress instructed the Social Security Administration to expand its review of those citizens receiving disability insurance benefits. State agencies, which carried out the reviews, had been doing between 20,000 to 30,000 cases a quarter. These same agencies were ordered to review 100,000 to 150,000 cases a quarter. As the number of people terminated increased, so did the legal appeals to have the terminations reversed, and the backlog of unresolved cases grew sharply. With the administrative system inundated with more cases than it could handle, the problems with the program reached crisis proportions.

Although obstacles to effective implementation create the impression that nothing succeeds, programs can and do work. Problems in the implementation process demonstrate why time, patience, and continual analysis are necessary ingredients of successful policymaking. To return to a term we used earlier, implementation is by its nature an incremental process in which trial and error eventually lead to policies that work.

Reforming the Bureaucracy: More Control or Less?

As we saw at the outset of this chapter, organization matters. The way in which bureaucracies are designed directly affects how effective they are in accomplishing their tasks.[31] Many different approaches to administrative reform have been used in recent years as the criticism of government has mounted.[32] A central question that overrides much of the debate over bureaucratic reform is whether we need to establish more control over the bureaucracy or less.

Deregulation

Many people believe that government is too involved in **regulation**, intervention in the natural workings of business markets to promote some social goal. For example, government might regulate a market to ensure that products pose no danger to consumers. Through **deregulation** the government reduces its role and lets the natural market forces of supply and demand take over. Some important movement toward deregulation took place in the 1970s and 1980s, notably in the airline, trucking, financial services, and telecommunications industries.[33]

In the case of the airlines, Congress passed a law in 1978 mandating deregulation of fares and routes, and the airlines became more competitive. In retrospect, it is clear that government had been overregulating the industry. Nevertheless, in the past few years there has been a trend toward dominance of the airline industry by a few large and healthy carriers. Open competition has forced the mergers and bankruptcies of a number of airlines, and just what the air travel market will look like in the future is unclear.

It is particularly difficult to decide on an appropriate level of deregulation of agencies dealing with health and safety issues. Companies within a particular industry may have legitimate claims that health and safety regulations are burdensome, making it difficult for them to earn sufficient profits or compete effectively with foreign manufacturers. The drug-licensing procedures used by the FDA illustrate the dilemma of deregulating these kinds of agencies. The pharmaceutical industry has been highly critical of the FDA, claiming that the licensing procedures are so complex that drugs of great benefit are kept from the marketplace for years, while people suffering from a particular disease are denied access to new treatments. The industry has encouraged the FDA to adopt faster procedures.

Although the FDA has been resistant to doing anything that would compromise what it sees as necessary precautions, in recent years the AIDS epidemic has brought about some concessions. New rules expediting the availability of experimental drugs have been issued, and, more generally, the FDA has adopted a somewhat speedier timetable for clinical tests of new drugs.[34]

Monitoring, Oversight, and Accountability

There is substantial support for making government smaller though reduction of its supervision of various industries and business activities. Further deregulation is championed by conservatives who see freedom in the marketplace as the best route to an efficient and growing economy. Yet making government smaller and reducing its role can entail serious risks. Nowhere are those risks more evident than in the collapse of the savings and loan industry.

S&L institutions, which were primarily designed to provide mortgages for a growing housing market, were tightly regulated by the fed-

Fly the Unfriendly Skies
With the deregulation of the airline industry, increased traffic on many routes has tested the capacity of the Federal Aviation Administration to ensure safety in the air. Air traffic controllers form the front line of the FAA's safety efforts. The responsibility of their job and the acute concentration it requires make the controllers' work extremely stressful.

eral government. Between 1980 and 1983, as the financial markets became much more complex and much more competitive, Congress approved a number of changes that significantly deregulated savings and loans. At the same time, the Reagan administration refused to allow the Federal Home Loan Bank Board, which then had the supervisory role over the industry, to hire the bank examiners that it felt it needed to monitor the health of the individual S&Ls. The administration was trying to shrink the size of government and didn't feel that so much money should be spent policing business practices. As the real estate market cooled off, so many commercial real estate developers ran into problems and couldn't repay their loans that a large number of S&Ls were plunged into insolvency. The federal bailout of the failed S&Ls will cost taxpayers hundreds of billions of dollars.

Although the S&L debacle is the most obvious example of the danger of removing government supervision of business markets, it is by no means an isolated case. The effort of the Reagan administration to get government "off the back" of American business and to make government less expensive led to problems at other agencies, such as the Department of Housing and Urban Development and the Farmers Home Administration. Unfortunately, one of the reasons big government exists is because to ensure the integrity of both government and markets, government has to expend significant resources on monitoring the behavior of bureaucrats and those people and groups regulated by bureaucrats. When waste, fraud, and abuse surfaces and the public demands reform, those reforms usually involve adding new layers of bureaucracy.[35]

Thus, there is a tension between the desire to make government lean, efficient, and unintrusive and the desire to protect citizens from fraud and unfair or unsafe business practices. This is in many ways a traditional dilemma between freedom and order. There is a strong case to be made for deregulated business markets, where free and unfettered competition benefits consumers and promotes productivity. The strength of capitalist economies comes from the ability of individuals and firms to compete freely in the marketplace. The regulatory state places restrictions on this freedom. But without regulation, there is nothing to ensure that marketplace participants will always act responsibly.

Summary

As the scope of government activity has grown during the twentieth century, so has the bureaucracy. The executive branch has evolved into a complex set of departments, independent agencies, and government corporations. The way in which these various bureaucracies are organized matters a great deal because their structure affects their ability to carry out their tasks.

Through the administrative discretion granted them by Congress, these bodies make policy decisions through rule making and adjudication that have the force of law. In making policy choices, agency decision makers are influenced by their external environment, especially the White House, Congress, and interest groups. Decision makers are also influenced by internal norms and the need to work cooperatively with others both within and outside their agencies.

The most serious charge facing the bureaucracy is that it is out of control. In fact, the White House, Congress, interest groups, and public opinion act as substantial controls on the bureaucracy. Nevertheless, to many Americans, the bureaucracy seems too big, too costly, and too intrusive. It is difficult to reduce the size and scope of bureaucratic activity because pluralism characterizes our political system. The entire executive branch may appear too large, and each of us can point to agencies that we believe should be reduced or eliminated, yet each bureaucracy has its supporters. The Department of Agriculture performs vital services for farmers.

Unions care a great deal about the Department of Labor. Scholars want the National Science Foundation protected. And home builders do not want HUD programs cut back. Bureaucracies survive because they provide important services to groups of people, and those people—no matter how strong their commitment to less government—are not willing to sacrifice their own needs to that commitment.

Policymaking in many areas can be viewed as an ongoing process of interaction between those in government and those outside it through issue networks. Each network is a means of communication through which information and ideas about a particular policy area are exchanged. Generally, these contemporary policy communities are more open to new participants than were the old iron triangles.

There is no shortage of reform plans for making the bureaucracy work better. Proponents of deregulation believe our economy will be more productive if we free the marketplace from the heavy hand of government supervision. Opponents believe that deregulation involves considerable risk and that we ought to be very careful in determining which markets and business practices can be subjected to less government supervision. To prevent disasters such as the S&L scandal, government bureaucracies need to be able to monitor the behavior of people inside and outside of government as well as supervise business practices in a wide range of industries.

Key Terms

bureaucracy
bureaucrat
departments
independent agencies
regulatory commissions
government corporations
civil service
administrative discretion

rule making
regulations
adjudication
issue network
iron triangles
implementation
regulation
deregulation

Selected Readings

Cater, Douglass. *Power in Washington*. New York: Vintage Books, 1964. Here is one reporter's view of how policy is formulated in Washington.

Chubb, John E. *Interest Groups and the Bureaucracy*. Stanford, Calif.: Stanford University Press, 1983. This is an ambitious analysis of interest group–agency interaction within various energy-policy communities.

Derthick, Martha. *Agency Under Stress*. Washington, D.C.: Brookings Institution, 1990. This is a study of how policymakers ignored the administrative capacity of the Social Security Administration when setting new goals for the agency.

Derthick, Martha, and Paul J. Quirk. *The Politics of Deregulation*. Washington, D.C.: Brookings Institution, 1985. The authors offer an interesting look at why some industries have undergone deregulation, while others have not.

Gormley, William T., Jr. *Taming the Bureaucracy: Muscles, Prayers, and Other Strategies*. Princeton, N.J.: Princeton University Press, 1989. Here is an incisive look at competing strategies for reform, with particular emphasis on whether the instruments for change should be mandatory controls or informal persuasion.

Harris, Richard A., and Sidney M. Milkis. *The Politics of Regulatory Change*. New York: Oxford University Press, 1989. This is a study of how the new regulatory regime of the Reagan years affected policymaking at the Federal Trade Commission and the Environmental Protection Agency.

Mackenzie, G. Calvin, ed. *The In-and-Outers*. Baltimore, Md.: Johns Hopkins University Press, 1987. This collection of essays examines the problems associated with the movement of people back and forth between the private sector and the executive branch.

Rourke, Francis E. *Bureaucracy, Politics, and Public Policy*. 3d ed. Boston: Little, Brown, 1984. This is an excellent introduction to bureaucracy, with a very useful analysis of the relationship between agencies and their clients.

Wilson, James Q., ed. *Bureaucracy*. New York: Basic Books, 1989. This book takes a comprehensive look at the operations of large, complex government organizations.

THE COURTS

11

When Chief Justice Fred M. Vinson died unexpectedly on September 8, 1953, Justice Felix Frankfurter commented, "This is the first solid piece of evidence I've ever had that there really is a God."[1] Frankfurter despised Vinson as a leader and disliked him as a person. Vinson's sudden death would bring a new colleague—and perhaps new hope—to the school segregation cases known collectively as *Brown* v. *Board of Education*.

The issue of segregated schools had arrived in the Supreme Court in November 1951. Although the Court had originally scheduled argument for October 1952, the justices elected a postponement until December 1952 and merged several similar cases. When a law clerk was puzzled by the delay, Frankfurter explained that the Court was holding the case for the outcome of the national election in 1952. "I thought the Court was supposed to decide without regard to the elections," declared the clerk. "When you have a major social political issue of this magnitude," replied Frankfurter, "we do not think this is the time to decide it."[2]

The justices were bitterly divided following the December argument, with Vinson supporting racial segregation in public education. Because the justices were still not ready to reach a decision, they sched-

Power Player on the Top Court   *Earl Warren (1891–1974) served as the fourteenth chief justice of the United States. A true liberal, Warren led the Supreme Court by actively preferring equality to freedom and freedom to order. These decisions occasionally brought calls from Congress for Warren's impeachment. He retired in 1968 after sixteen years of championship (critics might say controversial) activity.*

uled the cases for reargument the following year with instructions to address specific issues in the several lawsuits.

When the reargument of *Brown* v. *Board of Education* was heard in December 1953, a new chief justice, former California Governor Earl Warren, led the Court from division to unanimity on the issue of school segregation. Unlike his predecessor, Warren began the secret conference to decide the segregation issue with a strong statement: that segregation was contrary to the Thirteenth, Fourteenth, and Fifteenth Amendments to the Constitution. "Personally," remarked the new chief justice, "I can't see how today we can justify segregation based solely on race."[3] Moreover, if the Court were to uphold segregation, he argued, it could do so only on the theory that blacks were inherently inferior to whites. As the discussion proceeded, Warren's opponents were cast in the awkward position of appearing to support racism.

Five justices were clearly on Warren's side, making 6 votes; two were prepared to join the majority if Warren's opinion satisfied them. With only one clear holdout, Warren set about the task of responding to his colleagues' concerns. Finally, in April 1954, Warren approached Justice Stanley Reed, whose vote would make the opinion unanimous. "Stan," said the chief justice, "you're all by yourself in this now. You've got to decide whether it's really the best thing for the country." Ultimately Reed joined the others. On May 17, 1954, the Supreme Court unanimously ruled against racial segregation in public schools, signaling the end of legally created or governmentally enforced segregation of the races in the United States.[4]

Judges confront conflicting values in the cases before them, and tough cases call for fine distinctions among those values. In crafting their decisions, judges—especially Supreme Court justices—make policy. Their decisions become the precedents that other judges use to rule in similar cases. One judge in one court makes public policy to the extent that he or she influences other decisions in other courts.

The power of the courts to shape policy creates a difficult problem for democratic theory. According to that theory, the power to make law resides only in the people or in their elected representatives. Federal judges are not elected, yet court rulings—especially Supreme Court rulings—extend far beyond any particular case. Judges are students of the law, but they remain human beings. They have their own opinions about the values of freedom, order, and equality. And although all judges are constrained by statutes and precedents from expressing their personal beliefs in their decisions, some judges are more prone than others to interpret laws in light of those beliefs.

America's courts are deeply involved in the life of the country and its people. Some courts, such as the Supreme Court, make fundamental policy decisions vital to the preservation of freedom, order, and equality. Through checks and balances, the elected branches couple the courts to democracy, and the courts hitch the elected branches to the Constitution. But does this arrangement work? Can the courts exercise political power within the pluralist model? Or are judges simply sovereigns in black robes making decisions independent of popular control? In this chapter, we try to answer these questions by exploring the role of the judiciary in American political life.

Federal Judicial Supremacy

Section 1 of Article III of the Constitution created "one Supreme Court." The founders were divided on the need for other national courts, so they deferred to Congress the decision to create a national court system. Those who opposed the creation of national courts believed that the system would usurp the authority of the state courts.[5] Congress considered the issue in its first session and in the Judiciary Act of 1789 gave life to a system of federal, or national, courts that would coexist with the courts in each state but be independent of them. Federal judges would also be independent of popular influences because the Constitution provided for their virtual lifetime appointment.

In the early years of the republic, the federal judiciary was not considered a particularly powerful branch of government. It was especially difficult to recruit and keep Supreme Court justices. They spent much of their time as individual traveling judges ("riding circuit"); disease and transportation were everyday hazards. The justices only met as the Supreme Court for a few weeks in February and August.[6] John Jay, the first chief justice, refused to resume his duties in 1801 because he concluded that the Court could not muster the "energy, weight, and dignity" to contribute to national affairs.[7] But when John Marshall, an ardent Federalist, was appointed chief justice in 1801, a period of profound change began.

Judicial Review of the Other Branches

Shortly after Marshall's appointment, the Supreme Court confronted a question of fundamental importance to the future of the new republic: If a law enacted by Congress conflicted with the Constitution, which should prevail? The question arose in the case of *Marbury* v. *Madison* (1803), which involved a controversial series of last-minute political appointments made during the last days of John Adams's presidency.

The justices held, through Marshall's forceful argument, that the Constitution is "the fundamental and paramount law of the nation" and that "an act of the legislature repugnant to the constitution is void." In other words, when the Constitution—the nation's highest law—conflicts with an act of the legislature, that act is invalid. The last part of Marshall's argument vested in the judiciary the power to weigh the validity of congressional acts:

> It is emphatically the province and duty of the judicial department to say what the law is. Those who apply the rule to particular cases, must of necessity expound and interpret that rule. . . . If a law be in opposition to the constitution, if both the law and the constitution apply to a particular case, so that the court must either decide that case conformably to the law, disregarding the constitution; or conformably to the constitution, disregarding the law; the court must determine which of these conflicting rules governs the case. This is the very essence of judicial duty.[8]

The decision in *Marbury* v. *Madison* established the Supreme Court's power of **judicial review**—the power to declare congressional acts invalid if they violate the Constitution.* Subsequent cases extended the power to presidential acts.[9]

Marshall expanded the potential power of the Supreme Court to equal or exceed that of the other branches of government. Should a congressional act or, by implication, a presidential act conflict with the Constitution, the Supreme Court claimed the power to declare the act void. The judiciary would be a check on the legislative and executive branches, consistent with the principle of checks and balances embedded in the Constitution. Judicial review gave the Supreme Court the final word on the meaning of the Constitution.

---

* The Supreme Court had earlier upheld an act of Congress in *Hylton* v. *United States*, 3 Dallas 171 (1796). *Marbury* v. *Madison* stood for a component of judicial power that had never before been exercised: the power to invalidate an act of Congress.

The exercise of judicial review—an appointed branch checking an elected branch in the name of the Constitution—appears to run counter to democratic theory. In two hundred years of practice, however, the Supreme Court has invalidated fewer than 140 provisions of federal law, and only a small number have had great significance for the political system.[10] Moreover, there are mechanisms to override judicial review (constitutional amendment) and to control the action of the justices (impeachment). In addition, the Court can respond to the continuing struggle among competing interests (a struggle that is consistent with the pluralist model) by reversing itself.

Judicial Review of State Government

The establishment of judicial review of federal laws made the Supreme Court the umpire of the national government. When acts of the national government conflict with the Constitution, the Supreme Court can declare those acts invalid. But what about state laws? If they conflict with the Constitution, federal laws, or treaties, can the Court invalidate them as well?

The Supreme Court answered in the affirmative in 1796. *Ware* v. *Hylton* involved a British creditor who was trying to collect a debt from the state of Virginia.[11] Virginia law canceled debts owed British subjects, yet the Treaty of Paris (1783), in which Britain formally acknowledged the independence of the colonies, guaranteed that creditors could collect such debts. The Court ruled that the Constitution's supremacy clause (Article VI) nullified the state law.

The states continued to resist the yoke of national supremacy. Although advocates of strong states' rights conceded that the supremacy clause obligated state judges to follow the Constitution when it conflicted with state law, they maintained that the states were bound only by their own interpretation of the Constitution. The Supreme Court said no, ruling in *Martin* v. *Hunter's Lessee* (1816) that it had the authority to review state court decisions that called for the interpretation of federal law.[12] National supremacy required the Supreme Court to impose uniformity on federal law; otherwise, the Constitution's meaning would vary from state to state. The people, not the states, had ordained the Constitution; and the people had subordinated state power to establish a viable national government. In time, the Supreme Court would use its judicial review power in nearly twelve hundred instances to invalidate state and local laws on issues as diverse as abortion, the death penalty, the rights of the accused, and reapportionment.[13]

The Exercise of Judicial Review

The decisions in *Marbury*, *Ware*, and *Martin* established the components of judicial review:

- The power of the courts to declare national, state, and local laws invalid if they violate the Constitution

- The supremacy of federal laws or treaties when they conflict with state and local laws

- The role of the Supreme Court as the final authority on the meaning of the Constitution

But this political might—the power to undo decisions of the representative branches of national and state governments—lay in the hands of appointed judges, people who were not accountable to the electorate. Did judicial review square with democratic government?

Alexander Hamilton had foreseen and tackled the problem in "Federalist No. 78." Writing during the ratification debates surrounding the adoption of the Constitution (see Chapter 2), Hamilton maintained that, despite the power of judicial review, the judiciary would be the weakest of the three branches of government because it lacked "the strength of the sword or the purse." The judiciary, wrote Hamilton, had "neither FORCE nor WILL, but only judgment."

Although Hamilton was defending legislative supremacy, he argued that judicial review was an essential barrier to legislative oppression.[14] He recognized that the power to declare government acts void implied the superiority of the courts over the other branches. But this power, he contended, simply reflected the will of the people declared in the Constitution as compared with the will of the legislature declared in its statutes. Judicial independence, embodied in life tenure and protected salaries, minimized the risk of judges deviating from the law established in the Constitution by freeing the judiciary from executive and legislative control.* And if judges made a mistake, the people or their elected representatives had the means to correct the error through constitutional amendment and impeachment.

Life tenure does free judges from the direct influence of the president and Congress. And although mechanisms to check judicial power are in place, they require extraordinary majorities and have rarely been used. When judges exercise the power of judicial review, then, they can and occasionally do operate counter to majoritarian rule by invalidating the actions of the people's elected representatives. (Compared with What? 11.1 discusses the nature of judicial review in other governments, democratic and nondemocratic.) Are the courts out of line with majority sentiment? Or are the courts simply responding to pluralist demands—the competing demands of interest groups that turn to the courts to make public policy? We return to these questions later in this chapter.

---

* Hamilton also believed that the executive, recognizing the power stemming from judicial independence, would appoint judges with the skill and intelligence to carry out their interpretive function responsibly.

Judicial Review

The U.S. Constitution does not explicitly give the Supreme Court the power of judicial review. In a controversial interpretation, the Court inferred this power from the text and structure of the Constitution. Other countries, trying to avoid political controversy over the power of the courts to review legislation, explicitly define that power in their constitutions. For example, Japan's constitution, inspired by the American model, went beyond it in providing that "the Supreme Court is the court of last resort with power to determine the constitutionality of any law, order, regulation, or official act."

The basic objection to the American form of judicial review is an unwillingness to place judges, who are usually appointed for life, above representatives elected by the people. The European concept of judging involves principled decision making, not "creative" interpretation of constitutions or laws. Some constitutions explicitly deny judicial review. For example, Article 28 of the Belgian constitution (1831) firmly asserts that "the authoritative interpretation of laws is solely the prerogative of the Legislative authority."

The logical basis of judicial review—that government is responsible to higher authority—can take interesting forms in other countries. In some, judges can invoke a higher authority than the constitution—God, an ideology, or a code of ethics. For example, both Iran and Pakistan provide for an Islamic review of all legislation. (Pakistan also has the American form of judicial review.)

By 1985, sixty-five countries—mostly in Western Europe, Latin America, Africa, and the Far East—had adopted some form of judicial review. Australia, Brazil, Burma, Canada, India, Japan, and Pakistan give their courts a full measure of judicial review power. All but Japan have federal governments. Australia and Canada come closest to the American model of judicial review, but the fit is never exact. And wherever courts exercise judicial review, undoing it calls for extraordinary effort. For example, in Australia, the Federal Parliament has no recourse after a law is declared unconstitutional by the High Court but to redraft the offending act in a manner prescribed by the Court. In the United States, overruling judicial review by the Supreme Court requires a constitutional amendment.

Governments with relatively consistent experience with judicial review share some common characteristics: stability, competitive political parties, distribution of power (akin to separation of powers), a tradition of judicial independence, and a high degree of political freedom. Is judicial review the cause or the consequence of these characteristics? More likely than not, judicial review contributes to stability, judicial independence, and political freedom. And separation of powers, judicial independence, and political freedom contribute to the effectiveness of judicial review.

(continued)

Some constitutional courts possess extraordinary power compared with the American model. The German Constitutional Court, like the courts in the United States, has the power to strike down laws enacted by the legislature. But unlike the courts in the United States, the German Constitutional Court also has the power to invalidate the failure of the lawmakers to act. In 1975, for example, the German Constitutional Court nullified the legalization of abortion and declared that the government had a duty to protect unborn human life against all threats. The court concluded that the Constitution required the legislature to enact penal and nonpenal legislation to protect the unborn.

The Supreme Court of India offers an extreme example of judicial review. In 1967, the court held that the parliament could not change the fundamental rights sections of the constitution, even by constitutional amendment! The parliament then amended the constitution to secure its power to amend the constitution. The Supreme Court upheld the amendment but declared that any amendments that attacked the "basic structure" of the constitution would be invalid. In India, the Supreme Court is truly supreme.

Switzerland also has a federal form of government. However, its Supreme Federal Court is limited by the constitution to rule on the constitutionality of cantonal laws (the Swiss equivalent of our state laws). The Supreme Federal Court lacks the power to nullify laws passed by the national assembly. The Swiss people, through a constitutional initiative or a popular referendum, exercise the sovereign right to determine the constitutionality of federal law. In Switzerland, the people are truly supreme.

Sources: Henry J. Abraham, *The Judicial Process,* 5th ed. (New York: Oxford University Press, 1986), pp. 291–330; Chester J. Antineau, *Adjudicating Constitutional Issues* (London: Oceana, 1985), pp. 1–6; Jerold L. Waltman and Kenneth M. Holland, *The Political Role of Law Courts in Modern Democracies* (New York: St. Martin's Press, 1988), pp. 46, 99–100; and Robert L. Hardgrave, Jr., and Stanley A. Kochanek, India: *Government and Politics in a Developing Nation,* 4th ed. (New York: Harcourt Brace Jovanovich, 1986), p. 93.

The Organization of the Federal Courts Today

The American court system is complex, a function in part of our federal system of government. Each state runs its own court system, and no two are identical. In addition, we have a system of courts for the national government. These federal courts coexist with the state courts (see Figure 11.1). Individuals fall under the jurisdiction of both court systems. They can sue or be sued in either system, depending mostly on what their case is about. The vast majority of cases are resolved in the state courts.

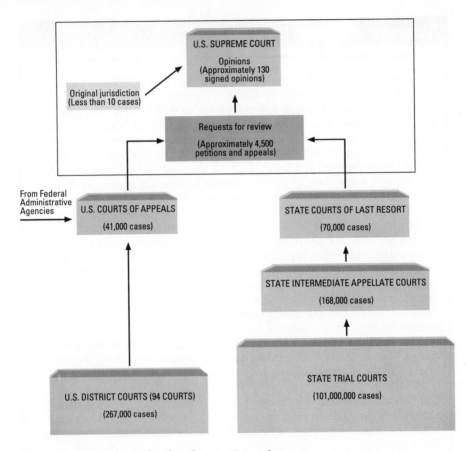

FIGURE 11.1 The Federal and State Court Systems
The federal courts have three tiers: district courts, courts of appeals, and the Supreme Court. The Supreme Court was created by the Constitution; all other federal courts were created by Congress. Most litigation occurs in state courts. The structure of state courts varies from state to state; usually there are minor trial courts for less serious cases, major trial courts for more serious cases, intermediate appellate courts, and courts of last resort. State courts were created by state constitutions. (Sources: State Court Caseload Statistics, Annual Report, 1990 *[Williamsburg, Va.: National Center for State Courts, 1992];* Annual Report of the Director of the Administrative Office of the United States Courts *[Washington, D.C.: Government Printing Office, 1990];* and Harold W. Stanley and Richard G. Niemi, Vital Statistics on American Politics, *2d ed. [Washington, D.C.: Congressional Quarterly, 1990];* Bureau of the Census, Statistical Abstract of the United States, 1990 *[Washington, D.C.: U.S. Government Printing Office, 1990], Table 311.)*

The federal courts are organized in three tiers, like a pyramid. At the bottom of the pyramid are the **U.S. district courts**, where litigation begins. In the middle are the **U.S. courts of appeals**. At the top is the U.S. Supreme Court. *To appeal* means to take a case to a higher court. The courts of appeals and the Supreme Court are appellate courts; with few exceptions, they review cases that have been decided in lower courts. Most federal courts hear and decide a wide array of cases; the judges in these courts are known as *generalists*.

The U.S. District Courts

There are ninety-four federal district courts in the United States. Each state has at least one district court, and no district straddles more than one state.[15] In 1990, nearly 550 full-time federal district court judges dispensed justice in various degrees in almost 267,000 criminal and civil cases.

The district courts are the entry point to the federal court system. When trials occur in the federal system, they take place in the federal district courts. Here is where witnesses testify, lawyers conduct cross-examinations, and judges and juries decide the fate of litigants. There may be more than one judge in each district court, but each case is tried by a single judge sitting alone.

Criminal and civil cases.   Crime is a violation of a law that forbids or commands an activity. Criminal laws are defined in each state's *penal code*, as are punishments for violations. Because crime is a violation of public order, the government prosecutes **criminal cases**. Maintaining public order through the criminal law is largely a state and a local function. Federal criminal cases represent only a fraction of all criminal cases prosecuted in the United States.

Courts decide both criminal and civil cases. **Civil cases** stem from disputed claims to something of value. Disputes arise from accidents, contractual obligations, and divorce, for example. Often the parties disagree over tangible issues (the possession of property, the custody of children), but civil cases can involve more abstract issues, too (the right to equal accommodations, damages for pain and suffering). The government can be a party to civil disputes when called on to defend or to allege wrongs.

Sources of litigation.   Today, the authority of U.S. district courts extends to

- federal criminal cases authorized by federal law (for example, robbery of a federally insured bank or interstate transportation of stolen securities).

- civil cases brought by individuals, groups, or government for alleged violation of federal law (for example, failure of a municipality to implement pollution-control regulations required by a federal agency).

- civil cases brought against the federal government (for example, enforcement of a contract between a manufacturer and a government agency).

- civil cases between citizens of different states when the amount in controversy exceeds $50,000 (for example, when a citizen of New York sues a citizen of Alabama in a U.S. district court in Alabama for damages stemming from an auto accident in Alabama).

Most of the cases scheduled for hearings in the U.S. district courts are never actually tried. One side may be using a lawsuit as a threat to exact a concession from the other. Often the parties settle their own dispute. Less frequently, cases end with **adjudication**, a court judgment resolving the parties' claims and ultimately enforced by the government. When district judges adjudicate cases, they usually offer written reasons to support their decisions. When the issues or circumstances of cases are novel, judges can publish **opinions**, explanations justifying their rulings.

The U.S. Courts of Appeals

All cases resolved by final judgments in the U.S. district courts and all decisions of federal administrative agencies can be appealed to one of the thirteen U.S. courts of appeals. These courts, with a corps of 158 full-time judges, handled approximately 41,000 cases in 1990. Each appeals court hears cases from a geographic area known as a *circuit*. The United States is divided into twelve circuits.*

Appellate court proceedings.   Appellate court proceedings are public, but they usually lack courtroom drama. There are no jurors, witnesses, or cross-examinations; these are features of the trial courts. Appeals are based strictly on the rulings made and procedures followed in the trial courts. Suppose, for example, that in the course of a criminal trial, a U.S. district judge allows the introduction of evidence that convicts a defendant. The defendant can appeal on the ground that the evidence was obtained in the absence of a valid search warrant and so was inadmissible. The issue on appeal is the admissibility of the evidence, not the defendant's guilt or innocence. If the appellate court agrees with the trial judge's decision to admit the evidence, then the conviction stands. If the appellate court disagrees with the trial judge and rules that the evidence is inadmissible, then the defendant must be retried without the incriminating evidence or be released.

It is common for litigants to try settling their dispute while it is on appeal. Occasionally, litigants abandon their appeals for want of resources or resolve. Most of the time, however, appellate courts adjudicate the cases.

The courts of appeals are regional courts. They usually convene in panels of three judges to render judgments. The judges receive written

---

* The thirteenth court, the U.S. Court of Appeals for the Federal Circuit, is not a regional court; it specializes in appeals involving patents, contract claims against the federal government, and federal employment cases.

arguments known as **briefs** (which are also sometimes submitted in trial courts). Often the judges hear oral arguments and question the attorneys to probe their arguments.

Precedent and decision making.   Following review of the briefs and, in many appeals, oral argument, the three-judge panel will meet to reach a judgment. The influence of published appellate opinions can reach well beyond the immediate case. For example, a lawsuit turning on the meaning of the Constitution produces a ruling that then serves as a **precedent** for subsequent cases; that is, the decision becomes a basis for deciding similar cases in the same way. At the appellate level, precedent requires that opinions be written.

Decision making according to precedent is central to the operation of our legal system and provides continuity and predictability. This bias in favor of existing decisions is captured by the Latin expression *stare decisis*, which means "Let the decision stand." But the use of precedent and the principle of **stare decisis** do not make lower-court judges cogs in a judicial machine. "If precedent clearly governed," remarked one federal judge, "a case would never get as far as the Court of Appeals: the parties would settle."[16]

Judges on the courts of appeals direct their energies toward correcting errors in district court proceedings and interpreting the law (in the course of writing opinions). When judges interpret the law, they often modify existing laws. In effect, they are making policy. Judges are politicians in the sense that they exercise political power, but the black robes that distinguish judges from other politicians signal constraints on the exercise of power.

Judges make policy in two different ways. Occasionally, in the absence of legislation, they employ rules from prior decisions. We call this body of rules the **common,** or **judge-made, law.** The roots of the common law lie in the English legal system. Contracts, property, and **torts** (an injury or wrong to the person or property of another) are common-law domains. The second area of judicial lawmaking involves the application of statutes enacted by Congress. The judicial interpretation of legislative acts is called **statutory construction.** To determine how a statute should be applied, judges first look for the legislature's intent, reading reports of committee hearings and debates in Congress. If these sources do not clarify the statute's meaning, the court does.

Uniformity of law.   Decisions by the courts of appeals ensure a measure of uniformity in the application of national law. The courts of appeals harmonize the decisions of district judges within their region so that laws are applied uniformly.

The regional character of the courts of appeals undermines uniformity somewhat, however, because the courts are not bound by the decisions of other circuits. The percolation of cases up through the federal system of courts virtually guarantees that at some point two or more

The Supreme Court, 1992 Term: The Starting Nine
*Pictured out of uniform, from left to right: (seated) John Paul Stevens and
Harry A. Blackmun; (standing) Clarence Thomas, Byron R. White, Chief Jus-
tice William H. Rehnquist, Anthony Kennedy, Sandra Day O'Connor, Antonin
Scalia, and David H. Souter. Justice White chose to retire at the end of the
1992 term.*

courts of appeals, working with a similar set of facts, are going to interpret the same law differently. However, the problem of conflicting decisions in the intermediate federal courts can be corrected by review in
the Supreme Court, where policymaking, not error correcting, is the
paramount goal.

The Supreme Court

Above the west portico of the Supreme Court building are inscribed the
words EQUAL JUSTICE UNDER LAW. At the opposite end of the building, above the east portico, are the words JUSTICE THE GUARDIAN
OF LIBERTY. These mottoes reflect the Court's difficult task: achieving
a just balance among the values of freedom, order, and equality. Consider how these values came into conflict in two controversial issues
the Court has faced in recent years.

Flag burning as a form of political protest pits the value of order—
the government's interest in maintaining a peaceful society—against

the value of freedom—the individual's right to vigorous and unbounded political expression. In the recent flag-burning cases (1989 and 1990), the Supreme Court affirmed constitutional protection for unbridled political expression, including the emotionally charged act of desecrating a national symbol.

School desegregation pits the value of equality—equal educational opportunities for minorities—against the value of freedom—the right of parents to send their children to neighborhood schools. In *Brown* v. *Board of Education*, the Supreme Court carried the banner of racial equality by striking down state-mandated segregation in public schools. The justices recognized the disorder their decision would create in a society accustomed to racial bias, but in this case equality clearly outweighed freedom. Twenty-four years later, the Court was still embroiled in controversy over equality when it ruled in the *Bakke* case (1978) that race could be a factor in university admissions (to diversify the student body).[17] In securing the equality of blacks, the Court then had to confront the charge that it was denying whites the freedom to compete for admission.

The Supreme Court makes national policy. Because its decisions have a far-reaching impact on all of us, it is vital that we understand how it reaches those decisions. With this understanding, we can better evaluate how the Court fits within our model of democracy.

Access to the Court

There are rules of access that must be followed to bring a case to the Supreme Court. Also important is a sensitivity to the interests of the justices. The idea that anyone can take a case all the way to the Supreme Court is true only in theory, not in fact.

The Supreme Court's cases come from two sources. A few (less than five in 1990) arrive under the Court's **original jurisdiction**, conferred by Article III, Section 2, of the Constitution, which gives the Court the power to hear and decide "all Cases affecting Ambassadors, other public Ministers and Consuls, and those in which a State shall be Party." Cases falling under the Court's original jurisdiction are tried and decided in the Court itself; the cases begin and end there. For example, the Court is the first and only forum in which legal disputes between states are resolved.

Most cases enter the Supreme Court from the U.S. courts of appeals or the state courts of last resort.* This is the Court's **appellate jurisdiction**. These are cases that have been tried, decided, and reexamined as

---

* On rare occasions, cases can be brought to the Supreme Court after judgment in a U.S. district court but before consideration by a federal court of appeals. This happened in *United States* v. *Nixon*, 418 U.S. 683 (1974). The urgency of an authoritative decision in the Watergate tapes case short-circuited a decision in the court of appeals.

far as the law permits in other federal or state courts. The Court exercises judicial power under its appellate jurisdiction only because Congress gives it the authority to do so. Congress may change (and, perhaps, eliminate) the Court's appellate jurisdiction. This is a powerful but rarely used weapon in the congressional arsenal of checks and balances.

Litigants in state cases who invoke the Court's appellate jurisdiction must satisfy two conditions: First, the case must reach the end of the line in the state court system. Litigants cannot jump at will from state to federal arenas of justice. Second, the case must raise a **federal question,** an issue covered under the Constitution, federal laws, or treaties. However, even most cases that meet these conditions do not reach the High Court. Since 1925, the Court has exercised substantial (today, nearly complete) control over its **docket,** or agenda. The Court selects a handful of cases (about 170) for consideration from the 4,200 requests it receives each year. For the vast majority of the cases left unreviewed by the Court, the decision of the lower court stands. No explanations accompany cases that are denied review, so they have little or no value as court rulings.

Review is granted only when four or more justices agree that a case warrants full consideration. This unwritten rule is known as the **rule of four.** With advance preparation by their law clerks, who screen petitions and prepare summaries, all nine justices make these judgments at conferences held twice a week.

The Solicitor General

Why does the Court decide to hear certain cases but not others? One theory suggests that the justices look for clues in the requests for review, for signs of an important case.[18] The most important sign is a recommendation by the solicitor general to grant or deny review.

The **solicitor general** represents the federal government before the Supreme Court. Appointed by the president, he is the third-ranking official in the U.S. Department of Justice (following the attorney general and deputy attorney general). His duties include determining whether the government should appeal lower-court decisions; reviewing and modifying, when necessary, the briefs filed in government appeals; and deciding whether the government should file an **amicus curiae brief*** in any appellate court.[19] His objective is to create a cohesive program for the executive branch in the federal courts. He is therefore a powerful figure in the legal system. His influence in bringing cases to the Court and arguing them there has earned him the informal title of the "tenth justice."

---

* Amicus curiae is Latin for "friend of the court." Amicus briefs can be filed with permission of the Court. They allow groups and individuals who are not parties to the litigation but have an interest in it to influence the Court's thinking and, perhaps, its decision.

Decision Making

Once the Court grants review, attorneys submit written arguments (briefs). Oral arguments usually follow. To conserve the justices' time and energy, these are limited to thirty minutes for each side. From October through April, the justices spend four hours a day, five or six days a month hearing arguments. They reach no collective decision at oral argument. A tentative decision is reached only after they have met in conference.

Our knowledge of the dynamics of decision making on the Supreme Court is all secondhand (see Feature 11.1). However, Justice Antonin Scalia, who joined the Court in 1986, remarked that "not much conferencing goes on." By *conferencing*, Scalia meant efforts to persuade others to change their views by debating points of disagreement. "In fact," he said, "to call our discussion of a case a conference is really something of a misnomer. It's much more a statement of the views of each of the nine Justices, after which the totals are added and the case is assigned [for an opinion]."[20] Votes remain tentative until the opinion announcing the Court's judgment is issued.

How do the justices decide how to vote on a case? According to some scholars, legal doctrines and past decisions explain the justices' votes. This explanation, which is consistent with the majoritarian model, anchors the justices closely to the law and minimizes the contribution of their personal values. Other scholars contend that the value preferences and resulting ideologies of each justice provide a more powerful interpretation of his or her voting. This explanation, which is consistent with the pluralist model, sees the justices as reflecting the public's values and acting on them.[21]

Judgment and argument. The voting outcome is the **judgment,** the decision on which side wins and which side loses. Justices often disagree not only on winners and losers but also on the reasons for the judgments.

After voting, the justices in the majority must draft an opinion setting out the reasons for their decision. The **argument** is the kernel of the opinion, its logical content separated from facts, rhetoric, and procedure. If all the justices agree with the judgment and the reasons supporting it, then the opinion is unanimous. A justice can agree with a judgment, upholding or striking down a claim, based on different reasons. This kind of agreement is called **concurrence.** Or a justice can **dissent** if she or he disagrees with a judgment. Both concurring and dissenting opinions may be drafted in addition to the majority opinion.

The opinion. After the conference, the chief justice writes the majority opinion or assigns that responsibility to another justice in the majority. If the chief justice is not in the majority, the writing or assigning responsibility rests with the most senior associate justice in the majority. (Remember, at this point votes are only tentative.)

Feature 11.1

Name Calling in the Supreme Court: When the Justices Vent Their Spleen, Is There a Social Cost?

Barely two months from now (on the first Monday in October), the Justices of the Supreme Court are scheduled to shake one another's hands and sit down around the conference table to begin the work of the new term. In light of the vituperative and personal tone that marked some of the major opinions of the term just ended, it seems fair to wonder whether the justices will be able to look one another in the eye, let alone get back to work.

What do you say to someone after you have told her in public that her views are "irrational" and "cannot be taken seriously"? (Justice Antonin Scalia to Justice Sandra Day O'Connor in *Webster* v. *Reproductive Health Services,* the Missouri abortion case.) Or after you have accused someone of "an Orwellian rewriting of history"? (Justice Anthony M. Kennedy to Justice Harry A. Blackmun in *County of Allegheny* v. *American Civil Liberties Union,* the Pittsburgh case that permitted the government to display a Hanukkah menorah but barred a Nativity scene.) Or after you have dismissed someone's opinions as "a regrettably patronizing civics lecture"? (Chief Justice William H. Rehnquist to Justice William J. Brennan, Jr. in *Texas* v. *Johnson,* the flag-burning case.)

The questions go beyond the Court's mood to its credibility. Unlike the other branches, which replenish their political capital periodically when officeholders face the voters, the Court's credibility depends on the public's belief that its members are engaged in principled judging rather than personal one-upmanship.

While this is hardly the first, or even the most, stressful period in the Court's history—it was Justice Oliver Wendell Holmes who described the Supreme Court half a century ago as "nine scorpions in a bottle"—[the 1988 Term was the nastiest in years.] Can the venom that was splattered across the pages of opinions really fade in the summer sun like so much disappearing ink?

It may not be easy to rattle Justice O'Connor. A former clerk for another Justice expressed doubt the other day that Justice O'Connor was particularly perturbed by Justice Scalia's verbal slings.

Shortly after Justice Scalia joined the Court in 1986, the ex-clerk recalled, the Justices met to discuss a pending case called *Johnson* v. *Santa Clara County,* which concerned the legality of an affirmative action program intended to benefit women. Justice Scalia treated his new colleagues to a 15-minute lecture on the evils of affirmative action, particularly affirmative action for women. When he finished, Justice O'Connor smiled and, addressing him by his nickname, said, "Why, Nino, how do you think I got my job?" Her eventual opinion supported the program; Justice Scalia attacked it in a long dissent.

(continued)

Feature 11.1 (Continued)

Students of the Court note that even when it is running smoothly, it has not been a very collegial place in recent years. A generation has passed since Chief Justice Earl Warren cajoled his colleagues to produce the unanimous opinion that marked the end of the era of segregation. Scholars now view the unanimity of *Brown* v. *Board of Education* as an indispensable element that gave the decision its moral weight.

"The country holds an ideal of the Court as a place where people sit down and reason together," Martha Minow, a Harvard law professor who clerked on the Court 10 years ago, said in a recent interview. "That's not true now even in the best of times. It's really nine separate courts. The Justices lead separate, even isolated lives. They deal with each other only in quite formalized settings. They vote the way they want to and then retreat to their own chambers."

With law clerks serving as ambassadors between the Justices' chambers, "the Justices have learned to run a Court quite well without talking to one another," another ex-clerk said.

The machinery works well enough to weather stormy periods like this one. The court can get by. Can it also inspire and lead? That is a question as important as any asked in the briefs now accumulating . . . and only the Justices have the answer.

Source: Linda Greenhouse, "At the Bar," *New York Times,* 28 July 1989, p. 21. Copyright © 1989 by The New York Times Company. Reprinted by permission.

The authoring justice distributes a draft opinion; the other justices read it and then circulate criticisms and suggestions. An opinion may have to be rewritten several times to accommodate colleagues who remain unpersuaded by the draft. Justices can change their votes, and perhaps alter the judgment, until the decision is officially announced.

Justices in the majority frequently try to muffle or stifle dissent to encourage institutional cohesion. Since the mid-1940s, however, unity has been more difficult to obtain.[22] Gaining agreement from the justices today is akin to negotiating with nine separate law firms. Nevertheless, the justices must be keenly aware of the slender foundation of their authority, which rests largely on public respect. That respect is tested whenever the Court ventures into areas of controversy. Banking, slavery, and Reconstruction policies embroiled the Court in controversy in the nineteenth century. Freedom of speech and religion, racial equality, and the right of privacy have led the Court into controversy in this century.

Strategies on the Court

The Court is more than the sum of its formal processes. The justices exercise real political power. If we start with the assumption that the justices are attempting to stamp their own policy views on the cases they review, then we should expect typical political behavior from them. Cases that reach the Supreme Court's docket pose difficult choices. Because the justices are grappling with conflict on a daily basis, they probably have well-defined ideologies that reflect their values. Scholars and journalists have attempted to pierce the veil of secrecy that shrouds the Court from public view and analyze these ideologies.[23]

The beliefs of most justices can be located on the two-dimensional model of political values discussed in Chapter 1 (see Figure 1.2). Liberal justices, such as Harry Blackmun, choose freedom over order and equality over freedom. Conservative justices—William Rehnquist and Antonin Scalia, for example—choose order over freedom and freedom over equality. These choices translate into policy preferences as the justices struggle to win votes or retain coalitions.

We know that the justices also vary in intellectual ability, advocacy skills, social graces, temperament, and the like. They argue for the support of their colleagues, offering information in the form of drafts and memoranda to explain the advantages and disadvantages of voting for or against an issue. And we expect the justices make occasional, if not regular, use of friendship, ridicule, and patriotism to mold their colleagues' views.

A justice might adopt a long-term strategy of influencing the appointment of like-minded colleagues to marshal additional strength on the Court. Chief Justice (and former President) William Howard Taft (1921–1930), for example, bombarded President Warren G. Harding with recommendations and suggestions whenever a Court vacancy was announced. Taft was especially determined to block the appointment of anyone who might side with the "dangerous twosome," Justices Oliver Wendell Holmes and Louis D. Brandeis. Taft said he "must stay on the Court in order to prevent the Bolsheviki from getting control."[24]

The Chief Justice

The chief justice is only one of nine justices, but he has several important functions based on his authority. And if he does not carry them out, someone else will.[25] Apart from his role in docket control decisions and his direction of the conference, the chief justice can also be a social leader, generating solidarity within the group. Sometimes, the chief justice can embody intellectual leadership. Finally, the chief justice can provide policy leadership, directing the Court toward a general policy position.

When he presides at the conference, the chief justice can exercise control over the discussion of issues, although independent-minded justices are not likely to succumb to his views. For example, as discussed in the chapter opening, at the end of the conference on *Brown* v. *Board of Education*, Chief Justice Warren skillfully dealt with the objections of his colleagues. Eventually, Warren's patriotic appeals had made both the decision and the opinion in *Brown* unanimous.[26]

Judicial Recruitment

Neither the Constitution nor federal law imposes formal requirements for appointment to the federal courts, except for the condition that, once appointed, district court and appeals judges must reside in the district or circuit to which they are appointed. The president appoints judges to the federal courts, and all nominees must be confirmed by the Senate. Congress sets, but cannot lower, a judge's compensation.

State courts operate somewhat similarly to federal courts. Governors appoint judges in nearly half the states. Other states select their judges by partisan, nonpartisan, or (rarely) legislative election.[27] Nominees in some states must be confirmed by the state legislature. In the rest, judges are confirmed in general elections held several years after appointment. Contested elections for judgeships are unusual.

The Appointment of Federal Judges

The Constitution states that federal judges hold their commissions "during good Behaviour," which in practice means for life.* A president's judicial appointments, then, are likely to survive his administration, a kind of political legacy. The appointment power assumes that the president is free to identify candidates and appoint judges who favor his policies.

Judicial vacancies occur when sitting judges resign, retire, or die. Vacancies also arise when Congress creates new judgeships to handle increasing caseloads. The president then nominates a candidate, who must be confirmed by the Senate. The president has the help of the Justice Department, which screens candidates before the formal nomination and subjects serious contenders to FBI investigation. The department and the Senate vie for control in the appointment of district court and appeals judges.

The advice and consent of the Senate. For district court and appeals vacancies, the practice of **senatorial courtesy** forces presidents to share the nomination power with members of the Senate. The Senate will not confirm a nominee who is opposed by the senior senator in the president's party in the nominee's state. The Justice Department searches for

---

* Only seven federal judges have been removed by impeachment in nearly two hundred years; nine resigned before formal impeachment charges could be lodged; and only five have ever been convicted of felonies (serious criminal conduct).

acceptable candidates and polls the appropriate senator for her or his reaction to them.

The Senate Judiciary Committee conducts a hearing for each judicial nominee. The chair exercises a measure of control in the appointment process beyond the power of senatorial courtesy. If a nominee is objectionable to the chair, he or she can delay a hearing or hold up other appointments until the president and the Justice Department consider some alternative. This kind of behavior does not win a politician much influence in the long run, however. So committee chairs are usually loathe to place obstacles in a president's path, especially when they may want presidential support for their own policies and constituencies.

The American Bar Association.   The American Bar Association (ABA), the largest organization of lawyers in the United States, has been involved in screening candidates for the federal bench since 1946.[28] Its role is defined by custom, not law. At the president's behest, the ABA's Standing Committee on the Federal Judiciary routinely rates prospective appointees using a four-value scale ranging from "exceptionally well qualified" to "not qualified."

To gather information about a candidate, the committee, in confidence, interviews lawyers and judges who know and are capable of evaluating the candidate. The committee's recommendation is supposed to address the candidate's "professional qualifications," which are defined as "competence, integrity, and judicial temperament." A candidate's politics and ideology should have no bearing on the committee's task.

Presidents do not always agree with the committee's judgment, in part because its objections can mask disagreements with a candidate's political views. Occasionally, a candidate deemed "not qualified" is nominated and even appointed, but the overwhelming majority of appointees to the federal bench since 1946 have had the ABA's blessing.

Recent Presidents and the Federal Judiciary

President Jimmy Carter wanted to make the judiciary more representative of the general population. He appointed substantially more blacks, women, and Hispanics to the federal bench than did any of his predecessors or his successors. Here his actions were consistent with the pluralist model, at least symbolically.

By comparison, political ideology, not demographics, lay at the heart of Ronald Reagan's judicial appointments. Reagan sought out nominees with particular policy preferences so he could leave his stamp on the judiciary well into the twenty-first century. Both Carter and Reagan used the nation's law schools the way major league baseball managers use farm teams. With the right statistics, a professor could move to the major leagues—in this case, one of the federal district or appellate courts. Carter's liberal values led him to look for judges who were committed to equality; Reagan's conservative values led him to appoint judges who were more committed to order. Reagan surpassed Carter in reshaping the federal courts: 262 lifetime appointments for Carter compared with 378 lifetime appointments for Reagan.

During his presidency, George Bush followed the example of his predecessor by nominating conservatives. In fact, Reagan's appointment of hundreds of judges in the district courts created a judicial minor league that enabled Bush to identify and nominate appellate court judges with some confidence in their value preferences and ideology.[29] In contrast, Bill Clinton assumed the presidency with a pledge to return to a policy of appointing individuals who reflected the diversity of the American population.

Appointment to the Supreme Court

The announcement of a vacancy on the High Court usually causes quite a stir. Campaigns for Supreme Court seats are commonplace, although the public rarely sees them. Hopeful candidates contact friends in the administration and urge influential associates to do the same on their behalf.

The president is not shackled by senatorial courtesy when it comes to nominating a Supreme Court justice. Appointment to the High Court attracts more intense public scrutiny than do lower-level appointments. This scrutiny limits a president's choices and focuses attention on the Senate's "Advice and Consent."

Of the 144 men and 1 woman nominated to the Court, 28—or about 1 in 5—have failed to receive Senate confirmation. The most important factor in the rejection of a nominee is partisan politics. The most recent nominee to be rejected on partisan and ideological grounds was Judge Robert Bork.

Since 1950, eighteen of twenty-two Supreme Court nominees have had judicial experience in federal or state courts. This "promotion" from within the judiciary may be based on the idea that a judge's past opinions are good predictors of future opinions on the High Court. After all, a president is handing out a powerful lifetime appointment; it makes sense to want an individual who is sympathetic to his views.

The resignation of Chief Justice Warren Burger in 1986 gave Reagan the chance to elevate Associate Justice William H. Rehnquist to the position of chief justice and to appoint Antonin Scalia, who was a judge in a federal court of appeals, as Rehnquist's replacement. Rehnquist faced stern questioning from liberal critics during his Senate confirmation hearings. (The testimony of Supreme Court nominees is a relatively recent phenomenon; it began in 1925.) But Rehnquist's opponents were unable to stop confirmation in the Republican-controlled Senate.

In 1987, when Justice Lewis F. Powell, Jr. resigned, Reagan had an opportunity to shift the ideological balance on the Court toward a more conservative consensus. He nominated Judge Robert H. Bork, a conservative, to fill the vacancy. Bork advocated **judicial restraint**, which rests on the premise that legislators, not judges, should make the laws. Ironically, the legislators who opposed Bork supported the concept of **judicial activism**, which allows judges to promote desirable social goals. Some of Bork's critics maintained that he was really an activist draped in the robes of judicial restraint. Bork's true purpose, these critics charged, was to advance his conservative ideology from the High Court.

The hearings concluded after several days of televised testimony from Judge Bork and a parade of witnesses. Liberal interest groups formed a rare coalition that included abortion rights, civil rights, feminist, labor, environmental, and senior citizen organizations. They put aside their disagreements and mounted a massive campaign to defeat the nomination, overwhelming conservative efforts to buttress Bork. At first, the public was undecided on Bork's confirmation; by the time the hearings ended, however, public opinion had shifted against him. Even though his defeat was a certainty, Bork insisted that the Senate vote on his nomination, hoping for a sober discussion of his record. But the rancor never abated. Bork was defeated by a vote of 58–42, the largest margin by which the Senate had ever rejected a Supreme Court nominee.

Federal appeals court judge Douglas H. Ginsburg was nominated shortly thereafter. Ginsburg had strong conservative credentials and youth (he was forty-one when nominated) on his side. Nine days after the nomination, Ginsburg's plans went up in smoke when he confirmed allegations that he had used marijuana while he was a student and a Harvard Law School professor. Ginsburg withdrew his nomination.

Subsequently, federal appeals court judge Anthony M. Kennedy was nominated and confirmed. The Senate examined Kennedy's views in detail, and the nominee did not duck questions that assessed his stand on constitutional issues. His winning combination of wholesomeness and ideological moderation netted him a place as the 104th justice of the Supreme Court.

The rules of the game for appointment to the High Court appeared to change in 1990 when President Bush plucked David Souter from relative obscurity to replace liberal Justice William J. Brennan, Jr. Souter fit the model of other nominees: He had extensive judicial experience as a justice on the New Hampshire Supreme Court and had recently been appointed to the federal court of appeals. But his views on provocative topics were undetectable because he had written little and spoken less on privacy, abortion, religious liberty, and equal protection. Furthermore, during Senate confirmation hearings, he successfully avoided or deflected the most controversial topics. Souter was confirmed by the Senate 90–9.

In 1991, George Bush nominated a black conservative judge, Clarence Thomas, to replace ailing Thurgood Marshall.[30] Thomas weathered days of questioning from the Senate Judiciary Committee. He declined to express opinions about policies or approaches to constitutional interpretation, which stymied his opponents. Thomas's nomination seemed assured until a last-minute witness, Professor Anita Hill, came forward

. . . The Truth and Nothing But the Truth
The Senate Judiciary Committee was moving toward the approval of the appointment of Judge Clarence Thomas to the Supreme Court when Professor Anita Hill, an attorney and one of Thomas's former co-workers, graphically leveled charges of sexual harassment against Thomas during nationally televised hearings. After hearing those charges and Thomas's rebuttal, in which he likened the hearings to a "high-tech lynching" of a black male, the Senate voted for confirmation by a vote of 52 to 48. Many observers believe the televised hearings contributed to the later success of women candidates in the 1992 election.

with charges that Thomas had sexually harassed her ten years earlier while she was working for him.

A transfixed nation watched the riveting testimony of Hill, then Thomas, and a parade of corroborating witnesses. After a marathon hearing, the committee failed to unearth convincing proof of Hill's allegations. In the end, the Senate voted 52 to 48 to confirm Thomas's nomination.[31]

The Consequences of Judicial Decisions

Of all the lawsuits begun in the United States, the overwhelming majority end without a court judgment. Many civil cases are settled, the parties give up, or the courts dismiss the claims because they are beyond the legitimate bounds of judicial resolution.

Most criminal cases end with a **plea bargain,** the defendant's admission of guilt in exchange for a less severe punishment. Only about 20 percent of criminal cases in the federal district courts are tried; an equally small percentage of civil cases are adjudicated. That a judge sentences a criminal defendant to ten years in prison or that a court holds a company liable for $11 billion in damages does not guarantee that the defendant or the company will give up either freedom or assets. In the case of the criminal defendant, an appeal following trial and conviction, if nothing else, serves to delay the day when no alternative to prison remains. In civil cases, the immediate consequence of a judgment may also be an appeal, which also delays the day of reckoning.

Supreme Court Rulings: Implementation and Impact

When the Supreme Court makes a decision, it relies on others to *implement* it, to translate policy into action. How a judgment is implemented rests in good measure on how it was crafted. Remember that in preparing opinions, the justices are working to hold their majorities together, to gain greater, if not unanimous, support for their arguments. This forces them to compromise in their opinions and moderate their arguments and creates uncertainty in many of the policies they articulate. Ambiguous opinions affect the implementation of policy. For example, when the Supreme Court issued its order in 1955 to desegregate public school facilities "with all deliberate speed,"[32] judges who opposed the Court's policy dragged their feet in implementing it. In the early 1960s, the Supreme Court struck down prayers and Bible reading in public schools. Yet state court judges and attorneys general reinterpreted the High Court's decision to mean that only *compulsory* prayer or Bible reading was unconstitutional and that state-sponsored voluntary prayer or Bible reading was acceptable.[33]

Because the Supreme Court confronts issues freighted with deeply felt social values or fundamental political beliefs, its decisions have an impact beyond the immediate parties in a dispute. The Court's decision in *Roe* v. *Wade* (1973) legalizing abortion generated heated public reaction. Groups opposing abortion vowed to overturn the decision; groups favoring abortion moved to protect the right they had won. Within eight months of the decision, more than two dozen constitutional amendments had been introduced in Congress, although none managed to carry the extraordinary majority required for passage.

Public Opinion and the Supreme Court

Democratic theorists have a difficult time reconciling a commitment to representative democracy with a judiciary that is not accountable to the electorate, yet has the power to undo legislative or executive acts. This difficulty may simply be a problem for theorists, however, because the policies coming from the Supreme Court rarely seem out of line with public opinion.[34] Surveys in several controversial areas reveal that the Court seldom departs from majority sentiment or the trend toward such sentiment.[35]

The evidence squarely supports the view that the Supreme Court holds close to public opinion at least as often as other elected institutions do. In a comprehensive study matching 146 Supreme Court rulings with nationwide opinion polls from the mid-1930s through the mid-1980s, the Court reflected public opinion majorities or pluralities in more than 60 percent of its rulings. However, the Court parted company with public opinion in about 33 percent of its rulings. For example, the Court clearly defied the wishes of the majority for decades on the issue of school prayer.

There are at least three explanations for the Court's consistency with majority sentiment. First, the modern Court has shown deference toward national laws and policies, which typically echo national public opinion. Second, the Court moves closer to public opinion during periods of crisis. Third, rulings that reflect the public view are subject to fewer changes than rulings that depart from public opinion.

Finally, the evidence also supports the view that the Court seldom influences public opinion. The Court enjoys only moderate popularity, and its decisions are not widely perceived by the public. With few exceptions, there is no evidence of shifting public opinion prior to and following its rulings.[36]

The Courts and Models of Democracy

How far should judges stray from existing statutes and precedents? Supporters of the majoritarian model argue that judges should refrain from injecting their own values into their decisions. If the law places too much (or not enough) emphasis on equality or order, then it is up to the elected legislature, not the courts, to change the law. In contrast, those who support the pluralist model maintain that the courts are a policy-making branch of government and that the individual values and interests of judges should advance the different values and interests of the population at large.

The argument that our judicial system fits the pluralist model gains support from a legal procedure called **class action**, which is a device for assembling the claims or defenses of similarly situated individuals so that they can be tried as a single lawsuit. A class action makes it possible for people with small individual claims and limited financial resources to aggregate their claims and resources to make a lawsuit viable. Since the 1940s, class action suits have been the vehicles through which groups have asserted claims involving civil rights, legislative apportionment, and environmental problems. For example, schoolchildren have sued (through their parents) under the banner of class action to rectify claims of racial discrimination on the part of school authorities, as in *Brown* v. *Board of Education.*

Abetting class action is the resurgence of state supreme courts in fashioning policies consistent with group preferences. State courts of all levels annually resolve millions of decisions. They exercise substantial influence over policies that affect citizens daily, including the rights and liberties enshrined in their state constitutions, statutes, and common law.[37]

State judges need not look to the U.S. Supreme Court for guidance on the meaning of similar state rights and liberties (see Table 11.1). A state court can avoid review by the U.S. Supreme Court by resting its decision solely on state law or by plainly stating that its decision rests on both state and federal law. If the U.S. Supreme Court is likely to render a restrictive view of a constitutional right, and the judges of a state court are inclined to a more expansive view, the state judges can employ the state court ground as a way of avoiding Supreme Court review. In a period when the nation's highest court has moved in a decidedly conservative direction, it should come as no surprise that some state courts have become safe havens for liberal values.

When judges reach decisions, they pay attention to the views of other courts, not just to the ones above them in the judicial hierarchy. State and federal court opinions are the legal granary from which judges regularly draw their ideas. Often the issues that affect individual lives—property, family, contracts—are grist for state courts, not federal courts.

State courts have become renewed arenas for political conflict with litigants, individually or in groups, vying to promote their own policies. The multiplicity of court systems with their overlapping state and federal responsibilities provides alternative points of access for individuals and groups to present and argue their claims. This description of the courts fits the pluralist model of government.

Summary

The power of judicial review, claimed by the Supreme Court in 1803, placed the judiciary on an equal footing with Congress and the president. The principle of checks and balances can restrain judicial power through several means, such as constitutional amendment and impeachment. But restrictions on that power have been infrequent, leaving the federal courts to exercise considerable influence through judicial review and statutory construction.

The federal court system has three tiers. At the bottom are the district courts, where litigation begins and most disputes end. In the middle are the courts of appeals. At the top is the Supreme Court. The ability of judges to make policy increases as one moves up the pyramid from trial courts to appellate courts.

Table 11.1 Protecting Rights and Liberties: U.S. Supreme Court Versus State Supreme Courts

Most Americans believe that the United States Supreme Court has the last word on their constitutional rights. But state constitutions also confer rights, many of them identical to the ones enshrined in the national Bill of Rights. The states cannot provide less protection for individual rights than the U.S. Constitution, but they can provide more. State court decisions are immune from subsequent challenge in the federal courts provided the decisions rest on adequate and independent reasons in the state constitutions.

At one time, liberals spurned state courts as conservative institutions; they preferred the ideological sympathy of the Warren Court for an expansion of constitutional guarantees. Today, liberals see state courts as safer havens for expanding rights and liberties than the nation's highest court.

Issue	U.S. Supreme Court ruling . . .	. . . and the state courts that have differed
Public funding for abortion	No	Calif., Mass., N.J.
Equalized school financing	No	Ark., Calif., Conn., Ky., N.J., Texas, Wash., W. Va., Wis., Wyo.
Leafleting in shopping centers	No	Calif., Mass., N.J., Pa., Wash.
Admitting evidence seized illegally but in good faith	Yes	Conn., N.C., N.J., N.Y.

Source: Time, October 8, 1990, p. 76. Copyright 1990 Time Inc. Reprinted by permission.

The Supreme Court, free to draft its own agenda through the discretionary control of its docket, harmonizes conflicting interpretations of national law and articulates constitutional rights. It is helped at this crucial stage by the solicitor general, who represents the executive branch of government before the High Court. His influence with the justices affects their choice of cases to review.

Once a case is placed on the docket, the parties submit briefs and the justices hear oral arguments. A tentative vote is taken in conference. Then the real work begins: crafting an opinion that satisfies the majority without sacrificing clarity or forcefulness.

The president and senators from his party share the power of appointment of federal district and appellate judges. The president has more leeway in the nomination of Supreme Court justices, although nominees must be confirmed by the Senate. Political allegiance and values are usually a necessary condition of appointment.

Courts inevitably fashion policy for each of the states and for the nation. They provide multiple points of access for individuals to pursue their preferences and so fit the pluralist model of democracy. Furthermore, class action enables people with small individual claims and limited financial resources to pursue their goals in court, reenforcing the pluralist model.

In addition to balancing freedom and order, judges must now balance freedom and equality. The impact of their decisions is much broader as well. Democratic theorists are troubled by the expansion of judicial power. But today's courts fit within the pluralist model and usually are in step with what the public wants.

As the U.S. Supreme Court headed in a more conservative direction, state supreme courts became safe havens for less restrictive policies on civil rights and civil liberties. The state court systems have overlapping state and federal responsibilities, offering groups and individuals many access points to present and argue their claims.

In its marble palace, the Supreme Court of the United States faces and tries to resolve the dilemmas of government. Within the columned courtroom, the justices work to balance conflicting values, to ensure an orderly, peaceful society. We examine some of these conflicts in Chapter 12.

Key Terms

judicial review
U.S. district courts
U.S. courts of appeals
criminal cases
civil cases
adjudication
opinions
briefs
precedent
stare decisis
common, or judge-made, law
torts
statutory construction
original jurisdiction
appellate jurisdiction

federal question
docket
rule of four
solicitor general
amicus curiae brief
judgment
argument
concurrence
dissent
senatorial courtesy
judicial restraint
judicial activism
plea bargain
class action

Selected Readings

Abraham, Henry J. *Justices and Presidents: A Political History of Appointments to the Supreme Court.* 2d ed. New York: Oxford University Press, 1985. This book examines the critical relationship between justices and presidents from the appointment of John Jay in 1789 through the appointment of Sandra Day O'Connor in 1981.

Baum, Lawrence. *American Courts: Process and Policy.* 2d ed. Boston: Houghton Mifflin, 1990. This comprehensive review of trial and appellate courts in the United States addresses their activities, describes their procedures, and explores the processes that affect them.

Bork, Robert H. *The Tempting of America.* New York: Free Press, 1990. This nationwide best-seller offers Judge Bork's view on the current state of legal scholarship and the political agenda he claims it masks. Bork also offers his candid view of the events surrounding his unsuccessful battle for a seat on the nation's highest court.

Ely, John Hart. *Democracy and Distrust.* Cambridge, Mass.: Harvard University Press, 1980. This appraisal of judicial review attempts to identify and justify the guidelines for the Supreme Court's application of a two-hundred-year-old constitution to conditions of modern life.

Friedman, Lawrence M. *American Law: An Introduction*. New York: Norton, 1984. This clear, highly readable introduction to the bewildering complexity of the law explains how law is made and administered.

Jacob, Herbert. *Law and Politics in the United States*. Boston: Little, Brown, 1986. This introduction to the American legal system emphasizes links to the political arena.

O'Brien, David M. *Storm Center: The Supreme Court in American Politics*. 2d ed. New York: Norton, 1990. This book is a primer on the Supreme Court, its procedures, personalities, and political impact.

Posner, Richard A. *The Federal Courts: Crisis and Reform*. Cambridge, Mass.: Harvard University Press, 1985. This provocative, comprehensive, and lucid analysis of the institutional problems besetting the federal courts was written by a distinguished law professor, now a federal appellate judge.

Wasby, Stephen L. *The Supreme Court in the Federal Judicial System*. 3d ed. Chicago: Nelson-Hall, 1988. This is a thorough study of the Supreme Court's internal procedures, its role at the apex of the national and state court systems, and its place in the political system.

CIVIL LIBERTIES AND CIVIL RIGHTS

12

In Cincinnati, Ohio, a retrospective exhibition of Robert Mapplethorpe's work opened several months after his death in 1989. Mapplethorpe was a critically acclaimed photographer whose subjects included celebrities, still lifes, nudes, children, and graphic sexual poses. The exhibition had traveled to several museums without incident. Then in 1990, Cincinnati's Contemporary Arts Center and its director were charged by local officials with pandering obscenity and illegal use of a minor. At issue were 7 photographs out of the 175 in the exhibit. Five photographs depicted homoerotic and sadomasochistic acts, which the city claimed were obscene. Two photographs used nude or partially nude children as subjects (one captured a toddler with her dress raised and her genitals exposed), which the city contended violated laws against child pornography. If convicted, the museum faced up to $10,000 in fines, and its director faced up to a year in jail and up to $2,000 in fines.

In Santa Clara County, California, Diane Joyce and Paul Johnson worked hard patching holes, shoveling asphalt, and opening culverts for the Santa Clara County Transportation Agency. In 1980, a skilled position as road dispatcher opened up. Joyce and Johnson competed along with ten other applicants for the job. At the time, all of the agency's 238 skilled positions were held by men.

Seven of the applicants, including Joyce and Johnson, passed an oral exam. Next, the agency conducted a round of interviews. Johnson tied for second with a score of 75; Joyce ranked third with a score of 73. After a second round of interviews with the top contenders, the agency gave the job to Johnson.

Joyce didn't let the matter rest. She filed a complaint with the head of the agency, invoking the county government's *affirmative action* policy. **Affirmative action** is a commitment by an employer, school, or other institution to expand opportunities for women, blacks, Hispanics, and members of other minority groups. The policy seeks to remedy the effects of former practices, intentional or not, that had restricted work opportunities for such people. Affirmative action embraces a wide range of policies from special recruitment efforts at one end to numerical goals and quotas at the other.

After reviewing its decision in light of the county's policy, the agency took the job away from Johnson and gave it to Joyce. A government-imposed equality policy thwarted Johnson's freedom to climb the ladder of success. Angered by the lost promotion, he sued.

In the case of the Mapplethorpe exhibition, the city used a criminal prosecution to maintain social order. The museum and its director—and countless others who came to their aid—responded with a vigorous defense of free expression. They maintained that the Mapplethorpe images were art and that the Constitution protected artistic expression from government interference and censorship. Ultimately, a court had to decide between the conflicting values of freedom and order. (The verdict was for acquittal.)

In the case of Diane Joyce and Paul Johnson, the conflict was between the values of equality and freedom. Laws and policies that promote equality inevitably come into conflict with demands for freedom.

In both cases, the exercise of one value would infringe on the exercise of another. And because each defended a value we recognize as vital to democratic rule, both sides had merit. How well do the courts respond to clashes that pit freedom against order in some cases and freedom against equality in others? Is freedom, order, or equality ever unconditional?

The value conflicts described in this chapter revolve around claims or entitlements that rest on law. Although we concentrate here on conflicts over constitutional issues, you should realize that the Constitution is not the only source of people's rights. Government at all levels can, and does, create rights through laws written by legislatures and regulations issued by bureaucracies. For example, Paul Johnson's suit involved provisions of the 1964 Civil Rights Act. Johnson argued that he was the victim of sex discrimination. **Discrimination** is the act of making or recognizing distinctions. When making distinctions between people, discrimination may be benign (that is, harmless) or invidious (harmful). The national government has enacted policies to prohibit invidious discrimination, which is often rooted in prejudice. Johnson invoked Title VII of the 1964 Civil Rights Act, which bars employment discrimination based on race, religion, national origin, or sex. He won the first round in a federal district court; Joyce's employer appealed and won a reversal. The final round was fought in the Supreme Court in 1987.[1] Joyce emerged the victor.

We begin this chapter with a look at the original struggle—the conflict between freedom and order—and the roles of the First Amendment, the due process clause of the Fourteenth Amendment, and the Ninth Amendment in that conflict. Then we examine the threat posed to the democratic process when judges transform policy issues into constitutional issues. We end with an examination of the Fourteenth Amendment's promise of equal protection, which sets the stage for the modern dilemma of government: the struggle between freedom and equality.

The Bill of Rights

You may remember from Chapter 2 that at first the framers of the Constitution did not include a list of individual liberties—a bill of rights—in the national charter. They believed that a bill of rights was not necessary because the extent of the national government's power was spelled out in the Constitution. But during the ratification debates, it became clear that the omission of a bill of rights was the most important obstacle to the adoption of the Constitution by the states. Eventually, twelve amendments were approved by Congress and sent to the states. In 1791, ten were ratified, and the nation had a bill of rights.

The Bill of Rights imposed limits on the national government but not on the state governments.* Over the next seventy-seven years, the Supreme Court was repeatedly pressed to extend the amendments' restraints to the states, but similar restrictions were not placed on the states until the adoption of the Fourteenth Amendment in 1868. Before then, protection from repressive state government had to come from state bills of rights.

The U.S. Constitution guarantees Americans a large constellation of liberties and rights. In this chapter, we explore a number of them. We use two terms, *civil liberties* and *civil rights*, interchangeably in this context, although their meanings are different. **Civil liberties** are freedoms guaranteed to the individual. These guarantees take the form of negative restraints on government. For example, the First Amendment declares that "Congress shall make no law . . . abridging the free-

---

* Congress considered more than a hundred amendments in its first session. One that was not approved would have limited the power of the states to infringe on the rights of conscience, speech, press, and jury trial in criminal cases. James Madison thought this amendment was the "most valuable" of the list, but it failed to muster a two-thirds vote in the Senate.

dom of speech." Civil liberties declare what the government cannot do; in contrast, civil rights declare what the government must do or provide.

Civil rights are powers or privileges that are guaranteed to the individual and protected from arbitrary removal at the hands of the government or other individuals. The right to vote and the right to jury trial in criminal cases are civil rights. Today, civil rights have also come to include the objectives of laws that further certain values. The Civil Rights Act of 1964, for example, furthered the value of equality by establishing the right to nondiscrimination in places of public accommodations and the right to equal employment opportunity.

Actually, the Bill of Rights lists both civil liberties and civil rights. When we refer to the rights and liberties of the Constitution, we mean the protections enshrined in the Bill of Rights and in the first section of the Fourteenth Amendment.[2] The list includes freedom of religion, freedom of speech and the press, the right to peaceable assembly and petition, the rights of the criminally accused, the requirements of due process, and the equal protection of the laws.

Freedom of Religion

> Congress shall make no law respecting an establishment of religion, or prohibiting the free exercise thereof.

Religious freedom was very important to the colonies and later to the states. That importance was reflected in its position in the Bill of Rights: first, in the very first amendment. The amendment guarantees freedom of religion in two clauses. The first, the **establishment clause,** prohibits laws establishing religion; the second, the **free-exercise clause,** prevents the government from interfering with the exercise of religion. Together they ensure that government can neither promote nor inhibit religious beliefs or practices.

The mingling of government and religion has a long history in America. At the time of the Constitutional Convention, many Americans, especially in New England, maintained that government could and should foster religion, certainly Protestantism. Many more Americans were in agreement, however, that this was an issue for state governments and that the national government had no authority to meddle in religious affairs. The religion clauses were drafted in this spirit.[3]

The Supreme Court has refused to interpret the religion clauses definitively. The effect of that refusal is an amalgam of rulings. Freedom to believe is unlimited, but freedom to practice a belief can be limited. Religion cannot benefit directly from government actions (for example, contributions to churches or synagogues), but it can benefit indirectly from those actions (for example, buying books on secular subjects for use in all schools—public, private, and parochial).

The Establishment Clause

The provision that "Congress shall make no law respecting an establishment of religion" bars government sponsorship or support of religious activity. The Supreme Court has consistently held that the establishment clause requires government to maintain a position of neutrality toward religions and to maintain that position in cases that involve choices between religion and nonreligion. However, the clause has never been held to bar all assistance that incidentally aids religious institutions. In this section, we consider the application of the clause to public support for parochial education and for religion in general and to prayer in the public schools.

Government support of religion.   In 1879, the Supreme Court contended, using Thomas Jefferson's words, that the establishment clause erected "a wall of separation between church and state."[4] That wall was breached somewhat in 1947 when the justices upheld a local government program that provided free transportation to parochial school students.[5] The breach seemed to widen in 1968 when the Court held constitutional a government program in which state-purchased textbooks were loaned to parochial school students.[6] The objective of the program, reasoned the majority, was to further educational opportunity. The loan was made to the students, not to the schools, and the benefits were realized by the parents, not by the church.

But in 1971, in **Lemon v. Kurtzman,** the Court struck down a state program that would have funded the salaries for teachers hired by parochial schools to give instruction in secular subjects.[7] The justices proposed a three-pronged test for constitutionality under the establishment clause:

- The law must have a secular purpose (such as lending books to parochial school students).

- Its primary effect must not be to advance or inhibit religion.

- It must not entangle the government excessively with religion.

A law missing any prong would be unconstitutional.

The program in *Lemon* failed on the last ground: To be sure that teachers of secular subjects did not include religious instruction in their lessons, the state would have had to constantly monitor them. This kind of supervision would entangle the government in religious activity.

School prayer.   The Supreme Court has consistently equated prayer in public schools with government support of religion. In 1962, it struck down the daily reading of this twenty-two-word nondenominational prayer in New York's public schools: "Almighty God, we acknowledge our dependence upon Thee, and we beg Thy blessings upon us, our parents, our teachers, and our country."[8]

In the years since that decision, new challenges on the issue of school prayer continue to find their way to the Supreme Court. In 1985, the Court struck down a series of Alabama statutes requiring elementary school teachers to observe a moment of silence for meditation or voluntary prayer each school day.[9] In 1992, the Court ruled, 5–4, that public schools may not include nondenominational prayers in graduation ceremonies.[10]

The establishment clause creates a problem for government. Support for all religions at the expense of nonreligion seems to pose the least risk to social order. Tolerance of the dominant religion at the expense of other religions risks minority discontent, but support for no religion (neutrality between religion and nonreligion) risks majority discontent.

The Free-Exercise Clause

The free-exercise clause of the First Amendment states that "Congress shall make no law . . . prohibiting the free exercise [of religion]." The Supreme Court has struggled to avoid absolute interpretations of this restriction so as not to violate its complement, the establishment clause. For example, suppose Congress grants exemptions from military service to individuals who have religious scruples against war. These exemptions could be construed as a violation of the establishment clause because they favor some religious groups over others. But if Congress forces conscientious objectors to fight—to violate their religious beliefs—the government runs afoul of the free-exercise clause. In fact, Congress has granted military exemptions to people whose religious beliefs lead them to oppose participating in war. The Supreme Court has avoided a conflict between the establishment and free-exercise clauses, however, by equating religious objection to war with any deeply held humanistic opposition to it.[11]

In the free-exercise cases, the justices have distinguished religious beliefs from actions based on those beliefs. Beliefs are inviolate, beyond the reach of government control; but antisocial actions are not protected by the First Amendment. Consider the conflicting values and preferred choices in saluting the flag, working on the sabbath, and using drugs as religious sacraments.

Saluting the flag.   The values of order and religious freedom clashed in 1940 when the Court considered the first of two cases involving compulsory flag saluting in the public schools. In *Minorsville School District* v. *Gobitis*, a group of Jehovah's Witnesses challenged the law on the ground that the action forced them to worship graven images, which their faith forbade.[12] Government order won in an 8–1 decision. The "mere possession of religious convictions," wrote Justice Felix Frankfurter, "which contradict the relevant concerns of a political society does not relieve the citizen from the discharge of political responsibilities."

Three years later, however, the Court reversed itself in *West Virginia State Board of Education* v. *Barnette.*[13] *Gobitis* was decided on the narrower issue of religious belief versus saluting of the flag. In *Barnette*, the justices chose to focus instead on the broader issue of freedom of expression. In stirring language, Justice Robert H. Jackson argued in the majority opinion that no one could be compelled by the government to declare any belief.

> If there is any fixed star in our constitutional constellation, it is that no official, high or petty, can prescribe what shall be orthodox in politics, nationalism, religion, or other matters of opinion or force citizens to confess by word or act their faith therein. If there are any circumstances which permit an exception, they do not now occur to us.

Working on the sabbath.   The modern era of free-exercise thinking begins with **Sherbert v. Verner** (1963). This case involved a Seventh-Day Adventist who was disqualified from unemployment benefits after declining a job that required working on Saturday, which was her sabbath. In a 7–2 decision, the Supreme Court ruled that the disqualification imposed an impermissible burden on Sherbert's free exercise of religion. The First Amendment, declared the majority, protected *observance* as well as belief. The additional burden on religion occasioned by the government regulation could be justified only if the government could demonstrate a compelling interest in not granting an exemption.[14] And government can rarely muster enough evidence to demonstrate a "compelling" interest.

Using drugs as sacrament.   The use of illegal substances as part of a religious sacrament forces believers to violate the law. For example, the Rastafarians and members of the Ethiopian Zion Coptic Church smoke marijuana in the belief that it is the body and blood of Christ. Obviously, the freedom to practice religion taken to an extreme can be used as a license for illegal conduct. However, government resistance to it is understandable. The inevitable result is a clash between religious freedom and social order.

In 1990, the Supreme Court, by a vote of 6 to 3, tipped the balance in favor of social order when two members of the Native American Church sought an exemption from an Oregon law that made the possession or use of peyote a crime.[15] (Peyote is a cactus that contains the hallucinogen mescaline. It has been used for centuries in Native American religious ceremonies.)

Justice Antonin Scalia, writing for the majority, examined the conflict between freedom and order through the lens of majoritarian democratic thought. He observed that the Court had never held that an individual's religious beliefs excused him or her from compliance with an otherwise valid law prohibiting conduct that government was free to regulate. Allowing exceptions to every state law or regulation affecting religion "would open the prospect of constitutionally required exemptions from civic obligations of almost every conceivable kind." Scalia cited as examples compulsory military service, payment of taxes, vaccination requirements, and child-neglect laws.

The conflict between the commands of one's religion and the demands of one's government must reside in the political process, reasoned Scalia:

> It may fairly be said that leaving accommodation to the political process will place at a relative disadvantage those religious practices that are not widely engaged in, but that unavoidable consequence of democratic government must be preferred to a system in which each conscience is a law unto itself.

Freedom of Expression

> Congress shall make no law . . . abridging the freedom of speech, or of the press; or the right of the people peaceably to assemble, and to petition the government for a redress of grievances.

The initial versions of the **speech clause** and the **press clause** of the First Amendment were introduced by James Madison in the House of Representatives on June 8, 1789. One was merged with the religion and peaceable assembly clauses to yield the First Amendment.

The sparse language of the First Amendment seems perfectly clear: "Congress shall make no law . . . abridging the freedom of speech, or of the press." Yet a majority of the Supreme Court has never agreed that this "most majestic guarantee" is absolutely inviolable.[16] Historians have long debated the framers' intentions regarding the **free-expression clauses**. The dominant view is that the clauses confer the right to unrestricted discussion of public affairs.[17] Other scholars, examining much the same evidence, conclude that few, if any, of the framers clearly understood the clause; moreover, these scholars insist that prosecution for seditious statements (statements inciting insurrection) is not ruled out by the First Amendment.[18]

Careful analysis of the records of the period supports the view that the press clause prohibited only the imposition of **prior restraint**—censorship before publication. Publishers could not claim protection from punishment if works that had already been published were later deemed improper, mischievous, or illegal. Today, however, the clauses are deemed to bar not only most forms of prior restraint but also after-the-fact prosecution for political and other discourse.

The Supreme Court has evolved two approaches to the resolution of claims based on the free-expression clauses. First, government can regulate or punish the advocacy of ideas but only if it can prove that the goal is to produce lawless action and that a high probability exists that such action will occur. Second, government may impose reasonable restrictions on the means for communicating ideas, which can incidentally discourage free expression.

Suppose, for example, that a political party advocates unilateral disarmament as part of its platform. (Unilateral disarmament is a policy of arms reduction or elimination without a corresponding reduction or elimination by any other nation.) Government cannot regulate or punish that party for advocating unilateral disarmament because the standards of proof—that the act be directed to inciting or producing imminent lawless action and that the act be judged likely to produce such action—do not apply. But government can impose restrictions on the way the party's candidates communicate what they are advocating. For example, government can bar them from blaring messages from loudspeakers in residential neighborhoods at 3:00 A.M.

Freedom of Speech

The starting point for any modern analysis of free speech is the **clear and present danger test** formulated by Justice Oliver Wendell Holmes in the Supreme Court's unanimous decision in *Schenck* v. *United States* (1919).[19] Charles T. Schenck and his fellow defendants were convicted under a federal criminal statute for attempting to disrupt World War I military recruitment by distributing leaflets claiming that conscription was unconstitutional. The government believed that this behavior threatened the public order. At the core of the Court's opinion, Holmes wrote:

> The character of every act depends upon the circumstances in which it is done. . . . The most stringent protection of free speech would not protect a man in falsely shouting fire in a theatre and causing a panic. . . . The question in every case is whether the words used are used in such circumstances and are of such a nature as to create a *clear and present danger* that they will bring about the substantive evils that Congress has a right to prevent. It is a question of proximity and degree. When a nation is at war many things that might be said in time of peace are such a hindrance to its effort that their utterance will not be endured so long as men fight and that no Court could regard them as protected by any constitutional right. [Emphasis added.]

Because the actions of the defendants in *Schenck* were deemed to create a clear and present danger to the United States at that time, the defendants' convictions were upheld. However, the test helps distinguish the *advocacy of ideas*, which is protected, from *incitement*, which is not.

In 1925, the Court issued a landmark decision in **Gitlow v. New York**.[20] Benjamin Gitlow was arrested for distributing copies of a "left-wing manifesto" that called for the establishment of socialism through strikes and class action of any form. Gitlow was convicted under a state criminal anarchy law; Schenck had been convicted under a federal law. The Court held, for the first time, that the First Amendment speech and press provisions applied to the states through the due process clause of the Fourteenth Amendment. Nevertheless, a majority of the justices affirmed Gitlow's conviction.

The protection of advocacy faced yet another challenge in 1948 when eleven members of the Communist party were charged with violating the Smith Act—a federal law making the advocacy of force or violence against the United States a criminal offense. The leaders were convicted, although the government introduced no evidence that they actually urged people to commit specific violent acts. The Supreme Court mustered a majority for its decision to uphold the convictions under the act, but it could not get a majority to agree on the reasons in support of that decision. The largest bloc of four justices announced the plurality opinion in 1951, arguing that the government's interest was substantial enough to warrant criminal penalties.[21] The justices interpreted the threat to government to be the gravity of the advocated action "discounted by its improbability." In other words, a single soap-box orator advocating revolution stands a low chance of success. But a well-organized, highly disciplined political movement advocating revolution in the tinderbox of world conditions stands a greater chance of success. In broadening the meaning of clear and present danger, the Court held that the government was justified in acting preventively rather than waiting until the revolution was about to occur.

By 1969, the pendulum had swung back in the other direction: That year, in *Brandenburg v. Ohio,* a unanimous decision extended the freedom of speech to new limits.[22] Clarence Brandenburg, the leader of the Ohio Ku Klux Klan, had been convicted under a state law for remarks he had made at a Klan rally. His comments, which had been filmed by a television crew invited to cover the meeting, included threats against government officials.

The Court reversed Brandenburg's conviction because the government had failed to prove that the danger was real. The Court went even further and declared that threatening speech was protected by the First Amendment unless the government could prove that such advocacy was "directed to inciting or producing imminent lawless action" and was "likely to produce such action."

Symbolic expression. **Symbolic expression,** or nonverbal communication, generally receives less protection than pure speech. But the courts have upheld certain types of symbolic expression. *Tinker v. Des Moines Independent County School District* (1969) involved three public school students who wore black armbands to school to protest the Vietnam War.[23] Principals in their school district had prohibited the wearing of armbands on the ground that such conduct would provoke a disturbance, so the students were suspended from school. The Supreme Court overturned the suspensions. Justice Abe Fortas declared for the majority that the principals had failed to show that the forbidden conduct would substantially interfere with appropriate school discipline.

Undifferentiated fear or apprehension is not enough to overcome the right to freedom of expression. Any departure from absolute regimentation may cause trouble. Any variation from the majority's opinion may inspire fear. Any word spoken, in class, in the lunchroom, or on the campus, that deviates from the views of another person may start an argument or cause a disturbance. But our Constitution says we must take this risk.

The flag is an object of deep veneration in our society, yet its desecration is also a form of symbolic expression protected by the First Amendment. In 1989, a divided Supreme Court struck down a Texas law that barred the desecration of venerated objects. Congress then enacted the Flag Protection Act of 1989 in an attempt to overcome the constitutional flaws identified in the Texas decision.

The Supreme Court nullified the federal flag-burning statute in **United States v. Eichman** (1990).[24] By a vote of 5 to 4, the justices reaffirmed First Amendment protection for all expression of political ideas. The vote was identical to the Texas case, with conservative justices Scalia and Kennedy joining with the liberal wing to forge an unusual majority. The majority applied the same freedom-preferring approach used in the Texas case: "'If there is a bedrock principle underlying the First Amendment, it is that the Government may not prohibit the expression of an idea simply because society finds the idea itself offensive or disagreeable.' Punishing desecration of the flag dilutes the very freedom that makes this emblem so revered, and worth revering."

The Court majority relied on the substantive conception of democratic theory, which embodies the principle of freedom of speech, to justify its invalidation of the federal law. Yet a May 1990 poll revealed that most people wanted to outlaw flag burning as a means of expressing political opinions and that a clear majority favored a constitutional amendment to that end.[25] The procedural conception of democratic theory states that government should do what the people want. In the case of flag burning, then, the people are willing to abandon the freedom-of-speech principle embodied in the substantive view of democracy.

Free speech versus order: Obscenity. Obscene material—words, books, magazines, films—is entirely excluded from constitutional protection. This exclusion rests on the Supreme Court's review of historical evidence surrounding freedom of expression at the time of the adoption of the Constitution. The Court observed that blasphemy, profanity, and obscenity were colonial crimes, but obscenity was not a developed area of the law at the time the Bill of Rights was adopted. Difficulties arise, however, in determining what is obscene and what is not.

In **Miller v. California** (1973), the Supreme Court's last major attempt to clarify constitutional standards governing obscenity, the Court declared that a work—play, film, or book—is obscene and may be regulated by government if (1) the work taken as a whole appeals to prurient interest (prurient means having a tendency to excite lustful thoughts), (2) the work portrays sexual conduct in a patently offensive way, and (3) the work taken as a whole lacks serious literary, artistic, political, or scientific value.[26] Local community standards govern application of the first and second prongs of the *Miller* test.

Recently the Court addressed the standard to be applied to the third prong. Speaking for the majority, Justice Byron White declared that the proper inquiry is not whether an "average" member of any given community would find serious value in material alleged to be obscene but "whether a reasonable person would find such value in the material, taken as a whole."[27] The law often uses the words *reasonable person* to denote a hypothetical person in society who exercises average care, skill, and judgment in conduct. The expectation is that a reasonable person may find serious value in works alleged to be obscene, whereas an average person may not. The decision here was an attempt by the Court to escape the nagging problem of reviewing state court obscenity rulings.

Feminism, free expression, and equality.   Traditionally, civil liberties conflict with demands for social order. However, civil liberties may also be viewed in conflict with demands for equality.

In the 1980s, city officials in Indianapolis, Indiana, influenced by feminist theorists, invoked equality principles to justify legislation restricting freedom of expression.[28] The ordinance focused on pornography and its impact on women's status and treatment. The ordinance banned pornographic material according to the following argument: Government interest in equality outweighs any First Amendment interest in communication. Pornography affects thoughts; it conditions society to subordinate women impermissibly. An ordinance regulating expression will regulate and control the underlying unacceptable conduct.

U.S. District Court judge Sarah Evans Barker, in her first case as a judge, declared the ordinance unconstitutional, stating that it went beyond the categories of unprotected expression (such as child pornography) to suppress otherwise protected expression. Although efforts to restrict behavior that leads to humiliation and degradation of women may be necessary and desirable, "free speech, rather than being the enemy, is a long-tested and worthy ally. To deny free speech in order to engineer social change in the name of accomplishing a greater good for one sector of our society erodes the freedom of all."[29]

Judge Barker thus confronted the trade-off between equality and freedom in a pluralist democracy. Interest groups using the democratic process to carve exceptions to the First Amendment benefit at the expense of everyone's rights.

In this recasting of a freedom-versus-order issue into a freedom-versus-equality framework, Judge Barker's trade-off protected freedom. Her judgment was affirmed by the U.S. Court of Appeals in 1985 and affirmed without argument by the Supreme Court in 1986. Also, in Bellingham, Washington, a similar ordinance was invalidated by a federal district court judge in 1989. However, in the next confrontation—and there will surely be others in a pluralist democracy—equality may prove the victor.

Freedom of the Press

The First Amendment guarantees that government "shall make no law ... abridging the freedom ... of the press." Although the amendment was adopted as a restriction on the national government, the free-press guarantee has been held since 1931 to apply to state and local governments as well.

The ability to collect and report information without government interference was (and still is) thought to be at the core of a free society. The print media continue to use and defend their freedom, which was conferred on them by the framers. The electronic media, however, have had to accept government regulation that stems from the scarcity of broadcast frequencies (see Chapter 4).

Defamation of character.   **Libel** is the written defamation of character.* A person who believes his or her name and character have been harmed by false statements in a publication can institute a lawsuit against the publication and seek monetary compensation for the damage. This kind of lawsuit can impose limits on freedom of expression; at the same time, false statements impinge on the rights of individuals. In a landmark decision in ***New York Times* v. *Sullivan*** (1964), the Supreme Court declared that freedom of the press takes precedence—at least when the defamed individual is a public official.[30] The Court unanimously agreed that the First Amendment protects the publication of all statements, even false ones, about the conduct of public officials except when statements are made with actual malice (with knowledge that they are false or in reckless disregard of their truth or falsity). Citing John Stuart Mill's 1859 treatise *On Liberty*, the Court declared that "even a false statement may be deemed to make a valuable contribution to public debate, since it brings about the clearer perception and livelier impression of truth, produced by its collision with error."

Three years later, the Court extended this protection to include suits brought by any public figures, regardless of whether they are public officials. **Public figures** are people who assume roles of prominence in the affairs of society or who thrust themselves to the forefront of public controversy—including officials, actors, writers, and television personalities. These people must show actual malice on the part of the pub-

---

* Slander is the oral defamation of character. The durability of the written word usually means that libel is a more serious accusation than slander.

lisher that prints false statements about them. Few plaintiffs prevail because the burden of proof is so great.

Prior restraint and the press.   In the United States, freedom of the press has primarily meant immunity from prior restraint, or censorship. The Supreme Court's first encounter with a law imposing prior restraint on a newspaper was in *Near* v. *Minnesota* (1931).[31] Jay Near published a scandal sheet in Minneapolis in which he attacked local officials, charging that they were implicated with gangsters.[32] Minnesota officials obtained an injunction to prevent Near from publishing his newspaper under a state law that allowed such action against periodicals deemed "malicious, scandalous, and defamatory."

The Supreme Court struck down the law, declaring that prior restraint was a special burden on a free press. The need for a vigilant, unrestrained press was expressed forcefully by Chief Justice Charles Evans Hughes: "The fact that the liberty of the press may be abused by miscreant purveyors of scandal does not make any the less necessary the immunity of the press from previous restraint in dealing with official misconduct." The Court recognized that prior restraint might be permissible in exceptional circumstances, but it did not specify those circumstances, nor has it yet done so. Consider the following case, which occurred in a time of war, a period when the tension between government-imposed order and individual freedom is often at a peak.

In 1971, Daniel Ellsberg, a special assistant in the Pentagon, delivered portions of a classified U.S. Department of Defense study to the *New York Times* and the *Washington Post*. By making the documents public, he hoped to discredit the Vietnam War and thereby end it. The highly secret study documented the history of U.S. involvement in the war. The U.S. Department of Justice sought to restrain the *Times* and the *Post* from publishing the documents, contending that publication would prolong the war and embarrass the government. The case was quickly brought before the Supreme Court.

Three days later, in a 6–3 decision in **New York Times v. United States** (1971), the Court concluded that the government had not met the heavy burden of proving that immediate, inevitable, and irreparable harm would follow publication.[33] The majority's view was expressed in a brief, unsigned *per curiam* (Latin for "by the court") opinion, although individual and collective concurring and dissenting views added nine opinions to the decision. Two justices maintained that the First Amendment offered absolute protection against government censorship, no matter what the situation. But the other justices left the door ajar for the imposition of prior restraint in the most extreme and compelling circumstances.

Freedom of expression versus maintaining order.   The courts have consistently held that freedom of the press does not override law enforcement. A Louisville, Kentucky, reporter who had researched and written an article about drug activities was called before a grand jury to identify people he had seen in possession of marijuana or in the act of processing it. The reporter refused to testify, maintaining that freedom of the press shielded him from inquiry. In a closely divided decision, the Supreme Court in 1972 rejected this position.[34] The Court declared that no exception exists to the rule that every citizen has a duty to give his or her government whatever testimony he or she is capable of giving.

The Supreme Court again confronted the conflict between free expression and order in 1988.[35] The principal of a St. Louis high school deleted articles on divorce and teenage pregnancy from the school's newspaper on the ground that the articles invaded the privacy of the students and families that were the focus of the stories. Three student editors filed suit in federal court, claiming that the principal's censorship interfered with the newspaper's function as a public forum, a role protected by the First Amendment. The principal maintained that the newspaper was just an extension of classroom instruction and therefore that it was not protected by the First Amendment.

In a 5–3 decision, the Court upheld the principal's actions in sweeping terms. Educators may limit speech that occurs in the school curriculum and might seem to bear the approval of the school provided their actions serve "any valid educational purpose."

The Right to Peaceable Assembly and Petition

The final clause of the First Amendment states that "Congress shall make no law . . . abridging . . . the right of the people peaceably to assemble, and to petition the Government for a redress of grievances." The right of peaceable assembly stems from the same root as free speech and free press and is held to be equally fundamental. Government cannot prohibit peaceful political meetings and cannot brand as criminals those who organize, lead, and attend such meetings.[36]

The rights of assembly and petition have merged with the guarantees of free speech and a free press under the more general freedom of expression. Having the right to assemble and to petition the government implies having the freedom to express one's thoughts and beliefs.

The clash of interests in cases involving these rights illustrates a continuing effort to define and apply fundamental principles. The concept of freedom has been tempered by the need for order and stability. And when there is a confrontation between freedom and order, the justices of the Supreme Court, who are responsible only to their consciences, strike the balance.

Applying the Bill of Rights to the States

Remember that the major purpose of the Constitution was to structure the division of power between the national government and the state governments. Even before the Constitution was amended, it had set some limits on both the nation and the states with regard to citizens' rights. Both governments were barred from passing **bills of attainder,** laws that make an individual guilty of a crime without a trial. They were also prohibited from enacting **ex post facto laws,** laws that declare an action a crime after it has been performed. And both nation and states were barred from impairing (and where necessary were required to enforce) the **obligation of contracts,** the obligation of the parties in a contract to carry out its terms.

Although initially the Bill of Rights seemed to apply only to the national government, various litigants pressed the claim that its guarantees reached beyond the national government to the states. In response to one such claim, Chief Justice John Marshall affirmed what seemed plain from the Constitution's language and "the history of the day" (the events surrounding the Constitutional Convention): The provisions of the Bill of Rights served only to limit national authority. "Had the framers of these amendments intended them to be limitations on the powers of the state governments," wrote Marshall, "they would have . . . expressed that intention."[37]

Change came with the Fourteenth Amendment, which was adopted in 1868. The due process clause of that amendment is the linchpin that holds the states to the provisions of the Bill of Rights.

The Fourteenth Amendment: Due Process of Law

All persons born or naturalized in the United States, and subject to the jurisdiction thereof, are citizens of the United States and of the State wherein they reside. No State shall make or enforce any law which shall abridge the privileges or immunities of citizens of the United States; nor shall any State deprive any person of life, liberty, or property, without due process of law.

Most freedoms protected in the Bill of Rights today apply as limitations on the states. And many of the standards that limit the national government serve equally to limit state governments. These changes have been achieved through the Supreme Court's interpretation of the due process clause of the Fourteenth Amendment: "Nor shall any State deprive any person of life, liberty, or property, without due process of law." Think of the due process clause as a sponge absorbing or incorporating the specifics of the Bill of Rights and spreading or applying them to the states.

The Fundamental Freedoms

In 1897, the Supreme Court declared that the states are limited by the Fifth Amendment's prohibition on taking of private property without just compensation.[38] The Court accomplished its goal by absorbing that prohibition into the due process clause of the Fourteenth Amendment, which applies to the states. Now one Bill of Rights protection—but only

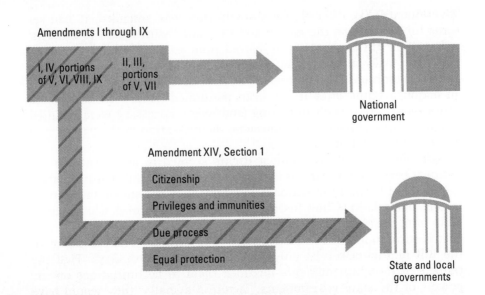

Amendments I through IX

I, IV, portions of V, VI, VIII, IX

II, III, portions of V, VII

National government

Amendment XIV, Section 1

Citizenship

Privileges and immunities

Due process

Equal protection

State and local governments

FIGURE 12.1   The Incorporation of the Bill of Rights
The Supreme Court has used the due process clause of the Fourteenth Amendment as a sponge, absorbing many—but not all—of the provisions in the Bill of Rights and applying them to state and local governments. All of the provisions in the Bill of Rights apply to the national government.

that one—limited both the states and the national government (see Figure 12.1).

The inclusion of other Bill of Rights guarantees within the due process clause faced a critical test in **Palko v. Connecticut** (1937).[39] Frank Palko had been charged with first-degree murder. He was convicted instead of second-degree murder and sentenced to life imprisonment. The state of Connecticut appealed and won a new trial; this time Palko was found guilty of first-degree murder and sentenced to death. Palko appealed the second conviction on the ground that it violated the protection against double jeopardy guaranteed to him by the Fifth Amendment. This protection applied to the states, he contended, because of the Fourteenth Amendment's due process clause.

The Supreme Court upheld Palko's second conviction. In his opinion for the majority, Justice Benjamin N. Cardozo formulated principles that were to direct the Court's actions for the next three decades. He noted that some Bill of Rights guarantees—such as freedom of thought and speech—are fundamental and that these fundamental rights are absorbed by the Fourteenth Amendment's due process clause and are applicable to the states. These rights are essential, argued Cardozo, because "neither liberty nor justice would exist if they were sacrificed." Trial by jury and other rights, although valuable and important, are not essential to liberty and justice and therefore are not absorbed by the due process clause. "Few would be so narrow or provincial," Cardozo claimed, "as to maintain that a fair and enlightened system of justice" would be impossible without these other rights. In other words, only some provisions of the Bill of Rights—the "fundamental" provisions—were absorbed into the due process clause and made applicable to the states. Because protection against double jeopardy was not one of them, Palko died in Connecticut's gas chamber in April 1938.

The next thirty years constituted a period of slow but perceptible change in the standard for determining whether a Bill of Rights guarantee was fundamental. The reference point was transformed from the idealized "fair and enlightened system of justice" in *Palko* to the more realistic "American scheme of justice" outlined in the decision in *Duncan* v. *Louisiana* (1968).[40] In case after case, as guarantees were tested they were found to be fundamental. By 1969, when *Palko* finally was overturned, most of the Bill of Rights guarantees had been found applicable to the states (see Table 12.1).

Criminal Procedure: The Meaning of Constitutional Guarantees

"The history of liberty," remarked Justice Frankfurter, "has largely been the history of observance of procedural safeguards."[41] The safeguards embodied in the Fourth through Eighth Amendments to the Constitution specify how government must behave in criminal proceedings. Their application to the states has reshaped American criminal justice in the last thirty years.

That application has come in two steps: The first step requires the judgment that a guarantee asserted in the Bill of Rights also applies to the states. The second step requires that the judiciary give specific meaning to the guarantee. The courts cannot allow the states to define guarantees themselves without risking different definitions from state to state and corresponding differences among citizens' rights. If the rights are fundamental, their meaning cannot vary.

But life is not quite so simple under the U.S. Constitution. The concept of federalism is sewn into the constitutional fabric, and the Supreme Court recognizes that there may be more than one way to prosecute the accused while heeding fundamental rights.

Consider, for example, the right to a jury trial in criminal cases, which is guaranteed by the Sixth Amendment. This right was made obligatory on the states in *Duncan* v. *Louisiana* (1968). The Supreme Court later held that the right applied to all nonpetty criminal cases—those in which the penalty for conviction was more than six months' imprisonment.[42] But the Court did not require that state juries have twelve members, the number required for federal criminal proceedings. Jury size was permitted to vary from state to state, although the

Table 12.1   Cases Applying the Bill of Rights to the States ▬▬

Amendment	Case	Date
1. Congress shall make no law respecting an establishment of religion,	*Everson* v. *Board of Education*	1947
or prohibiting the free exercise thereof;	*Cantwell* v. *Connecticut*	1940
or abridging the freedom of speech,	*Gitlow* v. *New York*	1925
or of the press;	*Near* v. *Minnesota*	1931
or the right of the people peaceably to assemble,	*DeJonge* v. *Oregon*	1937
and to petition the government for a redress of grievances.	*DeJonge* v. *Oregon*	1937
2. A well-regulated militia being necessary to the security of a free State, the right of the people to keep and bear arms shall not be infringed.		
3. No soldier shall, in time of peace, be quartered in any house without the consent of the owner, nor in time of war, but in a manner to be prescribed by law.		
4. The right of the people to be secure in their persons, houses, papers, and effects, against unreasonable searches and seizures, shall not be violated,	*Wolf* v. *Colorado*	1949
and no warrants shall issue but upon probable cause, supported by oath or affirmation, and particularly describing the place to be searched, and the persons or things to be seized.	*Aguilar* v. *Texas*	1964
5. No person shall be held to answer for a capital, or otherwise infamous crime, unless on a presentment or indictment of a grand jury, except in cases arising in the land or naval forces, or in the militia, when in actual service in time of war or public danger;		
nor shall any person be subject for the same offense to be twice put in jeopardy of life or limb;	*Benton* v. *Maryland*	1969
nor shall be compelled in any criminal case to be a witness against himself,	*Malloy* v. *Hogan*	1964
nor be deprived of life, liberty, or property, without due process of law;		
nor shall private property be taken for public use without just compensation.	*Chicago B.&Q.R.* v. *Chicago*	1897

(continued)

▬▬▬▬▬▬▬▬▬▬▬▬▬▬▬▬▬▬▬▬▬▬

minimum number was set at six. Furthermore, the federal requirement of a unanimous jury verdict was not imposed on the states.

Table 12.1   (Continued) ━━━━━━

Amendment	Case	Date
6. In all criminal prosecutions, the accused shall enjoy the right to a speedy	*Klopfer* v. *North Carolina*	1967
and public trial,	*In re Oliver*	1948
by an impartial	*Parker* v. *Gladden*	1966
jury	*Duncan* v. *Louisiana*	1968
of the State and district wherein the crime shall have been committed, which district shall have been previously ascertained by law,		
and to be informed of the nature and cause of the accusation;	*Lanzetta* v. *New Jersey*	1939
to be confronted with the witnesses against him;	*Pointer* v. *Texas*	1965
to have compulsory process for obtaining witnesses in his favor,	*Washington* v. *Texas*	1967
and to have the assistance of counsel for his defence.	*Gideon* v. *Wainwright*	1963
7. In suits at common law, where the value of the controversy shall exceed twenty dollars, the right of trial by jury shall be preserved, and no fact tried by a jury shall be otherwise reexamined in any court of the United States, than according to the rules of the common law.		
8. Excessive bail shall not be required, nor excess fines imposed,		
nor cruel and unusual punishments inflicted.	*Robinson* v. *California*	1962
9. The enumeration in the Constitution, of certain rights, shall not be construed to deny or disparage others retained by the people.	*Griswold* v. *Connecticut*	1965

In contrast, the Court left no room for variation in its definition of the fundamental right to an attorney, also guaranteed by the Sixth Amendment. Clarence Earl Gideon was a penniless vagrant accused of breaking into and robbing a pool hall. Because Gideon could not afford a lawyer, he asked the state to provide him with legal counsel. The state refused, and Gideon was subsequently convicted and sentenced to five years in the Florida State Penitentiary. From his cell, Gideon appealed to the U.S. Supreme Court, claiming that his conviction should be struck down because his Sixth Amendment right to counsel had been denied. (Gideon was also without counsel in this appeal; he filed a hand-lettered "pauper's petition" with the Court after studying law texts in the prison library. When the Court agreed to consider his case, he was assigned a prominent Washington attorney, Abe Fortas, who later became a Supreme Court justice.)[43]

In its landmark decision in **Gideon v. Wainwright** (1963), the Court set aside Gideon's conviction and extended to the states the Sixth Amendment right to counsel.[44] Gideon was retried, but this time, with the assistance of a lawyer, he was found not guilty. In subsequent rulings that stretched over more than a decade, the Court specified at what points a defendant was entitled to a lawyer in the course of criminal proceedings (from arrest to trial, appeal, and beyond).

During this period, the Court also came to grips with another issue involving procedural safeguards: informing suspects of their constitutional rights. Ernesto Miranda was arrested in Arizona for kidnapping and raping an eighteen-year-old woman. After the police questioned him for two hours and the woman identified him, Miranda confessed to the crime. He was convicted in an Arizona court on the basis of that confession—although he had not been told that he had the right to counsel and the right not to incriminate himself. Miranda appealed his conviction, which was overturned by the Supreme Court in 1966.[45]

The Court based its decision in *Miranda* v. *Arizona* on the Fifth Amendment privilege against self-incrimination. According to the Court, the police had forced Miranda to confess during in-custody questioning, not with physical force, but with the coercion inherent in custodial interrogation. Warnings were required, the Court argued, to dispel that coercion. Warnings were not necessary if a person was only in custody or if a person was only subject to questioning without arrest. But the combination of custody and interrogation was sufficiently intimidating to require warnings before questioning. These statements are known today as the **Miranda warnings.** Among them:

- You have the right to remain silent.
- Anything you say can be used against you in court.
- You have the right to talk to a lawyer of your own choice before questioning.
- If you cannot afford to hire a lawyer, a lawyer will be provided without charge.

The Fourth Amendment guarantees "the right of the people to be secure in their persons, houses, papers, and effects, against unreasonable searches and seizures." This right was made applicable to the states in *Wolf* v. *Colorado* (1949).[46] But although the Court found that protection from illegal searches by state and local government was a fundamental right, it refused to apply to the states the **exclusionary rule** that evidence obtained from an illegal search and seizure could not be used in a trial. Without that rule the protection was meaningless.

The justices considered the exclusionary rule again in **Mapp v. Ohio** (1961).[47] Dolree Mapp had been convicted of possessing obscene materials after an admittedly illegal search of her home for a fugitive. She appealed her conviction to the U.S. Supreme Court. In a 6–3 decision, the justices declared that "all evidence obtained by searches and seizures in violation of the Constitution is, by [the Fourth Amendment], inadmissible in a state court." The decision was historic. It placed the exclusionary rule within the confines of the Fourth Amendment and required all levels of government to operate according to the provisions of that amendment.

The struggle over the exclusionary rule took a new turn in 1984 when the Court reviewed *United States* v. *Leon.*[48] In this case, a judge had issued a search warrant without "probable cause" having been firmly established. The police, relying on the warrant, discovered large quantities of illegal drugs. The Court, by a vote of 6–3, established the **good faith exception** to the exclusionary rule. The justices held that evidence seized on the basis of a mistakenly issued search warrant *could* be introduced at trial. The exclusionary rule, argued the majority, was, not a right, but a remedy justified by its ability to deter illegal police conduct. Such a deterrent effect was not a factor in Leon: The police had acted in good faith. Hence, the Court decided, there was a need for an exception to the rule.

The exclusionary rule continues to divide the Supreme Court. In 1990, the justices again reaffirmed the rule, but by a bare 5–4 majority.[49] Since that time two additional conservative justices—Souter and Thomas—have been added to the Court.

The Ninth Amendment and Personal Autonomy

The enumeration in the Constitution, of certain rights, shall not be construed to deny or disparage others retained by the people.

The wording of the Ninth Amendment and its history remain an enigma. The evidence supports two different views. The amendment may protect rights that are not enumerated, or it may simply protect state governments against the assumption of power by the national government.[50] The meaning of the amendment was not an issue until 1965 when the Supreme Court used it to protect privacy, a right that is not enumerated in the Constitution.

Controversy: From Privacy to Abortion

In *Griswold* **v.** *Connecticut* (1965), the Court struck down, by a vote of 7 to 2, a seldom-used Connecticut statute that made the use of birth control devices a crime.[51] Justice William O. Douglas, writing for the majority, asserted that the "specific guarantees in the Bill of Rights have penumbras [areas of partial illumination]" that give "life and substance" to broad, unspecified protections in the Bill of Rights. Several specific guarantees in the First, Third, Fourth, and Fifth Amendments create a zone of privacy, Douglas argued, and this zone is protected by the Ninth Amendment and is applicable to the states by the due process clause of the Fourteenth Amendment.

Griswold established a zone of personal autonomy, protected by the Constitution, that was the basis for a suit to invalidate state antiabortion laws. In **Roe v. Wade** (1973), the Court in a 7 to 2 decision declared unconstitutional a Texas law making it a crime to obtain an abortion except for the purpose of saving the mother's life.[52] Justice Harry A. Blackmun, who authored the majority opinion, based the decision on the right to privacy protected by the due process clause of the Fourteenth Amendment. The Court declared that in the first three months of pregnancy, the abortion decision must be left to the woman and her physician. In the interest of protecting the mother's health, states may restrict but not prohibit abortions in the second three months of pregnancy. In the last three months of pregnancy, states may regulate or even prohibit abortions to protect the life of the fetus except when medical judgment determines that an abortion is necessary to save the mother's life. In all, the laws of forty-six states were affected by the Court's ruling.

The dissenters—Justices White and Rehnquist—were quick to point out what critics have frequently repeated since the decision: The Court's judgment was directed by its own dislikes, not by any constitutional compass. In the absence of guiding principles, they asserted, the majority justices simply substituted their views for the views of the state legislatures whose abortion regulations they invalidated.[53]

The composition of the Court shifted under President Ronald Reagan. His elevation of William Rehnquist to chief justice in 1986 and his appointments of Antonin Scalia in 1986 and Anthony Kennedy in 1988 raised new hope among abortion foes and old fears among abortion advocates.

A perceptible shift away from abortion rights materialized in **Webster v. Reproductive Health Services** (1989). In *Webster*, the Court upheld the constitutionality of a Missouri law that denied the use of public employees or publicly funded facilities in the performance of an abortion unless the mother's life was in danger. Furthermore, doctors were required to perform tests to determine whether fetuses twenty weeks and older could survive outside the womb. This was the first time that the Court upheld significant government restrictions on abortion.

The Court has since moved cautiously down the road toward greater government control of abortion policy. In 1990, the justices upheld two state parental notification laws. Then, in **Planned Parenthood v. Casey** (1992) a new coalition—forged by Reagan and Bush appointees O'Connor, Souter, and Kennedy—held that "the essential holdings of *Roe v. Wade* should be retained and once again affirmed." However, the Court upheld as constitutional elements of Pennsylvania's abortion law that placed additional restrictions on abortions. The test applied by the Court in determining the line between the state's "legitimate interests" in "protecting the life of the fetus" and a woman's rights was whether restrictions imposed "an undue burden" on a woman's ability to choose an abortion.[54] The Court remains deeply and bitterly divided on abortion.

Abortion pits freedom versus order. The decision to bear or beget children should be free from government control. Yet government has a legitimate interest in protecting and preserving life, including fetal life, as part of its responsibility to maintain an orderly society. Rather than make a clear choice between freedom and order, the majority on the Court has withdrawn the constitutional protection shrouding abortion rights and cast the politically divisive issue into the state legislative process, where elected representatives can thrash out the conflict.

Personal Autonomy and Sexual Orientation

The right-to-privacy cases may have opened a Pandora's box of divisive social issues. Does the right to privacy embrace private homosexual acts between consenting adults? Consider the case of Michael Hardwick, who was arrested in 1982 in his Atlanta bedroom while having sex with a man. In a standard approach to prosecuting homosexuals, he was charged under a state criminal statute with the crime of sodomy, which means any oral or anal intercourse. Hardwick sued to challenge the law's constitutionality. He won in the lower courts. However, in a bitterly divided ruling in 1986, the Supreme Court held in **Bowers** v. **Hardwick** that the Constitution does not protect homosexual relations between consenting adults, even in the privacy of their own homes.[55]

The appointments of conservative Associate Justices Anthony Kennedy, David Souter, and Clarence Thomas have halted the march toward increased personal freedom. A new concern for social order—for established patterns of authority—is evident.

Most likely, the direction toward personal autonomy will shift to the states, where groups can continue to assert their political power. The pluralist model, then, gives us one solution to dissatisfaction with Court rulings. If state legislatures can enact laws making certain acts punishable, then they can also repeal those laws. State courts also provide an avenue for change. The supreme courts of Kentucky, New York, and Pennsylvania each ruled that antisodomy laws violate privacy rights. Similar rulings were reached by lower courts in Michigan and Texas.

The Civil War Amendments

The Civil War amendments were adopted to provide freedom and equality to black Americans. The Thirteenth Amendment, which was ratified in 1865, provided the freedom: "Neither slavery nor involuntary servitude . . . shall exist within the United States, or any place subject to their jurisdiction." The Fourteenth Amendment was adopted three years later. It provided first that freed slaves were citizens: "All persons born or naturalized in the United States, and subject to the jurisdiction thereof, are citizens of the United States and of the State wherein they reside." Next, it prohibited the states from abridging the "privileges or immunities of citizens of the United States" or from depriving "any person of life, liberty, or property, without due process of law." The amendment then went on to protect equality under the law, declaring that no state could "deny to any person within its jurisdiction the equal protection of the laws." The Fifteenth Amendment, adopted in 1870, added a measure of political equality: "The right of citizens of the United States to vote shall not be denied or abridged by the United States or by any State on account of race, color, or previous condition of servitude."

American blacks were free and politically equal—at least according to the Constitution. But it would be many years before these constitutional rights were protected.

Congress and the Supreme Court: Lawmaking Versus Law Interpreting

In the years following the Civil War, Congress went to work to protect the rights of black citizens. In 1866, lawmakers passed a civil rights act that granted all citizens—white and black—the right to make and enforce contracts, sue or be sued, give evidence, and inherit, purchase, lease, sell, hold, or convey property. Later, in the Civil Rights Act of 1875, Congress attempted to guarantee blacks equal access to public accommodations (streetcars, inns, parks, theaters).

While Congress was passing laws to protect the civil rights of black citizens, the Supreme Court seemed intent on weakening those rights. In 1873, the Court ruled that the Civil War amendments had not changed the relationship between the state and national governments. In other words, state citizenship and national citizenship remained separate and distinct; the Fourteenth Amendment did not enlarge the rights guaranteed by U.S. citizenship. In effect, the Court stripped the amendment of its power to secure the Bill of Rights guarantees for black citizens.

In 1883, the Court struck down the public accommodations section of the Civil Rights Act of 1875.[56] The justices declared that the national government could prohibit only government action (also known as *state action*) discriminating against blacks; private acts of discrimination or acts of omission by a state were beyond the reach of the national government.

In case after case, the Court refused to see racial discrimination as a badge of slavery that the national government could prohibit. By tolerating racial discrimination, the justices abetted **racism,** a belief that inherent differences among races determine achievement and that one's own race is superior to and has a right to rule others.

The Court's decisions gave the states ample room to maneuver around civil rights laws. In the matter of voting rights, for example, states that wanted to bar black men from the polls simply used nonracial means to do so. One popular tool was the **poll tax,** first imposed by Georgia in 1877. This was a tax of $1 or $2 on every citizen who wanted to vote. The tax was not a burden for most whites. But many blacks were tenant farmers who did not have any extra money for voting. Other bars to black suffrage included literacy tests, minimum education requirements, and a grandfather clause that offered voter eligibility to those who could establish that their grandfather was eligible to vote before 1867 (three years before the Fifteenth Amendment declared that race could not be used to deny the right to vote).[57] Intimidation and violence were also used to keep blacks from the polls.

The Roots of Racial Segregation

Well before the Civil War, **racial segregation** was a way of life in the South: Blacks lived and worked separately from whites. After the war, southern states began to enact Jim Crow laws that *enforced* segregation. (*Jim Crow* is a derogatory term for a black person.) Once the Supreme Court nullified the Civil Rights Act of 1875, these kinds of laws proliferated. Blacks were required to live in separate and generally inferior areas; they were restricted to separate and inferior sections of hospitals, cemeteries, streetcars, and so forth. Each day in countless ways they were reminded of the inferior status accorded them by white society.

In 1892, Homer Adolph Plessy—who was seven-eighths Caucasian— took a seat in a "whites-only" car of a Louisiana train. He refused to move to the car reserved for blacks and was arrested. Plessy argued that Louisiana's law mandating racial segregation on its trains was an unconstitutional infringement on both the privileges and immunities and the equal protection clauses of the Fourteenth Amendment. The Supreme Court disagreed. The majority in **Plessy v. Ferguson** (1896) upheld state-imposed racial segregation.[58] They based their decision on the **separate-but-equal doctrine,** which held that separate facilities for blacks and whites satisfied the Fourteenth Amendment as long as those facilities were equal. The lone dissenter, John Marshall Harlan, who envisioned a "color-blind Constitution," wrote:

> We boast of the freedom enjoyed by our people above all other peoples. But it is difficult to reconcile that boast with a state of the law which, practically, puts the brand of servitude and degradation upon a large class of our fellow citizens—our equals before the law. The thin disguise of "equal" accommodations for passengers in railroad coaches will not mislead any one, nor atone for the wrong this day done.

Three years later, the Supreme Court extended the separate-but-equal doctrine to schools.[59] The justices ignored the fact that black educational facilities (and most other "colored-only" facilities) were far from equal to those reserved for whites.

By the end of the nineteenth century, racial segregation had been firmly and legally entrenched in the American South. Although constitutional amendments and national laws to protect equality under the law were in place, the Supreme Court's interpretation of those amendments and laws limited their effectiveness. Several decades would pass before there was any discernible change.

The Dismantling of School Segregation

By the middle of the twentieth century, public attitudes toward race relations were slowly changing. Black troops had fought with honor—albeit in segregated military units—in World War II. Blacks and whites were working together in unions and in service and religious organizations. Government-imposed segregation was assailable.

President Harry S Truman risked his political future with his strong support of black civil rights. In 1947, he established the President's Committee on Civil Rights. The committee's report, issued later that year, became the agenda for the civil rights movement over the next two decades. It called for national laws prohibiting racially motivated brutality, segregation, and poll taxes and for guarantees of voting rights and equal employment opportunity. In 1948, Truman ordered the **desegregation** (the end of authorized racial segregation) of the armed forces.

In 1947, the U.S. Department of Justice had begun to submit briefs to the courts in support of civil rights. Perhaps the department's most important intervention was in **Brown v. Board of Education** (1954).[60] This case was the culmination of twenty years of planning and litigation on the part of the National Association for the Advancement of Colored People to invalidate racial segregation in schools.

Linda Brown was a black child whose father tried to enroll her in a white public school in Topeka, Kansas. Brown's request was refused because of Linda's race. A federal district court found that the black public school was in all major respects equal in quality to the white school; therefore, by the *Plessy* doctrine, Linda was required to go to the black public school. Brown appealed the decision.

Brown v. *Board of Education* reached the Supreme Court in November 1951. The justices delayed argument on the sensitive race issue, placing it beyond the 1952 national election. The Court merged *Brown* with four similar cases. Each case was brought as a class action (see Chapter 11). And all were supported by the NAACP and coordinated by Thurgood Marshall, who would later become the first black justice to sit on the Supreme Court.

These five cases squarely challenged the separate-but-equal doctrine. By all tangible measures (standards for teacher licensing, teacher-pupil ratios, library facilities), the two school systems in each case—one white, the other black—were equal. The issue was legal separation of the races.

The cases were argued in late 1952, but they were set for reargument at the request of the justices. The sudden death of Chief Justice Fred M. Vinson in September 1953 added further delay. On May 17, 1954, Chief Justice Earl Warren, who had joined the Court as Vinson's replacement, delivered a single opinion covering four of the cases. Warren spoke for a unanimous Court when he declared that "in the field of public education the doctrine of 'separate but equal' has no place. Separate educational facilities are inherently unequal, depriving the plaintiffs of the equal protection of the laws." Segregated facilities generated in black children "a feeling of inferiority . . . that may affect their hearts and minds in a way unlikely ever to be undone." State-imposed public school segregation was found to violate the equal protection clause of the Fourteenth Amendment.

The Court deferred implementation of the school desegregation decisions until 1955. Then, in **Brown v. Board of Education II** (1955), it ruled that school systems had to desegregate "with all deliberate speed" and placed the process of desegregation under the direction of the lower federal courts.[61]

Some states quietly implemented the Brown decree. Others did little to desegregate their schools. And many communities in the South defied the Court, sometimes violently. This resistance, along with the Supreme Court's "all deliberate speed" order, placed a heavy burden on federal judges to dismantle what were by now fundamental social institutions in many communities.[62] Gradual desegregation under *Brown* was in some cases no desegregation at all. In 1969, a unanimous Supreme Court ordered that the operation of segregated school systems stop "at once."[63]

Two years later, the Court approved several remedies to achieve integration, including busing, racial quotas, and the pairing or grouping of noncontiguous school zones. But these remedies applied only to **de jure segregation,** government-imposed segregation (for example, government assignment of whites to one school and blacks to another within the same community). Court-imposed remedies did not apply to **de facto segregation,** segregation that was not the result of government influence (for example, racial segregation resulting from residential patterns).

Public opinion strongly opposed the busing approach, and Congress sought limits on busing as a remedy. In 1974, a closely divided Court ruled in **Milliken v. Bradley** that lower courts could not order busing across school district boundaries to achieve racial balance unless each district had practiced racial discrimination or unless school district lines had been drawn to achieve racial segregation.[64]

The Civil Rights Movement

Although the NAACP concentrated on school desegregation, it also made headway in other areas. The Supreme Court responded to the NAACP's efforts of the middle to late 1940s by outlawing the whites-only primary elections that were being held in the South, declaring them to be in violation of the Fifteenth Amendment. The Court also declared segregation on interstate bus routes and segregated restaurants and hotels in the District of Columbia to be unconstitutional. Despite these and other decisions that chipped away at existing barriers to equality, the realization of equality would require the political mobilization of people of all colors into what is now known as the **civil rights movement.**

Civil Disobedience

The call to action was first sounded by Rosa Parks, a black woman living in Montgomery, Alabama. That city's Jim Crow ordinances required blacks to sit in the back of the bus and empowered drivers to order blacks to vacate an entire row to make room for one white or to stand even when there were vacant seats. In December 1955, tired after the day's work, Parks took an available seat in the front of the bus; she refused to give up her seat when asked to do so by the driver and was arrested and fined $10 for violating the city ordinance.

Under the leadership of a charismatic twenty-six-year-old Baptist minister named Martin Luther King, Jr., Montgomery's black community responded to Parks's arrest with a boycott of the city's bus system. A **boycott** is a refusal to do business with a firm or individual as an expression of disapproval or as a means of coercion. A year after the boycott began, the federal courts ruled that segregated transportation systems violated the equal protection clause of the Constitution.

In 1957, King helped organize the Southern Christian Leadership Conference (SCLC) to coordinate civil rights activities. He was totally committed to nonviolent action to bring racial issues into the light. To that end, he advocated **civil disobedience,** the willful but nonviolent violation of unjust laws.

Martin Luther King, Jr. had risen to worldwide prominence by August 1963 when he organized and led a march on Washington, D.C., to show support for the civil rights movement. More than 250,000 people, black and white, gathered peaceably at the Lincoln Memorial to hear King speak. "I have a dream," he told them, "that my little children will one day live in a nation where they will not be judged by the color of their skin but by the content of their character"[65] (see Feature 12.1).

The Civil Rights Act of 1964

President Lyndon B. Johnson considered civil rights his top legislative priority. Within months after he assumed office, Congress passed the

Feature 12.1

A Preacher's Afterthought: A Dream of Freedom from Inequality

The Rev. Martin Luther King, Jr., gave Americans a vision of a society free from racial inequality in his famous "I Have a Dream" speech. But King's most memorable lines on the steps of the Lincoln Memorial in Washington, D.C., were not part of his prepared text. King ad-libbed.

King was the last speaker that day in Washington. He recited his prepared text until shortly near the end, when he decided not to deliver what one historian has labeled the lamest and most pretentious section. ("And so today, let us go back to our communities as members of the international association for the advancement of creative dissatisfaction.") Instead, he extemporized, urging his audience to believe that change would come "somehow" and that they could not "wallow in the valley of despair."

Voices from behind urged King on. Mahalia Jackson, the great gospel singer, added her voice: "Tell 'em about the dream, Martin." The dream device was one King had used in the past, in speeches and at the pulpit. It's not clear whether he heard Jackson's words or simply reached instinctively for a familiar and effective piece of oratory.

After the powerful "dream" sequence, King returned to a few sentences from his prepared text. But then he was off on his own again, reciting the first stanza from "My Country 'Tis of Thee," ending with "'let freedom ring.'" King continued: "And if America is to be a great nation, this must become true. So let freedom ring." King concluded with an old vision from the pulpit, born of enslavement but new to a world now riveted to his words: "And when this happens . . . we will be able to speed up that day when all God's children, black men and white men, Jews and Gentiles, Protestants and Catholics, will be able to join hands and sing in the words of the old Negro spiritual, 'Free at last! Free at last! Thank God Almighty, we are free at last!'"

From *Parting the Waters* by Taylor Branch. Copyright © 1988 by Taylor Branch. Reprinted by permission of Simon & Schuster, Inc.

Civil Rights Act of 1964, the most comprehensive legislative attempt ever to erase racial discrimination in the United States. Among its many provisions, the act

- Entitled all persons to "the full and equal enjoyment" of goods, services, and privileges in places of public accommodation without discrimination on the ground of race, color, religion, or national origin
- Established the right to equality in employment opportunities
- Strengthened voting rights legislation

A Modern-Day Moses
*Martin Luther King, Jr., was a Baptist minister who believed in the principles
of nonviolent protest practiced by India's Mahatma Gandhi. This photograph,
taken in 1963 in Baltimore, captures the crowd's affection for King, the man
many thought would lead the way to a new Canaan of racial equality. King,
who won the Nobel Peace Prize in 1964, was assassinated in 1968 in Memphis,
Tennessee.*

- Created the Equal Employment Opportunity Commission (EEOC),
  charging it to hear and investigate complaints of job discrimination*
- Provided that funds be withheld from federally assisted programs
  that were administered in a discriminatory manner.

Johnson's goal was a "Great Society." Soon a constitutional amendment and a series of civil rights laws were in place to help him meet his
goal.

- The Twenty-fourth Amendment, ratified in 1964, banned poll taxes
  in primary and general elections for national office.
- The Economic Opportunity Act of 1964 focused on education and
  training to combat poverty.

---

* Since 1972, the EEOC has had the power to institute legal proceedings on behalf of employees who allege that they have been victims of illegal discrimination.

- The Voting Rights Act of 1965 empowered the attorney general to send voter registration supervisors to areas in which fewer than half the eligible minority voters had been registered. This act has been credited with doubling black voter registration in the South in only five years.[66]

- The Fair Housing Act of 1968 banned discrimination in the rental or sale of most housing.

Restoration and Restriction

Civil rights on the books, however, do not ensure civil rights in action. Although Congress has tried to restore and expand civil rights enforcement, in recent years the Supreme Court has appeared to dismantle or confine it again. In a series of startling 5–4 decisions in 1989, the justices voted to limit the reach of longstanding civil rights decisions. The Court held that:

- Past societal discrimination alone could not serve as the basis for rigid racial quotas.[67]

- Affirmative action plan promotion decisions that favored African-Americans could be challenged years later by the affected whites who were not parties to the plan.[68]

- The burden of proving allegations of discrimination in hiring and promotion should shift from the employer to the employee, making it more difficult for plaintiffs to win.[69]

- An 1866 law that had been used by minorities to sue for private acts of discrimination barred discrimination only at the initial hiring stage, not on the job.[70]

These decisions (and others) signaled the ascendance of a new conservative majority more concerned with freedom than equality. Since the issues hinged on the Court's interpretation of federal law, civil rights advocates turned to Congress to restore, and perhaps enlarge, the earlier decisions by writing them into law. The result was a new civil rights bill. President Bush vetoed a 1990 version, asserting that it would force quotas in hiring and promotion. But a year later he approved a similar bill. The Civil Rights Act of 1991 will likely result in more awards for women and the disabled who sue for deliberate job bias and sexual harassment.

Civil Rights for Other Minorities

The civil rights won by black Americans apply to all Americans. Recent civil rights laws and court decisions protect members of all minority groups.

The Supreme Court underscored the breadth of this protection in an important decision in 1987.[71] The justices ruled unanimously that the

Civil Rights Act of 1866 (known today as Section 1981) offered broad protection against discrimination to all minorities. Heretofore, the law could not be invoked by members of white ethnic groups in bias suits. Under the decision, members of *any* ethnic group—Italian, Iranian, Norwegian, or Chinese, for example—can recover money damages if they prove they have been denied jobs, excluded from rental housing, or subjected to other forms of discrimination prohibited by the law. The 1964 Civil Rights Act offers similar protections to these ethnic groups, but the 1964 act has strict procedures for filing suits. These procedures tend to discourage litigation. Moreover, the remedies in most cases are limited. In job discrimination, for example, back pay and reinstatement are the only remedies. Section 1981 has fewer pitfalls and allows litigants to seek *punitive damages* (damages awarded by a court as additional punishment for a serious wrong).

Clearly the civil rights movement has had an impact on all minorities. Here we examine the civil rights struggles of three groups—Native Americans, Hispanic-Americans, and disabled Americans.

Native Americans

In 1924, Indians were finally given U.S. citizenship. Until that time, they were considered members of tribal nations whose relations with government were subject to treaties made with the United States. The agency system for administering Indian reservations kept Native Americans poor and dependent on the national government. And Indian lands continued to shrink through the 1950s and into the 1960s—in spite of signed treaties and the religious significance of portions of those lands.

Anger bred of poverty, unemployment, and frustration with an uncaring government exploded into militant action in November 1969 when several American Indians seized Alcatraz Island, an abandoned island in San Francisco Bay. The group cited an 1868 Sioux treaty that entitled them to unused federal lands; they remained on the island for a year and a half. In 1973, armed members of the American Indian Movement seized eleven hostages at Wounded Knee, South Dakota—the site of a tragic battle in 1890 between the Sioux and U.S. cavalry troops. They remained there, occasionally exchanging gunfire with federal marshals, for seventy-one days.

In 1946, Congress had passed legislation establishing an Indian claims commission to compensate Native Americans for land that had been taken from them. In the 1970s, the Native American Rights Fund and other groups used that legislation to win important victories. Lands were returned to tribes in the Midwest and in the states of Oklahoma, New Mexico, and Washington. In 1980, the Supreme Court ordered the national government to pay the Sioux $117 million plus interest for the Black Hills of South Dakota, which had been stolen from them a century before. Other cases involving land from coast to coast are still

Bury My Heart
Native American mourners gathered at Wounded Knee, South Dakota, on December 29, 1990, to remember a tragedy. On that site a hundred years earlier, two hundred Sioux—including women and children—were killed by Seventh Cavalry soldiers. Descendants of the survivors traveled by foot and horseback to mark the anniversary and honor their heritage.

pending. Litigation on behalf of Native Americans may prove to be their most effective weapon in the march toward equality.

Hispanic-Americans

Many Hispanic-Americans have a rich and deep-rooted heritage in America, but until the 1920s, that heritage was largely confined to the southwestern states and California. Then large numbers of Mexican and Puerto Rican immigrants came to the United States in search of employment and a better life. Like blacks who had migrated to northern cities, most of these immigrants found poverty and discrimination.

World War II gave rise to another influx of Mexicans, who this time were courted to work farms primarily in California. But by the late 1950s, most farm workers—whatever their race—were living in poverty. Those Hispanic-Americans who lived in cities fared little better. Yet millions of Mexicans continued to cross the border into the United States, both legally and illegally. The effect was to depress the value of farm labor in California and the Southwest.

The Hispanic-American population continues to grow. The 20 million Hispanics living in the United States in the 1970s were still mainly

Puerto Rican and Mexican-American, but they were joined by immigrants from the Dominican Republic, Colombia, Cuba, Ecuador, and elsewhere. Although civil rights legislation has helped them to an extent, they are among the poorest and least-educated groups in the United States.

Voter registration and voter turnout among Hispanics are lower than among other groups. With few or no Spanish-speaking voting officials, low registration levels may be inevitable. Voter turnout, in turn, depends on effective political advertising, and Hispanics are not targeted as often as other groups with political messages that they can understand. Despite these stumbling blocks, however, Hispanics have started to exercise a measure of political power. Hispanic-Americans have been elected mayor in San Antonio, San Diego, Denver, and Miami. In the 1992 election, seventeen Hispanics were elected to Congress. President Clinton appointed two Hispanics to his cabinet. Hispanics have also gained some access to political power through their representation in coalitions that dominate policymaking on minority-related issues.[72]

Disabled Americans

Millions of handicapped Americans gained recognition in 1990 as an oppressed minority with the passage of the Americans with Disabilities Act. The law extends the protections embodied in the Civil Rights Act of 1964 to people with physical or mental disabilities, including people with AIDS and recovering alcoholics and drug abusers. It guarantees access to employment, transportation, public accommodations, and communication services.

Advocates for the disabled found a ready model in the existing civil rights laws. Opponents argued that the changes mandated by the law (such as access for those confined to wheelchairs) could cost billions of dollars, but supporters replied that the costs would be offset by an equal or greater reduction in federal aid to disabled people who would rather be working.

A change in the law, no matter how welcome, does not assure a change in attitudes. Laws that end racial discrimination do not extinguish racism, and laws that ban biased treatment of the disabled will not mandate acceptance of the disabled. But attitudinal barriers toward the handicapped, like similar attitudes toward other minorities, will wither as the disabled become full participants in a society that once held them at bay.

Gender and Equal Rights: The Women's Movement

The ballot box and the lawsuit have brought minorities in America a measure of equality. The Supreme Court has expanded the array of legal

Moving Forward   *In 1990 the Americans with Disabilities Act brought people with physical or mental disabilities under the protections embodied in the Civil Rights Act of 1964. Mandated changes such as access to public places for those confined to wheelchairs now permit individuals such as this student on the campus of the University of California, Irvine to live fuller and more productive lives.*

weapons available to all minorities to help them achieve social equality. Women, too, have benefited from this change.

Protectionism

Until the early 1970s, laws that affected the civil rights of women were based on traditional views of the relationship between men and women. At the heart of these laws was **protectionism**—the idea that women must be sheltered from life's cruelties. And protected they were through laws that discriminated against them in employment and other areas. With few exceptions, women were also "protected" from voting until early in the twentieth century.

Protectionism reached a peak in 1908 when the Court upheld an Oregon law limiting the number of hours that women were allowed to work.[73] The decision was rife with sexist assumptions about the nature and role of women, and it gave wide latitude to laws that protected the "weaker sex." It also led to legislation that barred women from working more than forty-eight hours a week and from jobs that required workers to lift more than 35 pounds. In effect, women were locked out of jobs that called for substantial overtime (and overtime pay); instead, they were shunted to jobs that men believed suited women's abilities.

In 1991, the Supreme Court moved vigorously away from protectionism by striking down an employer's policy excluding women capable of bearing children from exposure to toxic substances that could harm a developing fetus. Relying on amendments to the 1964 Civil Rights Act, the Court declared that "women as capable of doing their jobs as their male counterparts may not be forced to choose between having a child and having a job."[74]

Political Equality for Women

In 1878, Susan B. Anthony, a women's rights activist, convinced a U.S. senator from California to introduce a constitutional amendment requiring that "the right of citizens of the United States to vote shall not be denied or abridged by the United States or by any State on account of sex." The amendment was introduced and voted down a number of times over the next twenty years. However, a number of states—primarily in the Midwest and West—did grant limited suffrage to women.

By the early 1900s, the movement for women's suffrage had became a political battle to amend the Constitution. The battle was won in 1920 when the **Nineteenth Amendment** gave women the right to vote in the wording first suggested by Anthony.

Utilizing that right in the election of 1992, women moved a bit closer to equality in Congress. In an election year that many had predicted would be "the year of the woman," female membership in the Senate rose from two to six. In the House it increased from twenty-eight to forty-seven.

Prohibiting Sex-based Discrimination

The movement to provide equal rights to women advanced a step with the passage of the Equal Pay Act of 1963. That act required equal pay for men and women doing similar work. However, state protectionist laws still had the effect of restricting women to jobs that were not usually taken by men. Where employment was stratified by sex, equal pay was an empty promise. To be free from the restrictions of protectionism, women needed equal opportunity for employment. They got it in the Civil Rights Act of 1964 and later legislation. The EEOC, which had been created by that law, was empowered to act on behalf of victims of sex discrimination, or **sexism.**

Subsequent presidential orders and legislation on women's rights were motivated by the pressure for civil rights as well as by the resurgence of the women's movement, which had subsided after the adoption of the Nineteenth Amendment. One particularly important law was Title IX of the Education Amendments Act of 1972, which prohibited sex discrimination in federally aided education programs. Another boost to women came from the Revenue Act of 1972, which provided tax credits for childcare expenses. In effect, the act subsidized parents with young children so that women could enter or remain in the work force.

Stereotypes Under Scrutiny

After nearly a century of broad deference to protectionism, the Supreme Court began to take a closer look at gender-based distinctions. In 1971, it struck down a state law that gave men preference over women in administering the estate of a person who had died without naming an administrator.[75] Two years later, the justices declared that the paternalism of earlier ages operated to "put women not on a pedestal, but in a cage."[76] They then proceeded to strike down several gender-based laws that either prevented or discouraged departures from "proper" sex roles. In 1976, the Court finally developed a workable standard for reviewing these kinds of laws: Gender-based distinctions were justified only if they served some important government purpose.[77]

The Equal Rights Amendment

Women have not enjoyed the same rights as men. Policies protecting women, based largely on sexual stereotypes, have been woven into the legal fabric of American life. That protectionism has limited the freedom of women to compete with men socially and economically on an equal footing. The Supreme Court has been hesitant to extend the principles of the Fourteenth Amendment beyond issues of race. If constitutional interpretation imposes such a limit, then it can be overcome only by a constitutional amendment.

The **Equal Rights Amendment (ERA)** was first introduced in 1923 by the National Women's party, one of the few women's groups that did not disband after the Nineteenth Amendment was passed. The ERA declared that "equality of rights under the law shall not be denied or abridged by the United States or any State on account of sex."

A national coalition of women's rights advocates generated enough support to get the ERA through the proposal stage in 1972. Its proponents had seven years in which to get the amendment ratified by thirty-eight state legislatures, as required by the Constitution. By 1977, they were three states short of that goal, and three states had rescinded earlier ratification. In an unprecedented action, Congress extended the ratification deadline. This action did not help. The ERA died on July 1, 1982, still three states short of adoption.

Why did the ERA fail? The amendment quickly acquired opposition, including many women who had supported women's rights legislation. As the opposition grew stronger, especially from women who wanted to maintain their traditional role, state legislators began to realize that there were risks involved in supporting the amendment. It takes an extraordinary majority to amend the Constitution, which means that it takes only a committed minority to thwart the majority's will.

Despite its failure, the movement to ratify the ERA produced real benefits. It raised the consciousness of women about their social position, it spurred the formation of the National Organization for Women (NOW) and other large organizations, it contributed to women's participation in politics, and it influenced major legislation affecting women.[78]

The failure to ratify the ERA stands in stark contrast to the quick passage of many laws that now protect women's rights. But in fact there was little audible opposition to women's rights legislation. If years of racial discrimination called for government redress, then so did years of gender-based discrimination.

For practical purposes, argue some scholars, the Supreme Court has implemented the ERA through its decisions. It has struck down distinctions based on sex and has held that stereotyped generalizations of sexual differences must fall.[79] In recent rulings, the Court has held that states may require employers to guarantee job reinstatement to women returning from maternity leave and that sexual harassment in the workplace is illegal.

Affirmative Action: Equal Opportunity or Equal Outcome?

In his vision of the Great Society, President Johnson linked economic rights with civil rights and equality of outcome with equality of opportunity. "Equal opportunity is essential, but not enough," he declared. "We seek not just legal equity but human ability, not just equality as a right and a theory but equality as a fact and equality as a result." This commitment led to affirmative action programs to expand opportunities for women, minorities, and the disabled.

Affirmative action embraces a range of public and private programs, policies, and procedures to bring about increased employment, promotion, or admission for members of designated groups. Such programs include recruitment, preferential treatment, and quotas in job training and professional education, employment, and the placement of government contracts. The goal of these programs is to move beyond equality of opportunity to equality of outcome.

Many arguments for affirmative action programs (from increased recruitment efforts to quotas) reduce to the following reasoning: In the past, certain groups suffered invidious discrimination that denied them educational and economic opportunities. To eliminate the lasting effects of such discrimination, the public and private sectors must take steps to provide access to good education and jobs. If the majority once used discrimination to hold groups back, then it is fair to use discrimination to benefit those groups now. Therefore, quotas are a legitimate means to provide a place on the ladder of success.[80]

Affirmative action opponents maintain that quotas for designated groups necessarily create invidious discrimination (in the form of reverse discrimination) against individuals who are themselves blameless. Moreover, quotas lead to admission, hiring, or promotion of the less qualified at the expense of the well qualified. Such policies thwart an individual's freedom to succeed in the name of equality.

Reverse Discrimination

The Supreme Court confronted an affirmative action quota program for the first time in **Regents of the University of California v. Bakke** (1978).[81] Allan Bakke, a thirty-five-year-old white man, had twice applied for admission to the University of California Medical School at Davis. He was rejected both times. The school had reserved sixteen places in each entering class of one hundred for "qualified" minorities, as part of the university's affirmative action program. Bakke's qualifications (college grade point average and test scores) exceeded those of any of the minority students admitted in the two years his applications were rejected. Bakke contended, first in the California courts and then in the Supreme Court, that he was excluded from admission solely on the basis of race. He argued that this reverse discrimination was prohibited by the equal protection clause of the Fourteenth Amendment and by the Civil Rights Act of 1964.

The Court's decision in *Bakke* contained six opinions and spanned 154 pages. But even after careful analysis of the decision, it was difficult to discern what the Court had decided: There was no majority opinion. Four of the justices contended that any racial quota system supported by government violated the Civil Rights Act of 1964. Justice Lewis F. Powell, Jr. agreed, casting the deciding vote ordering the medical school to admit Bakke. However, in his opinion, Powell argued that the rigid use of racial quotas as employed at the school violated the equal protection clause of the Fourteenth Amendment. The remaining four justices held that the use of race as a criterion in admissions decisions in higher education was constitutionally permissible. Powell joined that opinion as well, contending that the use of race was permissible as one of several admission criteria. So the Court managed to minimize white opposition to the goal of equality (by finding for Bakke) while extending gains for racial minorities through affirmative action.

Although the Court sent a mixed message, *Bakke* did contribute tangible benefits. The number of minority physicians doubled in the decade after the decision. Moreover, minority physicians tended to relocate to areas where there were critical health-care shortages. They also tended to serve significantly larger proportions of poor patients regardless of race or ethnicity.[82]

Other cases followed. In 1979, the Court upheld a voluntary affirmative action plan giving preferences to blacks in an employee training program.[83] Five years later, however, the Court held that layoffs had to proceed by seniority unless minority employees could demonstrate that they were actual victims of discrimination.[84]

Victims of Discrimination

The 1984 layoff decision raised a troublesome question: Do all affirmative action programs, not just layoffs, apply solely to actual victims of past discrimination? The Supreme Court delivered a partial answer in 1986 when it struck down a school board layoff plan giving preference to members of minority groups.[85] The layoff plan favored black teachers in an effort to redress general social discrimination and to maintain sufficient role models for black students. But the Supreme Court ruled that these objectives were insufficient to force certain individuals to shoulder the severe impact of layoffs. Hiring goals imposed a diffuse burden on society, argued Justice Powell for the Court. But layoffs of innocent whites, he continued, "imposed the entire burden of achieving racial equality on particular individuals."

The local chapter of a construction union in New York City practiced egregious racial discrimination for more than seventy-five years. When in 1975 a federal court concluded that the local had violated Title VII of the Civil Rights Act of 1964, and required it to accept equal numbers of white and nonwhite apprentices, the union took its case to the Supreme Court. The union argued that the membership goal ordered by the lower courts was unlawful because it extended race-conscious preferences to individuals who were not identified victims of the local's admittedly unlawful discrimination. In *Local 28 v. EEOC* (1986), the Court voted 6 to 3 in support of affirmative action that would benefit individuals who were not the actual victims of discrimination.[86] The majority held that the courts could order unions to use quotas to overcome a history of egregious discrimination and that black and Hispanic applicants could benefit from affirmative action even if they themselves had not been the victims of earlier bias.

Must affirmative action policies be limited to concerns over racial inequality? What about the conflict between Diane Joyce and Paul Johnson described at the beginning of this chapter? Johnson took his case all the way to the Supreme Court to argue that he was the victim of sex discrimination under Title VII of the Civil Rights Act of 1964, the provision that employers could not "limit, segregate or classify" workers so as to deprive "any individual of employment opportunities."

The justices decided *Johnson v. Transportation Agency, Santa Clara County* in 1987. They ruled, 6–3, that if women and minorities are underrepresented in the workplace, employers can act to remedy the imbalance. The decision was significant for at least two reasons. First, employers with affirmative action plans do not have to admit to a history of past discrimination. And second, employees who are passed over for promotions are nearly powerless to sue for reverse discrimination. The upshot of the decision is to encourage the adoption of affirmative action programs.

In a scathing dissent, Justice Antonin Scalia focused on two familiar themes: values in conflict and models of democracy. He declared that

We Shall Overcome *Gays and lesbians argue that their struggle for an equal place in society is a civil rights issue similar to that pursued by other minorities. Here speaking before a demonstration in support of lifting the ban on homosexuals in the military is gay sailor Keith Meinhold who had been removed from the Navy but was returned to duty after a federal judge ordered his reinstatement. The issue of whether to permit gays in the military was one of the most troublesome issues to confront President Clinton in the early months of his presidency.*

the majority converted "a guarantee that race or sex will *not* be the basis for employment determination, to a guarantee that it often *will*." The Court, continued Scalia, replaced the goal of a society free from discrimination with the incompatible goal of proportionate representation by race and by sex in the workplace. In simpler terms, equality trumped freedom.

Scalia then offered his observations about pluralism. The Court's decision would be pleasing to elected officials, he said, because it "provides the means of quickly accommodating the demands of organized groups to achieve concrete, numerical improvement in the economic status of particular constituencies." "The only losers in the process," he concluded, are the Paul Johnsons of the country, "predominantly unknown, unaffluent, unorganized—[who] suffer this injustice at the hands of a Court fond of thinking itself the champion of the politically impotent."

The conflict between freedom and equality continues as other individuals and groups press their demands through litigation and legislation. Americans want equality, but they disagree on the extent to which government should provide it.[87] In part, this ambivalence stems from confusion over equal opportunities and equal outcomes.

Two Conceptions of Equality

Most Americans support **equality of opportunity,** the idea that people should have an equal chance to develop their talents and that effort and ability should be rewarded. This form of equality glorifies personal achievement through free competition and allows everyone to climb the ladder of success starting at the first rung. Special recruitment efforts aimed at identifying qualified minority or female job applicants ensure that everyone has the same chance starting out. The competition for the promotion between Joyce and Johnson illustrates equality of opportunity.

Americans are less committed to **equality of outcome,** which means greater uniformity in social, economic, and political power. Equality of outcome can occur only if we restrict the free competition that forms the basis of equality of opportunity. One restriction comes by way of a limit on personal achievement. Preferential treatment in hiring is an apt example. That treatment prevented Johnson from climbing the ladder of success.

Quota policies generate the most opposition because they deny competition. Quotas limit advancement for some individuals and ensure advancement for others. They alter positions on the ladder of success without regard to ability. Policies that benefit minorities and women at the expense of innocent white men create strong opposition because they bring individual initiative into conflict with equal outcomes. In other words, freedom clashes with equality.

Summary

In establishing a new government, the framers were compelled to assure the states and the people, through the Bill of Rights, that their freedoms would be protected. In interpreting these ten amendments, the courts, especially the Supreme Court, have taken on the task of balancing freedom and order.

The First Amendment protects several freedoms: religion, speech and press, peaceable assembly and petition. The establishment clause demands government neutrality toward religions and between the religious and nonreligious. According to judicial interpretations of the free-exercise clause, religious beliefs are inviolate, but antisocial actions in the name of religion are not protected by the Constitution. Extreme interpreta-tions of the religion clauses could bring them into conflict with each other.

Freedom of expression encompasses freedom of speech and of the press and the right to peaceable assembly and petition. Freedom of speech and the press have never been held to be absolute, but they have been given far greater protection than other freedoms in the Bill of Rights. Exceptions to free-speech protections include some forms of symbolic expression and obscenity. Press freedom has had broad constitutional protection because a free society depends on the ability to collect and report information without government interference. The rights of peaceable assembly and petition stem from the same freedom protecting speech and press. Each of these freedoms is equally fundamental, but their exercise is not absolute.

The adoption of the Fourteenth Amendment in 1868 extended the guarantees of the Bill of Rights to the states. The due process clause became the vehicle for absorbing or incorporating specific provisions of the Bill of Rights, one at a time, case after case, and applying them to the states. The designation of a right as fundamental also called for a definition of that right.

As the Supreme Court fashioned new fundamental rights from the Constitution, it became embroiled in controversy. The right to privacy served as the basis for a woman's right to terminate a pregnancy, which in turn suggested a right to personal autonomy. The abortion controversy is still raging, and the justices have called a halt to the extension of personal privacy in the name of the Constitution.

The Civil War amendments—the Thirteenth, Fourteenth, and Fifteenth Amendments—were adopted to provide full civil rights to black Americans. Yet in the late nineteenth century, the Supreme Court interpreted the amendments very narrowly, declaring that they did not restrain individuals from denying civil rights to blacks and that they did not apply to powers reserved to the states. The Court's rulings had the effect of denying the vote to most blacks and of institutionalizing racial segregation, making racism a facet of daily life.

Through a series of court cases spanning two decades, segregation in the schools was slowly dismantled. The battle for desegregation culminated in the 1954 and 1955 *Brown* cases, in which a now-supportive Supreme Court declared segregated schools to be inherently unequal and therefore unconstitutional. The Court also ordered the desegregation of all schools and upheld the use of busing to do so.

Gains in other civil rights areas came more slowly. The motivating force was the civil rights movement, led by Martin Luther King, Jr. until his death in 1968. King believed strongly in civil disobedience and nonviolence, strategies that helped secure for blacks equality in voting rights, public accommodations, higher education, housing, and employment opportunity.

Civil rights activism and the civil rights movement worked to the benefit of all minority groups, in fact, of all Americans. Native Americans obtained some redress for past injustices. Hispanic-Americans came to recognize the importance of group action to achieve economic and political equality. Handicapped Americans won civil rights protections enjoyed by African-Americans and others. And civil rights legislation removed the protectionism that was, in effect, legalized discrimination against women in education and employment.

Despite legislative advances in the area of women's rights, the Equal Rights Amendment was not ratified. Nevertheless, the struggle for ratification produced several positive results, heightening the awareness of the role of women and mobilizing the political power of women through group activity. And legislation and judicial rulings implemented much of the amendment in practice, if not fact.

Affirmative action programs were instituted to counteract the results of past discrimination. These provide preferential treatment for women, minorities, and the handicapped in a number of areas that affect economic opportunity and well-being. In effect, such programs advocate discrimination to remedy earlier discrimination. A new conservative majority on the Supreme Court has now emerged to roll back the equality-preferring policies of a more liberal bench.

Americans want equality, but they disagree on the extent to which government should provide it. At the heart of this conflict is the distinction between equal opportunities and equal outcomes. We can guarantee equal outcomes only if we restrict the free competition that is an integral part of equal opportunity. Many Americans object to this idea.

Many of the civil liberties and civil rights that Americans enjoy today were defined by the courts. This raises a basic issue. By offering constitutional protection to public policies, the courts may be threatening the democratic process, which gives the people a say in government through their elected representatives. One thing is certain, however: The challenge of democracy requires the constant balancing of freedom and order.

Key Terms

discrimination
civil liberties
civil rights
establishment clause
free-exercise clause
Lemon v. Kurtzman
West Virginia State Board of
    Education v. Barnette
Sherbert v. Verner
speech clause
press clause
free-expression clauses
prior restraint
clear and present danger test
Gitlow v. New York
Brandenburg v. Ohio
symbolic expression
Tinker v. Des Moines Inde-
    pendent County School Dis-
    trict United States v.
    Eichman
Miller v. California
libel
New York Times v. Sullivan
public figures
New York Times v. United
    States
bills of attainder
ex post facto laws
obligation of contracts
Palko v. Connecticut
Gideon v. Wainwright
Miranda warnings

exclusionary rule
Mapp v. Ohio
good faith exception
Griswold v. Connecticut
Roe v. Wade
Webster v. Reproductive
    Health Services
Planned Parenthood v. Casey
Bowers v. Hardwick
racism
poll tax
racial segregation
Plessy v. Ferguson
separate-but-equal doctrine
desegregation
Brown v. Board of Education
Brown v. Board of Education
    II
de jure segregation
de facto segregation
Milliken v. Bradley
civil rights movement
boycott
civil disobedience
protectionism
Nineteenth Amendment
sexism
Equal Rights Amendment
    (ERA)
Regents of the University of
    California v. Bakke
Local 28 v. EEOC

*Johnson v. Transportation
Agency, Santa Clara
County*

equality of opportunity
equality of outcome

Selected Readings

Baer, Judith A. *Equality Under the Constitution: Reclaiming the Fourteenth Amendment.* Ithaca, N.Y.: Cornell University Press, 1983. Baer explores the early American concept of equality and re-examines the debates surrounding the adoption of the Fourteenth Amendment. The author points to new areas of struggle in the application of the equality principle to children, the aged, the disabled, and homosexuals.

Baker, Liva. *Miranda: Crime, Law and Politics.* New York: Atheneum, 1983. Baker uses *Miranda* as a vehicle for explaining the American legal system. She traces the case from its origin to its landmark resolution.

Barnett, Randy E., ed. *The Rights Retained by the People: The History and Meaning of the Ninth Amendment.* Fairfax, Va.: George Mason University Press, 1989. This excellent collection of writings on the Ninth Amendment includes a set of primary documents and a summary of the competing theories on this controversial area of constitutional jurisprudence.

Bass, Jack. *Unlikely Heroes.* New York: Simon and Schuster, 1981. Bass chronicles the efforts of four federal appellate judges in the Deep South to enforce the desegregation mandate in *Brown.*

Berger, Raoul. *Government by Judiciary: The Transformation of the Fourteenth Amendment.* Cambridge, Mass.: Harvard University Press, 1977. This provocative work argues that the framers of the Fourteenth Amendment had very narrow aims and that the Supreme Court, especially since 1954, has disregarded this historical legacy in promoting freedom and equality.

Branch, Taylor. *Parting the Waters: America in the King Years, 1954–1963.* New York: Simon and Schuster, 1988. This is a riveting, Pulitzer Prize–winning narrative history and biography of the King years.

Brigham, John. *Civil Liberties and American Democracy.* Washington, D.C.: Congressional Quarterly Press, 1984. Brigham surveys U.S. civil rights and liberties and organizes the discussion around basic concepts (privacy, entitlements).

Browning, Rufus P., Dale Rogers Marshall, and David H. Tabb. *Racial Politics in American Cities.* New York: Longman, 1990. This collection of essays documents the continuing struggle for minority access to political power in cities across the United States.

Deloria, Vine, Jr., and Clifford M. Lytle. *The Nations Within.* New York: Pantheon, 1984. This thorough discussion of Native American policies from the New Deal to the present examines the drive for Indian self-determination and self-government.

Haiman, Franklyn C. *Speech and Law in a Free Society.* Chicago: University of Chicago Press, 1981. In this thorough survey of the meaning of the First Amendment, Haiman argues that no special significance attaches to the separate speech and press clauses.

Hampton, Henry, and Steve Fayer with Sarah Flynn. *Voices of Freedom: An Oral History of the Civil Rights Movement from the 1950s Through the 1980s.* New York: Bantam, 1990. Herein are chronologically arranged interview excerpts recorded during the production of "Eyes on the Prize," the widely acclaimed public television series.

Kessler-Harris, Alice. *Out to Work: A History of Wage-earning Women in the United States.* New York: Oxford University Press, 1982. This is an informative analysis of the forces motivating women to work and the effect of work on family roles.

Levy, Leonard W. *The Establishment Clause: Religion and the First Amendment.* New York: Macmillan, 1986. This searching study of the establishment clause claims that the view that government can assist all religions is historically groundless. Levy argues that it is unconstitutional for government to provide aid to any religion.

Lewis, Anthony. *Gideon's Trumpet.* New York: Random House, 1964. This is a moving story of Clarence Earl Gideon's claim to assistance of counsel guaranteed by the Sixth Amendment.

Mansbridge, Jane J. *Why We Lost the ERA.* Chicago: University of Chicago Press, 1986. This is a valuable case study of organizations pitted for and against the Equal Rights Amendment in Illinois.

Polenberg, Richard. *Fighting Faiths.* New York: Knopf, 1987. By focusing on the famous case of *Abrams* v. *United States,* a noted historian examines anarchism, government surveillance, freedom of speech, and the impact of the Bolshevik Revolution on American liberals.

Prucha, Francis Paul. *The Great Father: The United States Government and the American Indians.* 2 vols. Lincoln: University of Nebraska Press, 1984. This is a definitive history of federal policy toward Native Americans from the beginning of the Republic to 1980.

Tribe, Laurence H. *Abortion: The Clash of Absolutes.* New York: Norton, 1990. Tribe seeks an accommodation in the clash of absolutes in the abortion debate through a historical, political and legal analysis of the issues.

Urofsky, Melvin I. *A Conflict of Rights: The Supreme Court and Affirmative Action.* New York: Scribner's, 1991. Here is an absorbing case study of the events, participants, and issues surrounding the landmark affirmative action decision of *Joyce* v. *Johnson.*

Williams, Juan. *Eyes on the Prize: America's Civil Rights Years, 1954–1965.* New York: Viking, 1987. This lucid account of black Americans' struggle for social and political equality contains vivid portraits of courageous blacks and the violence they had to endure in their fight for desegregation and the right to vote in the South.

APPENDICES

THE DECLARATION OF INDEPENDENCE
IN CONGRESS   JULY 4, 1776

The unanimous declaration of the thirteen
United States of America

When, in the course of human events, it becomes necessary for one people to dissolve the political bands which have connected them with another, and to assume, among the powers of the earth, the separate and equal station to which the laws of nature and of nature's God entitle them, a decent respect to the opinions of mankind requires that they should declare the causes which impel them to the separation.

We hold these truths to be self-evident: That all men are created equal; that they are endowed by their Creator with certain unalienable rights; that among these are life, liberty, and the pursuit of happiness; that, to secure these rights, governments are instituted among men, deriving their just powers from the consent of the governed; that whenever any form of government becomes destructive of these ends, it is the right of the people to alter or to abolish it, and to institute new government, laying its foundation on such principles, and organizing its power in such form, as to them shall seem most likely to effect their safety and happiness. Prudence, indeed, will dictate that governments long established should not be changed for light and transient causes; and accordingly all experience hath shown that mankind are more disposed to suffer, while evils are sufferable, than to right themselves by abolishing the forms to which they are accustomed. But when a long train of abuses and usurpations, pursuing invariably the same object, evinces a design to reduce them under absolute despotism, it is their right, it is their duty, to throw off such government, and to provide new guards for their future security. Such has been the patient sufferance of these colonies; and such is now the necessity which constrains them to alter their former systems of government. The history of the present King of Great Britain is a history of repeated injuries and usurpations, all having in direct object the establishment of an absolute tyranny over these states. To prove this, let facts be submitted to a candid world.

He has refused his assent to laws, the most wholesome and necessary for the public good.

He has forbidden his governors to pass laws of immediate and pressing importance, unless suspended in their operation till his assent should be obtained; and, when so suspended, he has utterly neglected to attend to them.

He has refused to pass other laws for the accommodation of large districts of people, unless those people would relinquish the right of representation in the legislature, a right inestimable to them, and formidable to tyrants only.

He has called together legislative bodies at places unusual, uncomfortable, and distant from the depository of their public records, for the sole purpose of fatiguing them into compliance with his measures.

He has dissolved representative houses repeatedly, for opposing, with manly firmness, his invasions on the rights of the people.

He has refused for a long time, after such dissolutions, to cause others to be elected; whereby the legislative powers, incapable of annihilation, have returned to the people at large for their exercise; the state remaining, in the mean time, exposed to all the dangers of invasions from without and convulsions within.

He has endeavored to prevent the population of these states; for that purpose obstructing the laws for naturalization of foreigners; refusing to pass others to encourage their migration hither, and raising the conditions of new appropriations of lands.

He has obstructed the administration of justice, by refusing his assent to laws for establishing judiciary powers.

He has made judges dependent on his will alone, for the tenure of their offices, and the amount and payment of their salaries.

He has erected a multitude of new offices, and sent hither swarms of officers to harass our people and eat out their substance.

He has kept among us, in times of peace, standing armies, without the consent of our legislatures.

He has affected to render the military independent of, and superior to, the civil power.

He has combined with others to subject us to a jurisdiction foreign to our constitution, and unacknowledged by our laws, giving his assent to their acts of pretended legislation:

For quartering large bodies of armed troops among us;

For protecting them, by a mock trial, from punishment for any murders which they should commit on the inhabitants of these states;

For cutting off our trade with all parts of the world;

For imposing taxes on us without our consent;

For depriving us, in many cases, of the benefits of trial by jury;

For transporting us beyond seas, to be tried for pretended offenses;

For abolishing the free system of English laws in a neighboring province, establishing therein an arbitrary government, and enlarging its boundaries, so as to render it at once an example and fit instrument for introducing the same absolute rule into these colonies;

For taking away our charters, abolishing our most valuable laws, and altering fundamentally the forms of our governments;

For suspending our own legislatures, and declaring themselves invested with power to legislate for us in all cases whatsoever.

He has abdicated government here, by declaring us out of his protection and waging war against us.

He has plundered our seas, ravaged our coasts, burned our towns, and destroyed the lives of our people.

He is at this time transporting large armies of foreign mercenaries to complete the works of death, desolation, and tyranny already begun with circumstances of cruelty and perfidy scarcely paralleled in the most barbarous ages, and totally unworthy the head of a civilized nation.

He has constrained our fellow-citizens, taken captive on the high seas, to bear arms against their country, to become the executioners of their friends and brethren, or to fall themselves by their hands.

He has excited domestic insurrection among us, and has endeavored to bring on the inhabitants of our frontiers the merciless Indian savages, whose known rule of warfare is an undistinguished destruction of all ages, sexes, and conditions.

In every stage of these oppressions we have petitioned for redress in the most humble terms; our repeated petitions have been answered only by repeated injury. A prince, whose character is thus marked by every act which may define a tyrant, is unfit to be the ruler of a free people.

Nor have we been wanting in our attentions to our British brethren. We have warned them, from time to time, of attempts by their legislature to extend an unwarrantable jurisdiction over us. We have reminded them of the circumstances of our emigration and settlement here. We have appealed to their native justice and magnanimity; and we have conjured them, by the ties of our common kindred, to disavow these usurpations, which would inevitably interrupt our connections and correspondence. They, too, have been deaf to the voice of justice and of consanguinity. We must, therefore, acquiesce in the necessity which denounces our separation, and hold them, as we hold the rest of mankind, enemies in war, in peace friends.

We, therefore, the representatives of the United States of America, in General Congress assembled, appealing to the Supreme Judge of the world for the rectitude of our intentions, do, in the name and by the authority of the good people of these colonies, solemnly publish and declare, that these United Colonies are, and of right ought to be, FREE AND INDEPENDENT STATES; that they are absolved from all allegiance to the British crown, and that all political connection between them and the state of Great Britain is, and ought to be, totally dissolved; and that, as free and independent states, they have full power to levy war, conclude peace, contract alliances, establish commerce, and do all other acts and things which independent states may of right do. And for the support of this declaration, with a firm reliance on the protection of Divine Providence, we mutually pledge to each other our lives, our fortunes, and our sacred honor.

JOHN HANCOCK
and fifty-five others

THE CONSTITUTION OF THE UNITED STATES OF AMERICA*

Preamble

We the people of the United States, in Order to form a more perfect Union, establish Justice, insure domestic Tranquility, provide for the common defense, promote the general Welfare, and secure the Blessings of Liberty to ourselves and our Posterity, do ordain and establish this Constitution for the United States of America.

Article I

Section 1 All legislative Powers herein granted shall be vested in a Congress of the United States, which shall consist of a Senate and a House of Representatives.

Section 2 The House of Representatives shall be composed of Members chosen every second Year by the people of the several States, and the Electors in each State shall have the Qualifications requisite for Electors of the most numerous Branch of the State Legislature.

No Person shall be a Representative who shall not have attained to the Age of twenty-five years, and been seven Years a Citizen of the United States, and who shall not, when elected, be an Inhabitant of that State in which he shall be chosen.

Representatives and direct Taxes shall be apportioned among the several States which may be included within this Union, according to their respective Numbers, *which shall be determined by adding to the whole Number of free persons, including those bound to Service for a Term of Years and excluding Indians not taxed, three fifths of all other Persons.* The actual Enumeration shall be made within three Years after the first Meeting of the Congress of the United States, and within every subsequent Term of ten Years, in such Manner as they shall by Law direct. The Number of Representatives shall not exceed one for every thirty Thousand, but each State shall have at Least one Representative; *and until such enumeration shall be made, the State of New Hampshire shall be entitled to choose three, Massachusetts eight, Rhode-Island and Providence Plantations one, Connecticut five, New-York six, New Jersey four, Pennsylvania eight, Delaware one, Maryland six, Virginia ten, North Carolina five, South Carolina five, and Georgia three.*

When vacancies happen in the Representation from any State, the Executive Authority thereof shall issue Writs of Election to fill such Vacancies.

The House of Representatives shall choose their Speaker and other Officers; and shall have the sole Power of Impeachment.

Section 3 The Senate of the United States shall be composed of two Senators from each State, *chosen by the Legislature threof,* for six Years; and each Senator shall have one Vote.

---

* Passages no longer in effect are printed in italic type.

Immediately after they shall be assembled in Consequence of the first Election, they shall be divided as equally as may be into three Classes. The Seats of the Senators of the first Class shall be vacated at the Expiration of the second Year, of the second Class at the Expiration of the fourth Year, and of the third Class at the Expiration of the sixth Year, so that one-third may be chosen every second year; *and if Vacancies happen by Resignation or otherwise, during the Recess of the Legislature of any State, the Executive thereof may make temporary Appointments until the next Meeting of the Legislature, which shall then fill such Vacancies.*

No Person shall be a Senator who shall not have attained to the Age of thirty Years, and been nine Years a Citizen of the United States, and who shall not, when elected, be an Inhabitant of that State for which he shall be chosen.

The Vice-President of the United States shall be President of the Senate, but shall have no vote, unless they be equally divided.

The Senate shall choose their other Officers, and also a President *pro tempore*, in the absence of the Vice-President, or when he shall exercise the Office of President of the United States.

The Senate shall have the sole Power to try all Impeachments. When sitting for that purpose, they shall be on Oath or Affirmation. When the President of the United States is tried, the Chief Justice shall preside: And no person shall be convicted without the Concurrence of two-thirds of the Members present.

Judgment in Cases of Impeachment shall not extend further than to removal from Office, and disqualification to hold and enjoy any Office of honor, Trust, or profit under the United States: but the Party convicted shall nevertheless be liable and subject to Indictment, Trial, Judgment and punishment, according to Law.

Section 4   The Times, Places and Manner of holding Elections for Senators and Representatives, shall be prescribed in each state by the Legislature thereof; but the Congress may at any time by Law make or alter such Regulations, except as to the Places of choosing Senators.

The Congress shall assemble at least once in every Year, and such Meeting *shall be on the first Monday in December, unless they shall by Law appoint a different Day.*

Section 5   Each House shall be the Judge of the Elections, Returns and Qualifications of its own Members, and a Majority of each shall constitute a Quorum to do Business; but a smaller number may adjourn from day to day, and may be authorized to compel the Attendance of absent Members, in such Manner, and under such Penalties, as each House may provide.

Each House may determine the Rules of its Proceedings, punish its Members for disorderly Behavior, and with the Concurrence of two-thirds, expel a Member.

Each House shall keep a Journal of its Proceedings, and from time to time publish the same, excepting such Parts as may in their Judgment require Secrecy; and the Yeas and Nays of the Members of either House on any question shall, at the Desire of one-fifth of those present, be entered on the journal.

Neither House, during the Session of Congress, shall, without the Consent of the other, adjourn for more than three days, nor to any other Place than that in which the two Houses shall be sitting.

Section 6   The Senators and Representatives shall receive a Compensation for their Services, to be ascertained by Law and paid out of the Treasury of the United States. They shall in all Cases except Treason, Felony and Breach of the Peace, be privileged from Arrest during their Attendance at the Session of their respective houses, and in going to and returning from the same; and for any Speech or Debate in either House, they shall not be questioned in any other place.

No Senator or Representative shall, during the Time for which he was elected, be appointed to any civil Office under the Authority of the United States, which shall have been created, or the Emoluments whereof shall have been increased, during such time; and no person holding any Office under the United States shall be a Member of either House during his continuance in Office.

Section 7   All Bills for raising Revenue shall originate in the House of Representatives; but the Senate may propose or concur with Amendments as on other bills.

Every Bill which shall have passed the House of Representatives and the Senate, shall, before it become a Law, be presented to the President of the United States; if he approve he shall sign it, but if not he shall return it with his Objections, to that House in which it shall have originated, who shall enter the Objections at large on their Journal, and proceed to reconsider it. If after such reconsideration two-thirds of that House shall agree to pass the bill, it shall be sent, together with the objections, to the other House, by which it shall likewise be reconsidered, and, if approved by two-thirds of that House, it shall become a law. But in all such Cases the Votes of both Houses shall be determined by Yeas and Nays, and the Names of the Persons voting for and against the Bill shall be entered on the Journal of each House respectively. If any bill shall not be returned by the President within ten Days (Sundays excepted) after it shall have been presented to him, the Same shall be a Law, in like Manner as if he had signed it, unless the Congress by their Adjournment prevent its Return, in which Case it shall not be a Law.

Every Order, Resolution, or Vote to which the Concurrence of the Senate and House of Representatives may be necessary (except on a question of Adjournment) shall be presented to the President of the United States; and before the Same shall take Effect, shall be approved by him, or being disapproved by him, shall be repassed by two-thirds of the Senate and House of Representatives, according to the Rules and Limitations prescribed in the Case of a Bill.

Section 8   The Congress shall have Power

To lay and collect Taxes, Duties, Imposts, and Excises, to pay the Debts and provide for the common Defense and general Welfare of the United States; but all Duties, Imposts and Excises shall be uniform throughout the United States;

To borrow money on the credit of the United States;

To regulate Commerce with foreign Nations, and among the several States, and with the Indian Tribes;

To establish an uniform Rule of Naturalization, and uniform Laws on the subject of Bankruptcies throughout the United States;

To coin Money, regulate the Value thereof, and of foreign Coin, and fix the Standard of Weights and Measures;

To provide for the Punishment of counterfeiting the Securities and current Coin of the United States;

To establish Post Offices and Post Roads;

To promote the Progress of Science and useful Arts by securing for limited times to Authors and Inventors the exclusive Right to their respective Writings and Discoveries;

To constitute Tribunals inferior to the Supreme Court;

To define and punish Piracies and Felonies committed on the high Seas and Offenses against the Law of Nations;

To declare War, grant Letters of Marque and Reprisal, and make rules concerning captures on land and water;

To raise and support Armies, but no Appropriation of Money to that Use shall be for a longer Term than two Years;

To provide and maintain a Navy;

To make Rules for the Government and Regulation of the land and naval forces;

To provide for calling forth the Militia to execute the Laws of the Union, suppress Insurrections, and repel Invasions;

To provide for organizing, arming, and disciplining the Militia, and for governing such part of them as may be employed in the Service of the United States, reserving to the States respectively the Appointment of the Officers, and the Authority of training the Militia according to the discipline prescribed by Congress;

To exercise exclusive Legislation in all Cases whatsoever, over such District (not exceeding ten Miles square) as may, by Cession of particular States, and the acceptance of Congress, become the Seat of the Government of the United States, and to exercise like Authority over all places purchased by the Consent of the Legislature of the State, in which the same shall be, for Erection of Forts, Magazines, Arsenals, dock-Yards, and other needful Buildings;— And

To make all Laws which shall be necessary and proper for carrying into Execution the foregoing Powers, and all other Powers vested by this Constitution in the Government of the United States, or in any Department or Officer thereof.

Section 9 *The Migration or Importation of such Persons as any of the States now existing shall think proper to admit shall not be prohibited by the Congress prior to the Year 1808; but a tax or duty may be imposed on such Importation, not exceeding ten dollars for each person.*

The privilege of the Writ of Habeas Corpus shall not be suspended, unless when in Cases of Rebellion or Invasion the public Safety may require it.

No Bill of Attainder or ex post facto Law shall be passed.

No capitation, or other direct, Tax shall be laid, unless in proportion to the Census or Enumeration herein before directed to be taken.

No Tax or Duty shall be laid on Articles exported from any State.

No Preference shall be given by any Regulation of Revenue to the ports of one State over those of another; nor shall Vessels bound to, or from, one State, be obliged to enter, clear, or pay Duties in another.

No Money shall be drawn from the Treasury, but in Consequence of Appropriations made by Law; and a regular Statement and Account of the Receipts and Expenditures of all public Money shall be published from time to time.

No Title of Nobility shall be granted by the United States: And no Person holding any Office or profit or Trust under them, shall, without the Consent of the Congress, accept of any present, Emolument, Office, or Title, of any kind whatever, from any King, Prince, or foreign state.

Section 10   No State shall enter into any Treaty, Alliance, or Confederation; grant Letters of Marque and Reprisal; coin Money; emit Bills of Credit; make any thing but gold and silver Coin a Tender in payment of Debts; pass any Bill of Attainder, ex post facto Law, or Law impairing the Obligation of Contracts, or grant any Title of Nobility.

No State shall, without the consent of Congress, lay any imposts or duties on imports or exports, except what may be absolutely necessary for executing its inspection laws: and the net produce of all duties and imposts, laid by any State on imports or exports, shall be for the use of the treasury of the United States; and all such laws shall be subject to the revision and control of the Congress.

No State shall, without the Consent of Congress, lay any duty of Tonnage, keep Troops or Ships of War in time of peace, enter into any Agreement or Compact with another State, or with a foreign power, or engage in War, unless actually invaded, or in such imminent Danger as will not admit of delay.

Article II

Section 1   The executive Power shall be vested in a President of the United States of America. He shall hold his Office during the Term of four years, and, together with the Vice-President, chosen for the same Term, be elected as follows:

Each State shall appoint, in such Manner as the Legislature thereof may direct, a Number of Electors, equal to the whole Number of Senators and Representatives to which the State may be entitled in the Congress; but no Senator or Representative, or person holding an Office of Trust or profit under the United States, shall be appointed an Elector.

The Electors shall meet in their respective States, and vote by Ballot for two persons, of whom one at least shall not be an Inhabitant of the same State with themselves. And they shall make a List of all the Persons voted for, and of the Number of Votes for each; which List they shall sign and certify, and transmit sealed to the Seat of Government of the United States, directed to the President of the Senate. The President of the Senate shall, in the Presence of the Senate and House of Representatives, open all the Certificates, and the Votes shall then be counted. The person having the greatest Number of Votes shall be the President, if such Number be a Majority of the whole Number of Electors appointed; and if there be more than one who have such Majority, and have an equal number of Votes, then the House of Representatives shall immediately choose by Ballot one of them for President; and if no person have a Majority, then from the five highest on the List said House shall in like Manner choose the President. But in choosing the President the Votes shall be taken by States, the Representation from each State having one Vote; a quorum for this Purpose shall consist of a Member or Members from two-thirds of the States, and a Majority of all the States shall be necessary to a Choice. In every Case, after the Choice of the President, the

Person having the greatest Number of Votes of the Electors shall be the Vice-President. But if there should remain two or more who have equal votes, the Senate shall choose from them by Ballot the Vice-President.

The Congress may determine the Time of choosing the Electors and the Day on which they shall give their Votes; which Day shall be the same throughout the United States.

No person except a natural-born Citizen, *or a Citizen of the United States at the time of the Adoption of this Constitution,* shall be eligible to the Office of President; neither shall any Person be eligible to that Office who shall not have attained to the Age of thirty-five years, and been fourteen Years a Resident within the United States.

In Case of the Removal of the President from Office or of his Death, Resignation, or Inability to discharge the powers and Duties of the said Office, the same shall devolve on the Vice-President, and the Congress may by Law provide for the Case of Removal, Death, Resignation, or Inability, both of the President and Vice-President, declaring what Officer shall then act as President, and such Officer shall act accordingly, until the disability be removed, or a President shall be elected.

The President shall, at stated Times, receive for his Services a Compensation, which shall neither be increased nor diminished during the period for which he shall have been elected, and he shall not receive within that Period any other Emolument from the United States, or any of them.

Before he enter on the execution of his Office, he shall take the following Oath or Affirmation:—"I do solemnly swear (or affirm) that I will faithfully execute the Office of the President of the United States, and will to the best of my Ability preserve, protect and defend the Constitution of the United States."

Section 2   The President shall be Commander in Chief of the Army and Navy of the United States, and of the Militia of the several States, when called into the actual Service of the United States; he may require the Opinion, in writing, of the principal Officer in each of the executive Departments, upon any subject relating to the Duties of their respective Offices, and he shall have Power to Grant Reprieves and Pardons for Offenses against the United States, except in Cases of Impeachment.

He shall have Power, by and with the Advice and Consent of the Senate, to make Treaties, provided two-thirds of the Senators present concur; and he shall nominate, and by and with the Advice and Consent of the Senate, shall appoint Ambassadors, other public Ministers and Consuls, Judges of the Supreme Court, and all other Officers of the United States, whose Appointments are not herein otherwise provided for, and which shall be established by Law: but Congress may by Law vest the Appointment of such inferior Officers, as they think proper, in the President alone, in the Courts of Law, or in the Heads of Departments.

The President shall have Power to fill up all Vacancies that may happen during the Recess of the Senate, by granting Commissions which shall expire at the End of their next Session.

Section 3   He shall from time to time give to the Congress Information of the State of the Union, and recommend to their Consideration such Measures as he shall judge necessary and expedient; he may, on extraordinary occasions, convene both Houses, or either of them, and in Case of Disagreement between them, with respect to the Time of Adjournment, he may adjourn them to such Time as he shall think proper; he shall receive Ambassadors and other public Ministers; he shall take Care that the Laws be faithfully executed, and shall Commission all the Officers of the United States.

Section 4 The President, Vice-President and all civil Officers of the United States shall be removed from Office on Impeachment for, and Conviction of, Treason, Bribery, or other high Crimes and Misdemeanors.

Article III

Section 1 The judicial power of the United States shall be vested in one supreme Court, and in such inferior Courts as the Congress may from time to time ordain and establish. The Judges, both of the supreme and inferior Courts, shall hold their offices during good Behavior, and shall, at stated Times, receive for their Services a compensation which shall not be diminished during their Continuance in Office.

Section 2 The judicial Power shall extend to all Cases, in Law and Equity, arising under this Constitution, the Laws of the United States, and treaties made, or which shall be made, under their Authority;—to all cases affecting ambassadors, other public ministers and consuls;—to all cases of admiralty and maritime Jurisdiction;—to controversies to which the United States shall be a party;—to Controversies between two or more States;—*between a State and Citizens of another State;*—between Citizens of different States;—between Citizens of the same State claiming Lands under Grants of different States, and between a State, or the Citizens thereof, and foreign States, Citizens or Subjects.

In all Cases affecting Ambassadors, other public Ministers and Consuls, and those in which a State shall be Party, the supreme Court shall have original Jurisdiction. In all the other Cases before mentioned, the supreme Court shall have appellate Jurisdiction, both as to Law and Fact, with such Exceptions, and under such Regulations, as the Congress shall make.

The trial of all Crimes, except in Cases of Impeachment, shall be by Jury; and such Trial shall be held in the State where said Crimes shall have been committed; but when not committed within any State, the Trial shall be at such Place or Places as the Congress may by Law have directed.

Section 3 Treason against the United States shall consist only in levying War against them, or in adhering to their Enemies, giving them Aid and Comfort. No person shall be convicted of Treason unless on the Testimony of two Witnesses to the same overt Act, or on Confession in open Court.

The Congress shall have power to declare the Punishment of Treason, but no Attainder of Treason shall work Corruption of Blood, or Forfeiture except during the Life of the Person attained.

Article IV

Section 1 Full Faith and Credit shall be given in each State to the public Acts, Records, and judicial Proceedings of every other State. And the Congress may by general Laws prescribe the Manner in which such Acts, Records, and Proceedings shall be proved, and the Effect thereof.

Section 2   The Citizens of each State shall be entitled to all Privileges and Immunities of Citizens in the several States.

A Person charged in any State with Treason, Felony, or other Crime, who shall flee from Justice, and be found in another State, shall on demand of the executive Authority of the State from which he fled, be delivered up, to be removed to the State having Jurisdiction of the crime.

No person held to Service or Labor in one State, under the Laws thereof, escaping into another, shall, in Consequence of any Law or Regulation therein, be discharged from such Service or Labor, but shall be delivered up on Claim of the party to whom such Service or Labor may be due.

Section 3   New States may be admitted by the Congress into this Union; but no new State shall be formed or erected within the Jurisdiction of any other State; nor any State be formed by the Junction of two or more States, or parts of States, without the Consent of the Legislatures of the States concerned as well as of the Congress.

The Congress shall have power to dispose of and make all needful Rules and regulations respecting the Territory or other property belonging to the United States; and nothing in this Constitution shall be so construed as to prejudice any Claims of the United States, or of any particular State.

Section 4   The United States shall guarantee to every State in this Union a Republican Form of Government, and shall protect each of them against Invasion; and on Application of the Legislature, or of the Executive (when the Legislature cannot be convened), against domestic Violence.

Article V

The Congress, whenever two-thirds of both Houses shall deem it necessary, shall propose Amendments to this Constitution, or, on the Application of the Legislatures of two-thirds of the several States, shall call a Convention for proposing Amendments, which, in either Case, shall be valid to all Intents and Purposes, as part of this Constitution, when ratified by the Legislatures of three-fourths of the several States, or by Conventions in three-fourths thereof, as the one or the other Mode of Ratification may be proposed by the Congress; provided *that no Amendment which may be made prior to the Year One thousand eight hundred and eight shall in any Manner affect the first and fourth Clauses in the Ninth Section of the first Article;* and that no State, without its Consent, shall be deprived of its equal Suffrage in the Senate.

Article VI

All Debts contracted and Engagements entered into, before the Adoption of this Constitution, shall be as valid against the United States under this Constitution, as under the Confederation.

This Constitution, and the Laws of the United States which shall be made in Pursuance thereof; and all Treaties made, or which shall be made, under the

Authority of the United States, shall be the supreme Law of the Land; and the Judges in every State shall be bound thereby, any thing in the Constitution or Laws of any State to the Contrary notwithstanding.

The Senators and Representatives before mentioned, and the Members of the several State Legislatures, and all executive and judicial Officers, both of the United States and of the several States, shall be bound by Oath or Affirmation to support this Constitution; but no religious Test shall ever be required as a qualification to any Office or public Trust under the United States.

Article VII

The Ratification of the Conventions of nine States shall be sufficient for the Establishment of this Constitution between the States so ratifying the same.

Done in Convention by the unanimous consent of the States present the Seventeenth day of September in the Year of our Lord one thousand seven hundred and Eighty-seven and of the Independence of the United States of America the Twelfth. In Witness whereof We have hereunto subscribed our Names.

GEORGE WASHINGTON
and thirty-seven others

Amendments to the Constitution*

Amendment I

Congress shall make no law respecting an establishment of religion, or prohibiting the free exercise thereof; or abridging the freedom of speech, or of the press; or the right of the people peaceably to assemble, and to petition the government for a redress of grievances.

Amendment II

A well-regulated militia being necessary to the security of a free State, the right of the people to keep and bear arms shall not be infringed.

Amendment III

No soldier shall, in time of peace, be quartered in any house without the consent of the owner, nor in time of war, but in a manner to be prescribed by law.

Amendment IV

The right of the people to be secure in their persons, houses, papers, and effects, against unreasonable searches and seizures, shall not be violated, and no

---

* The first ten amendments (the Bill of Rights) were adopted in 1791.

warrants shall issue but upon probable cause, supported by oath or affirmation, and particularly describing the place to be searched, and the persons or things to be seized.

Amendment V

No person shall be held to answer for a capital, or otherwise infamous crime, unless on a presentment or indictment of a grand jury, except in cases arising in the land or naval forces, or in the militia, when in actual service in time of war or public danger; nor shall any person be subject for the same offense to be twice put in jeopardy of life or limb; nor shall be compelled in any criminal case to be a witness against himself, nor be deprived of life, liberty, or property, without due process of law; nor shall private property be taken for public use without just compensation.

Amendment VI

In all criminal prosecutions, the accused shall enjoy the right to a speedy and public trial, by an impartial jury of the State and district wherein the crime shall have been committed, which district shall have been previously ascertained by law, and to be informed of the nature and cause of the accusation; to be confronted with the witnesses against him; to have compulsory process for obtaining witnesses in his favor, and to have the assistance of counsel for his defense.

Amendment VII

In suits at common law, where the value in controversy shall exceed twenty dollars, the right of trial by jury shall be preserved, and no fact tried by a jury shall be otherwise reexamined in any court of the United States, than according to the rules of the common law.

Amendment VIII

Excessive bail shall not be required, nor excessive fines imposed, nor cruel and unusual punishments inflicted.

Amendment IX

The enumeration in the Constitution, of certain rights, shall not be construed to deny or disparage others retained by the people.

Amendment X

The powers not delegated to the United States by the Constitution, nor prohibited by it to the States, are reserved to the states respectively, or to the people.

Amendment XI
[Adopted 1798]

The judicial power of the United States shall not be construed to extend to any suit in law or equity, commenced or prosecuted against one of the United States by citizens of another state, or by citizens or subjects of any foreign state.

Amendment XII
[Adopted 1804]

The electors shall meet in their respective States, and vote by ballot for President and Vice-President, one of whom, at least, shall not be an inhabitant of the same State with themselves; they shall name in their ballots the person voted for as President, and in distinct ballots the person voted for as Vice-President, and they shall make distinct lists of all persons voted for as President, and of all persons voted for as Vice-President, and of the number of votes for each, which lists they shall sign and certify, and transmit sealed to the seat of government of the United States, directed to the President of the Senate;—the President of the Senate shall, in the presence of the Senate and House of representatives, open all the certificates and the votes shall then be counted;—the person having the greatest number of votes for President shall be the President, if such number be a majority of the whole number of electors appointed; and if no person have such majority, then from the persons having the highest numbers not exceeding three on the list of those voted for as President, the House of Representatives shall choose immediately, by ballot, the President. But in choosing the President, the votes shall be taken by States, the representation from each State having one vote; a quorum for this purpose shall consist of a member or members from two-thirds of the States, and a majority of all the States shall be necessary to a choice. And if the House of Representatives shall not choose a President whenever the right of choice shall devolve upon them, before *the fourth day of March* next following, then the Vice-President shall act as President, as in the case of the death or other constitutional disability of the President.

The person having the greatest number of votes as Vice-President shall be the Vice-President, if such number be a majority of the whole number of electors appointed; and if no person have a majority, then from the two highest numbers on the list the Senate shall choose the Vice-President; a quorum for the purpose shall consist of two-thirds of the whole number of Senators, and a majority of the whole number shall be necessary to a choice. But no person constitutionally ineligible to the office of President shall be eligible to that of Vice-President of the United States.

Amendment XIII
[Adopted 1865]

Section 1   Neither slavery nor involuntary servitude, except as a punishment for crime whereof the party shall have been duly convicted, shall exist within the United States, or any place subject to their jurisdiction.

Section 2   Congress shall have power to enforce this article by appropriate legislation.

Amendment XIV
[Adopted 1868]

Section 1   All persons born or naturalized in the United States, and subject to the jurisdiction thereof, are citizens of the United States and of the State wherein they reside. No State shall make or enforce any law which shall abridge the privileges or immunities of citizens of the United States; nor shall any State deprive any person of life, liberty, or property, without due process of law; nor deny to any person within its jurisdiction the equal protection of the laws.

Section 2   Representatives shall be apportioned among the several States according to their respective numbers, counting the whole number of persons in each State, excluding Indians not taxed. But when the right to vote at any election for the choice of Electors for President and Vice-President of the United States, Representatives in Congress, the executive and judicial officers of a State, or the members of the legislature thereof, is denied to any of the male inhabitants of such State, being twenty-one years of age and citizens of the United States, or in any way abridged, except for participation in rebellion, or other crime, the basis of representation therein shall be reduced in the proportion which the number of such male citizens shall bear to the whole number of male citizens twenty-one years of age in such State.

Section 3   No person shall be a Senator or Representative in Congress, or Elector of President and Vice-President, or hold any office, civil or military, under the United States, or under any State, who, having previously taken an oath, as a member of Congress, or as an officer of the United States, or as a member of any State legislature, or as an executive or judicial officer of any State, to support the Constitution of the United States, shall have engaged in insurrection or rebellion against the same, or given aid or comfort to the enemies thereof. Congress may, by a vote of two-thirds of each house, remove such disability.

Section 4   The validity of the public debt of the United States, authorized by law, including debts incurred for payment of pensions and bounties for services in suppressing insurrection or rebellion, shall not be questioned. But neither the United States nor any State shall assume or pay any debt or obligation incurred in aid of insurrection or rebellion against the United States, or any claim for the loss of emancipation of any slave; but all such debts, obligations, and claims shall be held illegal and void.

Section 5   The Congress shall have power to enforce, by appropriate legislation, the provisions of this article.

Amendment XV
[Adopted 1870]

Section 1   The right of citizens of the United States to vote shall not be denied or abridged by the United States or by any State on account of race, color, or previous condition of servitude.

Section 2 The Congress shall have power to enforce this article by appropriate legislation.

Amendment XVI
[Adopted 1913]

The Congress shall have power to lay and collect taxes on incomes, from whatever source derived, without apportionment among the several States, and without regard to any census or enumeration.

Amendment XVII
[Adopted 1913]

Section 1 The Senate of the United States shall be composed of two Senators from each State, elected by the people thereof, for six years; and each Senator shall have one vote. The electors in each State shall have the qualifications requisite for electors of [voters for] the most numerous branch of the State legislatures.

Section 2 When vacancies happen in the representation of any State in the Senate, the executive authority of such State shall issue writs of election to fill such vacancies: *Provided,* that the Legislature of any State may empower the executive thereof to make temporary appointments until the people fill the vacancies by election as the Legislature may direct.

Section 3 This amendment shall not be so construed as to affect the election or term of any Senator chosen before it becomes valid as part of the Constitution.

Amendment XVIII
[Adopted 1919, repealed 1933]

Section 1 After one year from the ratification of this article the manufacture, sale or transportation of intoxicating liquors within, the importation thereof into, or the exportation thereof from the United States and all territory subject to the jurisdiction thereof, for beverage purposes, is hereby prohibited.

Section 2 The Congress and the several States shall have concurrent power to enforce this article by appropriate legislation.

Section 3 This article shall be inoperative unless it shall have been ratified as an amendment to the Constitution by the legislatures of the several States, as provided by the Constitution, within seven years from the date of the submission thereof to the States by the Congress.

Amendment XIX
[Adopted 1920]

Section 1 The right of citizens of the United States to vote shall not be denied or abridged by the United States or by any State on account of sex.

Section 2   The Congress shall have power to enforce this article by appropriate legislation.

Amendment XX
[Adopted 1933]

Section 1   The terms of the President and Vice-President shall end at noon on the 20th day of January, and the terms of Senators and Representatives at noon on the 3d day of January, of the years in which such terms would have ended if this article had not been ratified; and the terms of their successors shall then begin.

Section 2   The Congress shall assemble at least once in every year, and such meetings shall begin at noon on the 3d day of January, unless they shall by law appoint a different day.

Section 3   If, at the time fixed for the beginning of the term of the President, the President-elect shall have died, the Vice-President-elect shall become President. If a President shall not have been chosen before the time fixed for the beginning of his term, or if the President-elect shall have failed to qualify, then the Vice-President-elect shall act as President until a President shall have qualified; and the Congress may by law provide for the case wherein neither a President-elect nor a Vice-President-elect shall have qualified, declaring who shall then act as President, or the manner in which one who is to act shall be selected, and such persons shall act accordingly until a President or Vice-President shall have qualified.

Section 4   The Congress may by law provide for the case of the death of any of the persons from whom the House of Representatives may choose a President whenever the right of choice shall have devolved upon them, and for the case of the death of any of the persons from whom the Senate may choose a Vice-President whenever the right of choice shall have devolved upon them.

Section 5   Sections 1 and 2 shall take effect on the 15th day of October following the ratification of this article.

Section 6   This article shall be inoperative unless it shall have been ratified as an amendment to the Constitution by the Legislatures of three-fourths of the several States within seven years from the date of its submission.

Amendment XXI
[Adopted 1933]

Section 1   The eighteenth article of amendment to the Constitution of the United States is hereby repealed.

Section 2   The transportation or importation into any State, Territory, or Possession of the United States for delivery or use therein of intoxicating liquors, in violation of the laws thereof, is hereby prohibited.

Section 3   This article shall be inoperative unless it shall have been ratified as an amendment to the Constitution by conventions in the several States, as provided in the Constitution, within seven years from the date of submission thereof to the States by the Congress.

Amendment XXII
[Adopted 1951]

Section 1   No person shall be elected to the office of President more than twice, and no person who has held the office of President, or acted as President, for more than two years of a term to which some other person was elected President shall be elected to the office of President more than once. But this article shall not apply to any person holding the office of President when this article was proposed by the Congress, and shall not prevent any person who may be holding the office of President, or acting as President, during the term within which this article becomes operative from holding the office of President or acting as President during the remainder of such term.

Section 2   This article shall be inoperative unless it shall have been ratified as an amendment to the Constitution by the legislatures of three-fourths of the several States within seven years from the date of its submission to the States by the Congress.

Amendment XXIII
[Adopted 1961]

Section 1   The District constituting the seat of Government of the United States shall appoint in such manner as the Congress may direct:
    A number of electors of President and Vice-President equal to the whole number of Senators and Representatives in Congress to which the District would be entitled if it were a State, but in no event more than the least populous State; they shall be in addition to those appointed by the States, but they shall be considered for the purposes of the election of President and Vice-President, to be electors appointed by a State; and they shall meet in the District and perform such duties as provided by the twelfth article of amendment.

Section 2   The Congress shall have the power to enforce this article by appropriate legislation.

Amendment XXIV
[Adopted 1964]

Section 1   The right of citizens of the United States to vote in any primary or other election for President or Vice-President, for electors for President or Vice-President, or for Senator or Representative in Congress, shall not be denied or abridged by the United States or any State by reason of failure to pay any poll tax or other tax.

Section 2   The Congress shall have the power to enforce this article by appropriate legislation.

Amendment XXV
[Adopted 1967]

Section 1   In case of the removal of the President from office or of his death or resignation, the Vice-President shall become President.

Section 2   Whenever there is a vacancy in the office of the Vice-President, the President shall nominate a Vice-President who shall take office upon confirmation by a majority vote of both Houses of Congress.

Section 3   Whenever the President transmits to the President pro tempore of the Senate and the speaker of the House of Representatives his written declaration that he is unable to discharge the powers and duties of his office, and until he transmits to them a written declaration to the contrary, such powers and duties shall be discharged by the Vice-President as Acting President.

Section 4   Whenever the Vice-President and a majority of either the principal officers of the executive departments or of such other body as Congress may by law provide, transmit to the President pro tempore of the Senate and the Speaker of the House of Representatives their written declaration that the President is unable to discharge the powers and duties of his office, the Vice-President shall immediately assume the powers and duties of the office as Acting President.

Thereafter, when the President transmits to the President pro tempore of the Senate and the Speaker of the House of Representatives his written declaration that no inability exists, he shall resume the powers and duties of his office unless the Vice-President and a majority of either the principal officers of the executive department(s) or of such other body as Congress may by law provide, transmit within four days to the President pro tempore of the Senate and the Speaker of the House of Representatives their written declaration that the President is unable to discharge the powers and duties of his office. Thereupon Congress shall decide the issue, assembling within forty-eight hours for that purpose if not in session. If the Congress, within twenty-one days after receipt of the latter written declaration, or, if Congress is not in session, within twenty-one days after Congress is required to assemble, determines by two-thirds vote of both Houses that the President is unable to discharge the powers and duties of his office, the Vice-President shall continue to discharge the same as Acting President; otherwise, the President shall resume the powers and duties of his office.

Amendment XXVI
[Adopted 1971]

Section 1   The right of citizens of the United States, who are eighteen years of age or older, to vote shall not be denied or abridged by the United States or by any State on account of age.

Section 2   The Congress shall have power to enforce this article by appropriate legislation.

Amendment XXVII
[Adopted 1992]

No law, varying the compensation for the services of the senators and representatives shall take effect, until an election of representatives shall have intervened.

REFERENCES

Chapter 1 / Dilemmas of Democracy pp. 1–31

1. Center for Political Studies of the Institute for Social Research, *Election Study 1988* (Ann Arbor, Mich., University of Michigan, 1989).

2. *1977 Constitution of the Union of Soviet Socialist Republics*, Article 11, in *Constitutions of Countries of the World*, ed. A. P. Blaustein and G. H. Flanz (Dobbs Ferry, N.Y.: Oceana, 1971).

3. Karl Marx and Friedrich Engels, *Critique of the Gotha Programme* (New York: International Publishers, 1938), p. 10. This book was originally written in 1875 but was published in 1891.

4. See the argument in Amy Gutman, *Liberal Equality* (Cambridge: Cambridge University Press, 1980), pp. 9–10.

5. See John H. Schaar, "Equality of Opportunity and Beyond," in *Equality NOMOS IX*, ed. J. Roland Pennock and John W. Chapman (New York: Atherton Press, 1967), pp. 228–249.

6. *Gallup Report*, Nos. 282–283 (March–April 1989):8. See also Wesley G. Skogan, *Disorder and Decline: Crime and the Spiral Decay in American Neighborhoods* (New York: The Free Press, 1990), Chap. 2.

7. Milton Friedman, *Capitalism and Freedom* (Chicago: University of Chicago Press, 1962).

8. Lawrence Herson, *The Politics of Ideas: Political Theory and American Public Policy* (Homewood, Ill.: Dorsey Press, 1984), pp. 166–176.

9. "Five Children Killed as Gunman Attacks a California School," *New York Times*, January 18, 1989, p. A1; and

Robert Reinhold, "After Shooting, Horror But Few Answers," *New York Times*, January 20, 1989, p. B6.

10. *Gallup Report* (March–April 1989):2–5.

11. Joan Biskupic, "Anticrime Package Falters After Gun Ban Retained," *Congressional Quarterly Weekly Report*, May 26, 1990, pp. 1654–1656; Joan Biskupic, "Opponents of Gun Control Stall Crime Bill Action," *Congressional Quarterly Weekly Report*, June 9, 1990, pp. 1790–1791; and Joan Biskupic, "Death Penalty, Other Hot Issues Dumped from Crime Bill, *Congressional Quarterly Weekly Report*, October 27, 1990, p. 3615.

12. Austin Ranney and Willmoore Kendall, *Democracy and the American Political System* (New York: Harcourt Brace, 1956), p. 6.

13. This distinction is elaborated in ibid., pp. 12–13.

14. See C. B. Macpherson, *The Real World of Democracy* (New York: Oxford University Press, 1975), pp. 58–59.

15. Thomas E. Cronin, *Direct Democracy* (Cambridge, Mass.: Harvard University Press, 1989), p. 47.

16. Ibid., p. 80.

17. M. Margaret Conway, *Political Participation in the United States*, 2d ed. (Washington, D.C.: Congressional Quarterly, 1991), p. 44.

18. See Robert A. Dahl, *Dilemmas of Pluralist Democracy: Autonomy vs. Control* (New Haven, Conn.: Yale University Press, 1982), p. 5.

19. Michael Useem, *The Inner Circle* (New York: Oxford University Press, 1984). On a broader level, see Charles E. Lindblom, *Politics and Markets* (New York: Basic Books, 1977).

20. The most prominent study was Robert A. Dahl's research on decision making

in New Haven, Connecticut, in *Who Governs?* (New Haven, Conn.: Yale University Press, 1961). G. William Domhoff criticized Dahl's study in *Who Really Rules? New Haven and Community Power Re-examined* (New Brunswick, N.J.: Transaction Books, 1978). Nelson W. Polsby supported Dahl's basic findings in *Community Power and Political Theory: A Further Look at Problems of Evidence and Inference*, 2d ed. (New Haven, Conn.: Yale University Press, 1980).

21. See Robert A. Dahl, "A Critique of the Ruling Elite Model," *American Political Science Review* 52 (June 1958):466.

22. Peter Bachrach and Morton S. Baratz, "Two Faces of Power," *American Political Science Review* 56 December 1962):947–952; and John Gaventa, *Power and Powerlessness* (Urbana, Ill.: University of Illinois Press, 1980).

23. See Kenneth M. Dolbeare, *Democracy at Risk: The Politics of Economic Renewal* (Chatham, N.J.: Chatham House, 1984); and Edward S. Greenberg, *The American Political System: A Radical Approach* (Boston: Little, Brown, 1986).

24. See Kay Lehman Schlozman and John T. Tierney, *Organized Interests and American Democracy* (New York: Harper & Row, 1986).

25. G. Bingham Powell, Jr., *Contemporary Democracies* (Cambridge, Mass.: Harvard University Press, 1982), p. 3. Copyright 1982. Used by permission of Harvard University Press.

26. Arend Lijphart, *Democracies* (New Haven, Conn.: Yale University Press, 1984), p. 8. See also Robert Wesson, ed., *Democracy: A Worldwide Survey* (New York: Praeger, 1987), p. xi, for a similar count.

27. The Gallup Poll, *Public Opinion 1985* (Wilmington, Del.: Scholarly Resources, 1986), p. 32.

28. E. E. Schattschneider, *The Semi-sovereign People* (New York: Holt, Rinehart, and Winston, 1960), p. 35.

Chapter 2 / The Constitution
pp. 36–67

1. John Plamentz, *Man and Society*, vol. 1 (New York: McGraw-Hill, 1963), pp. 162–164.

2. Extrapolated from U.S. Department of Defense, *Selected Manpower Statistics, FY 1982* (Washington, D.C.: U.S. Government Printing Office, 1983), Table 2-30, p. 130; and *Statistical Abstract of the United States, 1985* (Washington, D.C.: U.S. Government Printing Office, 1985), Tables 1 and 2, p. 6.

3. Joseph T. Keenan, The Constitution of the United States (Homewood, Ill.: Dow Jones–Irwin, 1975).

4. David P. Szatmary, *Shays' Rebellion: The Making of an Agrarian Insurrection* (Amherst: University of Massachusetts Press, 1980), pp. 82–102.

5. Robert H. Jackson, *The Struggle for Judicial Supremacy* (New York: Knopf, 1941), p. 8.

6. Forrest McDonald, *Novus Ordo Seclorum: The Intellectual Origins of the Constitution* (Lawrence: University Press of Kansas, 1985), pp. 205–209.

7. Donald S. Lutz, "The Preamble to the Constitution of the United States," *This Constitution* 1 (September 1983):23–30.

8. Richard E. Neustadt, *Presidential Power: The Politics of Leadership* (New York: Wiley, 1960), p. 33.

9. Herbert J. Storing, ed., *The Complete Anti-Federalist,* 7 vols. (Chicago: University of Chicago Press, 1981).

10. Alexis de Tocqueville, *Democracy in America,* ed. J. P. Mayer and Max Lerner (New York: Harper and Row, 1966), p. 102.

11. Jerold L. Waltman, *Political Origin of the U.S. Income Tax* (Jackson: University Press of Mississippi, 1985), p. 10.

Chapter 3 / Federalism
pp. 71–96

1. Ronald Reagan, "National Minimum Drinking Age: Remarks on Signing

HR4616 into Law (July 17, 1984)," *Weekly Compilation of Presidential Documents,* July 23, 1984, p. 1036.

2. *South Dakota* v. *Dole,* 483 U.S. 203 (1987).

3. *Budget of the United States Government, FY 1992,* Part 4, p. 863.

4. Daniel J. Elazar, "Opening the Third Century of American Federalism: Issues and Prospects," *Annals of the American Academy of Political and Social Sciences* 509 (May 1990):14

5. William H. Stewart, *Concepts of Federalism* (Lanham, Md.: University Press of America, 1984).

6. Edward S. Corwin, "The Passing of Dual Federalism," *Virginia Law Review* 36 (February 1950):4.

7. See Daniel J. Elazar, *The American Partnership* (Chicago: University of Chicago Press, 1962); and Morton Grodzins, *The American System* (Chicago: Rand McNally, 1966).

8. *Baker* v. *Carr,* 369 U.S. 186 (1962); *Wesberry* v. *Sanders,* 376 U.S. 1 (1964); and *Reynolds* v. *Sims,* 377 U.S. 533 (1964).

9. Advisory Commission on Intergovernmental Relations, *A Catalog of Federal Grant-in-Aid Programs to State and Local Government: Grants Funded in FY 1989* (Washington, D.C.: U.S. Government Printing Office, 1990).

10. *McCulloch* v. *Maryland,* 4 Wheat. 316 (1819).

11. James T. Patterson, *The New Deal and the States: Federalism in Transition* (Princeton, N.J.: Princeton University Press, 1969).

12. *United States* v. *Butler,* 297 U.S. 1 (1936).

13. *Plessy* v. *Ferguson,* 163 U.S. 537 (1896).

14. *Brown* v. *Board of Education of Topeka,* 347 U.S. 483 (1954).

15. Advisory Commission on Intergovernmental Relations, *The Federal Role in the Federal System: The Dynamics of Growth* (Washington, D.C.: U.S. Government Printing Office, 1981), p. 101.

16. Richard M. Nixon, "Speech to National Governor's Conference, September 1, 1969," in *Congressional Quarterly Almanac* (Washington, D.C.: Congressional Quarterly Press, 1969), pp. 101A–103A.

17. Executive Order 12612—Federalism (October 26, 1987).

18. Thomas R. Dye, *American Federalism: Competition Among Governments* (Lexington, Mass.: Lexington Books, 1990).

19. Paul M. Weyrich, quoted in Neal Pierce, "Conservatives Weep as the States Make Left Turn," *National Journal,* October 10, 1987, p. 2559.

Chapter 4 / Public Opinion, Political Socialization, and the Mass Media   pp. 98–133

1. Richard G. Niemi, John Mueller, and Tom W. Smith, *Trends in Public Opinion: A Compendium of Survey Data* (Westport, Conn.: Greenwood Press, 1989), p. 138. The data for 1988 are from the *Gallup Report,* No. 280 (January 1989):27.

2. *New York Times,* July 3, 1976.

3. *Furman* v. *Georgia,* 408 U.S. 238 (1972).

4. *Gregg* v. *Georgia,* 248 U.S. 153 (1976).

5. Tom W. Smith and Paul B. Sheatsley, "American Attitudes Toward Race Relations," *Public Opinion* 7 (October–November 1984):15.

6. Ibid.

7. Ibid., p. 83.

8. Steven A. Peterson, *Political Behavior: Patterns in Everyday Life* (Newbury Park, Calif.: Sage Publications, 1990), pp. 28–29.

9. Paul Allen Beck, "The Role of Agents in Political Socialization," in *Handbook of Political Socialization Theory and Research,* ed. Stanley Allen Renshon (New York: Free Press, 1977), pp. 117–118.

10. W. Russell Neuman, *The Paradox of Mass Politics: Knowledge and Opinion in the American Electorate* (Cam-

bridge, Mass.: Harvard University Press, 1986), pp. 113–114.

11. M. Kent Jennings and Richard G. Niemi, *The Political Character of Adolescence: The Influence of Families and Schools* (Princeton, N.J.: Princeton University Press, 1974), p. 39. See also Stephen E. Frantzich, *Political Parties in the Technological Age* (New York: Longman, 1989), p. 152. Frantzich presented a table showing that more than 60 percent of children in homes where both parents have the same party preference will adopt their preference. When parents are divided, the children tend to be divided among Democrats, Republicans, and independents.

12. Robert D. Hess and Judith V. Torney, *The Development of Political Attitudes in Children* (Chicago: Aldine, 1967). But other researchers disagree. See Jerry L. Yeric and John R. Todd, *Public Opinion: The Visible Politics* (Itasca, Ill.: F. E. Peacock, 1989), pp. 45–47, for a summary of the issues.

13. Jarol B. Manheim, *The Politics Within* (New York: Longman, 1982), p. 83.

14. See Robert Huckfeldt and John Sprague, "Networks in Context: The Social Flow of Information," *American Political Science Review* 81 (December 1987):1197–1216. The authors' study of voting in neighborhoods in South Bend, Indiana, found that residents who favored the minority party were acutely aware of their minority status.

15. Theodore M. Newcomb, *Persistence and Social Change: Bennington College and Its Students After Twenty-Five Years* (New York: Wiley, 1967).

16. See Roberta S. Sigel, ed., *Political Learning in Adulthood: A Sourcebook of Theory and Research* (Chicago: University of Chicago Press, 1989).

17. This question has appeared for years in the National Opinion Research Center's General Social Survey. As usual, the question in 1990 had seven response categories ranging from "government should do something to reduce income differences between rich and poor" (Category 1) to "government should not concern itself with income differences" (Category 7). Categories 1 through 3 were combined to represent the "government should" response, and Categories 4 through 7 were combined to represent the "government should not" response.

18. The increasing wealth in industrialized societies may or may not be replacing class conflict with conflict over values. See the exchange between Ronald Inglehart and Scott C. Flanagan, "Value Change in Industrial Societies," *American Political Science Review* 81 (December 1987):1289–1319.

19. For a parallel analysis, see Neuman, *The Paradox of Mass Politics*, pp. 79–81.

20. For a recent review of these studies, see Robert S. Erikson, Norman R. Luttbeg, and Kent L. Tedin, *American Public Opinion*, 3d. ed. (New York: Macmillan, 1988).

21. Nathan Glazer, "The Structure of Ethnicity," *Public Opinion* 7 (October–November 1984):4.

22. Felicity Barringer, "Census Shows Profound Change in Racial Makeup of the Nation," *New York Times*, March 11, 1991, pp. 1 and 12.

23. Glazer, "The Structure of Ethnicity," p. 5.

24. These figures came from the 1990 General Social Survey and were kindly provided by Tom W. Smith, director of the survey.

25. John Robinson, "The Ups and Downs and Ins and Outs of Ideology," *Public Opinion* 7 (February–March 1984):12.

26. Angus Campbell et al., *The American Voter* (New York: Wiley, 1960), Chap. 10.

27. See Norman H. Nie, Sidney Verba, and John R. Petrocik, *The Changing American Voter*, 2d ed. (Cambridge, Mass.: Harvard University Press, 1979).

28. Some scholars believe that the methods used for classifying respondents as ideologues was too generous. See Robert C. Luskin, "Measuring Political Sophistication," *American Journal of Political Science* 31 (November 1987):878, 887–888. For a comprehen-

sive critique, see Eric R.A.N. Smith, *The Unchanging American Voter* (Berkeley and Los Angeles: University of California Press, 1989), especially Chap. 1.

29. Milton Rokeach also proposed a two-dimensional model of political ideology grounded in the terminal values of freedom and equality. See *The Nature of Human Values* (New York: Free Press, 1973), especially Chap. 6. Rokeach found that positive and negative references to these two values permeated the writings of socialists, communists, fascists, and conservatives and clearly differentiated the four bodies of writing from one another (pp. 173–174). However, Rokeach built his two-dimensional model only around the values of freedom and equality; he did not deal with the question of freedom versus order.

30. Pamela Johnston Conover, "The Origins and Meaning of Liberal-Conservative Self-Identifications," *American Journal of Political Science* 25 (November 1981):621–622, 643.

31. The relationship of liberalism to political tolerance was found by John L. Sullivan et al., "The Sources of Political Tolerance: A Multivariate Analysis," *American Political Science Review* 75 (March 1981):102. See also Robinson, "The Ups and Downs," pp. 13–15.

32. Herbert Asher, *Presidential Elections and American Politics* (Homewood, Ill.: Dorsey Press, 1980), pp. 14–20. Asher also constructed a two-dimensional framework, distinguishing between "traditional New Deal" issues and "new lifestyle" issues.

33. John E. Jackson, "The Systematic Beliefs of the Mass Public: Estimating Policy Preferences with Survey Data," *Journal of Politics* 45 (November 1983):840–865, at 857.

34. The second edition of *The Challenge of Democracy*, which used the 1987 General Social Survey, reported slightly different percentages for three of the four ideological tendencies. According to the 1987 data, populists accounted for 24 percent of the sample; libertarians, for 26 percent; conservatives, for 28 percent; and liberals, for 22 percent. The differences in percentages reflected a substantial shift in the 1990 sample of 7 percentage points away from firing a communist teacher (no doubt because of the collapse of the Soviet threat) and 6 points toward government equalizing of income. That shift is probably due to publicity about the growth of a gap between rich and poor during the Reagan administration. See Kevin Phillips, *The Politics of Rich and Poor: Wealth and the American Electorate in the Reagan Aftermath* (New York: Random House, 1990).

35. But a significant literature is developing on the limitations of self-interest in explaining political life. See Jane J. Mansbridge, ed., *Beyond Self-Interest* (Chicago: University of Chicago Press, 1990).

36. Aaron Wildavsky, "Choosing Preferences by Constructing Institutions: A Cultural Theory of Preference Formation," *American Political Science Review* 81 (March 1987):3–21.

37. David O. Sears and Carolyn L. Funk, "Self-Interest in Americans' Political Opinions," in Mansbridge, ed., *Beyond Self-Interest*, pp. 147–170.

38. Center for Political Studies, *1988 National Election Survey* (Ann Arbor, Mich.: Inter-University Consortium for Political and Social Research, 1989), pp. 281–291.

39. Times Mirror Center for the People and the Press, "Times Mirror News Interest Index" (July 12, 1990):2.

40. Smith, *The Unchanging American Voter*, p. 5. However, Smith then argued that the information component of the definition is more important than attitude consistency or level of conceptualization (pp. 224–227). For another attempt to measure political sophistication "by using a ten-word vocabulary test," see Lawrence Bobo and Frederick C. Licari, "Education and Political Tolerance: Testing the Effects of Cognitive Sophistication and Target Group Affect," *Public Opinion Quarterly* 53 (Fall 1989):285–308.

41. Neuman, *The Paradox of Mass Politics*, pp. 6–7. There is evidence that the educational system and parental practices hamper the ability of women to develop their political sophistication. See Linda L.M. Bennett and Stephen Earl Bennett, "Enduring Gender Differences in Political Interests," *American Politics Quarterly* 17 (January 1989):105–122.

42. Ibid., p. 81.

43. Pamela Johnston Conover and Stanley Feldman, "How People Organize the Political World: A Schematic Model," *American Journal of Political Science* 28 (February 1984):96. For an excellent review of schema structures in contemporary psychology—especially as they relate to political science—see Reid Hastie, "A Primer of Information-Processing Theory for the Political Scientist," in *Political Cognition*, ed. Richard R. Lau and David O. Sears (Hillsdale, N.J.: Erlbaum, 1986), pp. 11–39.

44. John Hurwitz and Mark Peffley, "How Are Foreign Policy Attitudes Structured? A Hierarchical Model," *American Political Science Review* 81 (December 1987):1099–1220.

45. Richard L. Allen, Michael C. Dawson, and Ronald E. Brown, "A Schema-based Approach to Modeling an African-American Racial Belief System," *American Political Science Review* 83 (June 1989):421–441.

46. See Milton Lodge and Ruth Hamill, "A Partisan Schema for Political Information Processing," *American Political Science Review* 80 (June 1986):505–519.

47. Arthur Sanders, *Making Sense Out of Politics* (Ames: Iowa State University Press, 1990).

48. Lee Sigelman, "Disarming the Opposition: The President, the Public, and the INF Treaty," *Public Opinion Quarterly* 54 (Spring 1990):37–47, at 46.

49. Benjamin I. Page, Robert Y. Shapiro, and Glenn R. Dempsey, "What Moves Public Opinion?" *American Political Science Review* 81 (March 1987):23–43.

50. Michael Margolis and Gary A. Mauser, *Manipulating Public Opinion: Essays on Public Opinion as a Dependent Variable* (Pacific Grove, Calif.: Brooks/Cole, 1989).

51. Doris A. Graber, *Mass Media and American Politics* (Washington, D.C.: Congressional Quarterly Press, 1984), pp. 78–79.

52. *Broadcasting Yearbook, 1990* (Washington, D.C.: Broadcasting Publications, 1990).

53. Harold W. Stanley and Richard G. Niemi, eds., *Vital Statistics on American Politics*, 2d ed. (Washington, D.C.: Congressional Quarterly Press, 1990), p. 69.

54. See Times Mirror Center for the People and the Press, "The American Media: Who Reads, Who Watches, Who Listens, Who Cares" (Washington, D.C.: Press release, July 15, 1990), p. 4; Doris A. Graber, *Processing the News: How People Tame the Information Tide*, 2d ed. (New York: Longman, 1988), p. 101; and Michael J. Robinson and Andrew Kohut, "Believability and the Press," *Public Opinion Quarterly* 52 (Summer 1988):174–189.

55. Times Mirror Center, "The American Media."

56. This fits with findings by Stephen Earl Bennett in "Trends in Americans' Political Information, 1967–1987," *American Politics Quarterly* 17 (October 1989):422–435. Bennett found that race was significantly related to level of political information in a 1967 survey but not in a 1987 survey.

57. Times Mirror Center for the People and the Press, "News Interest Index" (Washington, D.C.: Press release, March 1990), p. 125.

58. One seasoned journalist has argued instead that the technology of mini-cams and satellites has set back the quality of coverage. Now a television crew can fly to the scene of a crisis and immediately televise information, without knowing much about the local politics or culture, which was not true of the old foreign correspondents. See David R. Gergen, "Diplomacy in a Television Age: The Dangers of

Teledemocracy," in *The Media and Foreign Policy*, ed. Simon Serfaty (New York: St. Martin's Press, 1990), p. 51.

59. Bennett, "Trends in Americans' Political Information." Bennett's findings were supported by a national poll in 1990 that found only 40 percent of the sample read a newspaper "yesterday," compared with 71 percent asked the same question in 1965. Times Mirror Center, "The American Media," p. 100.

60. See Peter Clarke and Eric Fredin, "Newspapers, Television, and Political Reasoning," *Public Opinion Quarterly* 42 (Summer 1978):143–160; Joseph Wagner, "Media Do Make the Difference: The Differential Impact of Mass Media in the 1976 Presidential Race," *American Journal of Political Science* 27 (August 1983):407–430, at 415–417; and L. Harmon Zeigler and William Haltom, "More Bad News About the News," *Public Opinion* 12 (May–June 1989):50–52.

61. Graber, *Processing the News*, pp. 166–169.

62. Michael J. Robinson, "American Political Legitimacy in an Era of Electronic Journalism: Reflections on the Evening News," in *Television as a Social Force*, ed. Douglass Cater (New York: Praeger, 1975), pp. 97–139.

63. Graber, *Mass Media*, pp. 66–67; and Andrew Goodman, "Television Images of the Foreign Policy Process" (Ph.D. diss., Northwestern University, 1985), Chap. 11.

64. William Schneider, "Bang-Bang Television: The New Superpower," *Public Opinion* 5 (April–May 1982):13–15, at 13.

65. Page, Shapiro, and Dempsey, "What Moves Public Opinion?" pp. 23–43, at 31.

66. Shanto Iyengar and Donald R. Kinder, *News That Matters: Television and American Opinion* (Chicago: University of Chicago Press, 1987), p. 33.

67. Ibid., p. 60.

68. W. Russell Neuman, "The Threshold of Public Attention," *Public Opinion Quarterly* 54 (Summer 1990):159–176.

69. Richard Zoglin, "Is TV Ruining Our Children?" *Time*, October 5, 1990, p. 75. Moreover, much of what children see are advertisements. See "Study: Almost 20% of Kid TV Is Ad-Related," *Chicago Tribune*, April 22, 1991, p. 11.

70. John J. O'Connor, "Soothing Bromides? Not on TV," *New York Times*, Arts & Leisure Sec., October 28, 1990, pp. 1, 35.

71. For analysis of elections from 1964 to 1976, see S. Robert Lichter and Stanley Rothman, "Media and Business Elites," *Public Opinion* 5 (October–November 1981):42–46. For a study of the 1980 election, see L. Brent Bozell II and Brent H. Baker, eds., *And That's the Way It Isn't* (Alexandria, Va.: Media Research Center, 1990), p. 32.

72. Bozell and Baker, *And That's the Way It Isn't*, p. 38. Similar findings were found in a larger study of 2,703 reporters and editors in 1985. See William Schneider and I. A. Lewis, "Views on the News," *Public Opinion* 8 (August–September 1985):6–11, 58–59, at 7.

73. Elizabeth Kolbert, "For Bush, More TV News Is Also Good News," *New York Times*, September 22, 1992, p. 1.

74. Schneider and Lewis, "Views on the News," pp. 6–11, 58–59.

75. Stanley and Niemi, *Vital Statistics on American Politics*, p. 73.

76. Michael Robinson and Margaret Sheehan, *Over the Wire and on TV: CBS and UPI in Campaign '80* (New York: Russell Sage Foundation, 1983).

77. Michael J. Robinson, "The Media in Campaign '84: Part II; Wingless, Toothless, and Hopeless," *Public Opinion* 8 (February–March 1985):43–48, at 48.

78. Maura Clancey and Michael J. Robinson, "General Election Coverage: Part I," *Public Opinion* 7 (December–January 1985):49–54, 59, at 54.

79. Stanley Rothman and S. Robert Lichter, "Elite Ideology and Risk Perception in Nuclear Energy Policy," *American Political Science Review* 81 (June 1987):393.

80. For a historical account of efforts to determine voters' preferences before modern polling, see Tom W. Smith, "The First Straw? A Study of the Origin of Election Polls," *Public Opinion Polling* 54 (Spring 1990):21–36.

81. Michael R. Kagay, "The Use of Public Opinion Polls by the New York Times: Some Examples from the 1988 Presidential Election," in *Polling and Presidential Election Coverage*, ed. Paul J. Lavrakas and Jack K. Holley (Newbury Park, Calif.: Sage Publications, 1991), p. 19.

82. Jack K. Holley, "The Press and Political Polling," in ibid., p. 225.

83. Schneider and Lewis, "Views on the News," p. 11.

84. Times Mirror Center for the People and the Press, "The People, the Press and the War in the Gulf" (Washington, D.C.: January 31, 1991), p. 1.

Chapter 5 / Participation and Voting   pp. 137–163

1. Elaine S. Povich and Steve Daley, "Bush Turns Up Heat on Gulf Vote," *Chicago Tribune*, January 12, 1991, p. 1.

2. Jason DeParle, "On the Left, Voices Amid Confusion," *New York Times*, November 17, 1990, p. 5.

3. Michael deCourcy Hinds, "Drawing on Vietnam Legacy, Antiwar Effort Buds Quickly," *New York Times*, January 11, 1991, p. 1; Anthony DePalma, "On Campuses, Coordinated Antiwar Protests," *New York Times*, February 22, 1991, p. A8.

4. Janet Cawley and Ruth Lopez, "Rallies Draw Crowds Across U.S., Abroad," *Chicago Tribune*, January 22, 1991, sec. 1, p. 6; Jerry Adler, "The War Within," *Newsweek*, February 4, 1991, p. 58.

5. Jane Gross, "Anxious Nation Is Drawn Together," *New York Times*, January 18, 1991, p. A13.

6. Linda P. Campbell and Ruth Lopez, "To Illinois Protesters, War 'an Insane Move,'" *Chicago Tribune*, January 20, 1991, sec. 1, p. 8.

7. Lester W. Milbrath and M. L. Goel, *Political Participation* (Chicago: Rand McNally, 1977), p. 2.

8. *New York Times*, March 4, 1985.

9. Michael Lipsky, "Protest as a Political Resource," *American Political Science Review* 62 (December 1968):1145.

10. See Sidney Verba and Norman H. Nie, *Participation in America: Political Democracy and Social Equality* (New York: Harper and Row, 1972), p. 3.

11. Samuel H. Barnes and Max Kaase, eds., *Political Action: Mass Participation in Five Western Democracies* (Beverly Hills, Calif.: Sage Publications, 1979).

12. Stephen C. Craig and Michael A. Magiotto, "Political Discontent and Political Action," *Journal of Politics* 43 (May 1981):514–522. But see Mitchell A. Seligson, "Trust Efficacy and Modes of Political Participation: A Study of Costa Rican Peasants," *British Journal of Political Science* 10 (January 1980):75–98, for a review of studies that came to different conclusions.

13. Philip H. Pollock III, "Organizations as Agents of Mobilization: How Does Group Activity Affect Political Participation?" *American Journal of Political Science* 26 (August 1982):485–503. Also see Jan E. Leighley, "Social Interaction and Contextual Influence on Political Participation," *American Politics Quarterly* 18 (October 1990):459–475.

14. Arthur H. Miller et al., "Group Consciousness and Political Participation," *American Journal of Political Science* 25 (August 1981):495. See also Susan J. Carroll, "Gender Politics and the Socializing Impact of the Women's Movement," in *Political Learning in Adulthood: A Sourcebook of Theory and Research*, ed. Roberta S. Sigel (Chicago: University of Chicago Press, 1989), p. 307.

15. Russell J. Dalton, *Citizen Politics in Western Democracies* (Chatham, N.J.: Chatham House, 1988), p. 65.

16. M. Kent Jennings, Jan W. van Deth et al., *Continuities in Political Action:*

A Longitudinal Study of Political Orientations in Three Western Democracies (New York: Walter de Gruyter, 1990).

17. See James L. Gibson, "The Policy Consequences of Political Intolerance: Political Repression During the Vietnam War Era," *Journal of Politics* 51 (February 1989):13–35. Gibson found that individual state legislatures reacted quite differently in response to antiwar demonstrations on college campuses but that the laws passed to discourage dissent were not related directly to public opinion within the state.

18. See Joel B. Grossman et al., "Dimensions of Institutional Participation: Who Uses the Courts and How?" *Journal of Politics* 44 (February 1982):86–114; and Frances Kahn Zemans, "Legal Mobilization: The Neglected Role of the Law in the Political System," *American Political Science Review* 77 (September 1983):690–703.

19. See Verba and Nie, *Participation in America*, p. 69. See also John Clayton Thomas, "Citizen-initiated Contacts with Government Agencies: A Test of Three Theories," *American Journal of Political Science* 26 (August 1982): 504–522; and Elaine B. Sharp, "Citizen-initiated Contacting of Government Officials and Socioeconomic Status: Determining the Relationship and Accounting for It," *American Political Science Review* 76 (March 1982):109–115.

20. Elaine B. Sharp, "Citizen Demand Making in the Urban Context," *American Journal of Political Science* 28 (November 1984):654–670, at 654, 665.

21. Verba and Nie, *Participation in America*, p. 67; and Sharp, "Citizen Demand Making," p. 660.

22. *Brown v. Board of Education*, 347 U.S. 483 (1954).

23. Max Kaase and Alan Marsh, "Political Action: A Theoretical Perspective," in Barnes and Kaase, eds., *Political Action*, p. 168.

24. *Smith v. Allwright*, 321 U.S. 649 (1944).

25. *Harper v. Virginia State Board of Elections*, 383 U.S. 663 (1966).

26. Everett Carll Ladd, *The American Polity* (New York: Norton, 1985), p. 392.

27. Ivor Crewe, "Electoral Participation," in *Democracy at the Polls: A Comparative Study of Competitive National Elections*, ed. David Butler, Howard R. Penniman, and Austin Ranney (Washington, D.C.: American Enterprise Institute, 1981), pp. 219–223.

28. David B. Magleby, *Direct Legislation: Voting on Ballot Propositions in the United States* (Baltimore, Md.: Johns Hopkins University Press, 1984), p. 70.

29. Thomas E. Cronin, *Direct Democracy* (Cambridge, Mass.: Harvard University Press, 1989), p. 197.

30. Robert Reinhold, "Move to Limit Terms Gathers Steam After Winning in 14 States," *New York Times*, November 5, 1992, p. B16.

31. Magleby, *Direct Legislation*, p. 59.

32. "Fears on Economy Doom Environment Issues, Tax Cuts," *Chicago Tribune*, November 8, 1990, sec. 1, p. 22.

33. Robert Reinhold, "Complicated Ballot Is Becoming Burden to California Voters," *New York Times*, September 24, 1990, p. 1.

34. Cronin, *Direct Democracy*, p. x.

35. Ibid., p. 251.

36. *The Book of the States 1990–91*, vol. 28 (Lexington, Ky.: Council of State Governments, 1990), p. 85.

37. *Chicago Tribune*, March 10, 1985.

38. Crewe, "Electoral Participation," p. 232.

39. Warren E. Miller, Arthur H. Miller, and Edward J. Schneider, *American National Election Studies Data Sourcebook, 1952–1978* (Cambridge, Mass.: Harvard University Press, 1980).

40. Ibid.

41. Verba and Nie, *Participation in America*, p. 13.

42. Max Kaase and Alan Marsh, "Distribution of Political Action," in Barnes and Kaase, eds., *Political Action*, p. 186.

43. Milbrath and Goel, *Political Participation*, pp. 95–96.

44. Verba and Nie, *Participation in America*, p. 148. For a concise summary of the effect of age on voting turnout, see Michael M. Gant and Norman R. Luttbeg, *American Electoral Behavior* (Itasca, Ill.: F. E. Peacock, 1991), pp. 103–104.

45. Richard Murray and Arnold Vedlitz, "Race, Socioeconomic Status, and Voting Participation in Large Southern Cities," *Journal of Politics* 39 (November 1977):1064–1072; and Verba and Nie, *Participation in America*, p. 157. See also Bobo and Gilliam, "Race, Sociopolitical Participation, and Black Empowerment" *American Political Science Review* 84 (June 1990): 377–393. Their study of 1987 national survey data with a black oversample found that African-Americans participated more than did whites of comparable socioeconomic status in cities where the mayor's office was held by an African-American.

46. Carol A. Cassel, "Change in Electoral Participation in the South," *Journal of Politics* 41 (August 1979):907–917.

47. Ronald B. Rapoport, "The Sex Gap in Political Persuading: Where the 'Structuring Principle' Works," *American Journal of Political Science* 25 (February 1981):32–48.

48. Bruce C. Straits, "The Social Context of Voter Turnout," *Public Opinion Quarterly* 54 (Spring 1990):64–73.

49. Center for Political Studies, *1988 National Election Survey* (Ann Arbor, Mich.: Inter-University Consortium for Political and Social Research, 1989).

50. Michael Nelson, ed., *Congressional Quarterly's Guide to the Presidency* (Washington, D.C.: Congressional Quarterly, 1989), p. 170.

51. Stephen D. Shaffer, "A Multivariate Explanation of Decreasing Turnout in Presidential Elections, 1960–1976," *American Journal of Political Science* 25 (February 1981):68–95; and Paul R. Abramson and John H. Aldrich, "The Decline of Electoral Participation in America," *American Political Science Review* 76 (September 1981):603–620.

52. There is a sizable literature that attempts to explain the decline in voting turnout in the United States. Some authors have claimed to account for the decline with just a few variables, but their work has been criticized for being too simplistic. See Carol A. Cassel and Robert C. Luskin, "Simple Explanations of Turnout Decline," *American Political Science Review* 82 (December 1988):1321–1330. They contended that most of the post-1960 decline is still unexplained.

53. Abramson and Aldrich, "The Decline of Electoral Participation," p. 519; and Shaffer, "A Multivariate Explanation," pp. 78, 90. For a later, more complex analysis with similar conclusions, see Ruy A. Teixeira, *Why Americans Don't Vote: Turnout Decline in the United States, 1960–1984* (Westport, Conn.: Greenwood Press, 1987), pp. 107–108.

54. The negative effect of registration laws on voting turnout is argued in Frances Fox Piven and Richard A. Cloward, "Government Statistics and Conflicting Explanations of Nonvoting," *PS: Political Science and Politics* 22 (September 1989):580–588. Their analysis was hotly contested in Stephen Earl Bennett, "The Uses and Abuses of Registration and Turnout Data: An Analysis of Piven and Cloward's Studies of Nonvoting in America," *PS: Political Science and Politics* 23 (June 1990):166–171. Bennett showed that turnout declined 10 to 13 percent since 1960 despite efforts to remove or lower legal hurdles to registration. See Frances Fox Piven and Richard L. Cloward, "A Reply to Bennett," *PS: Political Science and Politics* 23 (June 1990):172–173, for their reply. You can see that reasonable people can disagree on this matter.

55. David Glass, Peverill Squire, and Raymond Wolfinger, "Voter Turnout: An International Comparison," *Public Opinion* 6 (December–January 1984):52.

56. G. Bingham Powell, Jr., "American Voter Turnout in Comparative Perspective," *American Political Science Review* 80 (March 1986):25.

57. See Charles Krauthammer, "In Praise of Low Voter Turnout," *Time*, May 21, 1990, p. 88. Krauthammer said, "Low voter turnout means that people see politics as quite marginal to their lives, as neither salvation nor ruin. . . . Low voter turnout is a leading indicator of contentment."

58. Crewe, "Electoral Participation," p. 262.

59. Barnes and Kaase, *Political Action*, p. 532.

60. *1971 Congressional Quarterly Almanac* (Washington, D.C.: Congressional Quarterly Press, 1972), p. 475.

61. Benjamin Ginsberg, *The Consequences of Consent: Elections, Citizen Control and Popular Acquiescence* (Reading, Mass.: Addison-Wesley, 1982), p. 13.

62. Ibid., pp. 13–14.

63. Ibid., pp. 6–7.

Chapter 6 / Political Parties, Campaigns and Elections pp. 166–206

1. "The Public Opinion and Demographic Report," *Public Perspective* 3 (July–August, 1992):84.

2. John B. Anderson, fund-raising letter dated April 30, 1980.

3. "The Major Election Polls," *Public Opinion* 3 (December–January 1981):19.

4. Center for Political Studies of the Institute for Social Research, *Election Study 1984* (Ann Arbor: University of Michigan, 1984).

5. Alan R. Gitelson, M. Margaret Conway, and Frank B. Fiegert, *American Political Parties: Stability and Change* (Boston: Houghton Mifflin, 1984), p. 317.

6. See Jerome M. Clubb, William H. Flanigan, and Nancy H. Zingale, *Partisan Realignment: Voters, Parties, and Government in American History*, vol. 108 (Beverly Hills, Calif.: Sage Publications, 1980), p. 163.

7. See Gerald M. Pomper, "Classification of Presidential Elections," *Journal of Politics* 29 (August 1967):535–566.

8. Clubb, Flanigan, and Zingale, *Partisan Realignment*, p. 99.

9. The following discussion draws heavily on Austin Ranney and Willmoore Kendall, *Democracy and the American Party System* (New York: Harcourt, Brace, 1956), Chaps. 18, 19.

10. See Steven J. Rosenstone, Roy L. Behr, and Edward H. Lazarus, *Third Parties in America: Citizen Response to Major Party Failure* (Princeton, N.J.: Princeton University Press, 1984), pp. 5–6.

11. Ibid., p. 8.

12. *Public Opinion* 7 (December–January 1985):26.

13. Measuring the concept of party identification has had its problems. For recent insights into the issues, see R. Michael Alvarez, "The Puzzle of Party Identification," *American Politics Quarterly* 18 (October 1990):476–491; and Donald Philip Green and Bradley Palmquist, "Of Artifacts and Partisan Instability," *American Journal of Political Science* 34 (August 1990): 872–902.

14. 1988 General Social Survey, provided by Tom W. Smith, director of the survey.

15. There is some dispute over how stable party identification really is when the question is asked of the same respondents over a period of several months during an election campaign. This literature is reviewed in Brad Lockerbie, "Change in Party Identification: The Role of Prospective Economic Evaluations," *American Politics Quarterly* 17 (July 1989):291–311. Lockerbie argued that respondents change their party identification according to their expectations of whether they think that the parties will help them personally in the future. But also see Green and Palmquist, "Of Artifacts and Partisan Instability."

16. Bill Keller, "As Arms Buildup Eases, U.S. Tries to Take Stock," *New York Times*, May 14, 1985.

17. See, for example, Gerald M. Pomper, *Elections in America* (New York: Dodd, Mead, 1968); Benjamin Ginsberg, "Election and Public Policy," *American Political Science Review* 70 (March 1976):41–50; Jeff Fishel, *Presidents and Promises* (Washington, D.C.: Congressional Quarterly Press, 1985); and Ian Budge and Richard I. Hofferbert, "Mandates and Policy Outputs: U.S. Party Platforms and Federal Expenditures," *American Political Science Review* 84 (March 1990):111–131.

18. Robert Harmel and Kenneth Janda, *Parties and Their Environments: Limits to Reform?* (New York: Longman, 1982), pp. 27–29.

19. Michael Nelson, ed., *Congressional Quarterly's Guide to the Presidency* (Washington, D.C.: Congressional Quarterly Press, 1989), p. 695.

20. See Ralph M. Goldman, *The National Party Chairmen and Committees: Factionalism at the Top* (Armonk, N.Y.: M. E. Sharpe, 1990). The subtitle is revealing.

21. William Crotty and John S. Jackson III, *Presidential Primaries and Nominations* (Washington, D.C.: Congressional Quarterly Press, 1985), p. 33.

22. John F. Bibby, "Party Renewal in the National Republican Party," in *Party Renewal in America: Theory and Practice*, ed. Gerald M. Pomper (New York: Praeger, 1980), pp. 102–115.

23. James L. Gibson, John P. Frendreis, and Laura L. Vertz, "Party Dynamics in the 1980s: Change in County Organizational Strength, 1980–1984," *American Journal of Political Science* 33 (February 1989):67–90. See also Paul S. Herrnson, "Reemergent National Party Organizations," in The Parties Respond: Changes in the American Party System, ed. L. Sandy Maisel (Boulder, Colo.: Westview Press, 1990), pp. 41–66.

24. David S. Broder, *The Party's Over: The Failure of Politics in America* (New York, Harper and Row, 1972); and William C. Crotty and Gary C. Jacobson, *American Parties in Decline* (Boston: Little, Brown, 1980).

25. Barbara Sinclair, "The Congressional Party: Evolving Organizational, Agenda-Setting, and Policy Roles," in *The Parties Respond*, pp. 227–248, at 227.

26. The model is articulated most clearly in a report by the American Political Science Association, "Toward a More Responsible Two-Party System," *American Political Science Review* 44 (September 1950). See also Gerald M. Pomper, "Toward a More Responsible Party System? What, Again?" *Journal of Politics* 33 (November 1971):916–940.

27. This is essentially the framework for studying campaigns set forth in Salmore and Salmore, *Candidates, Parties, and Campaigns*, pp. 10–11.

28. Martin P. Wattenberg, *The Rise of Candidate-Centered Politics: Presidential Elections of the 1980s* (Cambridge, Mass.: Harvard University Press, 1991).

29. Michael Gallagher, "Conclusion," in *Candidate Selection in Comparative Perspective: The Secret Garden of Politics*, ed. Michael Gallagher and Michael Marsh (London: Sage Publications, 1988), p. 238.

30. Kenneth Janda, *Political Parties: A National Survey* (New York: Free Press, 1980), p. 112.

31. *The Book of the States, 1990–91*, vol. 28 (Lexington, Ky.: Council of State Governments, 1990), pp. 234–235.

32. Gary R. Orren and Nelson W. Polsby, eds., *Media and Momentum: The New Hampshire Primary and Nomination Politics* (Chatham, N.J.: Chatham House, 1987), p. 23.

33. See James R. Beniger, "Winning the Presidential Nomination: National Polls and State Primary Elections, 1936–1972," *Public Opinion Quarterly* 40 (Spring 1976):22–38.

34. Quoted in E. J. Dionne, Jr., "On the Trail of Corporation Donations," *New York Times*, October 6, 1980.

35. Federal Election Commission, *The First Ten Years: 1975–1985* (April 14, 1985), p. 1.

36. Paul S. Herrnson, "Political Parties, Campaign Finance Reform, and Presidential Elections" (Paper prepared for presentation at the annual meeting of the Midwest Political Science Association, Chicago, Illinois, April 5–7, 1990), p. 11. See also Richard L. Berke, "In Election Spending: Watch the Ceiling, Use a Loophole," *New York Times*, October 3, 1988, pp. 1 and 13.

37. Salmore and Salmore, *Candidates, Parties, and Campaigns*, p. 11.

38. David Moon, "What You Use Depends on What You Have: Information Effects on the Determinants of Electoral Choice," *American Politics Quarterly* 18 (January 1990):3–24.

39. See "The Political Pages," *Campaigns & Elections* 10 (February 1990), which contains more than a hundred pages of names, addresses, and telephone numbers of people who supply "political products and services."

40. Stephen Ansolabehere, Roy L. Behr, and Shanto Iyengar, "Mass Media and Elections: An Overview," *American Politics Quarterly* 19 (January 1991):109–139.

41. Montague Kern, *30-Second Politics: Political Advertising in the Eighties* (New York: Praeger, 1989), p. 57.

42. News of the National Association of Broadcasters, 13 July 1987 (Washington, D.C.). A later study of campaign spending in the 1990 House and Senate elections found similar average levels of expenditures for advertising and media consultants combined: 25 percent for House candidates and 35 percent for Senate candidates. See Sara Fritz and Dwight Morris, "Burden of TV Election Ads Exaggerated, Study Finds," *Los Angeles Times*, March 18, 1991, pp. A1, A14. However, specialists warn that such averages, which include many uncontested elections, mask much higher levels of spending for media in contested elections. See Herbert E. Alexander and Monica Bauer, *Financing the 1988 Election* (Boulder, Colo.: Westview Press, 1991).

43. Bureau of the Census, "Popularly Elected Officials," *Government Organization*, vol. 1, no. 2 (Washington, D.C.: 1987 Census of Governments, January 1990), p. vi.

44. Michael Nelson, ed., *Congressional Quarterly Guide to the Presidency* (Washington, D.C.: Congressional Quarterly Press, 1989), p. 1427. You can find the other exceptions there, too.

45. Harold W. Stanley and Richard G. Niemi, *Vital Statistics on American Politics*, 2d ed. (Washington, D.C.: Congressional Quarterly Press, 1990), p. 132.

46. The 1988 National Election Study (data made available through the Inter-University Consortium for Political and Social Research).

47. Pamela Johnston Conover and Stanley Feldman, "Candidate Perception in an Ambiguous World: Campaigns, Cues, and Inference Processes," *American Journal of Political Science* 33 (November 1989):912–940.

48. Bruce Buchanan, *Electing a President: The Report on the Markle Commission on the Media and the Electorate* (Austin: University of Texas Press, 1991). These data came from Table 5.3 in excerpts from the book distributed by the Markle Commission, p. 21.

49. Ibid., Table 5.4, p. 27.

50. Ibid., Table 5.5, p. 32.

51. Stephen E. Frantzich, *Political Parties in the Technological Age* (New York: Longman, 1989), p. 167.

52. Michael M. Gant and Norman R. Luttbeg, *American Electoral Behavior* (Itasca, Ill.: F. E. Peacock, 1991), pp. 63–64. The literature on the joint effects of party, issues, and candidate is quite involved. See also David W. Romero, "The Changing American Voter Revisited: Candidate Evaluations in Presidential Elections, 1952–1984," *American Politics Quarterly* 17 (October 1989):409–421. According to Romero, research that finds a "new" American voter who votes according to issues is incorrectly looking at standardized, rather than unstandardized, regression coefficients.

53. Conover and Feldman, "Candidate Perception in an Ambiguous World," p. 938.

54. Party identification has been assumed to be relatively resistant to short-term campaign effects, but see Dee Allsop and Herbert F. Weisberg, "Measuring Change in Party Identification in an Election Campaign," *American Journal of Political Science* 32 (November 1988):996–1017. They concluded that partisanship is more volatile than we have thought.

55. Larry J. Sabato and David Beiler, "Mag . . . or Blue Smoke and Mirrors? Reflections on New Technologies and Trends in the Political Consultant Trade" (Northwestern University: Annenberg Washington Program in Communication Policy Studies, 1988), pp. 4–5.

56. Steven J. Rosenstone, *Forecasting Presidential Elections* (New Haven, Conn.: Yale University Press, 1983). Rosenstone, however, thought his model would increase the importance of campaigns, for it would help identify states where campaigns might decide the outcome.

Chapter 7 / Interest Groups
pp. 209–230

1. Jill Abramson, "Auto Makers Lobbied Hard Against Stricter Fuel Rules," *Wall Street Journal*, April 4, 1990, p. A15.

2. Michael Kranish, "Clean Air Measure Serves Some States' Special Interests," *Boston Globe*, April 9, 1990, p. 1. This account of deliberations over the Clean Air Act also draws upon Rose Gutfeld, "Senate Rejects, 50–49, Byrd Amendment to Clean Air Bill on Aid to Coal Miners," *Wall Street Journal*, March 30, 1990, p. C13; Phil Kuntz and George Hager, "Showdown on Clean-Air Bill," *Congressional Quarterly Weekly Report*, March 31, 1990, pp. 983–987; Rose Gutfeld and Barbara Rosewicz, "Battle Looms in the House as Senate Passes a Bill," *Wall Street Journal*, April 4, 1990, p. A1; John E. Yang, "Legislation Would Assist Corn Farms, Ethanol Firm," *Wall Street Journal*, April 4, 1990, p. A14; Neal Templin, "Environmentalists and Auto Makers Rev Up for Battle," *Wall Street Journal*, April 4, 1990, p. A14; Abramson, "Auto Makers Lobbied Hard"; and George Hager, "Clean Air: War About Over in Both House and Senate," *Congressional Quarterly Weekly Report*, April 7, 1990, pp. 1057–1061.

3. Jeffrey M. Berry, *The Interest Group Society*, 2d ed. (Glenview, Ill.: Scott, Foresman/Little, Brown, 1989), p. 4.

4. Alexis de Tocqueville, *Democracy in America*, ed. Richard D. Heffner (New York: Mentor Books, 1956), p. 198.

5. See Robert A. Dahl, *A Preface to Democratic Theory* (Chicago: University of Chicago Press, 1956), pp. 4–33.

6. This discussion follows from Berry, *The Interest Group Society*, pp. 6–8.

7. Steven Pressman, "Lobbying 'Star Wars' Flares as Movie Industry Fights Invasion of Video Recorders," *Congressional Quarterly Weekly Report*, June 4, 1983, pp. 1099–1103.

8. David B. Truman, *The Governmental Process* (New York: Knopf, 1951).

9. Herbert Gans, *The Urban Villagers* (New York: Free Press, 1962).

10. Robert H. Salisbury, "An Exchange Theory of Interest Groups," *Midwest Journal of Political Science* 13 (February 1969):1–32.

11. See Mancur Olson, Jr., *The Logic of Collective Action* (New York: Schocken, 1968); and Terry M. Moe, *The Organization of Interests* (Chicago: University of Chicago Press, 1980).

12. See Olson, *The Logic of Collective Action*.

13. See John Mark Hansen, "The Political Economy of Group Membership," *American Political Science Review* 79 (March 1985):79–96.

14. Robert H. Salisbury, "Washington Lobbyists: A Collective Portrait," in *Interest Group Politics*, 2d ed., ed. Allan J. Cigler and Burdett A. Loomis (Washington, D.C.: Congressional Quarterly, 1986), p. 155.

15. Paul Taylor, "Gladiators for Hire—Part I," *Washington Post*, July 31, 1983, p. A1. See also W. John Moore, "The Alumni Lobby," *National Journal*, September 9, 1989, pp. 2188–2195. Expertise gained in the executive branch can also be extremely lucrative for would-be lobbyists. See Pat Choate, *Agents of Influence* (New York: Knopf, 1990), especially pp. 49–63.

16. Carol Matlack, "Getting Around the Rules," *National Journal*, May 12, 1990, pp. 1138–1143.

17. Al Kamen and David Von Drehle, "Ethics Policy Toughened," *Washington Post*, December 10, 1992, p. A1.

18. Mark Green, "Political PAC–Man," *New Republic*, December 13, 1982, p. 24.

19. "PAC Activity Falls, in 1990 Election" Federal Election Commission, March 31, 1991, p. 2.

20. John R. Wright, "Contributions, Lobbying, and Committee Voting in the U.S. House of Representatives," *American Political Science Review* 84 (June 1990):417–438.

21. Common Cause data cited in Berry, *The Interest Group Society*, p. 122.

22. Nathaniel C. Nash, "Savings Unit Donations Criticized," *New York Times*, June 29, 1990, p. D4.

23. Elizabeth Drew, "Politics and Money—I," *New Yorker*, December 6, 1982, p. 147.

24. Kay Lehman Schlozman and John T. Tierney, *Organized Interests and American Democracy* (New York: Harper and Row, 1986), p. 150.

25. John E. Chubb, *Interest Groups and the Bureaucracy* (Stanford, Calif.: Stanford University Press, 1983), p. 144.

26. Berry, *The Interest Group Society*, p. 156.

27. Allan J. Cigler and John Mark Hansen, "Group Formation Through Protest: The American Agriculture Movement," in *Interest Group Politics*, ed. Allan J. Cigler and Burdett A. Loomis (Washington, D.C.: Congressional Quarterly, 1983), pp. 84–109.

28. David J. Garrow, *Protest at Selma* (New Haven, Conn.: Yale University Press, 1978).

29. Roger P. Kingsley, "Advocacy for the Handicapped" (Paper delivered at the annual meeting of the American Political Science Association, Washington, D.C., September 1984), p. 10.

30. Robert H. Salisbury et al., "Who Works with Whom?" *American Political Science Review* 81 (December 1987):1224–1228.

31. Anne Costain, "The Struggle for a National Women's Lobby," *Western Political Quarterly* 33 (December 1980):476–491.

32. Jack L. Walker, "The Origins and Maintenance of Interest Groups in America" (Paper delivered at the annual meeting of the American Political Science Association, New York, September 1981), p. 14.

33. Jeffrey M. Berry, *Lobbying for the People* (Princeton, N.J.: Princeton University Press, 1977), pp. 6–10.

34. Andrew S. McFarland, *Common Cause* (Chatham, N.J.: Chatham House, 1984).

35. David Vogel, *Lobbying the Corporation* (New York: Basic Books, 1978), pp. 21–68.

36. On the development of the New Right, see Jerome L. Himmelstein, *To the Right: The Transformation of American Conservatism* (Berkeley and Los Angeles: University of California Press, 1990).

37. See Allen D. Hertzke, *Representing God in Washington* (Knoxville: University of Tennessee Press, 1988).

38. Martha Joynt Kumar and Michael Baruch Grossman, "The Presidency and Interest Groups," in *The Presidency and the Political System*, ed. Michael Nelson (Washington, D.C.: Congressional Quarterly, 1984), pp. 293–294.

39. David Vogel, "How Business Responds to Opposition" (Paper delivered at the annual meeting of the American Political Science Association, Washington, D.C., December 1979.)

40. Monica Langley, "Feuding Lobbies Hinder Push to Write Comprehensive

Legislation," *Wall Street Journal,* March 24, 1986, p. 38.

41. Walter Dean Burnham, *Critical Elections and the Mainsprings of American Politics* (New York: Norton, 1970), p. 133.

42. *United States* v. *Harriss,* 347 U.S. 612 (1954).

43. See Matlack, "Getting Around the Rules."

44. Some argue, however, that the real dynamic at work is a decline in overall interest group power. See Robert Salisbury, "Paradox of Interest Groups in Washington—More Groups and Less Clout," in *The New American Political System,* 2d ed., ed. Anthony King (Washington, D.C.: American Enterprise Institute, 1990); and Paul E. Peterson, "The Rise and Fall of Special Interest Group Politics," *Political Science Quarterly* 105 (Winter 1990–1991):539–556.

Chapter 8 / Congress
pp. 233–261

1. This account of the Slaughter-Eckert race is taken from Linda L. Fowler and Robert D. McClure, *Political Ambition* (New Haven, Conn.: Yale University Press, 1989), pp. 204–217.

2. Clinton Rossiter, *1787: The Grand Convention* (New York: Mentor, 1968), p. 158.

3. *Wesberry* v. *Sanders,* 376 U.S. 1 (1964) (congressional districts within a state must be substantially equal in population); and *Reynolds* v. *Sims,* 377 U.S. 364 (1964) (state legislatures must be apportioned on the basis of population).

4. Norman J. Ornstein, Thomas E. Mann, and Michael J. Malbin, *Vital Statistics on Congress, 1989–1990* (Washington, D.C.: Congressional Quarterly Press, 1990), p. 59. See also David Mayhew, "Congressional Elections: The Case of the Vanishing Marginals," *Polity* 6 (Spring 1974): 295–317; and Gary C. Jacobson, *The Politics of Congressional Elections,* 2d ed. (Boston: Little, Brown, 1987), pp. 29–36.

5. *Gallup Report* (September 1988):21.

6. Norman Ornstein, "The Permanent Democratic Congress," *Public Interest* 100 (Summer 1990):24–44; and John A. Ferejohn, "On the Decline of Competition in Congressional Elections," *American Political Science Review* 71 (March 1977):166–176.

7. Timothy E. Cook, *Making Laws and Making News* (Washington, D.C.: Brookings Institution, 1989), p. 83.

8. "1990 Congressional Election Spending Drops to Low Point," *Federal Election Commission,* February 22, 1991, p. 4; and Alan I. Abramowitz, "Incumbency, Campaign Spending, and the Decline of Competition in U.S. House Elections," *Journal of Politics* 53 (February 1991):34–56.

9. Gary C. Jacobson, "Meager Patrimony: The Reagan Era and Republican Representation in Congress," in *Looking Back on the Reagan Presidency,* ed. Larry Berman (Baltimore, Md.: Johns Hopkins University Press, 1990), pp. 311–312.

10. On the historical dimensions and consequences of this trend, see David W. Brady, *Critical Elections and Congressional Policy Making* (Stanford, Calif.: Stanford University Press, 1988).

11. Ornstein, Mann, and Malbin, *Vital Statistics,* pp. 20–31.

12. Bob Benenson, "Arduous Ritual of Redistricting Ensures More Racial Diversity," *Congressional Quarterly Weekly Report,* October 24, 1992, pp. 3355–3361.

13. Election Supplement, *New York Times,* November 5, 1992, pp. B1–B13.

14. Walter J. Oleszek, *Congressional Procedures and the Policy Process,* 3d ed. (Washington, D.C.: Congressional Quarterly, 1989), p. 81.

15. Julie Kosterlitz, "Anguish and Opportunity," *National Journal,* April 28, 1990, pp. 1008–1015.

16. Roger W. Cobb and Charles D. Elder, *Participation in American Politics,* 2d ed. (Baltimore, Md.: Johns Hopkins University Press, 1983), pp. 64–65.

17. It was Woodrow Wilson who described the legislative process as the "dance of

legislation." Eric Redman used the phrase for the title of his case study of a health bill, *The Dance of Legislation* (New York: Touchstone, 1973).

18. Oleszek, *Congressional Procedures,* pp. 74–76.

19. Woodrow Wilson, *Congressional Government* (Boston: Houghton Mifflin, 1885), p. 79.

20. Lawrence D. Longley and Walter J. Oleszek, *Bicameral Politics* (New Haven, Conn.: Yale University Press, 1989), p. 4.

21. Leroy Rieselbach, *Congressional Reform* (Washington, D.C.: Congressional Quarterly, 1986), p. 47.

22. On some tentative steps toward recentralization, see Roger H. Davidson, "The New Centralization on Capitol Hill" (Paper delivered at the annual meeting of the Midwest Political Science Association, Chicago, April 1988).

23. Steven S. Smith and Christopher J. Deering, *Committees in Congress* (Washington, D.C.: Congressional Quarterly Press, 1984), p. 271.

24. Robert Weissberg, "Collective vs. Dyadic Representation in Congress," *American Political Science Review* 72 (June 1978):535–547.

25. See Richard L. Hall, "Committee Decision Making in the Postreform Congress," in *Congress Reconsidered,* 4th ed., ed. Lawrence C. Dodd and Bruce I. Oppenheimer (Washington, D.C.: Congressional Quarterly, 1989), pp. 197–223.

26. Robert L. Peabody, *Leadership in Congress* (Boston: Little, Brown, 1976), p. 9.

27. Charles O. Jones, *The United States Congress* (Homewood, Ill.: Dorsey Press, 1982), p. 322.

28. Oleszek, *Congressional Procedures,* p. 222.

29. Steven S. Smith, *Call to Order* (Washington, D.C.: Brookings Institution, 1989), p. 138.

30. Ibid.

31. This framework is adapted from John W. Kingdon, *Congressmen's Voting Decisions,* 2d ed. (New York: Harper and Row, 1981).

32. See David W. Rohde, "'Something's Happening Here, What It Is Ain't Exactly Clear': Southern Democrats in the House of Representatives" (Paper delivered at a conference in honor of Richard Fenno, Washington, D.C., August 1986).

33. David Rampe, "Power Panel in Making: The Hispanic Caucus," *New York Times,* September 30, 1988, p. B5.

34. Ornstein, Mann, and Malbin, *Vital Statistics,* pp. 132–136.

35. Michael Malbin, *Unelected Representatives* (New York: Basic Books, 1980).

36. Ibid., p. 240.

37. James Sterling Young, *The Washington Community* (New York: Harcourt, Brace, 1964).

38. Kingdon, *Congressmen's Voting Decisions,* p. 242.

39. Joel D. Aberbach, *Keeping a Watchful Eye* (Washington, D.C.: Brookings Institution, 1990), pp. 84–85.

40. Barry M. Blechman, "The New Congressional Role in Arms Control," *A Question of Balance,* ed. Thomas E. Mann (Washington, D.C.: Brookings Institution, 1990), pp. 109–145.

41. Richard F. Fenno, Jr., *Home Style* (Boston: Little, Brown, 1978), p. xii.

42. Ibid., p. 32.

43. Louis I. Bredvold and Ralph G. Ross, eds., *The Philosophy of Edmund Burke* (Ann Arbor: University of Michigan Press, 1960), p. 148.

44. Warren E. Miller and Donald E. Stokes, "Constituency Influence in Congress," *American Political Science Review* 57 (March 1963):45–57.

45. Julie Johnson, "Picking Over the Pork in the 1988 Spending Bill," *New York Times,* January 5, 1988, p. B6.

46. Weissberg, "Collective vs. Dyadic Representation."

Chapter 9 / The Presidency pp. 263–287

1. David Wessel and David Rogers, "Bush Appeals to the Public in Budget

Battle," *Wall Street Journal,* October 3, 1990, p. A3.

2. Louis W. Koenig, *The Chief Executive,* 4th ed. (New York: Harcourt Brace Jovanovich, 1981), p. 20.

3. Richard M. Pious, *The American Presidency* (New York: Basic Books, 1979), pp. 51–52.

4. Wilfred E. Binkley, *President and Congress,* 3d ed. (New York: Vintage Books, 1962), p. 155.

5. Barry M. Blechman, "The New Congressional Role in Arms Control," in *A Question of Balance,* ed. Thomas E. Mann (Washington, D.C.: Brookings Institution), pp. 109–145.

6. Richard E. Neustadt, *Presidential Power* (New York: John Wiley, 1980), p. 10.

7. Neustadt, *Presidential Power,* p. 9.

8. George C. Edwards III, *At the Margins* (New Haven, Conn.: Yale University Press, 1989). See also Jon R. Bond and Richard Fleisher, *The President in the Legislative Arena* (Chicago: University of Chicago Press, 1990).

9. See Edwards, *At the Margins,* pp. 101–125.

10. Jeffrey K. Tulis, *The Rhetorical Presidency* (Princeton, N.J.: Princeton University Press, 1987), p. 64ff.

11. Theodore J. Lowi, *The Personal President* (Ithaca, N.Y.: Cornell University Press, 1985).

12. Darrell M. West, *Congress and Economic Policymaking* (Pittsburgh: University of Pittsburgh Press, 1987), p. 33.

13. Kristen Renwick Monroe, *Presidential Popularity and the Economy* (New York: Praeger, 1984).

14. Charles W. Ostrom, Jr. and Dennis M. Simon, "Promise and Performance: A Dynamic Model of Presidential Popularity," *American Political Science Review* 79 (June 1985):334–358.

15. James W. Ceaser, "The Reagan Presidency and American Public Opinion," in *The Reagan Legacy,* ed., Charles O. Jones (Chatham, N.J.: Chatham House, 1988), pp. 172–210.

16. "Prepared Text of Carter's Farewell Address," *New York Times,* January 15, 1981.

17. Gary C. Jacobson, "Meager Patrimony: The Reagan Era and Republican Representation in Congress," in *Looking Back on the Reagan Presidency,* ed. Larry Berman (Baltimore: Johns Hopkins University Press, 1990), p. 300.

18. Gary King and Lyn Ragsdale, *The Elusive Executive* (Washington, D.C.: Congressional Quarterly Press, 1988), pp. 205–210.

19. *New York Times,* February 10, 1993, p. A8.

20. See Burt Solomon, "In Bush's Image," *National Journal,* July 7, 1990, pp. 1642–1647.

21. Kenneth T. Walsh, Matthew Cooper, and Carla Ann Robbins, "Clinton: Doing It All," *U.S. News and World Report,* December 28, 1992, pp. 18–20.

22. Richard F. Fenno, Jr., *The Making of a Senator: Dan Quayle* (Washington, D.C.: Congressional Quarterly Press, 1989); and Jack W. Germond and Jules Witcover, *Whose Broad Stripes and Bright Stars?* (New York: Warner Books, 1989), pp. 375–395.

23. Quoted in Thomas E. Cronin, *The State of the Presidency,* 2d ed. (Boston: Little, Brown, 1980), p. 253.

24. Terry M. Moe, "The Politicized Presidency," in *The New Direction in American Politics,* ed. John E. Chubb and Paul E. Peterson (Washington, D.C.: Brookings Institution, 1985), pp. 235–271.

25. *Public Papers of the President, Lyndon B. Johnson, 1965,* vol. 1 (Washington, D.C.: U.S. Government Printing Office, 1966), p. 72.

26. "Transcript of Second Inaugural Address by Reagan," *New York Times,* January 22, 1985, p. A1.

27. Kevin Phillips, *The Politics of Rich and Poor* (New York: Random House, 1990), p. 88.

28. John W. Kingdon, *Agendas, Alternatives, and Public Policies* (Boston: Little, Brown, 1984), p. 25.

29. Richard E. Neustadt, "Presidency and Legislation: The Growth of Central Clearance," *American Political Science Review* 48 (September 1954):641–671.

30. Seth King, "Reagan, in Bid for Budget Votes, Reported to Yield on Sugar Prices," *New York Times*, June 27, 1981, p. A1.

31. Martha Joynt Kumar and Michael Baruch Grossman, "The Presidency and Interest Groups," in *The Presidency and the Political System*, ed. Michael Nelson (Washington, D.C.: Congressional Quarterly Press, 1984), p. 309.

32. Sidney M. Milkis, "The Presidency and Political Parties," in Nelson, ed., *The Presidency and the Political System*, 2d ed., ed. Michael Nelson (Washington, D.C.: Congressional Quarterly Press, 1988), p. 337.

33. Fred Barnes, "Hour of Power," *New Republic*, September 3, 1990, p. 12.

34. Alexander George, "The Case for Multiple Advocacy in Making Foreign Policy," *American Political Science Review* 66 (September 1972):751–782.

35. John P. Burke and Fred I. Greenstein, *How Presidents Test Reality* (New York: Russell Sage Foundation, 1989).

36. Richard E. Neustadt and Earnest R. May, *Thinking in Time* (New York: Free Press, 1986), p. 143.

37. Gail Sheehy, "The Road to Bimini," *Vanity Fair*, September 1987, p. 132.

Chapter 10 / The Bureaucracy pp. 290–313

1. This account of the NEA controversy is based on Garrison Keillor, "Thanks for Attacking the N.E.A.," *New York Times*, April 4, 1990, p. A15; Richard Bernstein, "Subsidies for Artists: Is Denying a Grant Really Censorship?" *New York Times*, July 18, 1990, p. C11; Peter J. Boyer, "Mean for Jesus," *Vanity Fair* (September 1990):224ff; Bruce Selcraig, "Reverend Wildmon's War on the Arts," *New York Times Magazine*, September 2, 1990, p. 22ff; Richard L. Berke, "House Approves Compromise Bill to Continue Arts Endowment," *New York Times*, October 12, 1990, p. A1; and Martin Tolchin, "Senate Passes Compromise on Arts Endowment," *New York Times*, October 25, 1990, p. C17.

2. James Q. Wilson, *Bureaucracy* (New York: Basic Books, 1989), p. 25.

3. Bruce D. Porter, "Parkinson's Law Revisited: War and the Growth of American Government," *Public Interest* 60 (Summer 1980):50.

4. Keith Schneider, "Farmers to Face Patent Fees to Use Gene-altered Animals," *New York Times*, January 6, 1988, p. A1.

5. Philip Shabecoff, "Senator Urges Military Resources Be Turned to Environmental Battle," *New York Times*, June 29, 1990, p. A1.

6. Gary C. Jacobson, "Meager Patrimony," in *Looking Back on the Reagan Presidency*, ed. Larry Berman (Baltimore, Md.: Johns Hopkins University Press, 1990), p. 307.

7. Herbert Kaufman, *Are Government Organizations Immortal?* (Washington, D.C.: Brookings Institution, 1976).

8. John T. Tierney, "Government Corporations and Managing the Public's Business," *Political Science Quarterly* 99 (Spring 1984):73–92.

9. Bureau of the Census, *Statistical Abstract of the United States, 1990* (Washington, D.C.: U.S. Government Printing Office, 1990), pp. 324, 378.

10. Kenneth J. Meier, "Representative Democracy: An Empirical Assessment," *American Political Science Review* 69 (June 1975):532.

11. Census, *Statistical Abstract, 1990*, p. 326.

12. See Elizabeth Sanders, "The Presidency and the Bureaucratic State," in *The Presidency and the Political System*, 3d ed., ed. Michael Nelson (Washington, D.C.: Congressional Quarterly Press, 1990), pp. 409–442.

13. Doris A. Graber, *Mass Media and American Politics*, 3d ed. (Washing-

ton, D.C.: Congressional Quarterly Press, 1989), p. 51.

14. Jeffrey M. Berry, *Feeding Hungry People: Rulemaking in the Food Stamp Program* (New Brunswick, N.J.: Rutgers University Press, 1984).

15. "E.P.A. Drops Plan to Require Waste Incinerators to Recycle," *New York Times*, December 21, 1990, p. A33.

16. Terry M. Moe, "Control and Feedback in Economic Regulation: The Case of the NLRB," *American Political Science Review* 79 (December 1985):109–116.

17. Charles E. Lindblom, "The Science of Muddling Through," *Public Administration Review* 19 (Spring 1959):79–88.

18. Hugh Heclo, "Issue Networks and the Executive Establishment," in *The New American Political System*, ed. Anthony King (Washington, D.C.: American Enterprise Institute, 1978), p. 103.

19. Robert H. Salisbury et al., "Who Works with Whom? Interest Group Alliances and Opposition," *American Political Science Review* 81 (December 1987):1217–1234.

20. Douglass Cater, *Power in Washington* (New York: Vintage Books, 1964), p. 18.

21. Lawrence C. Dodd and Richard L. Schott, *Congress and the Administrative State* (New York: Wiley, 1979), p. 103.

22. Although the subgovernment concept has fallen on hard times, there are some political scientists who have tried to adapt it to contemporary politics. See Daniel McCool, "Subgovernments as Determinants of Political Viability," *Political Science Quarterly* 105 (Summer 1990):269–293.

23. Jeffrey M. Berry, "Subgovernments, Issue Networks, and Political Conflict," in *Remaking American Politics*, ed. Richard A. Harris and Sidney M. Milkis (Boulder, Colo.: Westview Press, 1989), pp. 239–260.

24. This account is based on Steven Coll, *The Deal of the Century* (New York: Atheneum, 1986); and Peter Temin with Louis Galambos, *The Fall of the*

Bell System (New York: Cambridge University Press, 1987).

25. Martha Derthick and Paul J. Quirk, *The Politics of Deregulation* (Washington, D.C.: Brookings Institution, 1985).

26. This discussion is drawn from Jeffrey M. Berry, *The Interest Group Society*, 2d ed. (Glenview, Ill.: Scott, Foresman/Little, Brown, 1989), pp. 189–193.

27. On recent conflicts, see Mike Mills, "Baby Bells' Fate Dangling Before Congress, Courts," *Congressional Quarterly Weekly Report*, February 23, 1991, pp. 458–463; and Margaret E. Kriz, "Ganging Up on the Bells," *National Journal*, September 1, 1990, pp. 2068–2071.

28. For an alternative perspective, see James A. Thurber, "Dynamics of Policy Subsystems in American Politics," in *Interest Group Politics*, 3d ed., ed. Allan J. Cigler and Burdett A. Loomis (Washington, D.C.: Congressional Quarterly Press, 1991), pp. 319–343.

29. Lauriston R. King and W. Wayne Shannon, "Policy Networks in the Policy Process: The Case of the National Sea Grant Program," *Polity* 19 (Winter 1986):213–231.

30. Edward O. Laumann et al., "Organizations in Political Action" (Paper presented at the annual meeting of the American Sociological Association, September 1986).

31. See generally Terry M. Moe, "The Politics of Bureaucratic Structure," in *Can the Government Govern?* ed. John E. Chubb and Paul E. Peterson (Washington, D.C.: Brookings Institution, 1989), pp. 267–329.

32. William T. Gormley, Jr., *Taming the Bureaucracy* (Princeton, N.J.: Princeton University Press, 1989).

33. Martha Derthick and Paul J. Quirk, *The Politics of Deregulation* (Washington, D.C.: Brookings Institution, 1985).

34. David Vogel, "AIDS and the Politics of Drug Lag," *Public Interest* 96 (Summer 1989):73–85.

35. See James A. Morone, *The Democratic Wish* (New York: Basic Books, 1990).

Chapter 11 / The Courts
pp. 316–342

1. Philip Elman (interviewed by Norman Silber), "The Solicitor General's Office, Justice Frankfurter, and Civil Rights Litigation, 1946–1960: An Oral History," 100 *Harvard Law Review,* 817–852, 840 (1987).

2. David M. O'Brien, *Storm Center,* 2d ed. (New York: Norton, 1990), p. 324.

3. Bernard Schwartz, *The Unpublished Opinions of the Warren Court* (New York: Oxford University Press, 1985), p. 446.

4. Ibid., pp. 445–448.

5. Felix Frankfurter and James M. Landis, *The Business of the Supreme Court* (New York: Macmillan, 1928), pp. 5–14; and Julius Goebel, Jr., *Antecedents and Beginnings to 1801,* vol. 1 of *The History of the Supreme Court of the United States* (New York: Macmillan, 1971).

6. Maeva Marcus, ed., *The Justices on Circuit, 1795–1800,* vol. 3 of *The Documentary History of the Supreme Court of the United States, 1789–1800* (New York: Columbia University Press, 1990).

7. Robert G. McCloskey, *The United States Supreme Court* (Chicago: University of Chicago Press, 1960), p. 31.

8. *Marbury* v. *Madison,* 1 Cranch 137, 177–178 (1803).

9. Interestingly, the phrase *judicial review* dates only to 1910; it was apparently unknown to Marshall and his contemporaries. Robert Lowry, *Clinton, Marbury v. Madison and Judicial Review* (Lawrence: University Press of Kansas, 1989), p. 7.

10. *Constitution of the United States of America: Annotated and Interpreted* (Washington, D.C.: U.S. Government Printing Office, 1987) and 1988 supplement.

11. *Ware* v. *Hylton,* 3 Dallas 199 (1796).

12. *Martin* v. *Hunter's Lessee,* 1 Wheat. 304 (1816).

13. *Constitution of the United States of America.*

14. Garry Wills, *Explaining America: The Federalist* (Garden City, N.Y.: Doubleday, 1981), pp. 127–136.

15. Charles Alan Wright, *Handbook on the Law of Federal Courts,* 3d ed. (St. Paul, Minn.: West, 1976), p. 7.

16. Linda Greenhouse, "Precedent for Lower Courts: Tyrant or Teacher?" *New York Times,* January 29, 1988, p. 18.

17. Regents of the University of California v. Bakke, 438 U.S. 265 (1978).

18. Joseph Tanenhaus et al., "The Supreme Court's Certiorari Jurisdiction: Cue Theory," in *Judicial Decision-Making,* ed. Glendon Schubert (New York: Free Press, 1963), pp. 111–132; and Gregory A. Caldiera and John R. Wright, "The Discuss List: Agenda Building in the Supreme Court," *Law and Society Review* 24 (1990):807–836.

19. Doris M. Provine, *Case Selection in the United States Supreme Court* (Chicago: University of Chicago Press, 1980), pp. 74–102.

20. "Rising Fixed Opinions," *New York Times,* February 22, 1988, p. 14.

21. Jeffrey A. Segal and Albert D. Cover, "Ideological Values and the Votes of U.S. Supreme Court Justices," *American Political Science Review* 83: 557–565.

22. Thomas G. Walker, Lee Epstein, and William J. Dixon, "On the Mysterious Demise of Consensual Norms in the United States Supreme Court," *Journal of Politics* 50 (1988):361–389.

23. See, for example, Walter F. Murphy, *Elements of Judicial Strategy* (Chicago: University of Chicago Press, 1964); and Bob Woodward and Scott Armstrong, *The Brethren* (New York: Simon and Schuster, 1979).

24. Henry J. Abraham, *Justices and Presidents: A Political History of Appointments to the Supreme Court,* 2d ed. (New York: Oxford University Press, 1985), pp. 183–185.

25. Stephen L. Wasby, *The Supreme Court in the Federal Judicial System,* 3d ed. (Chicago: Nelson-Hall, 1988), p. 241.

26. Schwartz, *The Unpublished Opinions,* pp. 446–447.

27. Lawrence Baum, *American Courts: Process and Policy*, 2d ed. (Boston: Hougton Mifflin, 1990), pp. 99–112.

28. Wasby, *The Supreme Court*, pp. 107–110.

29. "Bush Travels Reagan's Course in Naming Judges," *New York Times*, April 10, 1990, p. A1.

30. *New York Times*, July 2, 1991, pp. A1, A16.

31. Timothy M. Phelps and Helen Winternitz, *Capitol Games: Clarence Thomas, Anita Hill and the Story of a Supreme Court Nomination* (New York: Hyperion Press, 1992).

32. *Brown v. Board of Education II*, 349 U.S. 294 (1955).

33. Charles A. Johnson and Bradley C. Canon, *Judicial Policies: Implementation and Impact* (Washington, D.C.: Congressional Quarterly Press, 1984).

34. Alexander M. Bickel, *The Least Dangerous Branch* (Indianapolis: Bobbs-Merrill, 1962); and Robert A. Dahl, "Decision-Making in a Democracy: The Supreme Court as a National Policy-Maker," *Journal of Public Law* 6 (1962):279–295.

35. Thomas R. Marshall, *Public Opinion and the Supreme Court* (Boston: Unwin Hyman, 1989).

36. Ibid., pp. 192–193; and Gerald N. Rosenberg, *The Hollow Hope: Can Courts Bring About Social Change?* (Chicago: University of Chicago Press, in press).

37. William J. Brennan, Jr., "State Supreme Court Judge Versus United States Supreme Court Justice: A Change in Function and Perspective," *University of Florida Law Review* 19 (1966):225–237.

Chapter 12 / Civil Liberties and Civil Rights   pp. 346–388

1. *Johnson v. Transportation Agency, Santa Clara County*, 480 U.S. 616 (1987).

2. Learned Hand, *The Bill of Rights* (Boston: Atheneum, 1958), p. 1.

3. Leonard W. Levy, *The Establishment Clause: Religion and the First Amendment* (New York: Macmillan, 1986); Leo Pfeffer, *Church, State, and Freedom* (Boston: Beacon Press, 1953); and Leonard W. Levy, "The Original Meaning of the Establishment Clause of the First Amendment," in *Religion and the State*, ed. James E. Wood, Jr. (Waco, Tex.: Baylor University Press, 1985), pp. 43–83.

4. *Reynolds v. United States*, 98 U.S. 145 (1879).

5. *Everson v. Board of Education*, 330 U.S. 236 (1947).

6. *Board of Education v. Allen*, 392 U.S. 236 (1968).

7. *Lemon v. Kurtzman*, 403 U.S. 602 (1971).

8. *Wallace v. Jaffree*, 472 U.S. 38 (1985).

9. Ibid.

10. *Lee v. Weisman*, 505 U.S. ___ (1992).

11. Michael W. McConnell, "The Origins and Historical Understanding of Free Exercise of Religion," *Harvard Law Review* 103 (1990):1409–1517.

12. *Minersville School District v. Gobitis*, 310 U.S. 586 (1940).

13. *West Virginia State Board of Education v. Barnette*, 319 U.S. 624 (1943).

14. *Sherbert v. Verner*, 374 U.S. 398 (1963).

15. *Employment Division v. Smith*, 110 S. Ct. 1595 (1990).

16. Laurence Tribe, *Treatise on American Constitutional Law*, 2d ed. (St. Paul, Minn.: West, 1988), p. 566.

17. Zechariah Chafee, *Free Speech in the United States* (Cambridge, Mass.: Harvard University Press, 1941).

18. Leonard W. Levy, *The Emergence of a Free Press* (New York: Oxford University Press, 1985).

19. *Schenck v. United States*, 249 U.S. 46 (1919).

20. *Gitlow v. New York*, 268 U.S. 652 (1925).

21. *Dennis v. United States*, 341 U.S. 494 (1951).

22. *Brandenburg* v. *Ohio*, 395 U.S. 444 (1969).

23. *Tinker* v. *Des Moines Independent County School District*, 393 U.S 503 (1969).

24. *United States* v. *Eichman*, 110 S. Ct. 2404 (1990).

25. "Supreme Court Voids Flag Law," *New York Times*, June 12, 1990, p. A1.

26. *Miller* v. *California*, 415 U.S. 15 (1973).

27. *Pope* v. *Illinois*, 481 U.S. 497 (1987).

28. Donald Alexander Downs, *The New Politics of Pornography* (Chicago: University of Chicago Press, 1989).

29. *American Booksellers Ass'n* v. *Hudnut*, 598 F. Supp. 1316 (1984).

30. *New York Times* v. *Sullivan*, 376 U.S. 254 (1964).

31. *Near* v. *Minnesota*, 283 U.S. 697 (1931).

32. For a detailed account of the case and Near, see Fred W. Friendly, *Minnesota Rag* (New York: Random House, 1981).

33. *New York Times* v. *United States*, 403 U.S. 713 (1971).

34. *Branzburg* v. *Hayes*, 408 U.S. 665 (1972).

35. *Hazelwood School District* v. *Kuhlmeier*, 484 U.S. 280 (1988).

36. *DeJonge* v. *Oregon*, 299 U.S. 353, 364 (1937).

37. *Barron* v. *Baltimore*, 7 Pet 243 (1833).

38. *Chicago B.&O.R.* v. *Chicago*, 166 U.S. 226 (1897).

39. *Palko* v. *Connecticut*, 302 U.S. 319 (1937).

40. *Duncan* v. *Louisiana*, 391 U.S. 145 (1968).

41. *McNabb* v. *United States*, 318 U.S. 332 (1943).

42. *Baldwin* v. *New York*, 399 U.S. 66 (1970).

43. Anthony Lewis, *Gideon's Trumpet* (New York; Random House, 1964).

44. *Gideon* v. *Wainwright*, 372 U.S. 335 (1963).

45. *Miranda* v. *Arizona*, 384 U.S. 486 (1966)

46. *Wolf* v. *Colorado*, 338 U.S. 225 (1949).

47. *Mapp* v. *Ohio*, 307 U.S. 643 (1961).

48. *United States* v. *Leon*, 468 U.S. 897 (1984).

49. *James* v. *Illinois*, 110 S. Ct. 648 (1990).

50. Paul Brest, *Processes of Constitutional Decision-making* (Boston: Little, Brown, 1975), p. 708.

51. *Griswold* v. *Connecticut*, 381 U.S. 479 (1965).

52. *Roe* v. *Wade*, 410 U.S. 113 (1973).

53. See John Hart Ely, "The Wages of Crying Wolf: A Comment on Roe v. Wade," 82 *Law Journal* 920 (1973).

54. *Planned Parenthood* v. *Casey*, 505 U.S. ___ (1992).

55. *Bowers* v. *Hardwick*, 106 S. Ct. 2841 (1986).

56. *Civil Rights Cases*, 109 U.S. 3 (1883).

57. Mary Beth Norton et al., *A People and a Nation: A History of the United States*, 3d ed. (Boston: Houghton Mifflin, 1990), p. 490.

58. *Plessy* v. *Ferguson*, 163 U.S. 537 (1896).

59. *Cummings* v. *County Board of Education*, 175 U.S. 528 (1899).

60. *Brown* v. *Board of Education*, 347 U.S. 487 (1954).

61. *Brown* v. *Board of Education II*, 349 U.S. 294 (1955).

62. Jack W. Peltason, *Fifty-Eight Lonely Men*, rev. ed. (Urbana: University of Illinois Press, 1971).

63. *Alexander* v. *Holmes County Board of Education*, 369 U.S. 19 (1969).

64. *Milliken* v. *Bradley*, 418 U.S. 717 (1974).

65. Norton, et. al., *People and a Nation*, p. 943

66. *City of Richmond* v. *J.A. Croson Co.*, 109 S. Ct. 706 (1989).

67. *Martin* v. *Wilkes*, 109 S. Ct. 2180 (1989).

68. But see Abigail M. Thernstrom, *Whose Vote Counts? Affirmative Ac-*

tion and Minority Voting Rights (Cambridge, Mass.: Harvard University Press, 1987).

69. *Wards Cove Packing Co.* v. *Atonio,* 109 S. Ct. 2115 (1989).

70. *Patterson* v. *McLean Credit Union,* 109 S. Ct. 2363 (1989).

71. *Saint Francis College* v. *Al-Khazraji,* 481 U.S. 604 (1987).

72. Rufus P. Browning, Dale Rogers Marshall, and David H. Tabb, *Protest Is Not Enough* (Berkeley, Calif.: University of California Press, 1984).

73. *Muller* v. *Oregon,* 208 U.S. 412 (1908).

74. *International Union, United Automobile, Aerospace and Agricultural Implement Workers of America* v. *Johnson Controls, Inc.,* 1991 U.S. LEXIS 1715 (1991).

75. *Reed* v. *Reed,* 404 U.S. 71 (1971).

76. *Frontiero* v. *Richardson,* 411 U.S. 677 (1973).

77. *Craig* v. *Borden,* 429 U.S. 190 (1976).

78. Jane J. Mansbridge, *Why We Lost the ERA* (Chicago: University of Chicago Press, 1986).

79. Melvin I. Urofsky, *A March of Liberty* (New York: Knopf, 1988), p. 902.

80. Melvin I. Urofsky, *A Conflict of Rights: The Supreme Court and Affirmative Action* (New York: Scribner's, 1991), p. 29.

81. *Regents of the University of California* v. *Bakke,* 438 U.S. 265 (1978).

82. Steven N. Keith, Robert M. Bell, and Albert P. Williams, *Assessing the Outcome of Affirmative Action in Medical Schools* (Santa Monica, Calif.: Rand, 1987).

83. *United Steelworkers of America, AFL-CIO* v. *Weber,* 443 U.S. 193 (1979).

84. *Firefighters* v. *Stotts,* 467 U.S. 561 (1984).

85. *Wygant* v. *Jackson Board of Education,* 106 S. Ct. 1842 (1986).

86. *Local 28 of the Sheet Metal Workers' International Association* v. *EEOC,* 478 U.S. 421 (1986).

87. Sidney Verba and Gary R. Orren, *Equality in America: The View from the Top* (Cambridge, Mass.: Harvard University Press, 1985), especially pp. 1–51.

INDEX

Credits, *(continued)*